ECONOMICS BASICS

ECONOMICS BASICS

Volume 2

Labor Economics—
World Economies

Index

edited by
THE EDITORS OF SALEM PRESS

SALEM PRESS, INC.
Pasadena, California
Hackensack, New Jersey

Copyright © 1991, 1999, by SALEM PRESS, INC.
All rights in this book are reserved. No part of this work may be used or reproduced in any manner whatsoever or transmitted in any form or by any means, electronic or mechanical, including photo-copy, recording, or any information storage and retrieval system, without written permission from the copyright owner except in the case of brief quotations embodied in critical articles and reviews. For information address the publisher, Salem Press, Inc., P.O. Box 50062, Pasadena, California 91115.

Essays originally appeared in *Survey of Social Science: Economics*, 1991; new material has been added.

∞ The paper used in these volumes conforms to the American National Standard for Permanence of Paper for Printed Library Ma-terials, Z39.48-1992.

Library of Congress Cataloging-in-Publication Data
Economics basics / edited by the editors of Salem Press.
    p.   cm. — (Magill's choice)
Includes bibliographical references and index.
ISBN 0-89356-947-X (set: alk. paper). — ISBN 0-89356-948-8 (vol. 1: alk. paper). — ISBN 0-89356-949-6 (vol. 2: alk. paper)
    1. Economics. I. Salem Press. II. Series.
HB171.E269   1999
330—dc21   98-47089
                                                                          CIP

First Printing

TABLE OF CONTENTS
Volume 2

ECONOMICS BASICS

LABOR ECONOMICS

Type of economics: Labor and population
Field of study: Labor markets

Labor economics is intended to provide an understanding of how wages are determined in a market economy, why workers earn differing wages, and how the general level of employment is determined. Labor economics offers insight into why businesses hire workers and how households decide on the amount of labor time supplied to businesses.

Principal terms

DIMINISHING MARGINAL PRODUCTIVITY: a principle that states that, as additional units of labor are hired, the output of each additional worker will decline after some point
MARGINAL PRODUCT: the addition to total output attributed to the hiring of one more worker
MARGINAL RESOURCE COST: the addition to total labor costs from the hiring of each additional worker
PRODUCTIVITY: a measure of output per hour of work or labor input
VALUE OF MARGINAL PRODUCT: the addition to a firm's revenues as the additional output of successive workers is sold

Overview

The use of productive resources is required in order to produce the goods and services that are consumed on a daily basis. Those resources are land and its raw materials, capital (which is the tools and machinery utilized), and labor. Labor refers to both the mental and the physical capabilities of human beings. To employ these resources requires a payment. To hire labor, a business must pay wages. For an economic system to operate, two questions arise: How many workers will be hired? and What will be the level of wages?

To approach these questions, one begins by noting that the demand for labor by business is said to be a derived demand; that is, the demand for workers depends on, or is derived from, the demand for the products that workers produce. As consumers change their preferences for goods and services, businesses change their decisions on hiring workers. This derived demand for labor requires two elements to be effective. First, workers must have the capability to perform the tasks involved in production, which can be measured by the productivity of labor. Productivity is a measure of output per hour of labor time. Second, the product must have some value, which can be measured by the price the product commands in the marketplace.

In this process of hiring labor, the decision is made at the margin. This means that the decision is whether to hire an additional unit of labor. When hiring labor, the concern is how much that additional worker will add to the total output of the firm, which is known as the marginal product of labor. Not all workers possess similar abilities or carry similar credentials to the labor market; therefore, the marginal product of additional workers will vary. In the labor queue, businesses wish to hire the most productive labor first, the second most productive labor next, and so on. As this continues, the firm is faced with the concept of diminishing marginal productivity. That means that as additional labor is brought into the factory or office, the additional output associated with successive units of labor will begin to decline after some point. It is the limited or fixed size of capital that contributes to the law of diminishing marginal productivity.

Whatever is produced must have some value in the marketplace. Under competitive conditions, a business can sell all the output that it can produce, and it can sell at the market-determined price. If a firm is facing diminishing marginal product, but it can still sell all of its output at a constant price, then the value of the marginal product of labor will decline. The value of the marginal product is the price of the good sold multiplied by the marginal product of labor. What one discovers is that the marginal labor adds successively less value to a firm. Given this, one recognizes that firms will hire more workers if wages are reduced and fewer workers if wages are increased.

This derived demand will change if any of a number of factors change. First, if the demand for the product of labor were to change, then the derived demand for labor will be altered. This shift will be reflected in a change in the price of the product, altering the value of the marginal product of labor. Second, the marginal product of labor may be altered. This many come about by labor acquiring more education, undergoing a training program, or gaining more experience on the job. It also may be the result of improvements in the health of labor or even of changes in labor-management relationships. A third variable that may cause a shift in the demand for labor is a change in technology. The productivity of labor is dependent on the productivity of the other resources with which it is combined. An improvement in capital (goods used to produce other goods) will make labor more productive. This is a double-edged sword since capital is both a complement to labor (tools are required in order to work) and a substitute for labor (robots can replace welders on an assembly line). Any of these changes will result in either an increase or a decrease in the demand for labor.

The preceding offers an introduction to the demand side of a labor market, but with this information alone, one is still unable to determine the general level of wages or employment in a labor market. In order to make such a determination, an examination of the supply side of labor markets must be conducted. The potential supply of labor is dependent on, first, the size of the population that is willing and able to work. Also important is the age distribution of that population. If the population is particularly young or old, then a smaller potential supply of workers exists to produce goods and services. One may also consider the gender combination. This will be especially important if cultural biases exist regarding the division of labor between male and female members of the labor force. Finally, immigration policies and practices of a particular country will have an impact on the number of individuals available for employment.

On the microeconomic level, the amount of labor time available is an individual or family decision. This decision is based on the trade-off between how much income the family requires versus how much time it wants to spend in leisure. Leisure refers to the amount of time not spent at work for hire. The amount of time allocated for sale is directly related to the wage rate; that is, as wages increase, the number of hours allocated for work increases. When wages decrease, the number of labor hours available decreases. These changes in the quantity of labor supplied should be differentiated from changes in the aggregate supply of labor. As those factors referred to above (for example, population, age, and gender mix) change, the supply of labor either increases or decreases depending upon the direction of change in those variables.

Bringing together the demand variables with the supply factors allows one to determine wages and level of employment. The labor market is said to be in equilibrium when the decisions of buyers and sellers are mutually consistent; that is, if the wage being offered is acceptable to workers, then employment commences. Similarly, if the wage offered is unacceptable, or if the wage requested is unacceptable, then employment does not take place. Changes in wages and level of employment occur whenever alterations in the demand for or the supply of labor take place. For example, the formation of new businesses increases the demand for labor, thereby increasing both wages and employment. Similarly, as the population increases, wages decrease but employment grows. As changes in the labor market occur, the tendency is toward an equilibrium in which the buyers and sellers of labor agree on wages and employment.

Applications

Labor economics has a number of very useful applications. First, by considering demand side conditions, one may explain why a worker in one market earns more than a worker in another. The difference in earnings may be explained by the fact that one worker is more productive than another. Workers in the automobile, coal mining, and steel industries historically have earned higher wages than workers in other industries. Labor economics can explain this by the high productivity of these workers relative to workers elsewhere. The productivity of these workers has also improved over time because of improvements in the capital goods that they have at their disposal. Another explanation for the relatively higher productivity of some workers may be that they have more education than others, thereby earning higher wages. In general, college-educated labor earns higher wages because of the assumed improvements in its productivity. The conclusion to be drawn is that if one works longer, harder, or faster, then one earns higher wages. Labor economics captures this aspect in measuring the productivity of labor. Thus, if one individual or group is more productive, wages will be higher for that worker or group of workers.

The second explanation that labor economics can offer regarding wage differentials is in terms of the value of the product. Perhaps autoworkers, coal miners, and steel workers earn higher wages than clerks employed in retail trade, barbers, or tanning salon operators because the value of the goods produced by the former far exceeds the value of the latter. This higher value allows for higher wages for those workers.

Labor economics may also explain wage differentials from the supply side of the market. Since the mid-to late 1960's, the U.S. population has undergone some significant changes. Some of the population has moved from the snowbelt (the Northeastern United States) to the sunbelt (the Southeastern and Southwestern United States). As the supply of labor has shifted out of the snowbelt, the tendency has been for wages to rise. This occurs because businesses must bid up the price for the dwindling supply of labor. In contrast, the increasing supply of labor in the sunbelt has tended to push down the price of labor.

Another significant shift in the composition of the labor force, under supply-side considerations, has been an increasing female participation rate. Since the 1960's, more women have decided to enter the labor force rather than remain at home. The reasons for this shift are numerous. In some instances, women had to earn extra wages for a family to maintain a particular standard of living. In other cases, it was the increasing number of female-headed households that brought about the entrance of women into the paid-labor force. This trend may result from increasing divorce rates or women deciding to postpone or forgo marriage. The importance of these changes in the female labor force is that they have had a tendency to push down the general level of wages. It is the increasing number of women that has tended to lower women's wages relative to the wages earned by men. When comparing the wages of male and female workers, one can also note that men have traditionally held those jobs previously identified as the high-productivity jobs of the economy. Women have been relegated to the low-productivity or the less valuable sectors of the economy.

In summary, labor economics is useful for offering very broad generalizations to explain differences in wages and employment between disparate groups. First, differences in the productivity of workers, which arise from a variety of factors, influence the derived demand for workers. This is reflected in the wages and level of employment for some workers. Second, differences in the prices consumers are willing and able to pay for the products of labor are reflected in wages and employment. Finally, changes in the social fabric of life that influence the potential labor supply are reflected in wage and employment differentials among workers.

Context

The study of labor economics emerged in its present form in the late 1870's in the work of the neoclassical economists. There has been interest in fair wages and employment conditions, however, since the emergence of economics as a discipline in the social sciences. Given the nature of human labor, labor economics is perhaps the most unsettled area of the subject. It is more difficult to apply the principles of market operations to labor markets because of the peculiar nature of the commodity traded: human labor. A variety of factors influence labor and labor markets that are more difficult to capture in supply and demand principles. Relationships between groups of people may be influenced by cultural considerations more so than by economic considerations.

Even so, labor economics does provide significant generalizations that allow one to understand the employment situation. For one, labor economics is useful in explaining broad wage differentials between male and female, white and black, or young and old workers. It is also useful in explaining the employability of disparate workers. This will continue to be of acute interest as the continuous detailed division of labor occurs. That is, as jobs are further broken into smaller tasks with labor assigned to each subtask, labor economics will contribute to the understanding of wage and employment determination in these new work settings.

This subject has even broader implications when one considers economic justice within society. A good example to explore in this context is that of male and female wage differentials. It is estimated that in the 1880's women earned approximately 50 percent of the earnings of men. One hundred years later, women were earning approximately 65 percent of their male counterparts' earnings. Further estimates indicate that by the year 2000, women will have narrowed the wage gap to 74 percent of male earnings. Labor economics will offer an explanation of this slowly narrowing wage gap. It may also provide a basis from which policies may be developed to speed this process along, if desired.

As the fabric of capitalist society continues to change, other issues will present themselves for consideration. These will include an increasing demand by workers for flexible scheduling of hours as the number of two-wage-earner families and female-headed households increases. Developments in technology will allow employers to respond favorably to such requests, but to what extent is unknown. Another topic of interest to working people is that of job sharing, a situation in which two workers split the duties associated with a particular job. One may work in the morning, the other in the afternoon. This issue arises from responses to unemployment problems and the desire of some workers to work less than full-time.

Again, labor economics provides a foundation from which to examine the issues facing society and to develop responses to these issues. It helps economists to form opinions about and understand the world around them. Labor economics is likely to continue to break ground in the explanatory power of economics.

Bibliography

Blau, Francine D., Marianne A. Ferber, and Anne E. Winkler. *The Economics of Women, Men, and Work.* 3d ed. Upper Saddle River, N.J.: Prentice Hall, 1998. The authors explore in some detail the different experiences at work, in terms of wages and occupations, of men and women. They also explore the changing structure of the American family and how it has affected the employment situation.

Braverman, Harry. *Labor and Monopoly Capital.* New York: Monthly Review Press, 1974. The author views the outcome of labor economics as strongly influenced by the power of competing interest groups. He traces the origins of labor-management relations, the influence of technology upon work, and the changing composition of occupations within capitalist society.

Chamberlain, Neil W., Donald E. Cullen, and David Lewin. *The Labor Sector.* New York: McGraw-Hill, 1980. A very comprehensive text on labor economics, intended for those uninitiated in economics. Includes discussions of the influence of labor unions, labor's political activity, discrimination, and equality.

Galenson, Walter. *A Primer on Employment and Wages.* New York: Vintage Books, 1966. In clear, understandable language, this book explains the basic principles and practices of labor economics and labor market operations. The statistics are out of date, but that is easily remedied through use of current periodicals.

Kochan, Thomas A., Harry C. Katz, and Robert B. McKersie. *The Transformation of American Industrial Relations.* New York: Basic Books, 1986. The authors trace the development of the U.S. economy during the decade of 1975 to 1985. They explain the emergence of new industries and the demise of the basic infrastructure of the U.S. economy, examine these influences upon American workers, and explore some options for the future.

Sloman, John. *Essentials of Economics.* New York: Prentice Hall, 1998.

Dennis A. O'Connor

Cross-References

LABOR THEORY OF VALUE

Type of economics: General economics
Fields of study: Economic theory and history of economic thought

The labor theory of value holds that the value of a commodity is determined by the amount of socially necessary abstract labor time that is used in its production.

Principal terms

ABSTRACT LABOR: labor in general, undifferentiated from any particular form of labor in production and equivalent with all others when viewed from the perspective of society under capitalist social relations

CONCRETE LABOR: useful labor; productive activity of a definite kind and exercised with a definite aim

CONSTANT CAPITAL: the form that money capital takes when it is advanced for the purchase of the means of production by capitalists; its value reappears in commodity output as it depreciates or is used up in production

EXCHANGE VALUE: the quantitative worth of a commodity; the form of abstract human labor

LABOR POWER: the capacity to work that is exhibited by humans and that becomes a commodity under capitalism

MODE OF PRODUCTION: a historically specific way of organizing productive activity as defined by the particular manner in which humans interact with nature and one another in production

SOCIAL DIVISION OF LABOR: the distribution of the total labor of society to different concrete pursuits that are essential for the maintenance and reproduction of the entire society

USE VALUE: an object or an effect that meets a human need or want through its physical and nonphysical properties

VARIABLE CAPITAL: the money capital that is advanced for the purchase of labor power

Overview

To work in order to produce the goods and services that are necessary for sustaining human life is an absolute necessity that is imposed on humans by nature. Humans must continually interact with and transform nature with the aim of generating products suitable for assuring their subsistence and reproduction. For example, a farmer must plow the soil, sow the seed, and cultivate the seedling until its maturation into produce such as corn, in order to obtain it as food. Karl Marx highlighted this point: "Every child knows that a nation that ceased to work, I will not say for a year, but even for a few weeks, would perish."

Early in human society, a division of productive activity arose whereby different groups or individuals performed particular laboring tasks to ensure the survival of all. The total working time that was available to society was allocated to specific labors in definite, though not unchanging, quantities and proportions. Thus, the generation of the material foundation of human life requires humans not only to interact with and transform nature but also to rely on one another to perform particular activities in order to meet the material requirements of food, clothing, and shelter. The specific way in which productive tasks between humans and nature, and among humans, are organized defines a manner of producing, that is, a mode of production.

Capitalism is a historically specific mode of production with particular essential features. It is characterized by the fact that society grants the right to private persons to dictate how raw materials, tools, machines, and factories are to be used. In other words, private individuals own and control the means that all humans require for production and survival. The means of production came to be concentrated in the hands of a relatively small segment of society, identifiable by their ownership and control of the means of production: the capitalist class. The larger portion of society, which does not own or control the means of production, is known as the laboring class. This class possesses only one commodity—its labor power. Consequently, workers must sell their labor power to capitalists in exchange for wages in order to purchase the goods and services necessary for their continued existence. Therefore, under capitalism, production takes the form of class relations between workers and capitalists, and the ability to labor is turned into a commodity.

Given the imperative of the social division of labor, capitalism is also recognized by the specific manner in which it allocates the labor time of society. There is no a priori agreement for the allocation of labor time and, hence, no blueprint for the production and distribution of the various goods and services that result. Production is undertaken by private, apparently independent, producers without conscious regard of how the labor time at their disposal fits into the social division of labor.

Moreover, production under capitalism is undertaken with the generation of profit as its end, irrespective of the concrete form that the product takes in the labor process. Capitalists must then exchange these products in the market for money in order to realize a profit. Furthermore, some of this money that is acquired in exchange is used, in turn, to purchase the means to renew the production process on the same or extended scale. Exchange is an essential phase of the production process, indispensable for the reproduction of the system. Thus, capitalism takes as given a well-developed market in which goods and services may be bought and sold for money. The production and distribution of goods and services take place through this generalized process of exchange.

Under this particular form of the social organization of production, the products of labor become commodities. A commodity, according to Karl Marx (1818-1883), has a dual identity as a use value and an exchange value. As a use value, the commodity displays particular physical characteristics or nonphysical effects that make it usable to satisfy human needs or wants. Human brains, muscles, and nerves are expended in production with the intention that the product of that labor will be realized in a definite form, making it suitable for use. The consequence of the labor of a computer programmer is software that is capable of performing particular operations, just as the labor of the barber results in a haircut. In each case, the effect of the labor is a product that is identifiable by its physical qualities or nonphysical effects and characteristics, and as such, is a use value. The specific labor engaged in the production of these use values is an example of what Marx referred to as concrete labor.

Once produced, commodities enter circulation and are related to one another as given quantities of one commodity being the equivalent of a definite quantity of another. For example, one coat will exchange for two shirts; one coat is worth two shirts or two shirts exchange for one coat. Thus, this property of a commodity as having exchange value or

These autoworkers conducted a sit-down strike during the late 1930's to assert their demand for greater remuneration for their labor. (Sheldon Dick, courtesy Library of Congress)

quantitative worth, as being exchangeable for a definite quantity of another commodity, reveals itself in exchange. The concrete properties of two commodities are put out of sight when they are related to each other and, once done, an underlying commonality between them makes its existence known and appears as exchange value.

When these useful qualities are left out of consideration, the different qualities and specific operations of the labor that was expended in their production are also overlooked. Hence, nothing is left but what is common to them all—that of being products of one part of society's total labor. Consequently, they are all reduced to human labor in the abstract. Through the process of exchange, the mutual social dependence of labor is recognized and, in capitalist commodity production, the source of a commodity's exchange value is revealed as undifferentiated human labor, that is, abstract labor. Therefore, the source of a commodity's exchange value is homogeneous human labor, or what Marx called abstract human labor. When viewed from the perspective of being material depositories of part of society's undifferentiated human labor, commodities are values. It follows that, under capitalist social relations, it is abstract human labor that takes the form of exchange value. Individuals see the relations between people as being part of society's total homogeneous labor, as a relation between commodities as their exchange value.

Corresponding, then, to the dual nature of a commodity as a use value and an exchange value is a twofold character of labor as concrete and abstract human labor. Marx considered the uncovering of this duality his greatest contribution to political economy. It is in exchange that commodities shed their physical forms to reveal the underlying equality of being a receptacle of abstract human labor, that is, value. Given the social division of labor and the motivation of production, capitalist producers have no choice: They must produce for exchange. Therefore, human labor possesses value from the outset, acquiring this property in production and not in exchange.

The magnitude of the value of a commodity, then, is measured by the amount of abstract human labor that is contained in it, which is reckoned in time—minutes, hours, or days. It is only the human labor in the abstract, however, that is socially necessary to produce the commodity under normal conditions of production and with the average degree of skill and intensity that is consistent with existing technology. This condition requires that the indolent or lower efficiency labor of some workers is averaged in with the more efficient labor of others in order to determine a commodity's unit social value. The labor theory of value states that the value of a commodity is determined by the amount of socially necessary abstract human labor that is used for its production.

Applications

The labor theory of value can be used to explain the persistence of unemployment in the capitalist system. The point of departure for such an analysis is in the sphere of circulation, with the circuit of capital represented as $M - C \ldots P \ldots C' - M'$. The circuit begins with money (M) and ends with money (M'). Its essence is that more money (M' > M) can be extracted from exchange than was introduced into the process by the capitalist at the beginning. The capitalists advance money capital (M) for the purchase of commodity inputs (C), labor power, and other means of production in order to acquire the productive potential. This potential becomes actual production as laborers interact with and transform commodity inputs (C) through production (P) into commodity outputs (C'). Through this labor, the value of the means of production is merely transferred to the product through the intervention of human labor as these means are used up or depreciated in the course of production. Marx called means of production that are used in this way constant capital, as their value only reappears in the commodity output in proportion as it is used up or through wear and tear.

The exchange value of labor power is determined, as is the value of any other commodity, by the amount of socially necessary abstract labor time that is used in its production. In the case of labor power, its exchange value resolves itself into the value of the commodities that are required for the maintenance, regeneration, and reproduction of the laborer and his or her family. The money capital that is advanced for the purchase of labor power is known as variable capital. In this exchange of equivalent values, the capitalist parts with the exchange value of labor power in the form of variable capital and receives, in return, the labor's use value for a contracted period, such as an eight-hour day. Therefore, the use value of labor power, which creates value, belongs to the capitalist.

Commodity outputs are produced by combining labor and the means of production under the direction of the capitalist, but the labor process is also a value-creating process. The laborer transfers the value of constant capital to commodities through labor and also adds a value that is equal to the commodities that comprise the value of his or her contracted labor power over a given time period. The laborer thus returns to the capitalist, in the form of commodity outputs (C'), a value that is measured by a socially necessary abstract labor time that is equal to the variable capital (V) that was advanced for his or her labor power.

If a working day is eight hours long and the value of these commodities is equal to four hours of labor, however, then the remaining four hours belong to the capitalist. Value that is added by living labor (L) during eight hours to commodities in excess of the time that is required to reproduce the value of labor power (V) is surplus value (L – V). Surplus value forms the basis for profit and takes the form of the augmented money value, (M' – M), extracted through circulation by the capitalist. Marx thus uncovered the source of profit as surplus value and the source of surplus value as unpaid labor time. The ratio of surplus value (S) to variable capital (V) is what Marx called the rate of surplus value. Having purchased labor power for a given period, the capitalist proceeds to squeeze the maximum amount of surplus value from the labor process. This can be done by increasing S, that is, raising absolute surplus value, or by lowering V, that is, increasing relative surplus value.

The capitalist can increase absolute surplus value by lengthening the working day in two ways. The absolute number of hours that are worked can be extended, such as from eight to ten, and the amount of time that the laborer works for free for the capitalist raised, thus increasing surplus value in the form of the value that is added to commodities during these extra two hours. Alternatively, the capitalist can intensify the labor by forcing workers to work faster or harder through greater supervision, while using the same techniques, machines, and processes and without changing the physical character of the labor. The result of such intensification of labor is more commodities produced, more value generated, and more surplus value appropriated by the capitalist in a given amount of time.

There are physical and social limits, however, to augmenting absolute surplus value. Therefore the capitalist must rely on raising relative surplus value by lowering the value of commodities that comprise the value of labor power, and hence increase that part of the working day that the workers labor for free. This increase in relative surplus value takes the form of increasing the number of commodities that a given amount of living labor can produce in a given amount of time or of having a smaller quantity of living labor produce the same amount of commodities. Consequently, the value of both labor and commodities is lowered. This process appears, to the capitalist, to be raising the productivity of labor, but it will, in fact, have the effect of reducing the value of commodities.

When capital seizes control of production, it raises the productivity of labor by perfecting the labor process, which involves reorganization that is aimed at routinizing and subdividing the laboring task to its most elementary and repetitive motions and assigning it to a worker on a permanent basis. It is only a short step to replace the worker with a machine. Thus, workers are redundant from the point of view of capital. They become unemployed as a result of the insatiable quest by capitalists to increase surplus value or, as it appears to them as profit, by lowering cost. Hence, unemployment is a direct result of the normal, profitable operation of capitalism and is a ubiquitous feature of that mode of production.

Unemployment serves to help maintain labor discipline and to keep wages low. A substantial pool of unemployed workers discourages those threatening to strike over wages and working conditions by reminding them that they can be replaced. Furthermore, unemployment results when capitalists are successful in the war of competition with other capitalists. If, as a result of mechanization or a rising ratio of constant capital to variable capital, Japanese automobile producers are able to produce cars of a comparable and even better quality than U.S. automobile producers by using less than one-half of the labor time, then according to the labor theory of value, the Japanese cars will cost less to produce. Japanese firms can sell their cars for less and thus capture additional market shares and profits. This increased market share comes at the expense of U.S. carmakers, who then reduce production, close plants, and throw additional workers into unemployment. Unsuccessful participation in the capitalist war of competition will exacerbate the problem of unemployment. This conclusion is painfully obvious to unemployed automobile workers in Detroit.

A theory of unemployment that is based on a labor theory of value alerts one to a number of implications in addition to the existence of persistent unemployment. Losing the war of capitalist competition can exacerbate an already chronic problem. Furthermore, the preceding analysis implies that a single national economy is not the proper unit of analysis: Low rates of unemployment in Japan may be the result of higher rates in the U.S. and relatively low rates of unemployment in the U.S. may be related to even higher rates of unemployment in other less developed capitalist countries. Unemployment must be analyzed as it exists in the capitalist world as a whole and not only in one country's economy.

Context

The labor theory of value received its most developed form in the work of Marx. Marx's theory was based on a critical appropriation of David Ricardo's (1772-1823) labor theory, which was a critique and extension of Adam Smith's (1723-1790) labor theory. Smith's labor theory of value applied to that "early and rude state of society" before the private appropriation of land and the accumulation of capital. Smith argued that the differing amounts of labor that were required to obtain commodities seemed to be the only rule that could explain the quantities that were traded of each. At any period beyond this stage of society, however, the natural price of a commodity was composed of the wages of labor, the profits of capital, and the rent of the land-owner. Here, the value of a commodity is determined by the amount of labor that could be purchased in exchange for it.

Ricardo, in opposition to Smith, argued that the relative values of commodities were determined by the relative amounts of labor that were necessary for their production, even when land had been appropriated and capital accumulated. He argued that the general law of value determination should be modified under these circumstances, not overthrown or fused with another measure, as Smith had done. Marx showed that Ricardo was limited in his analysis because of his method of investigation. Ricardo was unable to discern the twofold character of labor and, hence, made no distinction between abstract labor and its appearance in the sphere of circulation as exchange value.

At least in part as a response to the radical uses to which Ricardian socialists put Ricardo's labor theory of value and demonstration by Marx that the source of surplus value was unpaid labor time, there arose a reaction against the classical school of political economy and Marx, and the central position that was held by the labor theory of value in the work of each. This reaction against Ricardo and Marx took the form of a shift replacing an objective theory of value, based on the measurement of a commodity's value as socially necessary abstract labor time, with a subjective theory of value, based on utility or degrees of satisfaction that were derived from the consumption of a good or service. This school of economists was known as the neoclassical school, according to which the value of commodity is determined by the opposing forces of supply and demand.

The publication of *Production of Commodities by Means of Commodities* by Piero Sraffa in 1960 led to a devastating critique of this neoclassical value theory and brought about a renewal of interest in an objective theory of value. In Sraffa's work, prices are determined by the conditions of reproduction and the requirement that resulting prices ensure the distribution of the product, such that production can continue in the same proportions on the same or an extended scale. The adherents of this method for calculating relative prices of production are known as neo-Ricardians.

Therefore, there are three competing theories as to the determination of the value of a commodity. Some economists subscribe to a Marxist labor theory of value, others to the neo-Ricardian/Sraffian theory, and the majority of economists to a neoclassical theory in which prices or values are determined subjectively, that is, by supply and demand.

Bibliography

Blau, Francine D., Marianne A. Ferber, and Anne E. Winkler. *The Economics of Women, Men, and Work.* 3d ed. Upper Saddle River, N.J.: Prentice Hall, 1998. The authors explore in some detail the different experiences at work, in terms of wages and occupations, of men and women. They also explore the changing structure of the American family and how it has affected the employment situation.

Braverman, Harry. *Labor and Monopoly Capital.* New York: Monthly Review Press, 1974. Chapters 1 through 4 provide a detailed analysis of labor and the labor process under capitalist social relations as it has appeared in recent history.

Carroll, Michael C. *A Future of Capitalism: The Economic Vision of Robert Heilbroner.* New York: St. Martin's Press, 1998.

Foley, Duncan K. *Understanding Capital.* Cambridge, Mass.: Harvard University Press, 1986. Written as a general introduction to Karl Marx's economic theory. The section on method is good, and chapter 4 provides an account of mechanization as an inherent feature of capitalist production. The references provide a nearly comprehensive list of pertinent literature on various subjects.

Heilbroner, Robert L. *The Worldly Philosophers.* 5th rev. ed. New York: Simon & Schuster, 1983. Subtitled "The Lives, Times, and Ideas of the Great Economic Thinkers," this is the best possible introduction to political economy, economists, and their analyses. It is written by one of the most elegant writers in economics. Strongly recommended for those without any background in economics.

Marx, Karl. *Capital.* Vol. 1. New York: International Publishers, 1967. There is no substitute for the original in any area of scientific study. Chapter 1 on commodities is Marx's explicit presentation of the labor theory of value. A challenging chapter, but worthwhile.

Meek, Ronald L. *Studies in the Labor Theory of Value.* New York: Monthly Review Press, 1956. A classic in the field of the history of economic thought. Meek provides an excellent analysis of the development of the labor theory of value from Adam Smith through David Ricardo to Karl Marx and the contributions made by the neoclassicals and Piero Sraffa to value theory. Should serve as background material for Marx's *Capital.*

Shaikh, Anwar. "Marx's Theory of Value and the 'Transformation Problem.'" In *The Subtle Anatomy of Capitalism,* edited by Jesse Schwartz. Santa Monica, Calif.: Goodyear, 1977. Begins with the centrality of production and its importance as a point of departure for the labor theory of value. The connection between values, direct prices, and prices of production, as well as the necessity of money, is analyzed with illuminating precision. A solution to the so-called transformation problem is presented.

_____. "The Transformation from Marx to Sraffa." In *Ricardo, Marx, Sraffa*, edited by Ernest Mandel and Alan Freeman. London: Verso, 1984. The centrality of labor in Marx's theory of value is established before analyzing the connection between value and money rates of profit and the determination of movements in relative prices by relative labor times. Empirical data are provided that support the validity of the labor theory of value as a price theory.

Jeffrey T. Stewart

Cross-References

Capitalism, 69; Classical Economics, 74; Labor Economics, 353; Marxist Economics, 412; Socialism, 544.

LAISSEZ-FAIRE

Type of economics: General economics
Field of study: History of economic thought

Laissez-faire, laissez-passer, or the doctrine of noninterference by the state in individual economic decision making and the underlying natural order of economic affairs, became the slogan of late eighteenth and nineteenth century liberal capitalism, of classical economic thought, and of economic liberalism. By the twentieth century, it had been modified by social reformers and the evolving field of welfare economics.

Principal terms

CAPITALISM: the economic theory that advocates organization of society on the basis of individuals' free pursuit of their economic self-interest and the ultimate subservience of governments to these individual aims

CLASSICAL ECONOMICS: developed between 1776 and 1875 in studies by Adam Smith, David Ricardo, Thomas Robert Malthus, and John Stuart Mill, the body of economic theory that rationalizes the operations and usefulness of capitalism

DEMOCRACY: historically, a system of majority rule as opposed to the organization of society to serve primarily individual interests

FREE TRADE: the relatively uninhibited flow of imports and exports without special restraints by governments

INVISIBLE HAND: an expression drawn from Adam Smith suggesting that, however conflicting and contradictory, the pursuit of economic self-interest is directed by God and thus results in improving the welfare of others

LIBERALISM: the organization of society best to serve and protect the pursuit of individual interests, as opposed to majority rule

NATURAL LAW: historically, the notion that God has endowed human beings with moral faculties that comprise human nature and help establish a natural order in human, and thus in economic, affairs

NATURAL RIGHTS: human beings' right freely to attempt the satisfaction of their self-interests and to acquire property, in the process discovering their own higher nature while contributing to the common good

OPEN MARKET: a conceptualization of individuals' ability to buy, sell, barter, or exchange without significant governmental or other interference

PHYSIOCRATS: an eighteenth century school of French economic thinkers who developed some of the ideas underlying economic liberalism

Overview

"Leave things alone, let things pass," or, laissez-faire, laissez-passer, was a commonplace eighteenth century French expression attributed variously, in its economic sense, to Vincent Gournay (1712-1759), Adrien-Marie Legendre (1752-1833), and the Marquis d'Argenson (1694-1757), friends of leading French mercantilist ministers such as Jean-Baptiste Colbert (1619-1683) and Anne Robert Jacques Turgot (1727-1781).

After the 1770's, the expression became a shorthand summary for the beliefs of the classical economists and for the emerging liberal capitalism that they sought to rationalize. Laissez-faire consequently became associated with what proved to be a pioneering school of economic thought with a distinctive economic system and political ideology. Laissez-faire embraced a profound set of moral and philosophical beliefs. These beliefs, in turn, significantly influenced the linkage of capitalist economic thought to political liberalism during the nineteenth and early twentieth centuries—especially in Great Britain and the United States, although such intertwined liberal and capitalist perspectives were also of importance in the rest of the English-speaking world, as well as in Western Europe.

Laissez-faire, or economic liberalism, was initially explained during the eighteenth century by a school of French thinkers known as the Physiocrats. Represented by François Quesnay, Victor Riqueti (the Marquis de Mirabeau), and Pierre-Samuel du Pont de Nemours, the Physiocrats developed the Western world's first comprehensive economic system. While they wanted to insure that a healthy agricultural establishment was the linchpin of national prosperity, their fundamental reasoning was rooted in the dogmatic conviction that all economic activity was governed by immutable, universal laws. Operation of these laws was therefore to be insulated against governmental interference; the marketplace was to be open, and trade was to be free. In eighteenth century authoritarian, mercantilist France, however, Physiocratic writings produced few tangible results; but that was not true elsewhere.

Instead, a number of moral philosophers and political economists in Great Britain between the late eighteenth and late nineteenth centuries gave full expression to laissez-faire, laissez-passer, fleshing out the details of economic liberalism. Among these figures were Adam Smith (1723-1790, whose *An Inquiry into the Nature and Causes of the Wealth of Nations*, 1776, practically and philosophically became one of the most influential writings of any age), Thomas Robert Malthus (1766-1834), David Ricardo (1772-1823), Nassau William Senior, (1790-1864), James Mill (1773-1836), and his precocious son, John Stuart Mill (1806-1873), along with Continental economists such as Jean-Baptiste Say (1767-1832) and Frédéric Bastiat (1801-1850). Although he was acquainted with and influenced by Quesnay and several other Physiocrats and could draw upon a rich British philosophical tradition (philosopher David Hume was a friend), Smith dominated classical thought. His writings and lectures epitomized justifications for liberal capitalism and for due regard by government authorities to laissez-faire.

As a moral philosopher, Smith premised his theory on the nature of the universe and on the biological and ethical nature of man. The universe, as he understood it, was governed by harmonious universal laws decreed by God. These laws were applicable to all human endeavors, existed whether or not they were manifest, but could be discovered in order to live happily and effectively. It was Smith's belief in the existence of such a natural order that permitted him to argue for the minimization of governments' roles or any other interferences (such as monopolies) in the natural operations of economic affairs.

Although by the twentieth century Smith was accused of being an apologist for liberal capitalism, his views on the ethical and moral nature of man fail to support such allegations. Smith's outlook on the human condition was grim: People were greedy, ambitious, arrogant, selfish, shortsighted, antisocial, and often ignorant of their real self-interest. He expected them to conspire in the marketplace against one another and against the common good. His confidence in a liberal, laissez-faire capitalist economy, however, rested on his assumption that it came closer than others, through the results of its operations, to producing a natural harmony. Left to open competition, people's vulgar, venal, and ill-motivated ambitions, as Smith saw them, tended to cancel one another and led ineluctably to a reconciliation of public and private interests.

The value of laissez-faire, according to Smith's version, also rested on a theory of natural rights, that is, the belief that people were endowed by their Creator with certain inalienable rights (a phrase incorporated in the American Declaration of Independence, wherein the term concerning rights is spelled with a "U") not only to life, liberty, and the pursuit of happiness, but also to the right to hold property. While base motives might characterize individual struggles for these rights, as well as for the realization of self-interest, the end result still brought people to a recognition of their own higher nature—though Smith did not say precisely how this would come about.

Smith shared the political conviction with classical economists that the best government is the one that governs least. Like most liberals, Smith thought the prime function of the state was to assure full protection to individualism, individual rights, individual self-expression, and free competition. Insofar as the state bore negative responsibilities, it was by way of preventing or curtailing interference in the marketplace by monopolies, chartered companies, corporations, and cabals. Government's more active obligations required it to serve or to assist the progress of private enterprise. While he was aware of disparate advantages favoring the privileged and middle classes, Smith's sympathies, like those of most liberals, lay with the less fortunate. He believed that improvement in the conditions of the classes would come from the effects of free economic and political competition.

Applications

Nowhere did laissez-faire, laissez-passer achieve greater prominence as a guide to economic change or as a slogan for the marketplace than during the nineteenth and early twentieth centuries in Great Britain and the United States. In both countries, liberal politics closely paralleled—or as Smith and many of his successors insisted, followed—liberal economics. Just as the ideal of free individual competition constituted the core of classical political economy, so too did the free individual, clothed with a host of natural rights, occupy the center of liberal politics. Neither aspect of liberalism, placed in an early nineteenth century context, was synonymous with democracy. Instead, liberalism, with its accent on individualism, tended to run counter to the majoritarian rule of democracy until democratization overwhelmed it by the twentieth century.

Liberal and democratic tendencies in laissez-faire economies nevertheless produced analogous results in Britain and the United States. Relatively free capitalist economies, for example, were matched politically by extensions of voting rights. Public pressures brought universal, white, manhood suffrage to most areas of the United States by 1845, and after the Reform Acts of 1832, 1867, and 1884, the same was true in Great Britain. Similarly, popular agitation insured virtual free trade in Great Britain after repeal of the Corn Laws in 1846; the same was true in the United States until 1862, when exclusionary tariffs reappeared. In each country, government was kept small and its role was minimized; taxation was light, since business communities thought moneys going to governments were wasted, drained potential investment capital, or were subject to less efficient uses than in the hands of private enterprise.

In the United States, popular antitrust legislation designed to break the power of alleged "monopolies" and restore competitive markets was enacted by the 1880's. Both British and American trade unionism was considered a form of interference in the free market and was purposely hampered by governmental and legal restrictions, as well as by public hostilities. Proposed regulatory and social legislation pertaining to wages, hours, or working conditions in each country was generally thought beyond government's responsibility and a matter for negotiation between employers and employees.

More positively, British and American governments during much of the nineteenth century acted as handmaidens to private ventures by extending loans, grants, subsidies, and special favors to canal builders, railroads, and mining and shipping interests. The U.S. federal government, for example, subsidized transcontinental railroad corporations by allocating 380 million acres, along with tens of thousands of dollars for each mile of construction. State and local governments followed suit. Moreover, in these liberal capitalist "systems," legislatures were weighted heavily toward representatives of business (including agricultural) interests and toward the influences of the upper class.

By the latter nineteenth century, classical economists, as well as liberal-democratic reformers, were modifying their theories to account for visible imbalances in laissez-faire political economies. By the 1870's, John Stuart Mill, although still retaining the core of his classical beliefs, wrote that advanced economies had conquered problems of production and should turn to corrective measures in regard to the distribution of wealth and improvements in the general standard of living. To achieve these goals, he advocated a more active legislative and regulatory career for government and a more positive attitude toward much-needed social and welfare legislation.

Mill offered five reasons for making exceptions to laissez-faire, each of which supported more extensive government intervention in national economic and political life. First, individuals were not always aware of their own self-interest, could not always promote it, and could not determine what self-interest would be in the distant future—thus affecting the fairness of contracts. Furthermore, any individual's interests might contravene those of others, in which case the state should have the right to restrict the interests of the few in behalf of the interests of the many. Mill supported the regulation of corporate interests such as canals, railroads, gas, and waterworks, which frequently inclined toward monopoly positions. When individuals were unable to act for themselves, Mill thought that the state should act for them (a view with special reference to the British Poor Laws and the dispensing of charity).

Government rather than the recipients should determine how charity was dispensed, always keeping those on welfare sufficiently needy to encourage them to work. He likewise argued that governments should control those who acted for others, not only those dispensing poor relief but also private investors in colonies, which however much they might profit individually, could hamper long-term colonial development. Finally, Mill sought to give the state rights of unlimited intervention on two grounds: first, when generally beneficial projects were unprofitable for private enterprise; and second, when shortsighted individual interests (governments presumably were farsighted) threatened the welfare of future generations.

Mill admired Claude-Henri de Rouvroy (1760-1825) and Auguste Comte (1798-1857), among other French socialists and positivist philosophers, and late in his career defended aspects of socialism and communism against what he regarded as unfair attacks. Mill likewise brilliantly sketched the problems of, and modifications required in, otherwise successful liberal capitalist economies. Nevertheless, he never surrendered his fundamental faith in laissez-faire and its underlying natural laws, or the sturdy individualism, undergirded by natural rights, around which political liberalism revolved.

Context

Historically, the theories, principles, and practices identified with laissez-faire, laisser-passer filled a vacuum. For centuries Europeans, then Americans, had struggled against authority, which almost invariably had assumed the guise of increasingly absolute monarchies whose rule over highly structured societies did not leave much room for individual initiatives. By the 1780's however, monarchical power had been drastically undermined, exemplified by Britain's Glorious Revolution of 1688, by the American Revolution of 1776-1783, and by the French Revolution of 1789.

Traditional order—previous impositions of absolutist political authority—was disappearing, thus creating the necessity for new order in all areas of life, especially in political and economic life. Because monarchies of the seventeenth and eighteenth centuries possessed carefully wrought justifications for God having sanctified their rule, their opponents took the providential ground of natural order, natural law, and natural rights. They asked why there was need for authority imposed by people when the universe (and people's place in the scheme of things) was already harmoniously governed by a natural order and natural laws. Kings and authoritarian order were unneccesary. Their opponents advocated discovering what the universal laws were, living by them, and letting things alone so that human affairs could adjust themselves automatically. Such laissez-faire positions were reinforced empirically by scientific revelations about the orderly, machinelike structure of the physical and biological world, revelations epitomized in the work of Sir Isaac Newton (1642-1727).

Modern economics, represented first by the Physiocrats and the classical economists, emerged partially to fill this void created by the erosion of absolutism and the decay of statist mercantilism. The economists' original task was to explain what the natural order was and how economic activity might be made compatible with it. To this end, they supported the aspects of capitalism through which people, in pursuit of individual self-interest, could operate in conformity with their own inner nature. It did not matter that avarice or self-interest menaced others; base actions would cancel one another and lead people to understand that the exercise of their higher virtues eventually paid best.

Political liberalism, the origins of which paralleled the acceptance of laissez-faire, placed the same emphasis upon natural order, natural rights, and the importance of the free play of individuals. Thus, for a time political liberalism dovetailed nicely with the precepts of the classical political economists. After the mid-nineteenth century, however, liberals were made increasingly aware of the broadly social imbalances and inconsistencies attending the practice of laissez-faire, such as maldistributions of wealth, persisting poverty, and harsh working conditions. Liberalism moved to ameliorate economic inequities through social legislation, selectively assisting society's underdogs through growing state interventionism, and by abetting the rise in popular expectations. Thus, as laissez-faire practices were weakened by their excesses, political liberalism was weakened by its diminished concern for individualism and by its attention to democratic precepts.

Bibliography

Carroll, Michael C. *A Future of Capitalism: The Economic Vision of Robert Heilbroner.* New York: St. Martin's Press, 1998.

Fried, Barbara H. *The Progressive Assault on Laissez-Faire: Robert Hale and the First Law and Economics Movement.* Cambridge, Mass.: Harvard University Press, 1998.

Gide, Charles, and Charles Rist. *A History of Economic Doctrines.* Translated by R. Richards. Boston: D. C. Heath, 1948. An authoritative, still eminently useful book. Not written for popular audiences, it is nevertheless clear, insightful, and authoritative, particularly in book 1, which deals with the Physiocrats, Adam Smith, Thomas Robert Malthus, and David Ricardo. There are no illustrative materials; the end-of-page footnotes are a rich source and an adequate replacement for a bibliography. Extensive index.

Grampp, William D. *The Classical View.* Vol. 2 in *Economic Liberalism.* New York: Random House, 1965. A clear, accurate, and critical synthesis of the subject, excellent for nonspecialists. While there are no illustrative materials, there are informative footnotes in place of a bibliography and a helpful index. Essential for introductory reading.

Heilbroner, Robert L. *The Worldly Philosophers.* 3d rev. ed. New York: Simon & Schuster, 1967. A critical and prolific political economist, Heilbroner provides an excellent exposition and critique of Adam Smith, Thomas Robert Malthus, and David Ricardo in chapters 1-4. The critical bibliographical essay is first-rate, and the index is helpful. Written for nonspecialists.

Heiman, Eduard. *A History of Economic Doctrines.* New York: Oxford University Press, 1945. A lively, scholarly account of the subject. Chapters 1-4, dealing with the Physiocrats, the classical economists, and their historical environments, are especially useful. There are no footnotes or illustrative materials, and the select bibliography is useless; the index is useful. With these minor exceptions, an excellent study.

Lekachman, Robert. *Varieties of Economics.* New York: Meridian, 1962. The early chapters are a valuable survey, which includes the classical economists' works in critical, summary fashion. Few notes; spare bibliography and index.

Polanyi, Karl. *The Great Transformation.* New York: Farrar and Rinehart, 1944. A brilliantly conceived, splendidly written, and provocative work of great value to specialists and nonspecialists alike. No one else has fastened so insightfully on the problems of acquainting the eighteenth century world with the idea of a market economy. Invaluable. Few footnotes; the bibliography and index are modest but helpful.

Clifton K. Yearley

Cross-References

Capitalism, 69; Classical Economics, 74; Economists, 164; Free Trade and Protection, 251; History of Economics, 295; Market Price, 401; Marxist Economics, 412; Regulation and Deregulation, 526; Socialism, 544; Wealth, 626.

LAW OF DIMINISHING RETURNS

Type of economics: General economics
Field of study: Economic theory

The law of diminishing returns shows that, as the amount of some productive input is increased in equal increments and technology and other inputs are held constant, the resulting increments in output will decrease beyond some point. The concept is important in helping to explain the behavior of all production processes over the short run.

Principal terms

AVERAGE COST: the total monetary costs divided by the quantity of output that is produced; the cost per unit

AVERAGE PRODUCT: the total output divided by the total input of productive factors; the output per unit of input

FACTOR OF PRODUCTION: an element that is used to produce a product or service including land, labor, capital, and entrepreneurship

FIXED COSTS: monetary costs that are incurred independently of the volume of production; commonly referred to as overhead costs

LONG RUN: a period of time, which may vary from one type of production to another, over which an enterprise can vary the quantity of all its factors of production

MARGINAL COST: the monetary cost of producing an additional unit of output

MARGINAL PRODUCT: the change in total output resulting from the addition of one unit of a variable factor of production

PRODUCTION FUNCTION: a function that identifies the maximum quantities of output that can be produced by different combinations of factor inputs, given the existing state of technology

SHORT RUN: a period of time, which may vary from one type of production to another, over which at least one productive agent cannot be changed

VARIABLE COSTS: monetary costs that vary or change with the level of production

Overview

The law of diminishing returns provides an important basis to an understanding of the production process, as the concept of diminishing returns applies, without exception, to any production process. Thus, it is as relevant to the production of commodities as it is to that of services, and it applies equally to the operations of business firms, government-owned enterprises and agencies, and nonprofit organizations. The law of diminishing returns is a concept that is completely independent of the social and political environment within which the production process takes place. Though the law of diminishing returns cannot be derived through deduction, it is a generalization based on empirical observation that is associated with every known system of production.

The law of diminishing returns, sometimes referred to as the law of variable proportions, states that, if equal increments of a factor of production (such as labor) are added to unchanging quantities of another factor or factors (such as capital, in the form of plant and equipment, or land), the resulting increments to output must eventually begin to decrease. Put another way, the marginal product (that is, the incremental contribution) of the variable factor will begin to decline at some point.

One of the key assumptions underlying the concept of diminishing returns is that technology is held constant; that is, the state of the art is given and no new technological methods are introduced during the time period to which the law applies. Technological advances would increase the output that is associated with any combination of factor inputs, and so inhibit the onset of diminishing marginal returns. A second key assumption is that all successive units of the variable factor of production are of equal quality. Indeed, such successive unit of the variable factor can be viewed as a clone of the preceding units. Thus, the declining marginal productivity of the variable input does not derive from any differences in the quality of the successive units of input.

Therefore, the law of diminishing returns applies only to what economists term the "short run." The notion of the short run does not refer to a specific time period, such as a number of weeks, months, or years, but rather to a time span in which the enterprise (or other productive unit) is unable to change the quantity of at least one factor of production. Clearly, this period of time will vary with the type of product or service. For example, in the production of automobiles, in which specialized plant and machinery are required that sometimes take years to plan, produce, and install, the short run is likely to be considerably longer than in the case of a local bakery or real estate office.

By contrast, the "long run" applies to the time period that would allow for the quantities of all productive inputs to change. In the long run, a similar sounding, but very different, economic concept applies—that of returns to scale. The notion of returns to scale deals with the relationship between proportional changes in all factor inputs and the resulting changes in output. By definition, therefore, all factors of production are assumed to be variable. In the face of proportional changes in all factor inputs, output can change in one of three ways: in like proportion, more than proportionately, or less than proportionately.

It is important to understand not only what the law of diminishing returns says but also what it does not say. It is sometimes misunderstood to mean that successive increments of the variable factor will cause the total output to decrease. This is not so: The law states only that additional increments of the variable factor will eventually cause output to increase at a decreasing rate. While it is possible for excessive increments of the variable input to result in absolute decreases of production, that result is not a part of the law. Also, the law of diminishing returns allows for initially increasing marginal returns; the law says only that marginal returns will "eventually" begin to decrease.

The law of diminishing returns also can be expressed in monetary terms. In the short run, a given level of fixed costs is assumed. These are monetary costs that do not depend on the level of output, such as rent, insurance, management salaries, or interest payments. Businesspeople and accountants sometimes refer to these as overhead costs. Given these fixed costs (and the fixed levels of factor inputs that they imply), changes in the level of production require altering the amounts, and therefore the total monetary cost, of the variable inputs. Typically, these include, but are not limited to, direct labor and raw materials.

The law of diminishing returns requires, at some level of output, that further equal increments of expenditure on variable inputs will cause output to begin increasing rate. From this, it follows that per-unit cost (average cost) must eventually begin to increase. This rise in short-run average cost is the inevitable consequence of requiring ever larger increments of variable inputs to generate constant increments of output.

The logic behind the law of diminishing returns is relatively straightforward. As equal increments of a variable factor of production, such as labor, are added to a fixed factor, such as capital, the initial effect is likely to be rapidly expanding levels of production. Each new increment of the variable factor allows for a more effective exploitation or utilization of the fixed factor through improved specialization and division of labor. In this first phase, marginal physical products will be increasing. At some point, however, further increases in the variable factor come to have a lesser impact on production, as the fixed factor constrains the opportunities for additional specialization and division of labor. When the output begins to increase at a slower rate, the marginal product of the variable factor will begin to fall.

Applications

The earliest applications of the concept of diminishing returns related to agriculture. Classical economists who wrote in the first half of the nineteenth century, such as Thomas Robert Malthus (1766-1834), David Ricardo (1772-1823), and Nassau William Senior (1790-1864), developed the concept and used it in their analyses of modern issues. Malthus used it to show the devastating consequences of unchecked population growth—a world in which the biological capacity of humanity to reproduce would eventually outstrip its ability to produce food for subsistence. Ricardo made the notion of diminishing returns central to his famous theory on rent, the essence of which was to suggest that land rents would continue to rise as the population grew.

Most economists of the period limited the application of diminishing returns to the agricultural sector. Indeed, many economists were so awed by the miracles of the Industrial Revolution that they thought an opposite law applied to manufactures. Not until the twentieth century was it generally understood that diminishing returns applied to all production processes. In addition, early advocates of the law of diminishing returns were not always clear about the critical assumption of an unchanging technology. Probably the first precise clarification of this assumption was made by Senior in 1836. (It was the same Senior, however, who most strongly expressed the view that diminishing returns applied only to agriculture.

Probably the most famous application of the law of diminishing returns was that made by Malthus in his theory of population. Malthus believed that, whenever the general level of wages exceeded subsistence (that is, rose above the level that was necessary to maintain survival), people would procreate at a rate that led to a population increase. With land fixed in quantity, Malthus argued that the marginal product of the additional labor would decline. Given his assumption that real wages would tend to equal the marginal product of labor, the effect of the population increase would be to lower wages back to their subsistence level. Thus, only through population control could humankind hope to experience any permanent improvement in its material condition.

For much of history, and for some parts of the modern world, this Malthusian specter has proved to be correct. In other parts of the world, however, such as Western Europe and the

United States, the Malthusian prediction has been avoided. This failure results from the fact that Malthus ignored an important caveat to the law of diminishing returns: He failed to foretell the important technological improvements that have revolutionized agriculture since the nineteenth century, improvements that were already in progress when he made his gloomy predictions. He also failed to foresee that the capital stock that is used in agriculture would increase at a rate that was far faster than that of labor, thereby also forestalling the onset of diminishing returns. Nevertheless, the Malthusian vision continues to haunt many people, particularly in certain Third World countries in which technology and capital have not been introduced.

The law of diminishing returns has become a centerpiece in the modern theory of microeconomics as it relates to the behavior of the enterprise over the short run. Thus, the concept of diminishing returns underlies the U-shaped short-run average cost curve. Increasing returns, characteristic of early stages of production when incremental units of the variable input allow for the more efficient exploitation of fixed inputs, account for the observable fall in per-unit costs. Similarly, the onset of diminishing returns signals the rise in per-unit costs. Also, diminishing returns explain the price increases that accompany increased demand, as it is through these price increases that producers have the incentive to incur the added marginal costs that will be realized as production is expanded.

The law of diminishing returns has also come to form the cornerstone of the modern theory of income distribution. An important predecessor was Ricardo's theory of land rent, in which he showed that land rent was determined by the productivity of the last unit of land in cultivation. Yet, it was the American economist John Bates Clark (1847-1938) who, in 1888, demonstrated the general applicability of that theory—that wages and interest are likewise determined by the marginal productivity of labor and capital, respectively. According to Clark, each factor of production would (and, most important, should) receive the value of its marginal product. This idea was to prove to be of the greatest importance, as marginalist theory was often used, particularly by Clark, to justify existing social and economic arrangements at the time. Thus, according to marginalist theory, low wages were largely the result of an excessive supply of labor. Moreover, just as there was something inevitable and inherently just about the share of income that went to labor, so was there something inevitable and just about the portion that accrued to capital and to land. According to marginalist theory, the demand for each factor of production depends on the marginal productivity of that factor and the price of the product or service that it is producing. Given the supply of the factor, its price is objectively and fairly determined. This assumption of an ethical distribution of income led, in turn, to strong support for the system of private property. It was to take a later generation of economists to show that distribution need not be governed by the same immutable laws that governed production.

The law of diminishing returns also helps to explain why factor inputs usually are not perfect substitutes, but rather can substitute for one another only on the basis of diminishing returns. Thus, in a production process in which two factors can be varied, increasing increments of one factor usually are required in order to substitute for each unit of the other if the level of output is to remain constant. This relationship has important practical implications. For example, the notion of diminishing marginal rates of factor substitution helps to explain why huge armies of lightly armored infantry are often outmatched by much smaller forces that are supported by "capital" in the form of aircraft, tanks, and other modern weaponry. In the same way, it helps to explain why there are limits to the ability to substitute legal assistants for attorneys and audiovisual equipment for classroom teachers. Carried further, this same idea also plays an important role in determining optimal resource combinations to be used in the production process.

Context

The law of diminishing returns is possibly the single most important insight on which modern microeconomic theory depends. The concept has played a pivotal role in production and distribution theory. Without it, economists could not begin to understand production functions and the relationship between costs and output. In addition, there would be no theory that was capable of explaining and predicting income distribution.

Furthermore, the law of diminishing returns, together with the notion of diminishing marginal utility (that each increment to the consumption of a good or service adds less to total satisfaction), provides the noneconomist with an "economic" way of thinking about economic and noneconomic issues. Central to the economic way of thinking is the idea that decisions are made at the margin. This is true of economic decisions, but it is equally true of all other decisions in which a cost-benefit analysis can be employed. All decisions involve an explicit or implicit calculation of the incremental benefits that are associated with a given action and the incremental costs of that action. The relevant cost concept is that of opportunity cost, which refers to the value (monetary or nonmonetary) of what has been sacrificed or given up. Thus, the cost of reading the evening paper is the value that might have been derived from watching a television program or from going to the gymnasium to exercise. What the law of diminishing returns suggests is that additional increments of a given action will usually involve increasing sacrifice or increasing opportunity cost.

Bibliography

Ahiakpor, James C. W., ed. *Keynes and the Classics Reconsidered*. Boston: Kluwer Academic Publishers, 1998.

Baumol, William J., and Alan S. Blinder. *Economics: Principles and Policy*. 5th ed. New York: Harcourt Brace Jovanovich, 1991. A basic textbook covering microeconomic and macroeconomic theory. Chapters 23 and 35 are particularly relevant. Suitable for college students.

Clark, John Bates. *The Distribution of Wealth*. New York: Macmillan, 1899. A classic work relating marginal productivity theory to income distribution. Suitable for college students.

Dolan, Edwin G., and David E. Lindsey. *Microeconomics*. 5th ed. New York: Dryden Press, 1988. A very good basic textbook covering all aspects of marginalist analysis. Chapters 8 and 13 are the most relevant. Suitable for college students.

Lekachman, Robert. *A History of Economic Ideas*. New York: Harper & Brothers, 1959. Readable and insightful look at the development of economic thought. Chapters on Thomas Robert Malthus, David Ricardo, and the marginalists are of particular interest. Suitable for the general reader and college students.

Schumpeter, Joseph A. *History of Economic Analysis*. New York: Oxford University Press, 1954. A brilliant and classic work. Contains an excellent discussion of the law of diminishing returns, its historical evolution, and its impact on the development of economic theory. Tough reading, but worth the effort. The relevant discussion is dispersed, so readers will need to consult the subject index.

Zilcha, Itzhak. *Understanding "Classical" Economics: Studies in Long-Period Theory.* Edited by Heinz D. Kurz and Neri Salvadori. New York: Routledge, 1998.

Martin R. Blyn

Cross-References

Classical Economics, 74; Economists, 164; History of Economics, 295; Marginal Principle, 390; Production and Cost Functions, 500; Production Theory, 507; Supply Function, 563.

LIQUIDITY

Type of economics: Monetary and fiscal theory
Field of study: Monetary theory

Liquidity refers to the ease and quickness with which an asset can be converted into a medium of exchange at a price that is near its maximum market price. The liquidity of assets depends on both the characteristics of the assets themselves and on general financial conditions.

Principal terms

FINANCIAL INTERMEDIARY: a firm that collects funds by issuing financial claims against itself and uses the funds to make loans or to purchase financial assets

LENDER OF LAST RESORT: the function performed by a central bank when it increases the quantity of its money in response to a generalized increase in the demand for liquidity

MEDIUM OF EXCHANGE: an asset that is generally acceptable in exchange for other assets or for goods and services

SECONDARY MARKET: a market in which the owners of previously issued assets can sell the assets to those who wish to acquire them

TERM TO MATURITY: the time that elapses before the issuer of a financial asset must pay its maturity value to the holder of the asset

Overview

Liquidity refers to the ease and speed with which an asset can be converted into a medium of exchange, that is, into spendable money. Only a relatively small number of assets are generally acceptable in exchange for all other assets, goods, and services. An asset that is not acceptable as a medium of exchange must be converted into money (which serves as the medium of exchange) before it can be used to make purchases. A number of factors affect the terms on which an asset can be converted into money.

One factor that affects the liquidity of assets is the existence or absence of organized secondary markets, institutional arrangements which bring together asset owners who want to sell their assets (convert them into money) and prospective purchasers of these assets. An organized secondary market increases the liquidity of an asset by providing information to both sellers and buyers on the quantity of assets being offered for sale and on the current market price of the assets. In general, the larger the number of prospective buyers, the greater the liquidity of the asset. A large number of prospective buyers enables a seller to obtain an offer near the maximum market value of the asset more quickly.

Another factor that affects the liquidity of an asset is the asset's term to maturity—the length of time remaining until the asset matures (is converted into money by the issuer). Financial assets such as bonds or bank certificates of deposit have specified maturity dates. On the specified date, the issuer of the bond or certificate of deposit pays the owner of the asset a specified amount of money (the maturity value). Other financial assets and all real assets lack maturity dates. Equities (commonly called stock), which are ownership claims against corporations, have no maturity dates; the ownership claim remains in force until the corporation ceases to exist. A real asset, such as a house, can remain in use for centuries if properly maintained. Assets without any specified maturity date are said to have infinite maturity.

The market value of an asset is affected by its term to maturity. The reason is straightforward: An asset with a specified maturity date pays its owner a specified sum of money on that date. Thus, the market value of such an asset reflects the certain future value of the asset. On the other hand, an asset with infinite maturity does not provide the owner with a guaranteed payment at any point in time. Assuming that the issuers of the assets meet their legal obligations, assets with specified maturity dates are less risky than assets with infinite maturity, because fluctuations in their market values are limited by the certainty of a specified payment when the asset matures.

In general, the longer the term to maturity of an asset, the greater the asset's secondary market price fluctuations can be. The price that a purchaser offers for an asset that matures in only three months reflects the fact that the purchaser will obtain a specified money payment very soon. The longer that a purchaser must wait in order to receive the maturity value of an asset, the more the secondary market price of the asset can vary. Because the variability of the secondary market prices of long-term assets is greater than the variability of short-term asset prices, short-term assets are (in general) more liquid than long-term assets. At any particular point in time, the owner of a short-term asset is more likely to be able to sell the asset for a price that is near its maturity value than is the owner of a long-term asset.

The degree of liquidity of any asset other than money depends on secondary market conditions. During normal economic conditions, when the number of people wishing to sell assets in secondary markets is matched by prospective buyers, many assets are quite liquid. During economic recessions or financial crises, however, the liquidity of assets often declines sharply. During a recession, total spending in the economy falls and unemployment rises. Consumers become cautious about their purchases, often postponing the purchase of real assets and long-term financial assets. Consequently, the secondary market prices of real assets (such as houses) and long-term assets (such as corporate equities) often fall by a large amount. Asset owners who are forced to liquidate such assets in a recession often incur large financial losses.

Similarly, during a financial crisis, when many borrowers default on their loans and the quality of financial assets is in doubt, the demand for assets in secondary markets falls sharply. Individuals, financial firms (such as banks and insurance companies), and other business firms all want to hold more money in order to ensure their ability to meet their upcoming payments. Relatively few buyers exist for assets that do not serve as the medium of exchange. Consequently, even short-term assets that are regarded as being very liquid during ordinary economic conditions may be illiquid during financial crises. The owners of such assets may be forced to sell them at very low prices to obtain the money they require to make their payments.

Applications

The concept of liquidity has both microeconomic and macroeconomic applications. At the microeconomic level, individual households and firms organize their asset holdings in a way that enables them to make unforeseen payments without selling assets at prices that may be well below their maximum market values.

Liquidity management is one of the most important aspects of the management of depository institutions, such as banks. Banks collect funds by issuing claims against themselves in the form of checkable deposits, savings deposits (with no maturity dates), and time deposits (with specified maturity dates). They use the funds to make loans and to purchase financial assets. Because the interest that is earned on loans and bonds is the major source of bank revenue, bankers attempt to use as large a portion of their funds as possible to make loans and to purchase bonds. The business of banking, however, requires banks to convert their checkable deposits and savings deposits into cash (central bank money) on demand. Thus, banks must maintain sufficient liquidity in order to meet the demands of their customers for cash.

Bankers address this problem of meeting these cash demands, while keeping as high a proportion of their funds in earning assets as possible, by keeping only enough cash on hand to meet the day-to-day needs of their customers. Further demands for cash are met by selling liquid assets. Banks typically hold more U.S. Treasury bills than cash. Should an unusually large demand for cash arise, bankers obtain the needed cash by selling Treasury bills on the secondary market. Individual banks also acquire cash for short periods of time by borrowing from other banks. This ability to borrow also contributes to a bank's liquidity.

The existence of financial intermediaries—firms which collect funds by issuing financial claims against themselves and use the funds to make loans and buy other financial claims—increases the liquidity of the entire economy. When a nonfinancial business borrows from a bank, the business converts its promise to repay the loan (with interest) in the future into money. The firm can use the borrowed money in order to hire workers and to purchase materials that it needs to produce its products. The ability to borrow from a bank increases the liquidity of the nonfinancial firm.

Because liquidity depends on financial market conditions, it has a macroeconomic dimension. Assets which do not serve as a medium of exchange are liquid only to the extent that they can be converted into money quickly, easily, and at a reasonable price. A generalized increase in the demand for liquidity (money), such as occurs during financial crises, cannot be met by selling assets in secondary markets. In such circumstances, the quantity of money in existence, or which the banking system can create on the basis of available cash reserves, is insufficient to meet the demand for liquidity. Only intervention by an agency capable of creating an asset that serves as the medium of exchange can satisfy a generalized increase in the demand for liquidity.

One of the most important functions of a central bank, which is a government bank that issues a nation's basic currency, is that of lender of last resort. A central bank acts as a lender of last resort when it responds to a generalized increase in the demand for liquidity by increasing the quantity of currency in the economy. A larger quantity of money in the central bank directly meets the demand for liquidity when it is held by individuals and nonfinancial businesses and indirectly meets the demand for liquidity by enabling banks to expand their loans and deposits when the banks acquire more cash reserves.

Context

Economists, financiers, and government officials have been concerned with liquidity issues for centuries. John Law (1671-1729), a Scotsman who became the top financial official in the French government, devised a scheme to turn land into a liquid asset. Through a number of semiofficial banks and agencies, Law issued large quantities of paper notes (inconvertible paper money) backed by the mortgage value of land. This, in effect, turned land into a liquid asset. Unfortunately, Law's program ended disastrously, as the huge increase in the French money supply generated rapid inflation and led to a financial crisis.

Nineteenth century British economists discussed the issues of credit and liquidity extensively. A number of economists associated with the Banking School, including Thomas Tooke (1774-1858), John Fullarton (1780?-1849), and John Stuart Mill (1806-1873), regarded credit as a more important determinant of total spending in the economy than the quantity of money in existence. In his book *On the Regulation of Currencies* (second edition, 1845), Fullarton ridiculed the idea that the government could control the total amount of spending by merely controlling the quantity of paper bank notes in circulation. Fullarton argued that it was credit itself that affected spending and that, if the quantity of bank notes were restricted, many types of liquid assets could serve as media of exchange if more liquidity were needed.

The history of American banking in the latter half of the nineteenth century is replete with financial crises caused by shortages of liquidity. The National Bank Act of 1863 sharply limited the quantity of paper currency in circulation. Bank notes could be issued only by national banks (banks chartered by the U.S. Comptroller of the Currency). National banks were required to hold a quantity of U.S. government bonds that was equal to the quantity of notes that they issued. In the 1860's, immediately following the Civil War, the quantity of bonds in existence was sufficient to back all the currency that Americans wanted to hold. During the following decades, however, the U.S. economy grew and, as the government paid off its war debts, the quantity of bonds that were outstanding shrank. The result was a series of banking crises arising from periodic increases in the demand for currency. Without the legal authority to issue more bank notes, banks could not convert their deposits into currency on demand. Bank failures caused by illiquidity caused a number of recessions in the late 1800's and early 1900's.

The Federal Reserve Act of 1913, which created the Federal Reserve System, recognized the importance of protecting the liquidity of the financial system. This act specified that one of the duties of the Federal Reserve was to act as the lender of last resort for the banking system. In the case of a generalized increase in the demand for liquidity, the Federal Reserve was to make loans to banks, accepting titles to inventories as security. The failure of the Federal Reserve to act as a lender of last resort in the early 1930's contributed to the banking crisis which turned the recession of 1929 into the Great Depression.

In 1936, English economist John Maynard Keynes (1883-1946) published a book that revolutionized economics. One of the innovative features found in Keynes's *The General Theory of Employment, Interest, and Money* was his theory of interest. Unlike previous writers who had argued that the interest rate is determined by the demand for and the supply of loans, Keynes argued that the interest rate is determined by the demand for liquidity relative to the quantity of money in circulation. In Keynes's liquidity preference theory, the interest rate is the payment that a person receives in return for parting with liquidity. The liquidity preference theory was widely accepted in the 1940's and 1950's and is still found in most economics textbooks. Under fairly general conditions, the liquidity preference theory and the loanable funds theory of the interest rate produce the same results.

Bibliography

Ahiakpor, James C. W., ed. *Keynes and the Classics Reconsidered*. Boston: Kluwer Academic Publishers, 1998.

Blinder, Alan S. *Central Banking in Theory and Practice*. Cambridge, Mass.: MIT Press, 1998.

Federal Reserve Bank of New York. *Funding and Liquidity: Recent Changes in Liquidity Management Practices at Commercial Banks and Securities Firms*. New York: Author, 1990. Provides a detailed examination of liquidity management practices at the level of an individual financial firm. Defines terms and explains concepts. Suitable for college students.

Friedman, Milton, and Anna Jacobson Schwartz. *A Monetary History of the United States, 1867-1960*. Princeton, N.J.: Princeton University Press, 1963. A monumental study of the factors affecting the U.S. money supply over a period of ninety-four years. The discussion of the banking collapse during the Great Depression—a massive liquidity crisis—is classic. Suitable for college students.

Keynes, John Maynard. *The General Theory of Employment, Interest, and Money*. London: Macmillan, 1936. The original statement of the theory of liquidity preference is presented in seemingly simple terms. Unfortunately, Keynes often smoothed over difficulties, making his ideas seem simpler than they really were. Suitable for college students.

Niehans, Jürg. *A History of Economic Theory: Classic Contributions, 1720-1980*. Baltimore: The Johns Hopkins University Press, 1990. Contains an excellent treatment of the ideas and policies of John Law on pages 48-51. Written at a level understandable by high school students.

Timberlake, Richard H. *The Origins of Central Banking in the United States*. Cambridge, Mass.: Harvard University Press, 1978. Examines the historical forces that led to the creation of the Federal Reserve System, including the banking crises of the late nineteenth century. Suitable for college students.

Neil T. Skaggs

Cross-References

MACROECONOMICS

Type of economics: Monetary and fiscal theory
Fields of study: Fiscal theory and public finance; monetary theory

Macroeconomics is a policy-oriented field that addresses the problems of the national economy as a whole. It principally addresses problems in which microeconomic markets (such as the labor market) do not clear and uses traditional microeconomic theories, such as partial and general equilibrium theories, as an input for analytical purposes.

Principal terms

BEHAVIORISTIC: refers to the predictions of human action that are statistically determined from previous activities and are not dependent on any theoretical rationale

CLASSICAL ECONOMICS: the doctrine associated mainly with a group of English and French political philosophers and certain bankers and businessmen around the turn of the nineteenth century; generally assumes full employment of labor, flexible prices, and a positive return from invested capital

GENERAL EQUILIBRIUM: an economic model in which all prices and quantities that are supplied and demanded may be variable

INFERIOR GOOD: a good whose demanded quantity decreases when consumers' income increases

MARGINAL PROPENSITY TO CONSUME: the fraction of income that is spent on consumption out of a given (small) increment of income

MICROECONOMICS: the study of the rational economic activity of individual consumers or firms that are faced with a given market structure; individual behavior in the face of multiple market general equilibrium

NEW-CLASSICAL ECONOMICS: a macroeconomic school, founded in the 1980's, that assigns prominence to classical postulates, most prominently that of market clearing, especially for the labor market

QUANTITY THEORY OF MONEY: the theory that monetary expenditure is proportionate to the total demand for goods, and that this expenditure must be equal to the quantity of money that is supplied by the government

Overview

Economics is the study of ways in which material welfare is achieved, given scarce resources. Macroeconomics confines this study to a general equilibrium setting in which a high degree of aggregation and few goods are assumed. The main purpose of these two restrictive assumptions is to study more carefully the problem of uncleared markets, that is, cases in which supply is not equal to demand in one or more markets. Macroeconomics is a study, as are all general equilibrium systems, of the feedback of the conditions in one market on the behavior in the other markets.

Although macroeconomics was not taught in the American college classroom until 1960, it was, in fact, one of the principal areas of study for such classical economists as David Ricardo (1772-1823), Thomas Robert Malthus (1766-1834), Jean-Baptiste Say (1767-

1832), and Karl Marx (1818-1883), and also for later mainstream scholars such as Knut Wicksell (1851-1926) and John Maynard Keynes (1883-1946).

While some of the classical economists were able to eliminate the major concern of macroeconomics by postulating that markets always clear, such as at full employment, there have always been economists who remained focused on the fact that aggregate markets do not always clear. These economists, notably Malthus, Marx, and Keynes, tried to understand

British economist John Maynard Keynes is credited with laying the foundations of modern macroeconomics. (Library of Congress)

the reasons for such phenomena and the possible policy prescriptions to correct them. If markets do unfailingly clear, however, then the general equilibrium interest in macroeconomic models reverts to problems of allocative efficiency and income distribution at full employment, which are traditional topics for microeconomics. For this reason, it is more useful to concentrate on the disequilibrium or uncleared market interpretation as it regards macroeconomics.

Traditionally, economists have used macroeconomic models with, at most, three markets or "sectors": first, the market for currently produced output, to be used domestically for current consumption, investment for the future, or international trading purposes; second, the financial market, including bonds, equities (stocks), and money itself; and third, the market for labor. This aggregation of the myriad activities that occur in a national economy seems to characterize the three main trouble spots at which market clearing might not occur. This is the main reason for thinking along macroeconomic lines, as well as the reason that economists have favored this three-part division since the time of Ricardo.

Ricardo, assuming that the labor market would clear, saw no macroeconomic problems in the current sense and instead pursued the policy problems that are connected with value and distribution in a long-run microeconomic equilibrium economy. Other classical era economists, however, did not follow Ricardo's lead. Malthus, in particular, saw the possibility that an economy could develop a chronic excess supply in the labor market that could not be corrected by lowering wages. Marx, who became famous as an advocate of labor revolution, actually espoused a theory of disequilibrium, in the general equilibrium sense, of goods and labor markets combined, as did the American economist of the same era, Henry George (1839-1897). Later, Wicksell introduced a truly original disequilibrium macroeconomic analysis of the financial and money markets, which then influenced Keynes, the most notable of the twentieth century macroeconomic theorists.

Keynesian economics is, in fact, the foundation of all modern macroeconomics, as taught in university courses and used for government policy formulation. Although much of the current literature in macroeconomics, such as the new-classical school, is a reaction to Keynesian precepts, even this reactionary conservative trend uses the basic Keynesian macroeconomic framework in discussing issues and policies. The major emphasis in the new-classical school is the assumption that the labor market clears at full (or nearly full) employment and that prices exist such that the other markets all clear at the same time. This market clearing assumption, especially for the labor market, constitutes a clear denial of Keynes's main theme. It is also unintuitive, as it is common to talk about unemployment as a frequent and conspicuous feature of the labor market.

Ideally, microeconomics should serve macroeconomics in the following manner: Traditional microeconomic theory is a nonbehavioristic logic of rational materialistic action or decision making. Economists believe that human action should not, and usually does not, violate this rationality. Hence, the behavioral postulates of macroeconomic models, such as the Keynesian consumption function, should not in any way contradict this rationality. This means, more formally, that macroeconomic theories must not violate the necessary conditions of this microeconomic logic. Yet, using the sufficient conditions for a particular form of microeconomic behavior as input for a macroeconomic theory is illogical, behavioristic, and therefore, inappropriate. Microeconomics serves macroeconomics only as a check on its logic.

Applications

The purpose of macroeconomics is completely practical, and its use of the tools of microeconomics is completely pragmatic. Macroeconomics is judged solely on its ability to improve practical policy.

In the 1980's in the United States, a debate occurred concerning the efficiency of a capital gains tax reduction for the purpose of increasing investment spending. This is an example of the relationship between the financial market and the investment sector of the goods market. In this model, there are three markets, as usual: first, for goods (consumption, plus investment, plus government expenditure); second, for financial claims on which the capital gains tax would or would not be imposed; and third, the labor market, which may or may not be at full employment equilibrium. Ordinarily, the advocates of capital gains tax reductions assume some unemployment of labor.

The policy problem is to decide whether to increase or decrease the tax on capital gains, which are the profits on financial market purchases and sales. A higher capital gains tax may reduce the incentive for channeling money income into the investment segment of the goods market and reduce growth and prosperity. This argument entails the microeconomic assumption, however, that the class of people who use the organized financial markets for the purpose of saving actually save more than the class of people who save by other means. In contrast, it is conceivable that a comparable reduction in the income tax on the persons who do not engage in financial market transactions (such as stocks and real estate) would actually produce a greater increase in net savings.

The problem for the macroeconomist is to decide which policy argument is correct. The advocates of the capital gains tax break tacitly assume that the incentive of higher after-tax profits is sufficient to increase total net capital formation. The advocates of reducing the income tax on the middle class assume that middle-class saving behavior more than makes up for investor-class behavior. Clearly, neither position can be "proved" from microeconomic theory alone.

One of the major macroeconomic postulates of Keynesian consumption theory is that aggregated consumption spending increases with consumer income. The postulate also suggests that consumer saving increases with consumer income, which makes the aggregate marginal propensity to consume a proper fraction. While neither of these postulates can be proved using microeconomic theory, both can be enlightened by it. Microeconomic theory claims that not all goods can be inferior; that is, the demand for at least one good must increase along with increases in income. If such goods (whose demand increases with income) are more or less evenly distributed between current consumption and future consumption (saving), and if inferior goods are similarly distributed, then the marginal propensity to consume currently produced goods will be a positive proper fraction, as will be the marginal propensity to save for consumption in the future. This powerful microeconomic conclusion was not available for application by the classical macroeconomists such as Malthus, but it was available for Keynes. Hence, this is an example of a convincing microeconomic contribution to macroeconomics.

The application of this result—that the marginal propensity to consume out of current aggregate income be less than one—to Keynesian theory was a critical microeconomic theory input for predicting movements in national income and employment. It provided, in effect, a rationale for government intervention in the demand, or purchase of national output, process. Keeping in mind the Keynes postulate that money wage reduction cannot clear the labor market, full employment depends on the aggregate demand for output being equal to the supply at some level of income. Because the increase of one dollar in consumer-laborer income contributes less than a dollar to the aggregate demand for output (the marginal propensity to consume being less than one), then, at arbitrarily large income levels, the remainder of demand must come from other sources, that is, investment and government spending. Therefore, at times when investment spending drops off, full employment can only be maintained by increases in expenditures by the government, as the government is the only alternative source of demand. This conclusion does not answer the argument, however, that government expenditures of output are often inefficient from an allocative point of view. Stated another way, the Keynesian argument is that, given the inability of the labor market to clear through wage reduction, the only way for full employment equilibrium to be achieved is for the aggregate demand for output to be supplemented by some kind of government expenditure in the goods market.

Macroeconomic modeling has not been particularly helpful in respect to the functioning of the financial market. Keynesian analysis seems to take financial market behavior as an input (that is, autonomous) to the happenings in the other two aggregate markets. More recent analysis suggests that financial markets are the quickest to clear. Consequently, no formal analysis has been done on the effects of financial bankruptcy on general equilibrium. Clearly, this is an important problem, considering the financial instability of U.S. savings and loan associations in the 1980's and earlier the bank failures during the Great Depression of the 1930's. Because financial bankruptcy is a serious macroeconomic problem, further application of macroeconomic theory to this phenomenon is likely to occur.

Context

Macroeconomics was a central issue during the heyday of classical economics, and while much formalization of the theory and certain policy refinements have been added during the intervening years, little real change has taken place in the original structure. This is probably a result of the extreme political importance of the conclusions of such a theory, and the concomitant political agendas of the various writers on the subject.

Macroeconomic analysis has always been conducted in general equilibrium terms, even for the classical school some eighty years before general equilibrium was "invented" in two different forms by Alfred Marshall (1842-1924) and Léon Walras (1834-1910). It is convenient to begin its history with Say, who discovered the "law of the market"—the aggregate supply in a set of markets could not exceed the aggregate demand in the same set of markets. This can mean that the "set of markets" includes the money and credit markets, that is, that the value of things that are bought must identically equal the value of things that are sold. If, however, the theory also includes a strict law as to the money-spending habits of the community, such as the quantity theory of money, then Say's law of the market applies, with flexible prices, to the set of markets that exclude money. Say's theory of markets makes this point clear, but his own political agenda advocated free markets, so that it has been the second (quantity theory) interpretation that has been employed by other free market advocates. Ricardo, for one, incorporated this second interpretation of Say's law into his own long-run theory of the workings of the economy. John Stuart Mill (1806-1873) adopted the first interpretation, allowing much indeterminacy in the demand for money and credit.

Marx abstracted his theories from the money and capital markets and concentrated on the disequilibrium in the labor market, which is caused not so much by capital market intrusion as by the domination of the economy by rent, in the sense that was used by Ricardo. Many have found Marx's analysis to be riddled with logical contradictions, many of which may be related to the terms and concepts that are embodied in Say's law of the market.

The next major contribution came from Wicksell, who attempted to sort out the market clearing problems of the money and capital markets. His system contained no real equilibrium solution, but his technique of analysis leads to Keynes's theory, which employs Wicksell's analysis of money (suggested by Mill's first interpretation of Say's law) coupled with a unique theory of wage adjustment in the labor market, leading to a macroeconomic equilibrium with less than full employment. Although Keynes's conclusions for the labor market are reminiscent of Marx's theories, the reasons that Keynes gives for unemployment are quite different, as is his political prescription of government activism. Finally, the new-classical theory of macroeconomics represents a nearly complete reversion of the second interpretation of Say's law. It assumes complete price flexibility, as well as full employment equilibrium in the labor market, and the money and capital markets are abstracted.

Bibliography

Ahiakpor, James C. W., ed. *Keynes and the Classics Reconsidered.* Boston: Kluwer Academic Publishers, 1998.

Blaug, Mark. *Economic Theory in Retrospect.* Homewood, Ill.: Richard D. Irwin, 1968. A standard work in the history of economic analysis. Contains a very concise treatment of classical macroeconomics, mostly in chapter 4. Also contains an adequate chapter on Karl Marx.

Hahn, Frank. *Equilibrium and Macroeconomics.* Cambridge, Mass.: MIT Press, 1984. A collection of essays by a prominent modern economist. Hahn is mostly critical of new-classical economics for its strict interpretation of Say's law.

Hicks, John R. *Value and Capital.* London: Oxford University Press, 1939. The most authoritative book on the relation of microeconomic theory to twentieth century macroeconomics. The appendices are very mathematical, but the text is generally readable.

Keynes, J. M. *The General Theory of Employment, Interest, and Money.* 1936. Reprint. London: Harcourt Brace Jovanovich, 1964. The most influential macroeconomics book of the twentieth century. The most important chapters are those on the classical labor market, the consumption function, and the demand for money. Follows a Marshallian general equilibrium approach.

Malinvaud, Edmond. *The Theory of Unemployment Reconsidered.* 2d ed. Cambridge, Mass.: Basil Blackwell, 1985. A short, nondoctrinaire treatment of macroeconomic policy in an economy which does not behave according to Say's law in a strong sense and, hence, may be amenable to government demand policy action.

Marshall, Alfred. *Principles of Economics.* 8th ed. Philadelphia: Porcupine Press, 1982. The bulk of Marshall's critique and interpretation of classical macroeconomics, especially that surrounding Say's law, is contained in appendix B of this monumental work. Contains many other insights.

Patinkin, Don. *Money, Interest, and Prices.* New York: Harper & Row, 1965. Patinkin attempts to collect the microeconomic (that is, the static rational) decision activity of individuals into a coherent explanation of macroeconomic behavior. He does this with limited success, but no one has done better. It is, however, instructive to go over just how Patinkin goes about this task.

Roll, Eric. *A History of Economic Thought.* Homewood, Ill.: Richard D. Irwin, 1974. Gives a particularly sympathetic treatment of the mid-nineteenth century reaction to classical macroeconomic conclusions, mostly in chapters 4, 5, and 6.

Schumpeter, Joseph A. *History of Economic Analysis.* New York: Oxford University Press, 1954. Schumpeter gives his usual in-depth analysis of the main players, David Ricardo, Jean-Baptiste Say, and John Stuart Mill. Nearly all of the history of macroeconomic thought to 1950 can be found in this book.

Yonay, Yuval P. *The Struggle over the Soul of Economics: Institutionalist and Neoclassical Economists in America Between the Wars.* Princeton, N.J.: Princeton University Press, 1998.

Peter Frevert

Cross-References

MARGINAL PRINCIPLE

Type of economics: General economics
Field of study: Economic theory

The marginal principle, as applied to economics, relies on the fundamentally important distinction between total utility (total revenues) and marginal utility (marginal revenues), that is, the additional utility (revenue) that results from the consumption (sale) of a small additional amount of a good. According to this principle, it is the marginal (as opposed to the total) utility (revenue) that determines the optimal amount to consume or output to produce.

Principal terms

EXTERNALITY: a side effect of consumption or production in which the consumption (production) of one person or firm affects the utility (output) of another

MARGINAL RATE OF SUBSTITUTION: the rate at which a consumer is willing to trade small amounts of any two goods, such that the combined satisfaction from consumption of both goods remains constant

MARGINAL RATE OF TECHNICAL SUBSTITUTION: the rate at which inputs (labor, machinery, and land) can be substituted for one another, holding output constant

MARGINAL RATE OF TRANSFORMATION: the rate at which the output of one product can be transformed into another product, given a fixed set of inputs

MARGINAL UTILITY: marginal satisfaction; the additional welfare that a consumer receives from consuming an additional unit of a good

MARGINAL VALUE PRODUCT: the contribution of an additional unit of an input to output when that contribution is valued using the market price of output

PARETO EFFICIENCY: a situation that exists when there is no way to make one person in an economy better off without making someone else worse off

PERFECTLY COMPETITIVE ECONOMY: an economy that is characterized by markets that operate without distortion, consumers and firms that are price takers, and no externalities or public goods

PUBLIC GOODS: goods that are nonexclusive; goods that can be consumed at the same time by more than one consumer

Overview

Marginal principles form the basis of most of the analysis of constrained decision making in neoclassical economic theory. The conceptual framework for marginalist analysis in economics entails purposeful (maximizing) choices and scarcity. Fundamental to the development of the marginal principle in economics is the assumption that consumers, firms, and policymakers make purposeful choices. Specifically, consumers are assumed to make choices that maximize the satisfaction that they receive from those goods that they consume. These choices include what combination of goods and services to purchase, how much to save for retirement, how much education to attain, what career to pursue, and how much to work. Firms are assumed to make choices that maximize profit and minimize costs. The choices of firms include how much output to produce given the product price and how to produce that output—how much labor, land, and machinery to use in the production process. Firms also choose which of many products to create and how much to invest in advertising and in research and development. Policymakers choose tax and subsidy laws, as well as how much of specific public goods (such as defense services, roads, and education) to provide. Furthermore, firms, consumers, and governments are constrained. They make their choices subject to the constraints that are imposed by the scarcity of resources. Consumers (and policymakers) face budget constraints and must choose how to allocate their incomes among goods and services that have fixed prices. Firms also have budget constraints and must choose how much output to produce given these constraints and the prices that they face, such as wage rates and rental rates on machines or land.

The marginal principle explains how consumers and firms make optimal, or maximizing, choices when they face constraints. In order to understand the basic reasoning that underlies the marginal principle, consider first the consumer's choice. Marginalist economic theory asserts that consumers behave according to a number of assumptions that amount to rationality or consistency in choice making, as well as diminishing marginal rates of substitution. The latter means that, as a consumer acquires more and more of a good (X), holding satisfaction constant, the amount of the other good (Y) that the consumer is willing to forgo in order to obtain an additional unit of the first good eventually declines. This is known as the marginal rate of substitution (MRS). In other words, the rate at which a consumer is willing to trade Y for X (that is, the MRS), holding utility constant, declines as the consumer obtains more of X.

If the marginal principle operates, then choices result in an allocation of goods to consumers such that the rate at which a consumer is willing to trade Y for X, holding satisfaction constant, is just equal to the rate at which the consumer can trade Y for X in a marketplace. Yet, the market terms of trade that the consumer faces are equal to the price of Y divided by the price of X (p_y/p_x). Thus, the marginal principle predicts that consumers maximize utility by choosing to consume any bundle of goods at which the MRS = p_y/p_x.

In order to examine this principle in more detail, consider the following example. Suppose that a consumer can purchase X at a price of $2.00 per unit and Y at a price of $1.00 per unit. Consequently, the consumer must give up two Y for each X that he or she consumes. Suppose that the consumer is willing to give up one Y for one X, holding satisfaction constant. Therefore, the consumer should take some X and trade it for some Y. Suppose that he or she takes one X and trades it (at market prices) for two Y. Then, the consumer will be better off, as he or she needed only one Y in return for one X in order to keep satisfaction constant. Furthermore, as the consumer increases Y consumption and reduces X consumption, the MRS increases and moves closer to the relative price ratio of two. This reasoning demonstrates that it is possible to increase satisfaction by reallocating goods in the consumption basket, unless the consumer's MRS = p_y/p_x, which constitutes the marginal condition for consumption.

Consider a firm that decides how much output to produce. If the firm produces one extra unit, then it can sell that unit at a fixed price (p) as firms are price takers in a perfectly competitive market. Then, if the additional revenue that the firm receives from producing one additional unit of output (that is, its marginal revenue, which equals the selling price of the good) is greater than the additional cost that is incurred from producing that unit (marginal cost), then it should produce that unit. Producing the unit adds a net amount to profits that is equal to the difference between marginal revenue (marginal price) and marginal cost. Profits can be increased by increasing output as long as the additional revenue from one more unit of output exceeds the additional cost of production. When the marginal revenue that is gained from producing one more unit of goods equals the marginal cost that is incurred in order to produce that good, profits are maximized. Accordingly, this is the output level at which the firm should produce.

In general, marginalist analysis distinguishes between total utility (total revenues) and marginal utility (marginal revenues) and demonstrates that the behavior that maximizes total utility (revenues) equates marginal increments of utility (revenues) to the additional cost of that marginal increment. This concept is the marginal principle. Given an initial distribution of income, marginal principles explain how goods are allocated to consumers, as well as how inputs are allocated to production, and what mix of products occurs in a perfectly competitive economy.

The following results can be derived using marginalist analysis: First is *optimal conditions for exchange:* The marginal rate of substitution for any two goods (and also the ratio of marginal utilities) equals the ratio of the prices for those goods. Second is *optimal conditions for production:* The marginal rate of substitution for any two productive factors for all firms in an industry equals the ratio of those input prices. Third is *optimal conditions for composition of output:* If the first and second conditions hold, then the marginal value product of each factor is the same in each industry, and the prices that are used to value them are the same prices that consumers face. Consequently, the marginal rate of substitution for consuming any two goods must equal the marginal rate of transformation of those two goods in production. Furthermore, if these marginal principles hold in a perfectly competitive economy with no distortions, then the result is an allocation of goods and services that is Pareto efficient. It should be noted that there exist many Pareto efficient allocations, each corresponding to the initial distribution of income.

Applications

Marginal principles have important implications for the design of economic policies when the aim is an efficient allocation of resources. The previous discussion maintains that, given an initial distribution of income in a perfectly competitive equilibrium, the allocation of resources is Pareto efficient. This result is the basic rationale for market-based economic policy recommendations, and it suggests that government intervention is not only unnecessary but also undesirable. That conclusion, however, follows only in the case of perfect competition with no externalities or public goods. In the event that the assumptions of perfect competition are violated (for example, if firms possess some price-setting power) or in the event that externalities or public goods exist, the resulting allocation of goods may no longer be efficient. Thus, there may arise a justification for intervention, and marginal principles can provide guidelines for a desirable policy intervention.

Typically, intervention entails taxation policies when production creates a negative side effect, such as in the case of polluting firms. Government intervention has also taken the form of the provision of some public goods (such as defense services) and the regulation of firms that have price setting power (such as airlines and telephone services). In these cases, marginal principles provide rules for intervention when the aim is to achieve Pareto efficiency. For example, the recommendation for the optimal government provision of a public good is to provide that amount of the good that maximizes the benefits that accrue from consuming the good. The marginal principle dictates that this benefit-maximizing amount of the public good occurs when the additional benefits that accrue from the last unit of the good just equal the additional cost of producing that unit. Because many consumers can consume the public good at the same time, however, there is no incentive to purchase the good; instead, consumers have the incentive to "free-ride" on the consumption of others. Yet, all consumers have this incentive and, consequently, the good will not be provided by market forces.

Because market forces do not ensure that the benefit-maximizing amount of the public good is forthcoming, there may be a justification for public provision of the good. While, in practice, it may be difficult to determine the benefit-maximizing quantity to provide (as measuring the benefits and costs of public goods consumption is difficult when consumers do not have incentives to reveal what the good is worth to them), marginalist analysis nevertheless provides the efficiency guideline for spending on public goods.

Secondly, marginal principles are used in the design of policy regarding side effects, or externalities. Consider pollution, a typical side effect that is created by firms that pollute the atmosphere in the process of production. A typical example of this type of side effect might occur in the pulp industry. In this case, pulp producers use society's resources above and beyond the resources (labor and capital) that are actually paid for by the firm. If the firms are not motivated to take account of the costs of this side effect, then the result is that too much of the good is produced, as the additional costs of the resources that are used in the production of the last unit of the good outweigh the additional benefits that are accrued because of that unit. Thus, total benefits can be increased by reducing output until the marginal costs that society incurs from production just equal the marginal benefits that society gains from the consumption of the last unit. One policy option is to induce firms in the industry to reduce output by imposing taxes that force firms to bear some of the costs of the externality that they create and to reduce output to the efficient level.

Marginal principles also provide regulatory guidelines for markets in which firms have price-setting power. When services are provided by one or a few firms (such as in electric or telephone services), the regulation of these firms may be necessary. The efficiency criteria for this regulation consist of marginal principles: The efficient output occurs when the additional costs that are incurred for the last unit equal the additional benefits that are accrued to this unit.

Marginal principles explain how a firm decides to produce, as well as how consumers choose to purchase goods. In practice, however, marginal principles do much more. Another application of marginalist economics consist of the conceptual basis for the demand curves that economists use to predict responses to alterations in prices of particular goods. These curves, in turn, are important for policy purposes (for example, to predict the response to the imposition of an excise tax on cigarettes or alcohol). The shape of the demand curve depends, in part, on marginal principles: the rate at which a consumer becomes satiated with goods. In addition, the shape of the demand curve determines how responsive consumers are to price changes, and, therefore, how much revenue will be gained and how much consumption discouraged by taxing a good such as alcohol.

Furthermore, a marginal principle is used to derive the firm's supply curve, which is used to analyze how firms react to different prices. Marginalist economics predicts that the price-taking firm that faces a new output price maximizes its profits by altering output until the additional cost of producing the (new) last unit that is produced equals the new output price. Thus, marginalist principles provide the basic reasoning underlying the derivation of a firm's supply curve. This supply curve can determine the responsiveness of firms to taxes imposed per unit of output.

Finally, as economic theory has extended its analysis to consider economic problems in a wide variety of settings, including intertemporal choice problems (choices made in the face of uncertainty and imperfect information), marginal principles have been extended to these types of problems. In the case of intertemporal choice, for example, marginal principles still apply. This problem can be framed in the terms of the prices of consumption in one time period compared to another, as well as preferences for consuming goods and services in one time period compared to consuming in another. Optimal consumption in each period will occur when the consumer's marginal rate of substitution for consumption in the second time period, compared to the first time period, equals the price of consuming in the second period, relative to the price of consuming in the first period.

Context

Economists have long been convinced that undistorted markets allocate scarce goods effectively. Adam Smith (1723-1790) proclaimed in *An Inquiry Into the Nature and Causes of the Wealth of Nations* (1776), for example, that self-interested behavior on the part of consumers and producers leads to desirable outcomes. Yet, marginal principles did not take explicit hold as a tool of economic analysis until late in the nineteenth century. What was required was the distinction between total satisfaction or utility (from consuming some amount of a good) and marginal utility (the increment to utility that results from consuming one extra unit of a good).

In *The Theory of Political Economy* (1871), William Stanley Jevons (1835-1882) described this distinction and analyzed the conditions for utility maximization in exchange. In order to do so, Jevons relied on the assumption of diminishing marginal utility—the general law that the increments of additional utility that accrue from consuming additional units of a good "ultimately decrease as that quantity increases." He justified this assumption on the grounds that "All our appetites are capable of *satisfaction* or *satiety* sooner or later...." Given the "law" of diminishing marginal utility, Jevons derived the condition for utility-maximizing exchange: that the ratio of marginal utility for any two goods must equal their relative prices.

After the exposition of marginalist principles in consumer theory late in the nineteenth century, it was some time before full marginalist analysis developed, mainly because of the difficulty of extending the analysis to production when factors of production can substitute for one another in production. In consumer theory, a further refinement developed in the twentieth century. This theory apparently called for measurable and cardinal marginal utility: It was expected that consumers not only rank consumption bundles but also assign utility or satisfaction numbers to these bundles. This expectation created conceptual, as well as measurement, problems because units of satisfaction are not measurable directly and utility cannot be compared across consumers.

Another type of analysis developed, however, that only required consumers to rank or order consumption bundles, not to measure their preferences between bundles numerically. Once these principles were developed, marginalist analysis was fully developed and accepted. At this point, mathematical techniques involving constrained optimization techniques were explicitly applied to the problems of consumer and producer choice. Optimization problems and techniques have become increasingly complex as economists attempt to introduce realism into economic problems by introducing intertemporal components, imperfect information, and uncertainty into choice problems.

Bibliography

Blaug, Mark. *Economic Theory in Retrospect.* Cambridge, England: Cambridge University Press, 1987. Contains a clear description of the development of marginalist economics in consumer theory, as well as of the theory of the firm. Suitable for general readers as well as college students.

Eijffinger, Sylvester, and Harry Huizinga, eds. *Positive Political Economy: Theory and Evidence.* New York: Cambridge University Press, 1998.

Hicks, John R. *Value and Capital.* Oxford, England: Clarendon Press, 1979. Presents an exposition of modern marginalist economics that is clear and accessible. Suitable for college students. The appendices contain mathematical expositions for more advanced readers.

Jevons, William Stanley. *The Theory of Political Economy.* 1871. Reprint. London, England: Penguin Books, 1970. One of the seminal works on marginal principles. Includes a fine introduction by R. D. Collison Black, the editor of Jevons' *Papers and Correspondence* (Clifton, N.J.: A. M. Kelley, 1972-1973).

Koopmans, T. C. *Three Essays on the State of Economic Science.* New York: McGraw-Hill, 1957. Examines the frontiers of modern neoclassical economics. Very accessible.

Palley, Thomas I. *Plenty of Nothing: The Downsizing of the American Dream and the Case for Structural Keynesianism.* Princeton, N.J.: Princeton University Press, 1998.

Silberberg, Eugene. *The Structure of Economics.* New York: McGraw-Hill, 1978. The first chapter of this textbook presents an overview of marginalist economics. Suitable for the general reader.

Sandra J. Peart

Cross-References

MARGINAL UTILITY

Type of economics: General economics
Fields of study: Consumer economics and economic theory

Marginal utility refers to the additional pleasure or satisfaction that is derived from consuming the last unit of a good or service. This concept is an important element of consumer demand theory and welfare theory.

Principal terms

ASSOCIATIVE MEASURE: a measure that assigns numbers in order to associate elements of one set to elements of a different set

CARDINAL MEASURE: a measure that can be expressed in an additive, as well as ordinal and associative, way

CONVEX PREFERENCES: consumer preferences that are characterized by preferring means to extremes

LAW OF DIMINISHING MARGINAL UTILITY: a principle that holds that, as more of a good is consumed, a point is eventually reached at which the marginal utility of added units of the good declines

OCCAM'S RAZOR: the scientific principle that a theory should rely on as few assumptions as possible in order to explain a phenomenon

ORDINAL MEASURE: a measure that assigns numbers in order to express a ranking of elements in a set

TOTAL UTILITY: the total amount of pleasure or satisfaction that is derived from having, owning, or consuming a given amount of a good or service

Overview

Marginal utility is an important concept in the development of the economic theory of consumer behavior. It is necessary to understand first the notion of total utility. Total utility refers to the total amount of pleasure or satisfaction that is derived from having, consuming, or owning goods or services. Goods such as automobiles, hamburgers, haircuts, and medical services all provide consumers with pleasure or satisfaction. The sources of the pleasure or satisfaction include aesthetic beauty, the convenience of use, functional usefulness, prestige, ego gratification, and many other possibilities. If an automobile is considered, for example, a Chevrolet may provide basic transportation that is reliable but a Mercedes-Benz provides both additional convenience of operation and prestige. These added features may make the Mercedes-Benz more desirable for some consumers, but not necessarily for all, and how much more desirable depends on the individual's tastes. Person A may like the prestige that Mercedes-Benz ownership confers. Person B may dislike the ostentation, and hence prefer the Chevrolet. Economists do not judge a consumer's reasons for wanting a product. While an ethical system may provide guidance as to whether one source of utility is justified and another is not, economics treats utility as utility, regardless of its subjective source. The implicit ethic of the economist, however, is that more satisfaction is better than less.

An immediate concern is how utility is measured. Early theorists believed that utility could be measured in a cardinal way, like temperature or distance. Therefore, a hamburger that provides one hundred utils (imaginary units of utility) is twice as good as one that provides fifty utils. It may provide additional utility because of its size, nutritional provision, flavor, speed of preparation, or any combination of these characteristics. Yet, the pleasure or satisfaction that is provided by a hamburger cannot be measured in such a cardinal way. An indication of the difficulty that is involved is the fact that the unit of measurement (utils) is imaginary. In addition, early theorists believed that the marginal utility of any good declined as more was consumed. They believed that, if the first hamburger provides one hundred utils, the second may provide eighty, and the third sixty. Utility was believed to be measurable in a cardinal way, which included additivity.

In the twentieth century, the assumption of cardinality of utility measurement was dispensed with. It is assumed, instead, that a consumer can provide a ranked order of all the options that are available. For example, when comparing hamburgers, a consumer may prefer a Big Mac to a Whopper and prefer a Whopper to a Wendy's hamburger. Another consumer may rank the burgers differently. All that is required is the rank ordering in order to establish the basic results of consumer theory. Thus, utility only needs to be ordinal in its measurement. It is sufficient to know that the Big Mac is preferred to the Whopper, which is in turn preferred to the Wendy's hamburger. From that information alone, the consumer's demand curve for hamburgers can be derived. Therefore, the questionable assumption that consumers possess a cardinal measure of satisfaction can be dropped.

Many introductory textbooks explain that marginal utility can be measured by the consumer's willingness to pay for added amounts of the good in question. By measuring the willingness to pay, the difficulties that are associated with measuring marginal utility in other units can be circumvented. The essence of this approach, however, is more substantive. By measuring marginal utility in money terms, the modern theory of marginal utility is being used, in which the marginal utility of the good in question is compared to the marginal utility of money. That ratio of marginal utilities (the marginal utility of the good divided by the marginal utility of money) is what is referred to as the marginal utility in money terms. Note that, if the marginal utility of the good, measured in utils per unit, is divided by the marginal utility of money, measured in utils per dollar, the resulting ratio is measured in dollars per unit. The units of measurement for utility cancel, solving the measurement problem. Absolute marginal utility is not needed, only the relative marginal utilities.

In modern axiomatic theory, consumer preferences are assumed to be convex, which means that consumers are assumed to prefer mean bundles of goods to extreme bundles of the same goods. For example, suppose that a consumer is confronted with selecting a house with some combination of bedrooms and bathrooms. It is assumed that the consumer would prefer a house with three bedrooms and three bathrooms to either a five-bedroom house with one bathroom or a five-bathroom house with one bedroom. The three-bedroom/three-bathroom house is a convex combination of the two extremes: one half of each, combined. In this sense, consumers are said to prefer means to extremes. This assumption has implications for the marginal utility of a bedroom. It implies that, the more bedrooms that a consumer has, relative to bathrooms, the smaller the marginal utility of the last bedroom, compared to the marginal utility of the last bathroom.

The importance of this result is that, at the outset, the traditional notion that is embodied in the law of diminishing marginal utility is not required. That law states that, eventually, the marginal utility declines. As a consumer buys more of any good, there comes a point at which the added satisfaction that is gained from the last unit purchased begins to decline. While earlier consumer theories asserted that the law of diminishing marginal utility applied to all goods and services, modern theory does not. Instead, modern theory assumes that preferences are convex, implying that the relative marginal utility declines.

Applications

Consumer demand curves rely on the concept of marginal utility. Demand theory begins with assumptions concerning consumer preferences. Those assumptions then have implications regarding the response of the consumer to changes in both income and prices.

In order to derive the demand curve for a product, one can confront a consumer with varying prices for a commodity and observe how the consumer's purchases vary. Then, by plotting the quantity that is demanded at each price, the demand curve for the product can be constructed. The resulting inverse relationship between price and quantity demanded reflects the underlying convexity of consumer preferences. Hence, the basic result of demand theory—that price and quantity demanded move in opposite directions—comes as a direct result of declining relative marginal utility. It is not necessary to assume that marginal utility declines in an absolute sense in order to derive this result. It is sufficient to assume that relative marginal utility declines.

Another application of the idea of marginal utility is found in the concept of progressive income taxation. If the marginal utility of income declines as a person's income rises, then each additional dollar of income provides smaller and smaller amounts of added satisfaction from the goods and services that can be purchased. In this case, by taxing additional dollars of income at higher rates as income rises, the reduction in total utility that is attributable to taxation can be minimized with a progressive tax structure. Consider a simple example of a community with two individuals. Person A has an income of $20,000 annually and a marginal utility of $1.00 for the last dollar of income. Person B has an income of $100,000 annually and a marginal utility of $0.50 for the last dollar of income. If the government needs to raise two additional dollars in tax revenue in order to pave a street, it has several choices. It can tax both individuals $1.00, or it could tax the higher-income individual at a higher rate. If both are taxed at the same rate, then the tax reduces social welfare by $1.50—$1.00 of lost marginal utility for Person A and $0.50 for Person B. If, on the other hand, Person B is taxed $2.00 and Person A is exempted from paying the tax, the same total tax revenue causes society's utility to decline by only $1.00.

Taxing higher-income individuals at higher marginal rates reduces the loss of utility caused by taxation. Keep in mind that the new pavement will benefit both people and that a full picture of the effects of the tax should include the benefits that come from the government provision of goods and services. Such arguments for progressive income taxation, in which the marginal tax rate rises as income rises, hinge on the assumption of the diminishing marginal utility of income as well as on the greater ability to pay taxes of high-income individuals.

A related example of the application of marginal utility is found in the policy of income redistribution. Suppose that the current distribution of income in a country is so uneven that a sense of fairness is violated. It is desired to redistribute some income from the very wealthy to the very poor. If the marginal utility of income is the same for everyone, then such a redistribution is pointless; by taking a dollar of income from one person and giving it to another no increase in social welfare is achieved. One person is made better off and another is made worse off, but it is difficult to say whether society as a whole benefits from such a redistribution. If, on the other hand, the marginal utility of income declines with income, then a strong incentive exists to redistribute income. By taking a dollar from a wealthy person with a small marginal utility of income and giving that dollar to a poor person with a larger marginal utility of income, total social welfare can be increased. Therefore, income redistribution schemes also rely on the concept of the declining marginal utility of income. It may be the case, however, that such a redistribution affects the incentives to work, save, and invest, altering the total output of the economy.

Context

Utility theory was developed initially by Jeremy Bentham (1748-1832) and others who regarded utility as a cardinal and absolute measurement of the pleasure or satisfaction that is derived from consuming goods and services. The concept of marginal utility received great emphasis during the late 1800's under the influence of the marginalists, an influential group of academics who assumed that utility is cardinal with an absolute zero. They developed the notion of the law of diminishing marginal utility. This led to policy recommendations for progressive income taxation and wealth redistribution, which followed the objective of maximizing total societal utility. Because they assumed that utility could be compared across individuals, a policy could be designed to redistribute resources as long as one person's increased utility because of the policy was greater than another person's decreased utility.

If marginal utility declines with income, then the loss of utility that is experienced by taking some income from a wealthy person is more than made up by giving that income to a poor person with greater marginal utility. The key development of the marginalist school of thought, however, was (according to Eugene Silberberg) that "it is possible to obtain answers regarding marginal quantities, i.e., how total quantities change, without specific investigation of individual preferences or how such preferences might be formed."

In the late 1800's, however, economists came to realize that a cardinal measurement of utility was not necessary for consumer theory. The work of Vilfredo Pareto (1848-1923) was important in this regard. The assumption of the cardinal measurement of utility was dropped in favor of ordinal measurement. It is sufficient to know how the consumer would rank commodity bundles, without regard for the intensity of satisfaction that is derived from those bundles, in order to derive refutable hypotheses. It is not necessary that specific cardinal measures of utility be assigned to those bundles, as no refutable implications are gained by the assumption of cardinal utility. Hence, Occam's razor (the principle that a theory should rely on as few assumptions as possible in order to explain a phenomenon) can be applied and the notion of a cardinal measurement of utility discarded.

In addition, modern microeconomic theory does not require the assumption of diminishing marginal utility. Axiomatic approaches, to consumer theory require only an ordinal ranking of commodity bundles, not cardinal measurement. From such rankings, and the assumption that preferences are convex, demand schedules for commodities can be derived and one can investigate how a consumer responds to changes in prices, income, and other factors.

Bibliography

Baumol, William, and Alan Blinder. *Economics: Principles and Policy.* 5th ed. New York: Harcourt Brace Jovanovich, 1991. A very good introductory text in economics that presents marginal utility as measured by a consumer's willingness to pay.

Canterbery, E. Ray. *The Making of Economics.* 3d ed. Belmont, Calif.: Wadsworth, 1987. Provides a very good history of the concept of utility and its role in economic theory. Discussion ranges from Jeremy Bentham and the early utilitarians to the marginalists to modern theorists.

Ferguson, C. E. *Microeconomic Theory.* Rev. ed. Homewood, Ill.: Richard D. Irwin, 1969. This classic microeconomics text explains, in a particularly clear way, the differences in approaches to applying utility theory.

Jha, Raghbendra. *Modern Public Economics.* New York: Routledge, 1998.

Katzner, Donald W. *Static Demand Theory.* New York: Macmillan, 1970. Modern axiomatic demand theory is presented in this highly mathematical volume, which represents a distillation of hundreds of years of thought on the concept of utility and its implications. The introduction contains a very good brief history of the development of utility theory.

Palley, Thomas I. *Plenty of Nothing: The Downsizing of the American Dream and the Case for Structural Keynesianism.* Princeton, N.J.: Princeton University Press, 1998.

Silberberg, Eugene, *The Structure of Economics: A Mathematical Analysis.* 2d ed. New York: McGraw-Hill, 1990. This mathematically oriented text in microeconomics presents modern consumer theory, including an excellent discussion of utility in chapter 10.

Solberg, Eric J. *Intermediate Microeconomics.* Plano, Tex.: Business Publications, 1982. A good modern undergraduate text in microeconomics in which Solberg clearly presents axiomatic consumer theory as distinct from the nineteenth century marginalist perspective, which still dominates many texts.

John E. Anderson

Cross-References

Capitalism, 69; Demand Function, 140; Income, 301; Marginal Principle, 390; Tax and Taxation, 569; Tax Systems, 575; Wealth, 626; Welfare Economics, 631.

MARKET PRICE

Type of economics: General economics
Fields of study: Economic theory and monetary theory

Market price is the equilibrium price in a free market, in which neither a shortage nor a surplus exists. It is the price at which quantity demanded is equal to quantity supplied.

Principal terms

ARBITRAGE: the simultaneous buying and selling of an item in order to earn sure and certain profit

CARTEL: an association of individual producers who act in concert in order to increase collective profits

COMMODITY: a good that is durable, divisible, and easily standardized as to grade or quality

DEMAND: the quantities of an item that buyers are willing and able to purchase at various prices

EFFICIENT MARKETS HYPOTHESIS: the idea that present prices fully incorporate all known information, so that future price movements are unpredictable

MARKETING ORDERS: the limits on the sales and/or production of individual members of a cartel

SHORTAGE: a continuing state of excess demand, caused by a price that is fixed below the equilibrium price

SUPPLY: the quantities of an item that its owners offer for sale at various prices

SURPLUS: a continuing state of excess supply, caused by a price that is fixed above the equilibrium price

Overview

The market price is that price which occurs naturally in a free market; consequently, it is often referred to as the "free market price." It is also the price which, once attained, will tend to continue; hence the name "equilibrium price" also applies.

In a free market, there are no restrictions, legal or otherwise, on the price that may be offered by potential sellers of a good. There are also no restrictions on the price that potential buyers may bid for the good. There would seem to be no reason, then, that the market price would simultaneously satisfy quantity demanded and quantity supplied. Yet it invariably does. To understand how this can occur requires a brief discussion of supply and demand.

As the market price increases, suppliers tend to offer more of the good for sale, for several reasons. They may decide to take the good out of inventory or storage, to produce a larger quantity because the profit per unit produced is higher, or to use a smaller amount of the good themselves, so that they may sell more. At the same time, buyers tend to reduce their intentional purchases when the market price increases. Buyers may decide to substitute other goods for the good whose price has risen or to do without the good in question until its price has fallen again. They may also feel poorer as a result of the price increase and reduce their purchases of the more expensive good, in addition to other goods.

As the market price increases, then, the quantity demanded tends to be reduced, while the quantity supplied tends to increase. Consequently, as the market price falls, the quantity demanded tends to rise, while the quantity supplied tends to fall. These facts virtually guarantee that, as long as some of the good is exchanged, the market price will reach an equilibrium between the quantity supplied and the quantity demanded.

Whenever price is above equilibrium, the quantity supplied exceeds the quantity demanded; there is excess supply. Sellers tend to offer a lower price in order to dispose of their unsold inventory. Buyers also tend to bid a lower price, aware that sellers cannot dispose of their stocks. In this way, excess supply leads to a lower market price. Whenever price is below equilibrium, the quantity supplied is less than the quantity demanded; there is excess demand. Buyers tend to bid a higher price, so that they are able to buy at least some of the good. Buyers also tend to raise their offered price, seeing that other buyers are clamoring for the offered quantity. In this way, excess demand tends to result in a higher market price.

Whenever market price is below equilibrium, excess demand tends to raise it; when market price is above equilibrium, excess supply tends to depress it. Both tendencies help to move the market price toward the equilibrium price, so that quantity demanded and quantity supplied are equal. In well-developed markets where many buyers and sellers deal in standardized commodities, the movement of market price to its equilibrium can be amazingly fast. The reason is that traders, alert to the divergence of market price from its equilibrium value, buy a commodity in excess demand (or sell a commodity in excess supply) not for their own use but to earn profits from the impending price change. This is very much like arbitrage. Although there is some elapsed time between the purchase and the sale of the commodity, it is usually short (a few minutes in some cases). The additional volume of offers to buy and sell on the part of traders adds to the responsiveness of market price to disequilibrium conditions and shortens the adjustment time.

Virtually all economists agree that, in free markets, shortages and surpluses cannot exist except momentarily, as the market price rises or falls to eliminate them. In order for a shortage to last, the market price must be held below its equilibrium value. Some buyers would have to receive a smaller quantity than they demand and some form of rationing would have to be implemented. Usually, the force of government is required to punish off-price selling, enforce rationing schemes, and police transactions. In order for a surplus to continue, the market price must be held above its equilibrium. In order for this to be accomplished, the excess supply, which is unwanted by market buyers at the high price, must be purchased and held back from sale, or sellers must be kept from offering what they desire to offer at the high price. Again, the force of government is almost always required to police transactions, punish offenders, buy and store surpluses, and enforce marketing orders.

Applications
The determination of market price and the analysis of its movements have many uses and many users. In agricultural markets, producers and consumers must ascertain the market price in order to maximize their profits. For example, ranchers must determine the market price of their cattle in order to know how much to produce, whether to sell outright or to hedge, and how to plan for the next production period. Baking companies must be able to determine the market price of flour in order to plan for the future production of bread.

Shipping companies must determine the market prices of diesel fuel, gasoline, jet fuel, or oil in order to calculate their costs. Therefore, many resources are devoted to market price discovery and the dissemination of this information.

Changes in market price can be profitable if they are predicted correctly. For example, if a trader believes that the market price of feeder cattle is due for an increase, then the trader may buy feeder cattle futures contracts. If the trader is correct—the market price of feeder cattle actually increases—then the futures contract position will be profitable. If the trader is wrong—feeder cattle prices actually decline—then the trader will suffer speculative losses.

To keep their costs from varying unnecessarily with unforeseen changes in the market price, users of commodities hedge their purchases of those commodities by using forward and futures contracts, call and put option positions, and swap contracts. In the case of a cattle feeder, who must unavoidably own cattle while they are being fed to marketable weight, a fall in the market price of live cattle may result in a loss rather than a profit. To ensure against this eventuality, cattle feeders commonly sell cattle futures contract or call options, or they may buy put options. If the market price of cattle at sale time is lower, then the value of the contracts or call options are lower as well. Because the contracts or call options were sold at higher market prices, however, the potential loss on the cattle sales is offset by the profit on the hedge.

An airline, which must buy aviation fuel, may purchase call options on heating oil, giving the airline the right to buy a certain amount of oil at a fixed price. If the market price of oil increases, then the operating cost of the airline's flights will increase. The increased cost will be offset, however, by the profit from the appreciation in the value of the call options that are owned by the airline.

Flour millers and cereal producers must, in the course of their businesses, purchase large stocks of grain. They almost always hedge their unavoidable ownership of grains against unforeseen fluctuations in the market price of grain by using futures contracts and options. A flour miller may have contracted to sell a certain quantity of flour at a certain price in two months' time. If the market price of wheat increases, then the difference between the wheat price and the flour price may not fully pay milling costs. If the wheat purchase intentions have been hedged by the purchase of wheat futures contracts, however, then the miller's profit is insulated from vagaries in the market price of wheat.

If the market price already reflects all the currently known information of value in the determination of the market price now and in the future, then the correct prediction of the future price is a matter of luck, not skill. Many economists, financial practitioners, and market observers maintain that current information is completely incorporated in market prices, so that only unforeseen (inherently unpredictable) information is capable of causing changes in market prices. In other words, they maintain the correctness of the efficient markets hypothesis. Yet, this does not prevent vast sums of money being spent on information and insight about future market price changes—information that is largely doomed to failure in the prediction of market price movements if the hypothesis is indeed correct.

If new information can be gained earlier or more accurately by private means, however, then insight into future market price movements can be turned to a profitable advantage. For example, several New York and Chicago trading firms subscribe to private weather forecasting services in the belief that more accurate forecasts are thereby available. In 1988, it happened that private forecasters were first in predicting the drought conditions in the Midwestern grain belt, which drove the market price of wheat and other grains to high levels in 1988 and 1989. It is said that the trading profits that accrued to those trading firms which subscribed to private weather forecasting services were quite large.

Context

An economic question of great importance to philosophers and common people alike has been the determination of the proper value of goods, services, and resources. The prices of things have, as often as not, been set in the past by emperors, kings, popes, guilds, commissars, potentates, and presidents as by free markets. Invariably, shortages and surpluses indicated the mistakes of those price setters. Inevitably, those price-setting activities were temporarily abandoned to the vicissitudes of free market prices. Prices then quickly rose or fell to quench the shortage or to soak up the surplus until the next episode of price fixing.

It is easy to fix market prices, but it is impossible to set them correctly. Many politicians long to set prices because it is a way to aid deserving constituents (at the expense of the less deserving) without being held responsible for increased government revenues. The political price is often widely removed from the market price, in direct proportion to the degree of deservingness of those to be aided.

From a long-term viewpoint, fixed prices are properly seen as temporary. If the fixed price is above the market price, then the inevitable surplus indicates that a return to market price is forthcoming and that it will be lower than the fixed price. If the fixed price is lower than the market price, the necessary shortage indicates the opposite. This fact holds for currencies as well as commodities. An overvalued dollar leads to a surplus of dollars and a forthcoming devaluation.

The things that are produced and sold are sold too cheaply; the things that are bought are too dear—it has always been that way and will continue to be that way. It has only been since Alfred Marshall (1842-1924), the great British economist of the early twentieth century, that the idea of the separation of market participants into buyers and sellers led to the concept of the market price, given by the determinants of supply and demand. When the market itself prices items, sellers and buyers can still complain that the price is too low or too high, but no surplus or shortage can continue.

It is likely that some prices will continue to be set by political means, by representatives of those having momentary political power. It is unlikely that pricing mistakes will be avoided. The inevitable appearances of surplus and shortage can always be eliminated, however, by a return to the free market price.

Bibliography

Amacher, Ryan, and Holly Ulbrich. *Principles of Microeconomics.* 4th ed. Cincinnati: South-Western, 1989. A popular introductory-level college textbook which is written to be brief in clear, concise English. Highly recommended as an introduction to the economic sciences. Chapters 3, 5, and 10 contain information explaining the concept of market price.

Crocker, David A., and Toby Linden, eds. *Ethics of Consumption: The Good Life, Justice, and Global Stewardship.* Lanham, Md.: Rowman & Littlefield, 1998.

Dorfman, Robert. *Prices and Markets.* Englewood Cliffs, N.J.: Prentice-Hall, 1978. One of Prentice-Hall's Foundations of Modern Economics series, written to be a basic core for a college course in economics. Dorfman develops the determinants of supply and demand, as well as market price determination under competition, monopoly, and oligopoly. The efficiency aspects of the free market pricing system are examined.

Hailstones, Thomas. *Basic Economics.* Cincinnati: South-Western, 1988. An economics textbook written for the beginning student or for those who require only a basic understanding of economic problems. The first half of the book is devoted to microeconomic topics, and the section on prices is especially well written. A good introductory text.

Heilbroner, Robert. *Behind the Veil of Economics.* New York: W. W. Norton, 1988. Heilbroner, as always in his many books, attempts to rehabilitate Marxist economics; as always, he fails, but in a thought-provoking and readable manner. Especially relevant are two essays, "The World of Work" and "The Problem of Value," both of which include a discussion of the labor theory of value.

Marshall, Alfred. *Principles of Economics.* 2 vols. 9th variorum ed. Annotations by C. W. Guillebaud. London: Macmillan for the Royal Economic Society, 1961. Marshall's magnum opus. Although written in 1890, this book is eminently readable. Marshall wrote it not for the professional economist but for the nonspecialist, and it has an accessible style. All notes and equations are contained in the second volume.

Mundell, Robert. *Man and Economics: The Science of Choice.* New York: McGraw-Hill, 1968. This small book is easy and pleasurable to read. Written by an eminent international economist for a general audience, it is full of anecdotes and trivia that illustrate and entertain. The determination of value, or market price, is well developed. Highly recommended.

O'Neill, John. *The Market: Ethics, Knowledge, and Politics.* New York: Routledge, 1998.

Palley, Thomas I. *Plenty of Nothing: The Downsizing of the American Dream and the Case for Structural Keynesianism.* Princeton, N.J.: Princeton University Press, 1998.

Shapiro, Milton. *Foundations of the Market-Price System.* New York: St. Martin's Press, 1983. A reprint of the author's Ph.D. dissertation. Introduces readers to the determination of market prices using supply and demand tools, and contains a bibliography that may be of some help to intermediate students. Difficult to read and definitely not for the novice.

Ralph C. Gamble, Jr.

Cross-References

MARKET STRUCTURE

Type of economics: Industrial economics
Fields of study: Industrial organization and public policy; industry studies

Market structure is an industry assessment concerning the degree of competition and monopoly, or simply the industrial organization of the firms in an industry that serves a given market. How these firms organize in production and price their products, the number of buyers and sellers, the similarities and differences in products, and the ease of entry and exit into the market determine market structure.

Principal terms

COMPETITION: the situation that exists when a large number of firms in a given industry vie for a share of the market

ECONOMIES OF SCALE: the situation that exists when the technology of production causes a firm's long-run average total cost curve to fall over a large range as production increases; mass-production assembly lines are an example

MONOPOLISTIC COMPETITION: the type of competition that results when there are many small firms in an industry, each producing a product that is slightly different or differentiated

MONOPOLY: an industry dominated by one seller who supplies an entire industry and who has no significant competitors

OLIGOPOLY: an industry dominated by a few large firms

PERFECT COMPETITION: a situation that exists when an industry is made up of a large number of buyers and sellers, none of which is dominant, who produce identical products

Overview

Market structure is an assessment of the organization of firms in their respective industries. The structure may be perfect competition, monopolistic competition, oligopoly, or monopoly.

Under the first condition, perfect competition, the number of firms is large enough that each firm cannot have a noticeable effect on the price of the output. Barriers to entry are small, so that each firm can easily enter and exit from the industry. The product is identical (homogeneous), such as grain, so that there is no product differentiation, as there would be with products such as automobiles. Therefore, competition is based on price, instead of on nonprice competition such as service or quality. The last requirement of perfect competition is that buyers have a perfect knowledge of the prices at which exchange takes place in the market. Therefore, sellers cannot charge more than the market price. There must also be many buyers, so that none of them has market power. Everyone is in essence a price taker (as opposed to a price maker), and no firm is large enough to influence price. Competition among firms is the ideal of a free market, because it brings prices down to the minimum average cost.

The agricultural industry comes closest to this description. There are more than one million farms in the United States, and each firm's output is, therefore, too small to affect the supply-demand equilibrium, which is the free market price. As a result, any one firm's demand curve is perfectly horizontal at the market price. The firm can choose to sell more or less of its product, but it will have no influence on the price of that product. Thus, it can be said that the firm has no market power and that the market can be characterized as the most competitive possible, or perfectly competitive. This market structure is also the most efficient, because this competition among firms brings the price down as low as possible. In the long run, only the most efficient firms survive and the price of the product will be equal to the minimum average cost to produce it, which includes the cost of capital and management. As a result, buyers can obtain the product at the lowest prices equal to their opportunity cost, reflecting the relative scarcity of the product.

Firms, in order to maximize profits, produce the social optimum at which marginal cost (the cost to produce one additional unit) has risen to equality with price. No excess profits exist, because if they did, new firms would enter the market and drive the price down again. Firms, in order to survive, must respond quickly to price changes, moving production to its most efficient use automatically and without costly bureaucracy. Adam Smith (1723-1790) called this direction or allocation of resources the "invisible hand" that guides the market. It directs consumers and producers alike in the most socially desirable fashion.

The most important category of industrial organization or market structure is monopolistic competition, as it contains more than 90 percent of all firms. These firms are small and are in the fields of retailing, wholesaling, and the service industries, which includes fast-food chains, restaurants, and legal and medical services. The reason that these firms are not perfectly competitive, even though there are many, is that their products are not identical but instead are differentiated. The word "monopolistic" is derived from the small amount of monopoly power that results from this product differentiation. In order to boost sales, each firm advertises its nonprice attributes, such as better or faster service and differences in style, warranty, shopping environment, location, packaging, and image. Firms in perfectly competitive industries do not advertise because one firm's product is identical to another's. Unless they produce a better product, monopolistically competitive firms cannot charge prices higher than cost for long, because there are no significant barriers to entry by potential rivals.

A large part of the manufacturing sector is made up of industries dominated by a few firms. Such a situation results in what is called oligopoly. Each firm is large, and therefore has a high market share, and each is mutually interdependent of its rivals in terms of price and output. Thus, nonprice competition is the norm. The auto, chemical, aircraft, petroleum refining, computer chip, and steel industries are examples of oligopolies. Barriers to competition such as economies of scale make entry difficult. As a result, the only entry into the U.S. auto market has been from firms overseas, as a large volume of output is required for any firm to reduce its costs (and its prices) to a competitive level. Because oligopolists differentiate their products wherever possible according to differences in styling, warranty, service, and reliability, many industries are called differentiated oligopolies.

Of the four general classifications of market structure, almost no perfectly competitive industries and few monopolies exist. A monopoly is one seller who, having no rivals, charges a monopoly price. To remain an only seller, however, such a firm must keep competitors out of its industry. This can be done through government protection such as copyright or patent laws or with government licensing, as with radio and television stations and medical and legal services. Technological changes render patents and some other governmentally sanctioned monopoly powers increasingly obsolete. Other monopolies are the result of control over a large share of natural resources, such as DeBeers in diamonds and the Organization of Petroleum Exporting Countries (OPEC) in oil. Natural monopolies exist in the utility industries, where the government grants exclusive franchises in water, local telephone, electric generation, and natural gas services. These franchises are granted because it would be more expensive to serve residences by two water lines rather than by one. As a result, natural monopolies are regulated by governmental agencies, with increasing input into these decisions coming from consumer groups.

Applications

In the United States, public policy has attempted to maintain economic efficiency (low prices and high output) associated with competition and in opposition to monopoly power in order to preserve economic freedom. The smaller the number of firms in an industry, the greater is their market power, which is the ability to raise prices above costs. As a result, mergers have been looked upon with suspicion and even terminated through the use of antitrust laws. Natural monopolies such as public utilities have their prices set by regulatory agencies. Agriculture, however, is exempt from antitrust laws.

Oligopolies possess some market power. There have been questions regarding the contribution of oligopolies to technological progress, as well as their conduct. On the issue of conduct, a classic case of price fixing in an oligopoly occurred in the 1950's, in which the two largest manufacturers of heavy electrical equipment agreed to fix prices through an organized bidding cartel. Each firm bid high or low on a contract according to the phases of the moon. These firms were convicted of price-fixing, and as a deterrent, their customers were awarded damages equal to three times the injury. In addition, their executives were sentenced to jail for criminal price fixing.

Antitrust policy has been directed not only at controlling price fixing and unfair practices of large firms but also at controlling the size of firms in a situation where the effect of a merger could substantially reduce competition. As a result, some mergers have been outlawed, and large firms such as International Business Machines (IBM) have been threatened with breakup. An examination of the global market and increased foreign competition resulted in the abandonment of the U.S. government's law suit. In a telephone monopoly case, American Telephone and Telegraph (AT&T) and the Reagan administration were able to reach an out-of-court settlement to split AT&T into eight local telephone firms. In this way, the long-distance telephone market was opened up to more competition, and local phone companies were given incentives to become more efficient.

In the airline industry, government regulation seems to have had the effect of protecting the oligopoly by fixing airfares for them and disallowing entry. Prior to deregulation, routes and prices on interstate flights were regulated by the Civil Aeronautics Board, and this board turned down all requests by new carriers for long-distance routes. Consequently, competition among airlines was reduced to non-price aspects. Airlines were said to be regulated for their own benefit as opposed to the public interest. Competition took on the form of better meals, free drinks, and on-time performance. Unregulated airfares within a state such as California were far cheaper than the regulated interstate flights in the Washington-New York corridor. When Congress passed the Airline Deregulation Act in 1978, airfares fell by 20 percent in 1978 alone, and travel increased by 40 percent. In subsequent years, more than a dozen new airlines entered the market as airfares fell further. It has been argued that regulation is counterproductive because the regulated firms have more clout and more to gain by influencing the regulators than by trying to influence a widely dispersed public.

Labor unions are also exempt from antitrust laws, and it has been claimed that they have a far greater power to fix the price of labor than even the largest of enterprises. Unions exercise their power further by restricting the entry of new trainees into skilled trades.

Governmental licensing of trade and professional associations has created medical and legal monopolies in which entry and the supply of practitioners is also restricted. Similar trade practices among real estate agents and architects bar the competitive determination of fees. Antitrust policy has moved only slowly in their direction. Competition from such parties as health maintenance organizations, paralegal services, and discount brokers, however, has moved faster.

Context

During the early nineteenth century, the U.S. economy was quite competitive because the business units and farms were small and each firm could not appreciably influence the price in the market. Corporate growth increased rapidly after the Civil War, however, as some firms grew rapidly internally and others merged.

The first large merger wave began in the 1880's and the 1890's and was characterized by horizontal mergers, in which corporations acquired their competitors in order to increase their market share. Large trusts and combinations were formed in oil, whiskey, sugar, lead, and cotton, initiating the period of the "robber barons." Standard Oil refined 90 percent of all domestically pumped crude oil and owned 80 percent of the pipelines. The Sherman Antitrust Act of 1890 and the Clayton Act of 1914 broke up many of these corporations.

The second merger wave took place in the 1920's. Those mergers were of the vertical kind, in which firms merged with their suppliers for greater control of the entire production and sales process of its own firm as well as of rivals. Competition was decreased because a rival firm owning the supplier could dictate supply prices.

The third distinct merger movement came in the 1960's. These were conglomerate mergers, in which firms merged with unrelated businesses in order to grow rapidly and diversify in order to reduce business risks. Giants such as International Telephone and Telegraph, Litton, Ling Tempco Vought, and Teledyne grew rapidly. Yet many of these large conglomerates became difficult to manage, lost their profitability, and either sold their unrelated businesses or filed for bankruptcy.

While Karl Marx (1818-1883) had predicted that capitalism would inexorably move in the direction of monopolies, other trends have dominated. Rapid technological change and innovation (particularly by small firms), increased competition from foreign firms, a global market, and an increase in the service economy relative to manufacturing have maintained a largely competitive and dynamic market structure.

It has become well recognized that the main determinants of market structure are competitive forces. Therefore, market structure in manufacturing is, to a large degree, reflected in scale economies and other efficiencies. Accordingly, industries in which con-centration is high in foreign countries are generally the same industries as those in which concentration is high in the United States. The industries that are not concentrated in foreign countries are generally the same as those which are not concentrated in the United States.

Legal protections such as patent, copyright, and trademark laws may yield further monopoly power and concentration. Concentration and collusion, however, may not be closely related. Government policies, such as the regulation of certain industries, may also contribute to market power. Furthermore, chance, mergers, and superior entrepreneurship may lead to different growth rates of firms and to different market structures. As a result of the strength of competitive forces and regardless of antitrust policies, the structure of American industry has changed surprisingly little since early in the twentieth century.

Bibliography

Brozen, Yale, ed. *The Competitive Economy.* Morristown, N.J.: General Learning Press, 1975. Brozen has edited a fine book of selected readings on imperfect competition, regulation, antitrust, and some applications of antitrust law with contributions from Kenneth J. Arrow, Arthur Laffer, Joseph Schumpeter, George J. Stigler, J. Fred Weston, and others. Excellent for nonspecialists and college students.

Clarkson, Kenneth W., and Roger Miller. *Industrial Organization.* New York: McGraw-Hill, 1982. Provides a good introduction to industrial organization, economic theory, evidence, and public policy, with examples of antitrust cases. Includes numerous graphs, tables, and charts. Excellent for college students as well as nonspecialists.

Douma, Sytse, and Hein Schreuder. *Economic Approaches to Organizations.* 2d ed. London: Prentice Hall, 1998.

Greer, Douglas F. *Industrial Organization and Public Policy.* 2d ed. New York: Macmillan, 1984. A very readable overview of industrial organization, from perfect competition to monopoly, including industry studies and both early and later antitrust cases. Presents a good discussion of advertising, business strategy, and technological change. Suitable for college students.

Hunt, E. K., and Howard J. Sherman. *Economics: An Introduction to Traditional and Radical Views.* 6th ed. New York: Harper & Row, 1990. Written from a Marxist historical perspective, this book is very readable, starting with economic evolution in ancient Greece; moving on to mercantilism, the corporate rise of capitalism, monopoly power, income distribution, and economic theories; and ending with comparative economic systems, such as market socialism and central planning in the Soviet Union. Fine for the general reader.

Palley, Thomas I. *Plenty of Nothing: The Downsizing of the American Dream and the Case for Structural Keynesianism.* Princeton, N.J.: Princeton University Press, 1998.

Scherer, F. M., and David Ross. *Industrial Market Structure and Economic Performance.* 3d ed. Boston: Houghton Mifflin, 1990. Probably the most comprehensive book (700 pages) on industrial organization, touching all topics, with reference to virtually all articles written on this topic. The perspective includes market structure and economic performance in Europe and other countries. Footnotes on antitrust cases and other studies sometimes take half a page. Excellent for graduate students.

Sharp, Ansel, Charles A. Register, and Richard H. Leftwich. *Economics of Social Issues.* 9th ed. Homewood, Ill.: Richard D. Irwin, 1990. Provides the reader with an excellent perspective on the economics of big business and monopoly power. Other topics are also discussed, including the history of airline regulation and deregulation as well as government control of prices, pollution, inflation, and poverty. Suitable for nonspecialists and college students.

Frank Billes

Cross-References

Antitrust Policy, 6; Average and Marginal Cost Pricing, 16; Classical Economics, 74; Competition, 91; Consumer Price Index, 97; Economies and Diseconomies of Scale, 158; Efficiency, 170; Equilibrium, 193; Forecasting, 246; Monopolies, 442; Oligopolies, 461; Price Fixing, 495.

MARXIST ECONOMICS

Type of economics: General economics
Fields of study: Economic theory and history of economic thought

The economic theories of Karl Marx, which are often equated with the term "communism," represent the most systematic challenge to both the theory and the visible results of the free enterprise system. Based on an assumption of the inevitable struggle between exploitative and exploited class interests, Marxist economics attempted to attain the "greatest good for the greatest number" by outlawing private property and to find a way to place the product of labor into the hands of the actual producers.

Principal terms

BOURGEOISIE: the key transitional class in the last stages of feudalism; by creating alternate sources of capital wealth, the bourgeoisie fosters, and then comes to dominate, the capitalist mode of production

MODE OF PRODUCTION: the concept of a totality of social, political, and strictly economic arrangements that, in the Marxist theory of historical materialism, constitute the "state" of humanity, or subsectors within humanity

PROLETARIAT: that segment of society whose economic existence depends solely on the "sale" of its labor for wages

SURPLUS VALUE: the "created" value, in the terms of market price, which is left to the controller of the key factors of production after all costs (materials, tools, labor) have been paid

USE VALUE: the direct practical value to actual producers, without reference to arbitrary market intermediaries, of a product that they have made through the application of their labor

Overview

It is difficult to separate the role and the content of Marxist economic theory from the other, equally consequential, legacies that were left by Karl Marx (1818-1883) to both the nineteenth and twentieth centuries. Clearly, Marx's theories contributed both to the theoretical field of political economy and to practical political history. The political ramifications of his ideas had already begun to take root—in the form of several European revolutionary uprisings—in the very year of his famous *Communist Manifesto*, 1848, written with Friedrich Engels (1820-1895). By the mid-twentieth century, different labels had been attached to Marxian ideological and economic ideas by the most famous mass revolutionary communist states, the Soviet Union (founded in 1917 under the banner of Marxist-Leninist theory) and the People's Republic of China (founded in 1948 under Marxist-inspired "Maoism"). These two attempted historic applications of Marxism contained the assumption that political control would be used to carry out economic programs based on the teachings of Marx. This characteristic of applied Marxism represented a departure from the original tenets of Marx's economic theories.

Reduced to its most essential tenets, Marxist economics is based on the assumption that production is the most important aspect of economic activity, and indeed of all human activity. The process of physical production in any given society must take precedence over other "practices" which, like the exchange of the goods that are produced or the use of currency, may or may not be deemed necessary in order to realize the most essential economic "goal," which is the material continuation of life. For this reason, Marxist economic theory rests on a careful comparative analysis of the modes of production.

A mode of production is defined in the terms of the degrees of access by different "members" of any economy to the key factors of production, namely capital (land, raw materials, tools) and labor. Complete economic self-sufficiency, according to Marx,

German economic philosopher Karl Marx in 1878. (AP/Wide World Photos)

would mean a direct application of individual or group labor to tools and resources (capital in the broadest sense) in order to obtain a product with direct use value for the producers without relying on intermediary influences. This concept implies varied and historically testable arrangements for obtaining access to the several key factors of production, and along with the added phenomenon of exchange or marketing, which is not considered as a factor of production, supplies Marxist economics with a comparative analytical framework for those arguments that led to a specifically communist basis for the "pure" Marxist system.

Although Marx offered analyses of early and obviously exploitative modes of production that were based on slavery and feudalism, the crux of his arguments for what would essentially be associated with the communist economic model stemmed from the modern workings of the capitalist mode of production. Two key factors—first the accumulation of capital (including money for investment) and factors of production (in the form of land, buildings, and machines) in a specific group's hands and, second, the transformation of labor into a commodity offered for sale (that is, salary)—are taken to characterize the capitalist mode of production. The accumulation of capital would yield what Marx referred to as the bourgeois class, whereas the increasing dependence of laborers on the "sale" of their labor to the bourgeoisie would create the proletarian class.

The primary characteristic of the proletariat (unlike the precapitalist peasantry) is that, lacking access to any of the essential factors of production, its role (as a factor of someone else's production) is manipulated by the means of contracts of their labor for wages. The latter, paid in money, provide the proletarian class with the necessary means to try to meet their basic economic needs by purchasing goods (most often the very ones their labor has produced, but to which they have no guaranteed access) on a market which is geared to the dominant force of the capitalist system: a profit margin.

Marx defined profit in the capitalist system as a phenomenon of surplus value. Stated simply, surplus value is the difference, calculated in money terms, between the costs incurred by capitalists (for raw materials, tools or machines, and labor's salary) and the market value of the commodity goods that have become their possessions. Surplus value for capitalists will be increased—to be used either for immediate profit or for reinvestment in the production process that they control—whenever the costs for labor or materials can be reduced.

Endeavors to increase surplus values and profits inevitably lead to exploitation of the proletarian class who, because of their dependency on wages as their sole means of providing for themselves, vie against one another in a supply and demand labor market. When the supply of labor exceeds demand, capitalists are free to lower pay amounts. A serious drop-off in the demand for labor can produce an "unhealthy" unemployment rate and therefore create a typical recessionary cycle. During such periods, the general unwillingness to maintain a critical level of investment (in labor and capital) cuts back the capitalists' very lifeline, which, ironically, is the demand that is reflected in the purchasing power of those whom they hire to buy the products that they produce. In extreme cases, as when a revised balance between the supply and demand of all the factors of production does not come about, depression conditions set in. These are the bane of capitalists and labor alike, and Marxist economists presume depressions to be the definite proof of the unworkability of the capitalist mode of production.

This brief sketch of Marx's view of the presumed pitfalls of the capitalist mode of production is sufficient to create a summary of what he proposed as an alternative. The Marxist economic system is based on the assumption that the class struggles which are associated with earlier modes of production, and the proletarian/bourgeois class struggle in particular, can be removed if private property and the exclusive private profit motive are abolished. Access to the factors of production is, theoretically, nonexclusive in a Marxist economy, as the fruits of production belong, again theoretically, not to the individual who produced them, but to society as a whole, and are "sold" only as a matter of monitoring the flow of goods back to producers who depend on them for their essential use value, not for profit.

Those most familiar with the communist model of the Soviet Union have consistently observed that the removal of profit-motivated "capitalists" did not yield Marx's "classless" society and an economy that was based on the fully integrated access by producers to the products of their labor. Rather, in the absence of any private property over means of production, all essential economic functions were vested in the state. Once the state "regulated" every act of production and compensation, the system became primarily political in nature and therefore did not constitute a true Marxist mode of production.

Applications

Although enormous amounts of literature both by and about Marx exist, actual applications of Marxist economics are relatively few in number. This stems, in large part, from the fact that, despite Marx's theory of the "inevitability" of a proletarian revolution against the capitalist mode of production, economic programs that can be considered significant attempts to apply Marx's system have involved not only specifically political revolutions but also the emergence and maintenance of a state apparatus that does not correspond to the revolutionary mode of production that Marx's theory envisaged.

Definitive economic programs that were based on Marxism were implemented in the nineteenth century, despite sporadic but unsuccessful revolutionary outbreaks that claimed to represent Marx's political and economic causes. Moreover, in the twentieth century, only a few revolutions actually led to substantial implementation of Marxist economic principles (in the Soviet Union until 1990, in the People's Republic of China after 1948, and in post-1958 Cuba). Because the latter two Marxist systems, as well as a number of other less important political experiments with Marxism, were founded on Russian precedents, it is most helpful to survey the Soviet experience during the heyday of its applied Marxism.

During the early years of the Soviet Marxist experiment, Vladimir Ilyich Lenin (1870-1924), his aides, and his successors wrestled in various ways with what became one of the main problems to confront the first full-fledged Marxist political and economic system, namely the overwhelmingly agricultural, not capitalist or industrial, nature of the system that was overthrown by the Bolsheviks. Although workers' *soviets*, or councils, were put in place with the presumed task of carrying out Marx's theory of producer control over labor and capital input into the industrial sector, the reality was that the vast bulk of Russia's production still came from rural lands. Expropriation of agricultural factors of production, because of the vast expanses of land in the Soviet Union, proved to be much more difficult than state "recruitment" of workers in centrally controlled industries. Initially, the Red Army was deployed by the Bolsheviks to seize the produce of *kulaks*, or small-to-medium-sized peasant proprietors, who tried to hold onto goods that they could market for profit instead of "fusing" their labor efforts with those of the salaried industrial sector.

Lenin found himself obliged to compromise with Marx's general economic plan when he created the "New Economic Policy" (NEP) in 1920. The NEP provided for limited restoration of private ownership in the consumer sector—specifically designed to assure that agriculturalists would continue to produce for an urban consumer market—but retained state control over large industry, transport, and foreign trade. When rural producers tried to use their market-earned income to purchase industrially produced goods, however, they discovered that central committee controls over prices had produced a completely uneconomic market: Industrial products from state factories cost three times as much as they had a few years before in the terms of what agricultural goods were worth compared to industrial labor equivalency. Resulting discontent led to expansion of NEP compromises: not only did more than 90 percent of agriculture continue to escape state expropriation to become state farms or, closer to the Marxist economic model, farm collectives but the denationalization of many firms that were not a part of the Soviet heavy industrial sector allowed them to participate in private economic interests as well. Three-quarters of all retail and two-fifths of wholesale trade were in such a position by the time of Lenin's death in 1924.

Initially, the Soviet economic system under Lenin's successor, Joseph Stalin (1879-1953), retained the main features of the NEP, mainly because Stalin needed to be certain that his political success would not be thwarted through alienation of some of Lenin's key supporters, especially Nikolai Bukharin (1888-1938). By the late 1920's, however, especially after the elimination of his more staunchly leftist ideological rival Leon Trotsky (1879-1940), Stalin introduced major changes in the application of Marxist economics to the Soviet system.

In part, Stalin reoriented the economic dimensions of Marxism away from lingering "proto-Marxist" views that, in order to succeed, economic Marxism had to be an international revolutionary movement. By 1929, he was set in his idea of realizing a massive economic transformation in the Soviet Union itself. Arguing that such a transformation could occur only if the country relied on its own resources alone, Stalin proceeded to expand the state-controlled industrial sector and forcefully collectivize the agricultural sector.

In the industrial domain, one could say that Stalinist economic methods were not actually realizations of "true" Marxist principles, as the state used its power over its own giant industrial concerns to seize scarce capital out of what had been left as smaller scale competitive enterprises by the NEP. Because their enterprises had no access to capital resources in order to maintain their activities, they essentially disappeared from what henceforth became a state monopoly over the industrial market. In the agricultural domain, Stalin's version of Marxist economics was even more harsh, as not only the means of production fell to forced and often violent expropriation (to comprise state farms, or *sovkhozy*, and "peasant-owned" collectives, or *kolkhozy*), but also a large part of the rural population was faced with violence. Any individual or group resistance to Stalin's policies led to political prison camps or even death.

All these developments need to be placed in another essential context that is associated, not necessarily with the theory, but certainly with the application of Marxist economics. This is the inevitable adoption, by the state political authority, of a monolithic economic plan into which all productive subsectors are made to fit. Although the Soviet Union had experienced fairly rigid state economic planning under the NEP, it was during the Stalin years that formal five-year plans were imposed. Under the regime of central economic plans, all semblance of the originally conceived Marxist economic order disappeared in the presumably Marxist-inspired states that were created during the twentieth century. So-called Marxist plans that were based on specific sector priorities and obligatory quotas of production—not for the benefit of the population as a whole, but for the strengthening of that state and military apparatus—would certainly have been denounced by Marx not as the "dictatorship of the proletariat" (an often-quoted phrase drawn from Marxist revolutionary rhetoric) but as what it was in fact: dictatorship by the state for the state.

Context

One must approach Marxist economic theory in two contexts, one representing the socio-economic, as much as the political, environment of the nineteenth century in which Marx lived and wrote, and the second representing a later conjuncture of twentieth century circumstances that would call for the formal political adoption and application of Marxist social and economic theories in ways that Marx himself might not have recognized.

It is not unreasonable to state that there is no Marxist economic context or theoretical formula without the presence of the most basic unit that is required for any economic system to function: physical labor. More specifically, Marxist economic analysis depends on the centrality of the physically laboring wage-earning class, or proletariat. In Marx's day, this group and the role it played in the representative Western economies of the mid-nineteenth century was just developing and was certainly not yet dominant. Perhaps it was a factor—involving a dynamic shift in economic functions that was occurring at the time—that induced Marx to pinpoint labor as the linchpin of his theory. Perhaps because wage labor was engaged in the first serious phase of its struggle to stand on its own at the time of *The Communist Manifesto*, Marx, in effect, chose that moment to declare that the stage was set for the historical realization of the shift from the capitalist to the communist mode of production, a shift that would be essential for his economic theory to work.

Largely because Marx saw this imminent revolution in modes of production almost entirely in the terms of dynamic economic relationships, however, essential political dimensions—namely, the role of the state in bringing about necessary changes in the existing capitalist bourgeois mode of production—seem not to have been addressed in real-world terms. One result of this, as far as prospects for the actual application of revolutionary Marxist economic principles in practice were concerned, was that the proponents of the maintenance of the status quo used their essential control of mid-nineteenth century state political systems in order to suppress dissent.

This peculiarity of the nineteenth century context—the apparently completely mutual incompatibility between Marxist revolutionary economic methods and existing state political systems—must be compared with what occurred in the twentieth century. What one finds is quite paradoxical: After "winning" revolutions against the alliance between status quo capitalist class interests and the state, the Marxist systems that emerged seem to have imposed systems that could not have existed without new forms of non-Marxist state (that is, political) and economic alliances that were imposed with even greater force than had existed beforehand.

Beginning with the first successful erection of a revolutionary communist regime in the Soviet Union in 1917, an apparently necessary ingredient was added to the Marxist economic program that would guarantee its application: a monolithic state power. Original Marxist theory did not espouse formal participation of the state in the economic process; to the contrary, the "pure" communism of Marx and his idea of the direct control of the factors of production by the producers themselves envisaged the eventual "withering away of the state." The fact of twentieth century Marxist regimes, however, is that producers were systematically excluded from determining the disposition of the results of their labor. In this respect, the most significantly altered socioeconomic condition between the mid-nineteenth and mid-twentieth centuries—the fact of the establishment of the proletarian, or wage-earning working class, as a numerically and politically dominant reality throughout the world—did not contribute substantially to Marxism's chances of becoming established as a practical, as opposed to a purely theoretical and idealized, mode of production.

Bibliography

Arthur, Christopher J., and Geert Reuten, eds. *The Circulation of Capital: Essays on Volume Two of Marx's "Capital."* New York: St. Martin's Press, 1998.

Bellofiore, Riccardo, ed. *Marxian Economics—A Reappraisal: Essays on Volume Three of "Capital."* New York: St. Martin's Press, 1998.

Berlin, Isaiah. *Karl Marx: His Life and Environment.* 3d ed. New York: Oxford University Press, 1963. A very complete biography of Marx which places his work as an economic theorist in a wider context. Examines not only his career as a journalist and researcher, but also the mid-nineteenth century political organizations under which he lived, both in Germany and in England.

Caatephores, George. *An Introduction to Marxist Economics.* New York: New York University Press, 1989. This comprehensive review of the key factors of economic analysis that are contained in Marxism begins with the theory of historical materialism, the labor theory of value, and the question of money and growth. Also focuses on the way in which, according to Marxist theory, capitalism was responsible for the distortion in these areas.

Lipset, Seymour M. *The Sociology of Marxism.* Berkeley: University of California Press, 1963. A brief essay in response to *Marxism: An Historical and Critical Study* (New York: Praeger, 1961), by George Lichtheim. As the title of Lipset's essay suggests, the treatment of Marxism as a theory of social, as well as economic, organization receives primary attention.

Strachey, John. *The Nature of Capitalist Crisis.* New York: Covici, Friede, 1935. A distinctly pro-Marxist tract which sets out to explain how the capitalist world created the conditions that led to the Great Depression of the 1930's. Offers Marxist solutions, based heavily on the content of Marx's major work, *Das Kapital* (1867; *Capital*, 1886).

Vygodski, V. S. *The Story of a Great Discovery: How Karl Marx Wrote "Capital."* Translated by Christopher S. V. Salt. Turnbridge Wells, England: Abacus Press, 1974. A translation from the original Russian. Vygodski's essay is representative of mid-twentieth century Marxist estimates of the importance of Marx's original theories.

Wood, John Cunningham, ed. *Karl Marx's Economics: Critical Assessments.* London: Croom Helm, 1988. A multivolume work belonging to a series of edited works on major economic questions of worldwide importance. Its coverage of topics is very impressive, including literally hundreds of individual contributions, all brief and gauged for easy understanding by the educated reader, that are focused on the meaning of certain of Marx's writings, as well as criticism of other theorists' attempts to analyze Marx's theories.

Byron D. Cannon

Cross-References

Capitalism, 69; Classical Economics, 74; Communism, 80; History of Economics, 295; Labor Economics, 353; Labor Theory of Value, 358; Socialism, 544.

MICROECONOMICS

Type of economics: General economics
Fields of study: Economic theory; industrial organization and public policy

Microeconomics is that segment of economics which deals with the individual parts of an economy (such as firms, industries, and households), with separate markets, with goods and services within these markets, and with prices. Macroeconomics, on the other hand, deals with the sum of these parts and with government, presenting a total picture of the economy.

Principal terms

AGGREGATE DEMAND: the total amount of goods and services for which expenditures are made at different price levels

AGGREGATE SUPPLY: the total amount of goods and services that are produced and offered for sale at different price levels

DEMAND: the behavior of individuals or firms that indicates their desire for a good or service

FACTOR MARKET: the market in which resources that are used to produce goods and services are bought and sold

GROSS NATIONAL PRODUCT: the total output of goods and services that are produced by an economy within a specified period of time, usually one year; measured in the amount of purchases

MARKET ECONOMY: the type of economic structure in which consumers and producers are free to make their decisions as to what and how much to buy and sell

PRODUCT MARKET: the market in which goods and services are offered for sale and are bought

SUPPLY: the amount of a good that is offered in a market at different prices

UTILITY: the satisfaction that a consumer obtains from the purchase of a product

Overview

Microeconomics describes the area of economics dealing primarily with the individual parts of an economy, such as individual households, firms, and industries. Each of these units represents a separate market, and the behavior of these units involving specific goods and services needs to be analyzed and understood. As goods and services are bought and sold within these markets, particular prices are involved.

In any of these individual markets, two elements are at work—the forces of supply and demand. Thus, in any market, there are two sides, which are called the demand side and the supply side. Generally speaking, those individual units on the demand side desire to have goods and/or services and are willing to pay a price for them. The amount of goods that would be purchased would therefore depend on the price of the good, and also on whether the person or firm has sufficient money to pay for them. Logically then, if the price of the product is low, then a larger quantity would probably be bought, and if the price is high, then a smaller quantity would probably be bought. Each purchaser would want the largest quantity for the amount of money spent. From the supply side, if the price is low, then a smaller quantity of the good or service would be offered, but if the price is high, then a larger quantity would be made available. The seller would be most happy to sell large quantities at high prices and collect a large revenue. As the seller and the buyer negotiate quantity and price, each tries to gain the greater advantage. When the decision is reached, however, the quantity demand must equal the quantity supplied and one price (an equilibrium price) is reached.

An individual householder sells labor or resources to another person or to a business and receives a wage or salary in compensation. This wage or salary is really the agreed-upon price. Armed with this income, the householder will spend a part of it and save a part of it. The portion spent is used to buy goods and services from a particular firm or business. If there are a number of these firms, the individual will generally choose the firm which offers the product at the lowest price, assuming that the quality of these products is the same.

From the standpoint of the firm, a business tries to produce goods at the lowest possible cost. Therefore, the firm seeks to buy labor and materials which can produce its products at the lowest possible price. It then attempts to sell its product to the consumer at the highest price possible, and the firm will obtain a profit if the selling price is greater than the cost price.

The forces of demand and supply are constantly at work in any market, and this results in a decision of a given quantity of goods to be bought and sold at a particular price. Because resources are scarce (limited), and human desires (wants) are unlimited, the aim of economics is to utilize resources in order to produce the largest quantity of goods possible. The economy is made up of many types of markets for a variety of goods and services, but one condition is necessary in all markets: Buyers and sellers must be in contact with one another. This concept is the essence of microeconomics.

On one level, microeconomics examines the individual firm, the individual household, and the interaction of the forces of supply and demand that is reflected in prices. National leaders (in both business and government), however, are interested in the total picture: how much is produced and sold, the number of citizens that are employed, and their incomes and patterns of spending. This is the function of macroeconomics. Thus, macroeconomics focuses on the gross national product (the total output of goods and services), the total amount of goods consumed, the amount of investment goods that business firms have made, the total amount of income and savings, the amount of exports and imports for the nation, the total amount of government purchases of goods and services, the total tax revenue, and economic growth.

These aggregate (total) figures of macroeconomics are extremely important, as they provide the necessary information for decision making at the top levels of business firms and the government. In fact, the decisions of such individual economic entities affect the total output of business. Furthermore, the total output of all units will influence the decision and output of each unit. Thus, the individual entity (microportion) is integrally related to the total (macroportion); whatever affects the total economy will affect each unit within that economy. If the total demand for exported goods falls, then that condition will affect the firm which produces goods for export. In response to the change in aggregate (total) demand, the firm may have to reduce its output so that it will not have a surplus supply on hand. Hence, macroeconomic changes have microeconomic effects and, similarly, microeconomic adjustments will have macroeconomic effects. Although these two areas of economic under-standing often are treated separately, they are, in fact, interdependent. The total picture cannot be ascertained without analyzing both standpoints.

Applications

At first glance, it would appear that microeconomic issues and macroeconomic issues are distinct or conflicting parts of economics. Such an idea is false, as both macroeconomics and microeconomics are involved with the same information yet represent different perspectives of presentation. Macroeconomics examines the dimensions of the economy as a whole, while microeconomics focuses on the individual elements.

Within an economy, there are two major markets, the resources or factor market and the product market, yet all markets are subject to the forces of supply and demand, which are reflected in the prices that are paid in these markets. The major participants in both markets are business firms, individual households, and the government. For example, in the factor market, households supply the resources of labor, land, and capital, while business firms demand these resources. The intensity of supply and demand for resources is reflected in the price paid. In the product market, households demand the products made and express the intensity of their demand by the price that they are willing to pay. Businesses, on the other hand, supply the goods that households want at a price that they are willing to accept. Thus, one price clears the market. If the amount that is supplied is smaller than the amount that households demand, then the price of the product will rise. If the amount that is offered is larger than what is demanded, there will be a surplus of supplies and the price will fall. This is the kind of behavior that exists within a free market if there are no obstacles to affect the flow of goods between the participants in the market.

Normally, if the price of a good rises, consumers will buy a smaller quantity. If the goods are a necessity, however, they will buy the same amount no matter what the offered price. Economists describe this relationship of consumers to price changes as the price elasticity of demand. There is also a price elasticity of supply from the producer's side. This microeconomic concept indicates how consumers and producers interact in their exchanges of various products.

Another microeconomic concept regarding industries refers to the number of firms that make a similar or identical product. Industries which are composed of a large number of firms are called competitive industries. Firms in this type of industry that are aggressive to satisfy the consumer offer their products at attractively low prices, and consumers benefit not only from the price itself but also from the large quantity that is available. Generally, the larger the number of competitors, the better the quality of the product. On the other hand, a firm that is the only producer of a specific product or service is known as a monopoly. By varying the quantity of the goods that are offered in the market, this type of firm maintains such a high price that only a limited number of consumers may be able to afford its products. In addition, some industries contain only a few firms (an oligopoly), and they can, by group agreement or behavior, influence the price that a consumer pays.

In a market economy, one finds that both the householder and the business operate under the driving force of self-interest. The householder (consumer) wants the highest income possible in order to purchase the largest quantity of goods and to obtain the greatest satisfaction or utility from such purchases. At the same time, each business firm aims to obtain the largest profits possible by reducing costs and increasing sales. As each unit in the market works toward this end, both consumers and producers unwittingly contribute to the betterment of society, even though that was never part of their original intention, as indicated by the well-known economist Adam Smith (1723-1790). A large volume of production tends to lower the price of the product and therefore the consumer benefits. Moreover, as each firm becomes more efficient through competitive activity in its attempts to obtain a larger share of the market or output, the cost of the product falls.

From a macroeconomic standpoint, if the values of all resources that are used in a year are added, this sum is the aggregate (total) supply for the economy. On the other hand, if the amount of money that is spent on goods and services for all units for the same year is totaled, this sum is the aggregate (total) demand for the economy, which is generally referred to as the gross national product (GNP). The GNP is simply the total amount of goods and services that were produced during that year.

There are many policies that the government employs which may affect all households and business firms. For example, if the government levies a tax on production, this affects both the consumer and the producer. Furthermore, if the amount of money that is available in the economy in order to facilitate the exchange of goods and services and borrowing keeps increasing rapidly, this will tend to push prices up and create an inflationary situation, which is bad for the economy and will affect each producer and consumer. In addition, if a nation engages in international trade, the volume and money value of exports and imports affect each firm and individual.

A nation finds that it is very important to monitor its total output, money supply, employment, price level changes, taxes, revenue and spending by the government sector, and interest rates in order that correct decisions may be made. These macroeconomic elements will have an impact on the microeconomic elements. For example, if the government increases tax rates on certain products and resources, the cost to the consumer and the producer would increase. This increased cost could result in decreased sales, which could further cause the layoffs of workers and an increase in the level of unemployment in the economy. If people are unemployed, their income falls, and they will eventually be forced to reduce their purchases. From the above analysis, it clearly can be seen that microeconomic and macroeconomic issues and policies are inseparable and interrelated.

Context

With the beginning of economic thought and philosophy, microeconomics became an integral part of economic literature. At first, individual householders were self-sufficient and provided themselves with goods and services, but because people possess different talents, specialization in different occupations was inevitable. The consequent process resulted in a desire for the exchange of goods and services, which, in turn, involved the forces of supply and demand. Such a development resulted in the further expansion of economic activity, which included the process of bartering (exchanging one good for another). Bartering became cumbersome, however, and led to the invention of money in order to simplify the process of exchange.

Propelled by self-interest to maximize production and profits, individuals founded business firms, their major concern being to keep costs low and to be competitive. A successful business unit accumulated wealth and profits, and, consequently, other business units arose, either producing a competing substitute or starting entirely new business units as new wants in the society developed.

A further expansion of economic activity resulted in the cooperative development of groups of individuals who formed larger economic and political units—analogous to the evolution from the individual to the tribe and then to the nation state. As this change occurred, attention had to be paid to the total needs of the society. Thus, macroeconomic issues involving such items as roads, port facilities, defense capabilities, and tax revenues became necessary. It was soon recognized that central control and authority were required, and power was vested in a ruler.

By taking a closer look at the evolutionary change of such a society, the relationship between microeconomics and macroeconomics can be observed. The individual household's supply of resources and demand for goods and services, as well as the firm's supply of goods and services and demand for resources, provides the aggregate information on which policy decisions must be made. Such policies include the decisions as to the supply of money in an economy, the actions that ensure stable prices, economic growth, and full employment, and the revenues and expenditures of the government. If macroeconomic actions result in either inflation or a recession, this will affect individual units. If prices rise, some firms might experience a reduction in sales and eventually may be forced to lay off workers, causing unemployment to rise. As unemployment increases, tax revenues fall because of the decreased incomes of the unemployed.

A further interesting relationship can be seen by examining the international trading patterns of nations. Within these nations, individual firms are the units that produce goods for export to other countries. If there is free trade between nations, goods will be purchased from the firms that offer the product at the lowest price, assuming that the quality is the same among competing nations. As the exports of a nation increase, there is an increase in output, employment, and income for that nation, which produces further economic growth.

As nations continue to grow, many will need to increase their output of existing products or to develop new products in order to satisfy new consumer demands. Such a change involves the individual firm—the microeconomic setting—and the growth of output that is measured by the sum total of all productive units—macroeconomics. Invariably, one will not exist without the other.

Bibliography

Carson, Robert B. *Microeconomic Issues Today: Alternative Approaches.* New York: St. Martin's Press, 1983. The main strength of Carson's work is that it points out significant microeconomic issues with which the reader may identify. In addition, he presents opposing viewpoints which provide alternative perspectives about the issues of energy, consumer protection, monopoly power, and income distribution.

Eggert, Jim. *What Is Economics?* Los Altos, Calif.: Kaufmann, 1987. Treats both microeconomic and macroeconomic principles and ideas in a manner which the general reader will appreciate and understand. The illustrations are not too difficult and tend to emphasize concerns that are universal and timeless. A good work.

Evensky, Jerry. *Economic Ideas and Issues: A Systematic Approach to Critical Thinking.* Englewood Cliffs, N.J.: Prentice-Hall, 1987. Presents economic ideas and issues in a bit more advanced level and style, using graphical illustrations. Yet, the explanation of microeconomic theories is quite clear and suitable for both high school seniors and undergraduate students. Also presents background theories that underlie economic analysis. Some items in the appendix will interest the general reader.

Freixas, Xavier, and Jean-Charles Rochet. *Microeconomics of Banking.* Cambridge, Mass.: MIT Press, 1997.

McConnell, Campbell R., and Stanley L. Brue. *Economics: Principles, Problems, and Policies.* New York: McGraw-Hill, 1990. A classic economics text which presents macroeconomic and microeconomic issues in depth. A challenging work which contains a glossary of terms that is a good source for explanations of the language of economics, especially to the general reader. On the other hand, the general reader would find the theoretical analysis a bit too rigorous.

Starr, Philip C. *Economics: Principles in Action.* Belmont, Calif.: Wadsworth, 1988. Starr presents economic principles in a traditional format but with analytical illustrations which might be too difficult for the general reader. Nevertheless, he presents a clear statement of the link between microeconomics and macroeconomics. Also contains a good glossary of economic terms.

Thomas, Robert Paul. *Microeconomic Applications: Understanding the American Economy.* Belmont, Calif.: Wadsworth, 1981. Presents microeconomic issues in a simple and concise style which the general reader will understand. Avoids the use of graphical analysis, and the examples that are used are clear and direct. The key points at the end of each chapter provide good highlights.

Veseth, Michael. *Introductory Macroeconomics.* Orlando, Fla.: Academic Press, 1984. Veseth's book provides a good standard analysis for the collegiate student of the principles of the aggregate picture. The section which treats problems, goals, and trade-offs gives a short and interesting account and assessment for the general reader.

Llewellyn M. Mullings

Cross-References

Business Organization, 57; Classical Economics, 74; Competition, 91; Demand Function, 140; Elasticity, 175; Gross National Product: Real and Nominal, 275; Macroeconomics, 383; Supply Function, 563.

MODELS

Type of economics: General economics
Fields of study: Econometrics and mathematical models; economic theory

An economic model is a description, in abstract terms, of interdependencies among some of the individuals, functions, and activities in an entire economic system or some part of it.

Principal terms

DYNAMICS: a formal description of the way in which an economic system or subsystem evolves as time passes

ECONOMETRIC MODEL: a mathematical description of an economic system or subsystem, including random variates, in terms of equations estimated by statistical methods

EQUATION: a description of an economic (or other numerical) relationship in mathematical terms which states that the two quantities must be equal when the relationship holds

EQUILIBRIUM: a condition in a model that corresponds to the steady values of the key variables that make up the model

MODEL: a description, in abstract terms, of interdependencies among some of the individuals, functions, and activities in an entire system or some part of it

MULTIVARIATE: an equation that allows more than one variable to influence the value of another variable

RANDOM VARIATE: a variable that changes unpredictably ("at random") from time to time

SIMULTANEOUS SOLUTION: a condition in which two or more equations are fulfilled at the same time; often used to characterize an equilibrium

VARIABLES: numerical measures that may take on a range of values either predictably or unpredictably, depending on circumstances

Overview

All economic theory relies on models as a means of dealing with the complexity of real-life economies. In a modern economic system, individuals, companies, markets, and even nations are interdependent. A model (of a particular subsystem of the economic system) is a description of these interdependencies in terms of mathematics, pictures, a computer programming language, or some similar descriptive language, together with a theory of the dynamics of the subsystem. Models are usually somewhat more complex than theories, and a theory may be only one part of a model. Like theories, however, models are abstract and must ignore some aspects of the system that they describe.

In economics, a model will most likely take the form of a list of variables and one or more relationships among the variables. These variables and relationships describe the interdependence among people and their activities of production, consumption, and distribution. Examples will serve best to make this clear. One of the best-known models in economics is the supply-and-demand model, a model which is applicable to the determination of the price and sales in any highly competitive market—for example, the market for Maine potatoes. The "language" in which this model is expressed may be the language of pictures or of mathematics.

The interdependencies between buyers and sellers of potatoes are summarized in a limited number of variables: the price of potatoes (of standard quality), the physical quantity of Maine potatoes bought and sold, the average income of the consumers of potatoes, the population of potato consumers, and the total rainfall during the growing season in Maine. Next, the model assumes that there are two relationships among these variables: a demand relationship and a supply relationship. The demand relationship determines the quantity demanded, that is, the number of pounds of potatoes that people want to buy, while the supply relationship determines the quantity supplied, that is, the number of pounds that people want to sell. Economic theory (and common sense) suggest that the relationship between the price of potatoes and the quantity that people will want to buy is inverted—the higher the price, the less demanded. Accordingly, in the familiar supply-and-demand diagram, this relationship is expressed as a downward-sloping line or curve. Similarly, because it is likely that a higher price will motivate farmers to sell more potatoes, the supply relationship (between price and quantity supplied) is expressed as an upward-sloping line.

It is necessary to say something about the dynamics of the model. It is assumed that the price of potatoes will rise whenever people want to buy more than people want to sell, and that the price will fall whenever people want to sell more than people want to buy. This means the price will be stable only when "supply is equal to demand," or the market has reached its "equilibrium price." In terms of the diagram, the equilibrium price is the price at which the demand line (downward-sloping line) intersects the supply line (upward-sloping line) (see figure). The quantity sold at that price is the equilibrium quantity sold. Taken together, the two variables (price and quantity sold), the two relationships (demand relationship and supply relationship), and the idea of equilibrium, all expressed in terms of the picture, make up the "model" of the supply and demand for potatoes, in its simplest form.

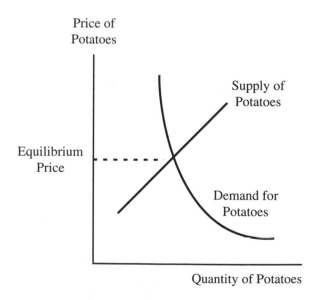

THE SUPPLY AND DEMAND FOR POTATOES

This model can also be expressed in the language of algebra. The demand relationship then would be expressed as an equation. This equation has quantity demanded on the left-hand side and price on the right-hand side, and is called the demand equation. The supply relationship is expressed as a second equation (the supply equation). The result is a "system" of two equations in two unknowns. The equilibrium can be computed from the simultaneous solution of the two equations, a basic method from algebra. The simultaneous solution for the price and the quantity sold is the equilibrium price and quantity. Taking the two variables, the two equations, and their simultaneous solution together produces a "mathematical model" of the market for potatoes. This mathematical model may also include some variables which are random, in order to allow for the uncertainty of real economic life.

In summary, an economic model consists of a list of variables, some of which may be "random," a series of relationships among the variables, and some assumptions about the way in which the relationships interact (concepts of "equilibrium" and "dynamics"). The relationships and the concept of equilibrium may be expressed as pictures, as algebraic equations with or without real numbers, or in a computer programming language.

Applications

An economist might draw a diagram of supply and demand in order to think through a question of economic policy, such as "Who will bear the burden of the sales tax?" In this sense, models play a role in every branch of economics. The most important applications of economic models in business and government, however, make use of computerized mathematical and statistical (econometric) models. The mathematical approach has four advantages. First (in the context of the supply-and-demand example), this approach makes it relatively easy to allow for the fact that the quantity that people want to buy depends on some other variables besides the price. It may also depend, for example, on the population of potential potato consumers and the average income of these potato consumers. Using the mathematical approach, it is possible to express this by making our demand equation a multivariate equation, that is, an equation with more than one variable on the right-hand side. Thus, there will be the quantity demanded on the left-hand side, and on the righthand side, there will be three variables: price, average income, and population. If the values for the population and the average income are known, they can be substituted in the demand and supply equations. These equations can be solved simultaneously, and the equilibrium can be determined. The result is a new model of the market for potatoes which is more complete, as it allows for changing populations and average incomes.

Second, using the mathematical approach, it is possible to allow for the fact that some of the variables that influence supply and demand are very unpredictable, such as the rainfall in the Maine potato country. This factor can be taken into account by adding a "random variable" (a basic concept from statistics) to the right-hand side of the supply equation. This random variable represents the effects of rain (and other unpredictable influences on supply). In practice, it is best to add a random variable to the right-hand side of the demand equation, as there will be unpredictable influences on the quantity demanded as well. These additions create a third, still more complete, model of the supply of and demand for potatoes. It is an "econometric" model, that is, a mathematical model which allows for both the predictable and the unpredictable influences on the price and quantity sold of potatoes.

Third, because it includes random variables, an econometric model can be "estimated" by statistical methods. That is, while it was guessed before that when the price of potatoes rose, such as by 10¢ per pound, the quantity demanded would decrease, it had not been determined how much the quantity demanded would decrease. With an econometric model, statistical methods can give an approximate answer to that question, so that the model will be much more exact. Finding numerical answers to questions such as "How much will the quantity decrease when the price goes up 10¢?" is the major purpose of the specialization called econometrics.

Fourth, a mathematical or econometric model can be very easily translated from mathematics and statistics into a computer programming language. Thus, it is possible to arrive at a computer model of the market for potatoes from a picture model, by way of mathematical and econometric models.

These models may be used for at least four interrelated purposes. First is inference, as the models may be used to infer answers to questions about the structure of markets—in the example, the market for potatoes. Second is forecasting; in the potato example, the model might be used to forecast changes in the price and production of potatoes. The models can also be used to answer questions of the "what if" variety, such as "What if there were to be a drought in the Maine potato country? What would that do to the price and quantity of potatoes?" Third is regulation and control; in the potato example, the government might use the model to determine the impact of a tax on potatoes and use this information in making the decision whether or not to tax. Fourth is experimental design, as the model may help to determine what information is needed at the next stage of research.

Similarly, a model of the petroleum industry might be used to answer the question "What if there should be another long war in the Middle Eastern countries which produce petroleum? How much would the price of oil rise, and how long would it take?" Companies and government agencies might use this sort of information to decide whether to build up their reserves of oil. Models of the macroeconomic system help to answer such questions as "What will happen to unemployment and inflation if the government increases taxes in order to cut the government deficit?" Computerized macroeconomic models of this kind may have as many as several hundred equations and variables. Large enterprises such as Data Resources, Inc., and the WEFA group specialize in selling advice to businesses, based on the results that they get from their large, computerized econometric models.

Context

Models have been a part of economic theory since before Adam Smith (1723-1790). Smith's teacher, David Hume (1711-1776), was one of the discoverers of the "price specie-flow mechanism," a model of the influence of international trade on price levels under the gold standard. Also before Smith, an Italian economist wrote a mathematical model of the impact of import tax rates on tax revenues and smuggling, which may have been the first mathematical model in economics and certainly was an early instance of "supply-side economics." Smith's conception of the "natural price" can also be thought of as a model, as can his "labor theory of value." Both Smith and Thomas Robert Malthus (1766-1834) had "models" of economic growth.

These models, however, have little numerical content. From the numerical point of view, they are vague, which was true of most economic models until the twentieth century. Two nineteenth century developments, however, made greater numerical precision possible. One is the development of statistics, which has provided the methods by which this precision can be obtained. Another was the development of modern microeconomics by such scholars as William Jevons (1835-1882), Léon Walras (1834-1910), and Alfred Marshall (1842-1924). These new theories lent themselves to numerical methods, and Jevons is known to have estimated a model of the demand for grain, though it is not known whether he estimated it by statistical methods.

Beginning quite early in the twentieth century, statistical estimates of economic models began to be made. Since then, two further influences have pushed economic models toward more numerical precision. The first is the economic theories of John Maynard Keynes (1883-1946), which (rightly or wrongly) persuaded economists that government policies could improve the performance of the economy, provided that numerical models could be provided to "fine-tune" these policies. The controversy between Keynesians and monetarists brought about improvements in both economic models and statistical methods. A second influence has been the development of electronic computers since the 1940's, which has made possible both the statistical estimation and the solution of very large and complicated models. Thus, the Nobel Prize in Economic Sciences was awarded to Trygve Haavelmo for putting Keynes's theory into terms suitable to be estimated by statistical methods and to Lawrence R. Klein for an early computerized estimate of such a model. Several other economists have been honored with Nobel Prizes for their contributions to economic models of this kind.

Bibliography

Backhouse, Roger. *Explorations in Economic Methodology: From Lakatos to Empirical Philosophy of Science*. New York: Routledge, 1998.

Bacon, Robert. *A First Course in Econometric Theory*. Oxford, England: Oxford University Press, 1988. A textbook on econometric methods and models, with emphasis on the applications and the use of models and on the methods of intermediate levels of difficulty. Assumes a knowledge of basic economics and mathematics.

Begg, Iai, and S. G. B. Henry, eds. *Applied Economics and Public Policy*. New York: Cambridge University Press, 1998.

Brennan, Michael J., and Thomas M. Carroll. *Preface to Quantitative Economics and Econometrics*. 4th ed. Cincinnati: South-Western, 1987. This 550-page text introduces the student to mathematical, statistical, and econometric methods and models in economics. A knowledge of basic economics, but no knowledge of college-level mathematics, is assumed.

Case, Karl E., and Ray C. Fair. *Principles of Economics*. Englewood Cliffs, N.J.: Prentice-Hall, 1989. Most introductory texts in economics have some brief discussion of the role of models in economics. Chapter 1 presents one of the best.

Chiang, Alpha. *Fundamental Methods of Mathematical Economics*. 3d ed. New York: McGraw-Hill, 1984. A standard textbook of mathematical economics in most graduate and undergraduate programs in economics in the United States. Defines the range of mathematical modeling tools which modern economists are expected to know. A large, difficult, but rewarding book.

Clower, Robert W., Philip E. Graves, and Robert L. Sexton. *Intermediate Microeconomics*.

San Diego: Harcourt Brace Jovanovich, 1988. The appendix to chapter 3 offers a good introduction to econometric models in the specific context of supply and demand.

Fossati, Amedeo, and John Hutton, eds. *Policy Simulations in the European Union.* New York: Routledge, 1998.

Intriligator, Michael D. *Econometric Models: Techniques and Applications.* Englewood Cliffs, N.J.: Prentice-Hall, 1978. Chapter 2 presents perhaps the best overall introduction to models in economics, stressing econometric models. The discussion assumes a knowledge of intermediate economic theory and mathematical analysis.

Roemer, John E. *Equality of Opportunity.* Cambridge, Mass.: Harvard University Press, 1998.

Roger A. McCain

Cross-References

Classical Economics, 74; Demand Function, 140; Economists, 164; Factor Analysis, 218; Forecasting, 246; History of Economics, 295; Indicators, 311.

Monetary Policy

Type of economics: Monetary and fiscal theory
Field of study: Monetary theory

Monetary policy involves any action taken by a central bank to influence the national economy by manipulating a nation's money stock and the level of interest rates. The ultimate objectives of monetary policy are to help stabilize the price level, keep unemployment low, promote economic growth, and influence a country's exchange rate.

Principal terms

DISCOUNT RATE: the interest rate that the central bank charges banks to which it lends reserves
MONEY: the currency and checking deposits held by people and businesses
OPEN-MARKET OPERATIONS: the purchase and sale of securities, usually government securities, by the central bank
RESERVE REQUIREMENT: a required ratio of certain bank assets, called reserves, to bank checking deposit liabilities
RESERVES: generally, the vault cash holdings of banks plus their deposits at the central bank

Overview

Monetary policy is a collection of actions by a central bank designed to affect directly the money stock and interest rates, and ultimately to promote national economic health. The precise measures used to influence the economy vary from nation to nation dependent upon its economic and financial institutions. Generally, there are three main techniques—the reserve requirement, the discount rate, and open market operations—employed to affect the money stock and interest rates, and all three of these are connected with the reserve position of the nation's banks and how money is created.

Money consists of the currency and checking deposits held by people and businesses. These are the principal assets that can be used directly to purchase goods and services. The main component of money is checking deposits, and these deposits are created by banks when they make loans and investments. Banks must have sufficient reserves to cover the deposits they create. These reserves primarily consist of a bank's own deposit holdings at the central bank. In many nations, including the United States, a bank's holdings of cash in its own vaults also is included in its reserves.

Bank reserve positions are important because when the reserves of the banking system expand (contract), the ability of banks to make loans and create deposits expands (contracts), and such expansions and contractions can have adverse effects upon the economy. For example, when bank reserves expand during periods of full employment, bank expansion of loans and money leads to inflation. Initially interest rates fall because banks have more reserves and desire to put them to use. This reduction in interest rates induces people and businesses to borrow and spend. The demand for national output rises, but because the economy is at full employment, it is difficult to increase output to meet the added demand, and inflation follows. This is one of the main problems that cause many central bankers to stress the importance of monitoring and controlling bank reserve positions.

One means of controlling these positions is for the central bank to set and manipulate the reserve requirement, which is defined as a required ratio of certain bank assets, called reserves, to bank checking deposit liabilities. The requirement is fractional; that is, for every dollar a bank owes its depositors in checking accounts, it needs to hold somewhat less than a dollar in reserves. For example, if banks have $50 billion in reserves and the reserve requirement is 10 percent, then the amount of checking deposit money in the economy could be $500 billion. The total amount of money would consist of the $500 billion plus the volume of currency held by people outside banks. If banks actually had $500 billion in checking deposit liabilities and if the central bank in an inflationary period chose to raise the reserve requirement from 10 to 12 percent, then banks would be $10 billion short in reserves, holding $50 billion instead of the required $60 billion. To overcome this shortage of reserves, banks might raise interest rates in order to discourage people and businesses from obtaining more loans. The repayment of loans would exceed the granting of new loans. Because people repay loans with checking deposits, the amount of checking deposit money in the economy would contract, thereby reducing the amount of reserves that is needed by banks to cover their reserve requirement.

A second policy instrument is the discount rate. This is the interest rate that the central bank charges banks to which it lends reserves. Generally, the central bank raises the discount rate when it wishes to increase banks' interest rates on loans and discourage banks from borrowing reserves. Should this occur, businesses and individuals may reduce their own borrowing and spending. Conversely, the central bank generally lowers the discount rate when it wishes to encourage banks to borrow reserves and to lower their lending rates. Should this occur, businesses and individuals may be encouraged to increase their own borrowing and spending.

The third and, for most nations, the most important policy instrument of a central bank is open-market operations. This refers to the central bank's purchase or sale of securities, usually government securities. The central bank is only one participant, although the most important, in the market for securities. It buys and sells, along with the general public, in the government securities market. A purchase by the central bank from the public at large is paid for by a credit to the checking deposit accounts of the sellers and to the reserves of the sellers' banks. Conversely, a sale of securities by the central bank results in a decrease in the checking deposits of the security purchasers and in the reserves of the purchasers' banks. The open-market purchase and sale of securities by the central bank is the most critical instrument of monetary policy because its use directly and immediately affects bank reserves. Many central banks employ this instrument daily, seeking to adjust interest rates and the money stock and, hopefully, to accomplish the ultimate policy objectives of low inflation, low unemployment, significant real economic growth, and an appropriate exchange rate.

Applications

The techniques for accomplishing the purposes of monetary policy appear to be clear. For example, during an economic boom the central bank can restrain inflation through using some combination of the open-market sale of government securities, an increase of the discount rate, and an increase in the reserve requirement. Theoretically, these actions will reduce bank reserve positions and force banks to raise interest rates which, in turn, will lower the public's demand for goods. At the same time as interest rates rise, bank lending will be reduced and the growth of the money stock will be restrained, thereby further directly reducing the demand for goods and inflationary pressures. Similarly, during economic recession the central bank can use the reverse of the policy just described: It can purchase government securities, lower the discount rate, and lower the reserve requirement in an effort to increase demand and reduce unemployment. Unfortunately, monetary policy processes and their results are not as simple as just described. Ultimate policy objectives are often in conflict with each other, and there are variable lags in the effects of monetary policy on the economy.

Consider the anti-inflationary policy previously mentioned. It is important that the reduction in the demand for goods stemming from contractive monetary policy not be excessive. If it is, then the demand for goods and services may contract the economy so much that it may be thrown into recession and increased unemployment. A classic case of such a consequence occurred in the United States from 1936 to 1938. The country was in recovery from the Great Depression of the 1930's. Banks had very ample reserves. The Federal Reserve Board was responsible for implementing central bank policy in the United States. The Board believed that, if the banking system used its excess reserves to finance the economic expansion that was then under way, it could cause price inflation. Consequently, the Board sharply raised the reserve requirement, an action that may have caused the 1937-1938 recession in the middle of the Great Depression.

Anti-inflationary policy not only may cause unemployment but also may reduce real economic growth. High interest rates reduce investment expenditures, and such expenditures result in increased plant and equipment and in improved technology, the source of added potential output. Yet here is a supreme irony: A restrictive monetary policy, which raises interest rates and reduces inflation in the short run, may reduce the growth of the supply of goods and thereby keep prices higher than they might otherwise be in the long run.

Comparable complications exist for expansive monetary policy designed to reduce unemployment during a recession. When a central bank follows an expansive policy, the demand for goods and services rises, leading to output, profit margin, and price increases. Some price rises are inevitable when economic policy is expansive. Since the end of World War II, many Western nations have focused their policies on maintaining high employment levels instead of on reducing inflation. Associated with these expansive policies has been rising prices. For example, the annual rate of price inflation in the United States was 4.7 percent from 1946 through 1990, whereas in 1945 the price level was almost the same as it had been in 1800.

The phenomenon of a trade-off between inflation and unemployment is known as the Phillips curve, named after A. W. Phillips (1914-1975), who first discussed it in 1958. Most economists believe that, in the short run, an expansive policy results in a reduction of unemployment at the expense of added inflation, and that a contractive policy results in reduced inflation at the cost of added unemployment. In the long run, there is little evidence for any trade-off, as wage changes approximately parallel price changes.

Conflict may also exist between a country's domestic and international economic objectives. A nation may have a persistent adverse balance of trade, that is, its imports may exceed its exports of goods. One means of reducing the difference is to lower the value of the country's currency in international money markets. This would increase the cost of foreign goods and lead to a reduction of imports. It would also lower the cost of domestic goods to foreigners and lead to an increase in exports. One means the central bank can use to accomplish this is to lower interest rates. A possible fall in interest rates will cause foreigners to lend less to the country, thereby reducing the demand for the country's currency in international money markets. A decrease in the international value of the country's currency should then occur.

Typically, a domestic monetary policy of lowering interest rates is used when a country has less than full employment, and it becomes a domestic expansion policy. Yet if the central bank works to lower interest rates in order to eliminate an adverse balance of trade, there will be conflict between the external and domestic objectives of policy if there is at the same time full employment. Economic boom calls for rising, not declining, interest rates.

Finally, the lag in the effect of monetary policy calls into question the efficacy of countering the business cycle. For example, it is recognized by most economists that an expansive policy undertaken to correct a mild recession may intensify the next inflation if the effects of the policy are not felt until recovery is already under way. Similarly, a contractive monetary policy designed to reduce inflation in a full employment economy may not affect the economy until the next recession has begun. If the lag in the effect of monetary policy is highly variable and hard to specify, then countercyclical policy may not be feasible. Some economists believe that the central bank should reduce its policy objectives to one: the use of policy instruments to stabilize the growth of bank reserves. This is the view of those economists known as "monetarists." They believe that a steady growth of bank reserves (a growth rate keyed to the potential real annual growth of output) would provide a stable financial environment for the attainment of the long-run goals of policy, such as higher real output and economic welfare.

Context

The modern monetary policy objectives of central banks are a relatively recent development, dating back to the period between the two world wars. Central banks first developed in the seventeenth century with the establishment of the Bank of Sweden in 1668 and the Bank of England in 1694. These banks, and their counterparts as they were formed in the next two centuries, were frequently private commercial banks that were extended a monopoly of note issue in their respective countries. In exchange for special privileges, these banks became their government's banker and provided financial assistance to their governments in times of crisis.

Given their close connection to the government, these banks gradually gained dominance over other private commercial banks, regulating their deposit and loan creation ability. As this took place, the banks favored by the government came to be called central banks by the middle of the nineteenth century. In some nations there was intense rivalry between commercial banks and the governmentally favored private central banks. For example, both the First Bank of the United States (1791-1811) and the Second Bank of the United States (1816-1836) made loans and regulated the notes created by other banks. There was strong opposition to these Banks of the United States from liberal lending private banks as well as from commercial businesses and rural interests who wanted easy credit. The result was that the United States government did not renew their charters. There was no central bank in the United States from 1836 to 1913, when the Federal Reserve System was established.

Gradually, all central banks had their private charters removed and became public institutions. Those central banks that were established in the late nineteenth century and through most of the twentieth century were almost always public banks.

A principal function of a central bank was and continues to be to act as a lender of last resort and to supervise private banks. Their goal is to help maintain the soundness of the financial system, not directly to affect employment, inflation, output, and exchange rates through changing bank reserve positions. Obviously, there is a link between the financial well-being of the economy and the broad objectives of monetary policy. The regulatory function of a central bank as a lender of last resort is, in large part, designed to prevent bank panics. Financial collapse can lead to price deflation and depression. As already noted, however, the monetary objectives were developments of the period between the two world wars. Monetary policy techniques affect the financial system and the economy as a whole. A central bank as a bank supervisor and lender of last resort engages in regulatory practices that directly affect an individual bank.

In its role as a regulator, a central bank is a "banker's bank." It examines the books of the private financial institutions, holds their reserves, makes recommendations to the institutions for adjusting the composition of their loan and investment portfolios, and above all, provides financial assistance to solvent banks that are temporarily short of funds. This has been the traditional regulatory role of a central bank. Starting in the 1980's, however, a different view emerged among some economists: that a central bank should also lend to insolvent banks, especially when those banks are large and if their failure could result in a loss of confidence in the banking system by the general public. A contrary position is that this view, if implemented, could result in the making of increasingly risky loans by banks, as bankers would know that their institutions would not be permitted to fail. The net result could be increased bank reserves, loans, and inflation.

Bibliography

Bordo, Michael D. "The Lender of Last Resort: Alternative Views and Historical Experience." *Economic Review* (Federal Reserve Bank of Richmond, Virginia), January/February, 1990, 18-29. A nontechnical article outlining the lender-of-last-resort function of central banks and arguing that this function, when applied to solvent banks, can prevent a banking panic.

Broaddus, Alfred. *A Primer on the Fed.* Richmond, Va.: Federal Reserve Bank of Richmond, 1988. A booklet, intended for the layperson, outlining the structure, functions, and monetary policy actions of the Federal Reserve System. One of the best short (74-page) nontechnical books on the Federal Reserve. Includes a bibliography.

Friedman, Milton. "Monetary Policy: Theory and Practice." *Journal of Money, Credit, and Banking* 13 (February, 1982): 98-118. Friedman, the leading monetarist of the twentieth century, presented this paper as a lecture in 1981. He examines the actual practices of monetary policy and gives the reasons for its frequent lack of success. Written with conviction and humor.

Friedman, Milton, and Anna J. Schwartz. *A Monetary History of the United States, 1867-1960.* New York: National Bureau of Economic Research, 1963. A monumental narrative study of the behavior of money in the United States. Includes author and subject indexes, many charts, and tables. A classic book.

Goldenweiser, E. A. *American Monetary Policy.* New York: McGraw-Hill, 1951. An examination of Federal Reserve monetary policy from 1914 through 1950. An earlier and somewhat less critical view of the Federal Reserve. Includes an index and charts.

Goodhart, Charles. *The Evolution of Central Banks.* Cambridge, Mass.: MIT Press, 1988. A paperback book on the development of central banks by a former economic adviser (1968-1985) on domestic monetary affairs in the Bank of England. Strongly advocates the importance of the lender-of-last-resort function of a central bank. Includes a bibliography and an index.

Guttmann, Robert, ed. *Reforming Money and Finance: Toward a New Monetary Regime.* 2d ed. Armonk, N.Y.: M. E. Sharpe, 1997.

Klein, John J. *Money and the Economy.* 6th ed. New York: Harcourt Brace Jovanovich, 1986. A 560-page text written for a college-level course in money and banking. Describes financial institutions as well as monetary theory and policy. Also suitable for the general reader. Includes author and subject indexes, references, figures, and tables.

Maisel, Sherman J. *Managing the Dollar.* New York: W. W. Norton, 1973. A delightful and realistic paperback book written by a former member of the Federal Reserve Board. Recounts his experiences and reflections on the operations of the Federal Reserve. A nonmonetarist perspective. Includes an index.

Meulendyke, Ann-Marie. *U.S. Monetary Policy and Financial Markets.* New York: Federal Reserve Bank of New York, 1989. Meulendyke is a manager and senior economist assigned to the Federal Reserve Bank of New York's trading desk, where open market operations take place. Examines the evolution of U.S. monetary policy and practices. Includes charts.

Selgin, George A. *Bank Deregulation and Monetary Order.* New York: Routledge, 1996.

John J. Klein

Cross-References

Banks, 29; Credit, 124; Currency, 129; Federal Reserve Bank, 223; Gold and the Gold Standard, 257; Interest and Interest Rates, 323; Interest Rates and Monetary Policy, 329.

MONEY SUPPLY

Type of economics: Monetary and fiscal theory
Field of study: Monetary theory

The money supply is the total quantity of currently available objects which fulfill the functions of money. Its basic function is to serve as a "medium of exchange"; thus, the money supply includes everything that can be spent directly, that which is widely acceptable as a means of payment in the purchase of goods or services.

Principal terms

ELECTRONIC FUNDS TRANSFER SYSTEM: a technology for transferring money electronically rather than by checks

LIQUIDITY: the degree to which an asset can be easily turned into a medium of exchange without loss in nominal value

M-1: the value of all the paper currency, coin, and transactions deposits that are held by the public

MEDIUM OF EXCHANGE: that which is accepted as payment for purchasing goods and services

MONETARY AUTHORITY: an agency that is responsible for controlling the money supply

Overview

Most economies practice a substantial amount of specialization in production because of the larger outputs that result. Specialization, however, means that no economic unit (household, firm, region) can be completely self-sufficient; thus, trade between units is required. While barter—the direct exchange of goods or services—is possible, one fundamental problem with barter led to the introduction of money: There must be a "double coincidence of wants" for exchange to occur. In other words, if two people wish to trade, each must have something that the other wants. If not, several intermediate trades may be required before a deal can be consummated. This inefficiency makes a medium of exchange an attractive innovation: People can exchange their goods for a medium of exchange which is acceptable to anyone for any other good. The need for intermediate transactions is eliminated and a higher level of efficiency is achieved.

Because money is the medium of exchange, it can also be considered a store of generalized purchasing power or a store of value. The two concepts associated with money—its role as a medium of exchange and the notion that it may be a store of value—lead to two different approaches to defining and measuring the supply of money.

The first approach, called the transactions approach, follows from the medium of exchange function of money. According to this view, the supply of money is made up of all currently available assets which can be spent directly in the purchase of goods or services without intermediate transactions. If an asset cannot itself be used directly in transactions, it is not "money" and therefore is not a part of the money supply. A country's currency and coin are obviously a part of its money supply, but so too would be transactions deposits, which are accounts on which a check can be written. From this perspective a checking account is part of the money supply, but a passbook savings account is not, because in order to buy something using a savings account, it must first be transformed into a medium of exchange—it cannot be spent directly.

Because money is a store of generalized purchasing power, a second way to define and measure the money supply is to concentrate upon those assets which are currently serving the store of value function. This approach is called the liquidity approach. Following this view, the distinguishing feature of money is not that it can be spent directly but instead that it is a highly liquid asset. An asset is said to be liquid if it can be transformed quickly and easily, at terms that are known in advance, into a medium of exchange. The transactions money supply is already a medium of exchange; thus it is the most liquid asset. A one-dollar bill is always worth one dollar in transactions, as are four quarters, ten dimes, or one dollar in a checking account. Note, however, that one dollar in a passbook savings account is also worth one dollar in goods or services transactions. It has to be withdrawn from the account before it can be spent, but its value in transactions is known and access to it easily gained. Thus, the liquidity approach to defining money leads to the inclusion of some assets which are not directly spendable.

A problem with the liquidity approach is that all assets possess the quality of liquidity to some degree. A diamond ring or a condominium also may be turned into a medium of exchange; the difference between money and "nonmoney" is not perfectly distinct. Conceptually, all assets may be placed along a liquidity continuum or spectrum ranging from the most to the least liquid of assets. At one end of the continuum are currency, coin, and checkable deposits which are already media of exchange. Next there are assets which guarantee a fixed money value (for example, a savings account), followed by financial and other assets which are less and less liquid. The point at which assets are no longer "money," as one moves down the spectrum, is a matter for discussion.

The determination of which of these two concepts of the money supply is superior depends on the resolution of two issues. These issues directly concern the interest in defining the money supply: the belief that the amount of money affects the level of economic activity. Thus, the money supply ought to reflect that concept of money which is most clearly related to important economic variables, such as the level of spending and the levels of output and prices, and which can be controlled most directly by the monetary authority.

Proponents of the transactions approach stress the role of money in spending. They argue that individuals hold money principally because it is a medium of exchange (often at the cost of lower investment earnings than would result if assets were held in another form). Therefore, when the money supply increases, individuals are likely to spend rather than hold the additional money. This will likely increase output and/or prices. These economists stress a predictable relationship between the money supply and the nominal value of output in the economy. Furthermore, they argue that the transactions money supply can be controlled with some precision by a country's monetary authority. In the United States, this agency is the Federal Reserve System.

The liquidity approach, on the other hand, is based on an assumption that individuals prefer to hold a portfolio of assets of different types and varying liquidity, such as currency, checking accounts, savings accounts, bonds, stocks, and real estate. If most people are content with the composition of their portfolios, an increase in the money supply by the monetary authority will introduce a disequilibrium because these portfolios would become too liquid. In order to adjust, the public will purchase assets which are less liquid, such as bonds, corporate stocks, and real estate. These adjustments in portfolios will cause higher levels of spending by households and higher levels of financial and nonfinancial investment; thus the level of economic activity will change. Any asset which is liquid may be considered a part of the money supply according to this approach, and the monetary authority may be viewed as having some control over the supply of liquidity in the economy in its monetary policy adjustments.

Applications

In the United States, the Federal Reserve issues official measures of the money supply. Both the transactions approach and the liquidity approach are used to construct these estimates.

The term "money supply," when it is used without a qualification, usually means M-1, the Federal Reserve's measure of the money supply using the transactions approach; M-1 includes all financial assets which can be used directly in exchange for goods and services: currency (paper money), coins, transactions deposits, and traveler's checks. Included among transactions deposits are any accounts on which unlimited checks may be written. Demand deposits, Negotiable Order of Withdrawal (NOW) accounts, automatic transfer service accounts (whether held at commercial or savings banks or at savings and loan associations), and credit union share drafts are examples of transactions accounts which the Federal Reserve includes in M-1.

In addition, the Federal Reserve also publishes measures of the money supply using the liquidity approach. The most frequently encountered is M-2. M-2 includes, in addition to all items in M-1, additional highly liquid assets, most of which have a fixed nominal value or can also be used in transactions but only to a limited degree. Examples of these types of assets are savings-type deposits at all depository institutions, small-denomination (less than $100,000) time deposits, money-market deposit accounts (typically with limited check writing privileges) and money-market mutual funds held by individuals, and some overnight deposits and other accounts. Accounts which are intended to be held for longer periods, such as Individual Retirement Accounts (IRAs), are not included.

Moving further down the liquidity spectrum and broadening the money supply using the liquidity approach, the Federal Reserve also calculates M-3, adding to M-2 (which includes M-1) liquid assets which have either a longer term to maturity, are held primarily by institutions rather than individuals, or are of a large size (over $100,000).

Finally, the Federal Reserve issues L, a measure of the total liquidity in the economy in the broadest sense. All items in M-3 are included in L, as well as U.S. savings bonds, Treasury bills, and some short-term business obligations.

Context

Because it is widely believed that the amount of money may have an impact on the level and quality of a society's economic activity, professional economists, business-people, and government policymakers have been interested in determining, measuring, and controlling the money supply.

A precise definition of a money supply which is related in a predictable and stable manner to the ultimate economic objectives of society is particularly desirable, as is an aggregate over which the monetary authority has some control. Although there has been a fair amount of agreement concerning the general principles of monetary measurement, such as the transactions or liquidity approaches, the actual assets which are included in the money supply have changed over time as payment methods have evolved.

Beginning around 1975, the pace and scope of financial innovation began to increase. Before 1980, financial institutions in the United States were regulated under a system which had changed little since it was implemented during the Great Depression of the 1930's. This system featured very little competition between financial institutions of different types which were, by statute, narrowly proscribed in the services that they could offer. In addition, little interest rate competition was allowed between institutions of the same type. For example, commercial banks were the only institutions which were allowed to offer a checking account, and these institutions also did the commercial lending. Savings and loan associations were limited, for the most part, to making mortgage loans. Credit unions were limited to making consumer loans to their own members. The latter two types of institutions could offer only savings-type accounts. At the same time, ceilings were set on the interest rate which could be paid on all accounts of different types (no interest was allowed on checking accounts).

As inflation rates reached levels which were high by historical standards, market interest rates began to exceed the limits which banks and other institutions were allowed to pay on their deposits. A result was a dramatic increase in financial innovation: New types of financial institutions began to spring up and new types of financial instruments were invented in an attempt to circumvent the legal rate ceilings.

Whenever a new financial instrument appears, questions arise concerning whether it is "money" and where it should be placed in the liquidity spectrum. The money supply has become a changing aggregate. To complicate matters, many new financial instruments were hybrids—instruments which might serve both as a medium of exchange and as a store of value. An example is the NOW account, on which checks may be drawn and on which interest is paid. A more complex case is money-market mutual fund shares at an investment company on which higher money-market interest rates are earned. These shares may be a good store of value, but checks may also be drawn on them, although typically of a certain minimum (often $500) amount. As a result, the items within the money supply have become less homogeneous and less distinct from instruments not in the money supply. Also, M-1 has become more volatile, more sensitive in size to interest-rate changes, and much more difficult for the monetary authority to control.

During this same period and continuing into the present and future, a profound ongoing revolution is occurring in the way in which funds are transferred in the economy. The system was primarily paper-based; that is, the principal method of transferring funds was by check. There has been increasing use of electronic methods of fund transfer. This innovation has led to new and further complications in defining the supply of money. Automatic teller machines, point of sale terminals, and wire transfer of funds have changed the way in which money is viewed and will continue to raise new issues about its definition. Yet to be answered is the question of which concept of the money supply, under these new conditions, is most closely related to economic activity and which can be most closely controlled for policy purposes by the Federal Reserve System.

Bibliography

Federal Reserve Bank of Chicago. *Modern Money Mechanics.* Chicago: Author, 1982. A pamphlet, intended for the general public, which describes the mechanical process of money creation. Includes a concise description of the characteristics of money, as well as how the Federal Reserve System attempts to control it. Available free to the public.

Flannery, Mark J., and Dwight M. Jaffee. *The Economic Implications of an Electronic Monetary Transfer System.* Lexington, Mass.: Lexington Books, 1973. One of the earlier books on the electronic transfer of funds. Describes the nature of these types of transfers, discusses their broader implications, and speculates about the future course of this system. Chapter 2 includes an excellent description of various systems of exchange in historical perspective. Largely in nontechnical language.

Guttmann, Robert, ed. *Reforming Money and Finance: Toward a New Monetary Regime.* 2d ed. Armonk, N.Y.: M. E. Sharpe, 1997.

Miller, Rozen LeRoy, and Robert W. Pulsinelli. *Modern Money and Banking.* 2d ed. New York: McGraw-Hill, 1989. One of the better textbooks concerning money and banking. Assumes some prior knowledge of economics, but is straightforward and very readable. Chapter 3 contains a detailed description of the changing definition of the money supply.

Robertson, Dennis Holme. *Money.* 1922. Reprint. Cambridge, England: Cambridge University Press, 1961. A charming classic in economics. Develops the theory of the value of money in nonmathematical terms. The chapters are headed by quotations from Lewis Carroll's *Alice's Adventures in Wonderland* (1865) and *Through the Looking-Glass and What Alice Found There* (1871).

Selgin, George A. *Bank Deregulation and Monetary Order.* New York: Routledge, 1996.

United States. Board of Governors of the Federal Reserve System. *The Federal Reserve System: Purposes and Functions.* Washington, D.C.: Author, 1985. A comprehensive yet succinct description of the Federal Reserve System and its activities which is intended for the general public. Chapter 2 reviews monetary policy and the measurement of the various official versions of the money supply. Available free to the public.

Earl W. Adams

Cross-References

Banks, 29; Bonds, 40; Currency, 129; Federal Reserve Bank, 223; Financing, 228; Interest and Interest Rates, 323; Liquidity, 378; Monetary Policy, 431.

MONOPOLIES

Type of economics: Industrial economics
Field of study: Industrial organization and public policy

A monopoly is a marketplace in which there is only one seller, and the resulting absence of competition can adversely affect the allocation of a society's resources. Though governments in market economies may encourage monopolies in special circumstances, public policy generally focuses on limiting monopoly power.

Principal terms

ANTITRUST: a government policy that prevents cooperation between sellers, unilateral acts by sellers, or mergers that reduce the level of competition in markets
COLLUSION: any cooperation between sellers to set prices, sales levels, sales territories, or other business variables with the intention of raising prices or harming other competitors
COMPETITIVE MARKET: a marketplace in which many sellers, none of which is large enough to affect the market price unilaterally, compete for the business of many buyers
ENTRY BARRIERS: technical, legal, or financial conditions that prevent additional sellers from entering the market
EXCESS PROFITS: profits in excess of the amount necessary for a seller to remain in business
MARKET STRUCTURE: the production technology, demand conditions, entry barriers, number and size of sellers, geographic area, and nature of the product unique to a single market

Overview

The word "monopoly" has Latin and Greek roots; literally, it means single (*mono*) seller (*polium* or *polion*). Any market in which buyers have only one seller from which to purchase a good or service is a monopoly market, and that single seller is called a monopolist. No other good or service is an acceptable substitute for the monopolist's product, and sellers wishing to compete for the monopolist's customers are unable to do so because of entry barriers.

As with other types of sellers, it is generally assumed that a monopolist wishes to maximize its profits. Unlike firms in competitive markets, however, the monopolist can unilaterally dictate the quantity, quality, and price of the good or service it provides. The monopolist's unchallenged market position gives it the leverage needed to earn very high profits. Buyers have only two choices: make a purchase at the price and quality decided by the monopolist, or do without the good or service.

The behavior most characteristic of a profit-maximizing monopolist is to restrict the quantity of goods or services it supplies to the market. The resulting shortage of goods drives up the price in the market—because no other sellers or substitute products are available, buyers can make a purchase only by outbidding other buyers. Even though the monopolist makes fewer sales at this high price, the monopolist earns a higher profit from each unit it sells by raising the price above the cost of producing that unit. By carefully observing buyers' purchasing behavior, the monopolist can set price and quantity to maximize its profits. The final price will be higher, and the quantity supplied lower, than would have occurred in a market with competing firms.

Mainstream economic theory and policy condemn monopoly markets as undesirable institutions that inefficiently allocate society's resources, unfairly redistribute wealth from buyers to sellers, and hinder technological progress. Monopoly markets have the capability to concentrate a dangerous amount of political power in the hands of a relatively small number of citizens. Three types of inefficiencies are identified with monopoly markets.

First, by choosing to restrict its output, the monopolist excludes from the market some buyers who otherwise would have made a purchase. While the monopolist could sell more units by reducing price, the monopolist would rather not serve these additional customers—by doing so, its total profits would be lower. By restricting output, the monopolist inefficiently allocates society's resources—it produces too little of the good.

Second, the monopolist is prone to inefficiencies in production. All else equal, holding down costs contributes to higher profits. The monopolist may have difficulty maintaining low production costs, however, because it is not pressed to remain efficient by competition. In a competitive market, sellers that do not produce efficiently will lose most of their customers to more efficient sellers who can afford to sell at lower prices. The monopolist, who does not face this competitive pressure to keep costs down, has less incentive to minimize the amount of society's resources that it uses.

Third, without vigorous competition, the monopolist faces less pressure to make the investments in quality control, research, and product development that are needed in order to maintain a quality product. As a result, improvements in existing products and in production techniques occur slowly or not at all, and new products and technologies may go undiscovered. As knowledge tends to spread to other markets, these long-run inefficiencies can hinder technical progress in other markets as well.

In addition to being inefficient, the distribution of income between buyers and sellers in monopoly markets is considered by many social commentators to be unfair. While competition drives prices down to levels that allow sellers just enough profits to remain in business, the monopolist's price generates excess profits. These profits are a pure transfer of income from buyers to the monopolist. Those who view this redistribution as unfair believe that buyers, who have no alternative sources for the product, are being exploited by the monopolist. Others believe that the redistribution can threaten the workings of democratic government by concentrating a disproportionate amount of society's wealth in the hands of a few individuals, who could use it to gain political power and influence.

Despite the inefficiencies and inequities of monopoly markets, they can produce beneficial results in some circumstances. For example, even while restricting its output, a monopolist may be producing more output than any single competitive seller could. Depending on the product being produced, operating at a large scale can allow the monopolist to achieve economies unavailable to smaller firms. In other circumstances, monopolies may be more likely to invest in cost-reducing innovation than competitive firms. This condition results from the fact that the monopolist is able to keep the profits from any cost reduction, while firms in highly competitive markets see profits from cost savings competed away through replication by other firms and by price competition. Yet, sellers in most markets can gain these two benefits without having a monopoly position. Only in rare cases, such as natural monopolies and patent monopolies, do these advantages outweigh the severe inefficiencies and perceived unfairness of the monopoly market.

Applications

The pure monopoly described above is rarely found in free markets because the structure of a monopoly market—a single seller, absolutely no substitute products, and no chance of entry by other firms—is so exclusive. When pure monopolies do exist, they produce only a tiny percentage of total free market output. An airport that has only one restaurant or a small college town with only one bookstore are examples of virtual monopolies, but even in these cases the monopoly is not pure because some buyers can find substitutes.

Because of this, economists are less concerned with the existence of pure monopoly markets than with the existence of monopoly power. Monopoly power is the ability of a seller or a group of sellers to restrict market output and maintain price at monopoly levels. Sellers may be able to use monopoly power even if the structure of a market does not exactly fit the definition of pure monopoly. The extent of the inefficiencies and unfairness that result depends on both the structure of the market and the behavior of the sellers in that market.

A market with multiple sellers can perform exactly like a monopoly market if the sellers cooperate and act jointly as a monopolist. The polar example of this type of collusion is a cartel. In a cartel, all sellers have specific production quotas, which when added together equal the monopoly quantity. The resulting monopoly price ensures the highest possible profits, which are divided between the colluding sellers. The stability of a cartel depends upon the number and relative sizes of sellers in the cartel, the type of product being produced, the ease with which prices can be observed by other sellers, and other market characteristics. Unfortunately for cartel members, there is usually an incentive for one or all of the sellers to "cheat" on its quota by overproducing. The Organization of Petroleum Exporting Countries (OPEC) is a classic example. Because collusion is illegal in the United States through antitrust laws, collusive agreements have to be made in private, increasing the chance that the agreement will break down.

When society stands to benefit greatly from one of the few positive characteristics of a monopoly, the government may grant a monopoly right to a single firm. A monopoly right is an artificial entry barrier that keeps other sellers out of the market. The two classic cases of this are natural monopolies and patent monopolies.

Some production processes require a seller to operate at a very large scale in order to produce at the lowest possible cost per unit. In some markets, a seller of this size becomes large enough to service all the potential buyers. This situation is called a natural monopoly. In such cases, society benefits from having all production done by a single, large, efficient seller rather than from several smaller, less efficient producers. Granting a monopoly right to a single seller guarantees an efficient-sized producer, but it makes possible inefficiencies from monopoly power. This problem is usually addressed through government regulation of price and quantity.

A good example of such a natural monopoly is a local electric utility. Kilowatts of electricity produced by a set of small, competing firms are very expensive, because the large fixed costs of each seller's power plant and system of power lines must be spread out over a relatively small amount of output. In addition, in order to gain access to customers, competing firms must duplicate each other's systems of electric poles and underground cables. A single monopoly firm reduces the cost for each customer by producing electricity for the entire city and dividing up the fixed cost of the power plant over more customers. The monopolist can also build a single electric grid network for the entire city to avoid the wasteful duplicate use of society's resources. It is the policy of state governments in the United States to award electric utility companies monopoly rights for defined geographic areas, in exchange for charging prices set by a state commission and agreeing to serve all the buyers in the geographic area. Thus, the scale economy cost savings are achieved without allowing the utility to exercise its monopoly power to restrict output and charge excessively high prices.

A patent monopoly is also a policy designed to encourage more efficient uses of society's resources. The government promises a patent to the first seller that develops a new product or process. This patent gives the seller the exclusive right to produce, use, and/or sell the patented product or process free of competition. Patent rights under U.S. law typically last for seventeen years. The patent monopoly and the monopoly power that accompanies it are the rewards for the seller's increased research and development of new products and technologies. In this case, the monopolist is rewarded for using society's resources more efficiently than its less innovative competitors.

Note that in the case of a regulated natural monopoly, monopoly exists but monopoly power is not exercised. In a patent monopoly, the seller holding the patent can exercise monopoly power—indeed, the potential for monopoly profits encourages the seller to innovate.

Context

The chief reason that economists are interested in monopoly markets is to prevent monopolies from forming and prevent nonmonopoly sellers from exercising monopoly power. Most Western nations limit or prohibit the extent of monopoly in their economies. In the United States, monopoly, attempts to gain monopoly, and acts of collusion that restrain trade are illegal under the Sherman Antitrust Act (1890). Mergers that substantially reduce competition or create a monopoly are illegal under the Clayton Act (1914). These antitrust laws are enforced by the Justice Department and the Federal Trade Commission. Though the Supreme Court's interpretation of these laws has evolved over time, its rulings have been motivated more by the income distribution effects of monopoly and monopoly power than by concerns about inefficiencies.

Since the 1960's, an alternative view of antitrust policy has emerged. Known as the Chicago School of antitrust, this movement criticizes laws against monopoly on the grounds that sellers gain and maintain monopoly or monopoly power because they are more efficient or offer better goods and services than other sellers. Outlawing monopolies thus penalizes sellers who have found ways of using society's resources most efficiently. Members of this school of thought believe that the antitrust laws should be used primarily to punish firms that collude, as collusion represents a direct stifling of the beneficial forces of competition.

The Chicago antitrust scholar places paramount importance on the belief that significant entry barriers do not exist in most markets, so that competitive forces naturally produce an efficient marketplace. Any firm with monopoly power is under constant pressure from potential competitors to remain efficient. Any misstep by that seller—a price that is too high or a level of product quality that is too low—will cause it to lose sales to other firms. Along these same lines, any attempts by government to redistribute income more "fairly" by breaking up large firms or limiting the size of mergers only serve to reduce efficiency. Likewise, artificial entry barriers erected by the government, such as licensing requirements or monopoly rights, insulate sellers from competitive market forces and allow those sellers to exercise monopoly power.

The free market theories of the Chicago School were key factors behind the easing of government regulation of industry in the United States during the 1980's. These ideas influenced Congress to deregulate the trucking, airline, energy, and financial services markets. The antitrust agencies were similarly influenced—as a result, more and larger mergers were allowed during the decade, in stark contrast to the restrictive antitrust practices of the 1960's.

Bibliography

Caves, Richard. *American Industry: Structure, Conduct, Performance.* 6th ed. Englewood Cliffs, N.J.: Prentice-Hall, 1987. Provides a compact (124-page) overview of the structure-conduct-performance model of markets, the mainstream framework for analyzing nonmonopoly markets in which firms have market power. Easily accessible to readers having only an introductory exposure to economics, providing an excellent introduction to entry barriers, collusion, cartels, mergers to monopoly, natural monopoly, patents, market efficiency, and the social consequences of monopoly power.

Douma, Sytse, and Hein Schreuder. *Economic Approaches to Organizations.* 2d ed. London: Prentice Hall, 1998.

Ottosen, Garry K. *Monopoly Power.* Salt Lake City, Utah: Crossroads Research Institute, 1990. This monograph provides an excellent and very readable introduction to monopoly power. Part 1 focuses on numerical measurements of monopoly power and how they are used by the antitrust authorities. Part 2 examines the extent of current and historical monopoly power in the U.S. economy, incorporating views from across the political spectrum. The more difficult mathematical exposition is relegated to the appendices.

Posner, Richard A. *Antitrust Law: An Economic Perspective.* Chicago: University of Chicago Press, 1976. Posner is a judge on the U.S. Court of Appeals and a leading member of the Chicago School. While the book assumes no background in economics on the part of its reader, it is somewhat difficult to read. Nevertheless, the effort is well worth it: Posner's arguments for overhauling U.S. antitrust laws and policy are compelling, and the work remains one of the definitive statements of the Chicago School's view of antitrust.

Samuelson, Paul A., and William D. Nordhaus. *Economics.* 12th ed. New York: McGraw-Hill, 1985. This textbook is among the best-written and best-received college-level introductory texts. Chapter 23, "Imperfect Competition: Monopoly and Regulation," develops the theory of the profit-maximizing monopolist with graphical and numerical examples. Also included is a discussion of natural monopoly and its regulation, data on concentration and scale economies in several important U.S. industries, and a brief discussion of the inefficiencies of monopoly markets.

Sloman, John. *Essentials of Economics.* New York: Prentice Hall, 1998.

Waldman, Don E. *The Economics of Antitrust: Cases and Analysis.* Boston: Little, Brown, 1986. A thorough introduction to the field of antitrust economics. The strength of this work is its historical analysis of major antitrust laws, cases, and policies, particularly the judiciously selected excerpts of Supreme Court opinions. The sections on monopolization, horizontal mergers, horizontal agreements, and patents are particularly applicable. Chapter 1 assumes that its reader is familiar, at the introductory level, with microeconomics, but it can be skipped without much loss.

Robert E. DeYoung

Cross-References

Antitrust Policy, 6; Competition, 91; Economies and Diseconomies of Scale, 158; Oligopolies, 461; Production Theory, 507.

MORTGAGES AND MORTGAGE RATES

Type of economics: Monetary and fiscal theory
Fields of study: Consumer economics and monetary theory

A mortgage is a contract between a lender or financial institution and a borrower, who is usually a homeowner. The borrower receives funds and promises to pay a monthly stream of payments over some future time period. The contract may have many features, but the most important one is the mortgage or interest rate.

Principal terms

ADJUSTABLE-RATE MORTGAGE: a long-term loan that has an interest rate that varies with changes in short-term interest rates

AMORTIZATION: the rate of decrease of the outstanding balance

CONVENTIONAL MORTGAGE: a long-term loan that has one nominal interest rate set at the beginning of the contract for the life of the loan; also known as a fixed-rate mortgage

GRADUATED-PAYMENT MORTGAGE: a loan for which the payments begin at a low level but gradually rise over time; sometimes referred to as a negative amortization mortgage

INFLATION: the rate of increase in the price of goods

NOMINAL INTEREST: the rate of increase in the dollar amount of funds that is owed

POINTS: a device that makes the amount that is loaned less than the original balance

PRESENT VALUE: the amount of funds that is equivalent to the discounted value of a stream of future funds

PRICE LEVEL-ADJUSTED MORTGAGE: a loan for which the interest rate is set in real terms, with the outstanding balance and nominal payments indexed to the price level

REAL INTEREST RATE: the difference between the nominal rate and inflation; the increase in the amount of goods that is owed

Overview

In most cases, a prospective home buyer does not possess enough holdings of money to meet the price of a house. In fact, most barely have enough for a down payment. A consumer in this position may obtain the rest of the needed funds from a bank by taking out a mortgage if he or she agrees to repay or amortize the balance, plus pay interest charges on the outstanding balance over the next thirty years or other term of the mortgage. Any home-owner who does take out a mortgage to buy a house can view these monthly payments as replacing the rent that he or she would have to pay in order to live in a house.

Once a homeowner and a bank have agreed on the amount to be loaned and the interest rate, the amount of monthly payments or the house note can be determined, which will be income for the bank and an expense for the borrower. This stream of future cash flows can be found by using the agreed on interest rate and adjusting the cash flows such that their present value equals the outstanding balance of the loan. In the absence of points, the original balance equals the amount that is loaned.

Points is a device of raising the effective interest rate. The lender bases the house note on an original balance but then takes a small percentage of that balance from the amount that is loaned as a kind of service charge. In relationship to the amount that is actually loaned, the borrower pays a higher effective interest rate.

While the lender views the house note as income or a return to a mortgage asset, the homeowner might see the interest expense as a form of implicit rental payment, as owning a house means living there rent free. Typically, house notes include both interest and amortization. As the loan is amortized, the outstanding balance declines so the interest component declines with more of the fixed house note representing amortization. The declining amount of interest expense that is actually paid may be viewed as analogous to a saving plan that earns compound interest.

Many types of mortgages exist, but the most common is the conventional mortgage. Conventional mortgages have a fixed term, a fixed nominal interest rate, and a fixed dollar payment or cash flow to be paid each month. The usual term is thirty years. Variable-rate and renegotiated-rate mortgages are similar, except the interest rate is periodically adjusted to reflect current market information about short-term interest rates. Graduated payment mortgages, on the other hand, usually have an agreed on set of nominal interest rates but allow the cash flow to begin at a low level and rise over the term of the loan.

Regardless of the type of mortgage, five issues are critical: the expected return or expense; liquidity implications; inflation and interest-rate risk; default risk; and tax implications. Each of these issues will be important to both the homeowner and the bank regarding two decisions: whether to make the mortgage contract and the type of mortgage to make. The bank is concerned with the return on its asset, which is the mortgage contract. The return is the interest rate in the absence of points and default. Points tend to raise the return above the stated interest rate, while defaults tend to lower the return to a portfolio of mortgages. The homeowner is concerned with not only the interest expense but also the liquidity implications of the dollar outlays each month that are mandated by the mortgage contract.

Applications

Suppose that the contract has already been written with a given nominal interest rate (i). If it is a conventional mortgage with no points, finding the periodic cash flows (C) is an example of the annuity problem of present value. For simplicity, assume that the house note is paid yearly for thirty years, rather than monthly for 360 months. Also assume that it includes only interest and amortization, and not escrow payments for taxes and insurance. In general, let the outstanding balance be labeled PV for present value and the stream of cash flows $C_1, C_2, C_3, \ldots C_n$, whether they are constant or not. The term of the mortgage is n years, so $n = 30$ in this example. PV equals the discounted sum of future cash flows, or $C_t/(1 + i)^t$, where i is the discount rate and t is the time period. For the annuity, the cash flows are equal, so one can reverse the present value formula to read $C = PV/D$, where $D = 1/(1 + i)^t$. The actual calculation of D is complex, and most business or real estate finance texts have tables that provide the value of D for a given discount rate (i) and term (n).

As an example, let the mortgage be $200,000 (PV) and the interest rate be $i = 4$ percent per year with term $n = 30$ years. Because $D = 17.292$, the annual house note is PV/D = $11,566/year. In the first year, most of this house note represents flow interest income for the lender and interest expense for the homeowner. Given an original balance of $200,000 and $i = 4$ percent, the interest income/expense is $8,000/year, with the remaining $3,566 being debt repayment or amortization. If the value of the house has not changed, then the homeowner could view the amortization as a form of saving. Over the life of the loan, the outstanding balance declines, so the amount of interest expense declines. Because the house note is constant, the amount of amortization per year increases over time.

If the contracted interest rate is higher, the cash flows will also be higher. For example, a 5 percent interest rate for $n = 30$ implies $D = 15.372$, so if PV = $200,000, then the cash flow is $13,011/year, which is $1,445/year in additional expense. This increase is less than the increase in interest rate multiplied by the original balance, but this is because the balance over the life of the mortgage is declining. The amount of first year amortization has been reduced to only $3,011. If the interest rate rises to 14 percent and $n = 30$, then D falls to 7.003, which pushes up the yearly house note to $28,559/year. These examples seem to confirm the view that higher interest rates raise the cost of housing.

Often, mortgage contracts have origination fees and other points. A point is a percentage deduction from the original balance before the loan is made. For example, if the original balance is $200,000 but the bank deducts two points (2 percent), then the homeowner only receives $196,000. If $i = 4$ percent and $n = 30$, then cash flows still equal $11,566/year even though the amount that is borrowed is lower. Points increase the effective interest rate. For a given PV, the house note is $C = PV/D(1 - f)$, where f is the percentage of original balance that represents points. If the household wished to borrow $200,000 and $f = 0.02$ (two points), then the original balance would be $204,081.63 (= $200,000 ÷ 0.98), with a cash flow of $C = $11,802/year. The effective interest rate in this case is closer to 4.4 percent.

One way of viewing the nominal interest rate on mortgages is to separate it into three components: a risk-free real rate, plus a risk premium, plus an expected inflation for the life of the mortgage. The bank charges an interest rate that is above deposit rates because of default and interest-rate risk. Let r_d = the real rate on deposits, a = the risk premium, r_m = the real rate on mortgages ($= r_d + a$), and p^e = expected inflation. If mortgages were one-period loans, then the nominal rate would be simply $i_m = r_d + a + p^e$ while nominal deposit costs would be $i_d = r_d + p^e$. The bank's profits margin would be $i_m - i_d = a$, reflecting only a default risk premium and perhaps additional returns for the cost of intermediation. In this case, banks bear no inflation or interest-rate risk. The maturity of mortgages, however, is very long term, while the maturity of deposits is often very short term. The bank must set mortgage rates equal to the average of expected short-term rates plus the desired margin. To do so requires expectations of both future inflation and future short-term real deposit rates. If actual rates equal expected rates, at least on average, then the bank earns the expected spread. If future short-term deposit rates unexpectedly rise, perhaps because future inflation exceeded the expectation at the time of the contract, then bank profits would be below expectation and could easily be negative. Such a situation can exist whenever a bank issues long-term loans with a fixed nominal return but raises funds by attracting short-term deposits.

In the above scenario, banks bear both inflation risk and real deposit-rate risk. It is sometimes argued that borrowers do not face interest-rate risk under conventional mortgages. While it is true that borrowers are insulated from surprise changes in real deposit rates, they still face inflation risk under the assumption that borrowers care about the real interest rate $i_m - p$, where p is actual inflation. If inflation unexpectedly rises, then lenders lose while borrowers gain, but if inflation unexpectedly falls, then the reverse is true. For example, in the early 1980's, nominal mortgage rates in the United States were set at 15 percent because inflation was hovering around 10 percent. If households expected the 10 percent inflation to continue, then they expected to pay a 5 percent real interest rate. Actual inflation, however, fell to around 4 percent, implying an actual real rate of 11 percent.

One could argue that, if inflation surprisingly falls, lowering the nominal rate on any new contract, then the household could avoid paying these 11 percent real rates by prepaying the old contract and refinancing. If households could costlessly refinance, then this would be the case, but points and prepayment penalties cause the effective interest rate to be higher for early payment of the mortgage and partially offset this effect.

The other major risk for lenders involves the possibility of default. If borrowers do repay, then let the lender's yield be the contractual rate (i). If the borrower defaults, then the return for the lender may be negative, and the extent to which the return is negative depends on such factors as the amount of collateral that is pledged. Let c equal the percentage of principal that is recovered in default and b equal the percentage of mortgages that go into default. A one-period example would give the actual return to be $i^a = [i(1 - b)] - [b(1 - c)]$. If collateral is 100 percent or less and if some of the loans do go into default, then the actual return is less than the contracted rate. For most mortgages, however, the outstanding balance is below the original purchase price because of down payments and amortization. Does this imply that c exceeds 100 percent? In many cases, a mortgage is more than fully collateralized with a loan/value ratio that is less than one. The rate of principal recovery, however, might be less than this "value" of the house for two reasons: first, the legal and transactions costs of foreclosure, and second, the possibility that the auction price might be less than the assumed value of the house. In fact, the bank may not know with certainty either the recovery rate or the percentage of defaults. By interpreting c and b as expected values, however, one can find the required contract rate for any given target return (i^e) as $i = [i^e + b(1 - c)] \div (1 - b)$. Note that, as the probability of default rises or the rate of recovery falls, the required contract rate rises.

The conventional mortgage has certain desirable features under low and certain inflation that disappear if inflation is either variable or high. If the variability of short-term nominal rates were only from inflation uncertainty, then both lenders and borrowers would bear inflation risk. This risk could also be eliminated for both parties under several types of indexation. Adjustable-rate mortgages, for example, allow the bank to reset the mortgate rate annually to be some index rate, which is some short-term rate plus some agreed on margin. If the index rate exactly follows short-term deposit rates, then the bank spread does not vary at all. Banks bear neither inflation risk nor real-rate risk. This discussion, however, ignores caps to adjusting the variable rate, which make the rate behave as a conventional fixed rate once the cap is reached. From the viewpoint of the borrower, the inflation risk is also eliminated, but now borrowers bear real-rate risk.

Rollover or renegotiable-rate mortgages periodically allow the parties to reset the mortgage rate to current market conditions. If current market conditions reflect current inflation, then these rollover mortgages alleviate inflation risk, with the issue of real-rate risk being unclear. A price level-adjusted mortgage (PLAM), however, sets the real interest rate for the loan at the beginning of the contract. In doing so, it eliminates risk and transfers real deposit-rate risk away from the borrower to the lender. The PLAM offers a liquidity advantage as well.

The liquidity issue, known as "forward tilt" or "front-end loading," occurs merely because inflation exists, and it is a problem for both conventional and variable-rate mortgages. In fact, these types of mortgages act in the same manner if inflation is both predictable and steady. Suppose, for example, that inflation is 10 percent for the entire life of the mortgage so that a 4 percent real rate translates into a 14 percent nominal rate for either contract. Comparing the house note of this contract to one for which inflation is zero and $i = 4$ percent suggests that the cost of housing is higher in periods of higher inflation and higher nominal interest rates. The real interest rate, however, is the same in these two cases. Therefore, if real rates are the right measure for the costs over the life of the contract, then equal increases in nominal rates and inflation do not effect the cost of housing over the thirty years.

The liquidity issue, however, involves the early burden of the mortgage. Suppose that a family earns $50,000/year and takes out a $200,000 mortgage in an environment of no inflation with $i = 4$ percent. Its house note ($11,566) represents approximately 23 percent of its income. If its desired consumption were $35,000/year, or 70 percent of income, then it has almost 7 percent of income left over for a financial saving plan. Next, consider the case of 10 percent inflation, so that $i = 14$ percent. This same mortgage would have a nominal house note of $28,559/year, or approximately 57 percent of the first-year income. Over time, inflation will gradually increase both the price level and nominal income if household real income does not erode. The nominal house note, however, is constant, so it falls in real terms or as a percentage of income. If the family is able to borrow on future income in order to finance current desired consumption at a 4 percent real rate, then this forward tilting does not create problems, but this is not always the case.

Several devices have been constructed to reduce the cash flow that is required in the early years of a mortgage. One simple device is to lengthen the term of the mortgage. For example, Japanese mortgages have been written for one hundred-year terms. This term requires that not only the parents but also the children and grandchildren be held accountable for the loan. If only the parents can be held responsible, then setting the term length above forty years may not be feasible. Even so, there is only a small reduction in cash flow. If $i = 14$ percent and $n = 40$, then $D = 7.105$ and the house note would be $28,149/year, or 56.3 percent of initial income. In fact, even an infinite term or interest-only loan would require annual payments of $28,000/year, or 56 percent of income.

Balloon payments would be another device to lower the annual house note. In this case, the borrower agrees to pay a fixed amount at some future date that essentially retires the outstanding balance in exchange for lower annual payments. The hope is that there will be some nominal capital gain to the house that will allow the homeowner to refinance later and still keep the house. There is the danger that the nominal capital gain will not be realized, however, and the homeowner will not be able to refinance. The homeowner will then have to sell the house, and even then there may not be sufficient funds to repay the mortgage.

Graduated-payment mortgages are a natural way of altering the tilt of a mortgage. Suppose that the borrower agreed to pay ever-rising house notes on the anticipation of rising nominal income. Let g be the expected growth of nominal income, which will also serve as the rate of increase in the house note. In this case, one would calculate the house note by using $i - g$ as the discount rate in the present value approach. As an example, let PV = $200,000, $i = 14$ percent, and $g = 10$ percent. The original note is $11,566/year, or 23 percent of income, just as in the $i = 4$ percent and $g = 0$ case. In dollar terms, however, the outstanding balance has risen to $216,434 because the nominal interest expense was $28,000 for the first year. If nominal income does rise by 10 percent, however, then the mortgage/income ratio behaves exactly as in the $i = 4$ percent, $g = 0$ case. Even though the mortgage begins with negative nominal amortization, after a few years, the rising house note will exceed the interest expense on the outstanding balance. If all proceeds according to original expectations, then the mortgage will be retired in thirty years.

If g is the inflation rate, then this mortgage is a price level-adjusted mortgage, or PLAM. If inflation continues at 10 percent, then the real cash flows will be $11,566/ year while real income is $50,000/year. Therefore, the PLAM acts like a conventional mortgage under zero inflation.

Context

A mortgage is one type of financial contract. The principles of finance theory and optimal contracting are applicable to analyzing the design of an ideal mortgage. In the United States, mortgage design has a special place in public policy discussions for three reasons: the public policy concern over housing; the often-cited claim that one's house is one's most important investment; and the concern over the health of the savings and loan industry. In fact, savings and loan associations (S&Ls) were once the almost exclusive holders of mortgages.

The chief concerns for homeowners are inflation risk and liquidity. For banks and S&Ls, the chief concerns are inflation risk and default. Some economists advocate the use of the PLAM to eliminate inflation risk and the liquidity problem of conventional mortgage designs. The question then becomes why the PLAM is not offered by banks. In addition to legal impediments, two reasons are often given. One reason is the differential tax treatment. Homeowners are allowed to deduct nominal interest expenses from their income before calculating income taxes. They do not have to include the implicit rental income, so this tax break is an advantage to homeowners that applies to both real and inflation components of the nominal rate under conventional and variable rate plans. It is unclear, however, what the tax rules for a graduated or PLAM plan would be. If homeowners could also deduct the increase in nominal value of the outstanding balance that occurs because of the inflation indexing, then the tax treatment for borrowers would be the same. If not, the tax law presents a disadvantage for PLAM. The second reason is that there is another tax disadvantage that occurs when lenders must pay taxes on income as it accrues. A PLAM gives the bank deferred nominal income in order to compensate if for inflation. Even though the cash flows are actually received in the future, the tax obligations are due in the present.

Banks view graduated payment plans as entailing more default risk because of their negative nominal amortization features. One could easily understand this fear for the case of negative real amortization, which is possible if the rate of payment graduation exceeded the inflation rate. With a PLAM, however, the real outstanding balance declines over time. Therefore, the PLAM offers no greater default risk than does a conventional mortgage under zero inflation. One could claim, however, that banks really desire an even more rapid real amortization in order to guard against the possibilities that the real value of the house or the borrower's real income might decline. Given the coincidence of the S&L crisis and the fall in property values, this issue of default risk could be considered as important as the liquidity implications of various mortgage designs.

Bibliography

Chinloy, Peter. *Real Estate: Investment and Financial Strategy.* Boston: Kluwer Academic Publishers, 1988. An advanced treatment of the financial and legal aspects of both the borrower and the lender in the mortgage market, with an especially good focus on the problems of conventional mortgages and the role of alternative mortgage design. Appropriate for advanced undergraduates and graduate students.

Dickens, Ross N. *Contestable Markets Theory, Competition, and the United States Commercial Banking Industry.* New York: Garland, 1996.

Fitch, Thomas P. *Dictionary of Banking Terms.* 3d ed. Hauppauge, N.Y.: Barron's Educational Series, 1997.

Jaffe, Austin J., and C. F. Sirmans. *Real Estate Investment Decision Making.* Englewood Cliffs, N.J.: Prentice-Hall, 1982. An intermediate presentation of the financial and legal aspects of buying property. Appropriate for advanced undergraduates.

Rose, Peter S. *Money and Capital Markets.* 3d ed. Homewood, Ill.: Richard D. Irwin, 1989. Chapter 19, entitled "The Residential Mortgage Market," describes the historical, institutional, and legal environment behind the mortgage market. Also gives a brief description of alternative mortgages and ways in which banks can make their mortgages more liquid. This text is intended for undergraduates, but the descriptive approach of this chapter is accessible to a general audience.

Sirmans, C. F. *Real Estate Finance.* New York: McGraw-Hill, 1989. The book describes itself as a "comprehensive coverage of real estate finance within a decision-making framework. Both the borrower's and lender's perspective are examined—making it of interest to students and readers of all backgrounds." This description is essentially accurate, especially because the book gives thorough discussions of both the legal environment and the financial analysis that are involved in buying property. Its presentation of the present value and other financial analysis is covered in a textbook style that might be difficult for the general reader.

J. Harold McClure, Jr.

Cross-References

Banks, 29; Financing, 228; Inflation, 316; Interest and Interest Rates, 323; Saving, 539.

NATIONAL DEBT

Type of economics: Monetary and fiscal theory
Fields of study: Fiscal theory and public finance; monetary theory

The national debt of a country is the total accumulated borrowing of the government of that country. It exists in the form of government bonds, notes, bills, or other obligations, all of which are usually held by the public. Government borrowing must take place whenever the government spends more money than it collects in taxes or other revenues.

Principal terms

BALANCED BUDGET: a budget that exhibits an equality between spending and revenue
BUDGET: a statement of a government's proposed spending programs and expected revenue from taxes and other sources for its next year of operation
BUDGET DEFICIT: a budget that displays spending that is greater than revenue collections
BUDGET SURPLUS: a budget that shows that spending will be less than revenue collections
FISCAL POLICY: the use of the government's budget as a way to influence the total level of production in the economy
GOVERNMENT SECURITIES: debt obligations issued by a government in the form of bills, notes, or bonds

Overview

"National debt" is the popular term that is used to refer to the total debt obligations of a country's government at any given time. In the United States, the federal government's total debt outstanding is called the public debt, and it is represented by Treasury securities (that is, bonds, notes, and bills) that are held by the public. The term "public debt" is also used in the writings of professional economists.

A government is placed in debt when it runs a budget deficit, as it must borrow the additional funds it needs to cover its spending. When there is a budget surplus, a government can used unspent funds to pay off some of its debt. The total national debt at any given time is the net total of borrowing minus the debt payment over the course of the government's existence. A national debt indicates a history in which deficits and borrowing exceeded surpluses. In the United States, for example, the federal government has had a debt ever since it was formed in 1790, when it agreed to take over the debt accumulated by the Continental Congress and the states during the Revolutionary War; only once in its history, in 1837, was the U.S. federal government out of debt. The government need not repay its national debt, as long as it is able to refinance that debt by selling new securities in order to borrow the money needed to redeem any loans that have become due.

Government budget deficits result when the government does not raise enough tax revenue to meet its spending needs, usually the result of unusual circumstances such as emergencies and economic recessions. The typical example of an emergency is a war, but there are others, such as natural disasters. War has been the cause of most periods of government borrowing.

When a war takes place, the government needs resources, such as soldiers and equipment, to fight it. In democratic, market-based societies, the government cannot simply take those resources from its citizens—it must buy them. To obtain the funds it needs for wartime purchases, a government could raise the taxes it collects from its citizens. Even if citizens were willing to pay higher taxes, however, there are limits to how quickly taxes can be increased and by how much. Individuals need to retain some of their incomes for their own purchases, so a rapid increase in taxes may be too much for them to bear. Instead, the

Opponents of high government spending erected a "National Debt Clock" in New York City that constantly calculated the total national debt. On November 14, 1995, it stopped at $4,985,567,071.20 because a budget impasse in the federal government temporarily shut down many government functions. (AP/Wide World Photos)

government borrows the money it needs, so that those who are best able to help finance the war can do so.

When a budget deficit is caused by an economic recession, there are even greater problems involved with raising taxes. A recession takes place when the total production in the economy declines for a period that usually exceeds six months. During the course of a recession, individuals lose their jobs and businesses suffer reductions in sales and profits. The reduction in sales and the income normally derived from them will lead to a decline in government tax collections. At the same time, government spending on welfare programs and unemployment benefits will increase. This explains how a recession can cause a budget deficit. Eliminating a budget deficit during a recession can be counterproductive, however, because an increase in taxes will give consumers and businesses even less money to spend. At the same time, cutting government programs will also mean that less money is being spent when more spending is needed in order to end the recession.

The tendency for governments to run a budget deficit during a recession has been common. Since the 1940's, governments have operated under a fiscal policy in which they allow their budgets to show a deficit during a recession in order to increase the amount of spending in the economy. Under this policy, taxes may be reduced to give individuals more money to spend, and the government may increase its spending, all to stimulate the economy. In pursuing this policy, governments are following the economic theories of John Maynard Keynes (1883-1946). In the United States, the Employment Act of 1946 gave the government the responsibility of keeping the economy growing to avoid recessions. Deficit finance became more acceptable under Keynesian policies.

A government finances its deficits by selling its securities. To minimize the impact that the sale of these securities may have on financial markets, the government must manage carefully how and when those securities are issued. It must also ensure that its securities will be attractive to borrowers in terms of the rate of interest offered, the time until the debt will be repaid, and the ability of the purchaser to sell the securities on the open market. In the United States, there are two categories of government securities. Marketable securities consist of bills (to be repaid in less than one year), notes (to be repaid in one to ten years), and bonds (to be repaid in ten to thirty years); marketable securities are sold through an auction by the Treasury Department at prevailing rates of interest and can be bought and sold by individuals once they have been purchased from the Treasury. Nonmarketable securities (savings bonds) are sold for the Treasury by a variety of institutions and are redeemable only by turning them in to the Treasury. All recordkeeping of the ownership, the paying of interest and principal, and the accounting for outstanding totals of government securities in the United States is done by the Bureau of the Public Debt, an agency within the Treasury Department.

Applications

The main economic issue concerning the national debt is its impact on the economy as a whole. Whenever a government spends, it is purchasing resources that its citizens may also wish to purchase. If the government were to finance its purchases strictly by taxation, then these taxes would reduce the spending of individuals by an amount that would be equal to the amount that the government wanted to spend, unless individuals paid part of the tax from their savings.

A program that finances government purchases with debt can have a variety of effects on the economy, subject to differing interpretations. A popular view is that the burden of government debt falls on the future generation, which will have to repay it. The view common among economists is that, no matter how the government finances its purchases, the direct impact is the resources that citizens must relinquish to the government. In this view, the impact of governmental spending for World War II was the cars and refrigerators that were not manufactured so that planes and tanks could be produced. When the money that was borrowed to buy those tanks and planes is paid back, it will merely represent a financial transaction among citizens of the country.

It has also been argued there is no burden imposed on a present generation by governmental borrowing because the purchasers of government securities either used money that they were not spending (savings) or voluntarily curtailed their consumption to earn the interest on those securities. If the debt is paid off by a tax in the future, the payers of that tax, because they will involuntarily cut spending to pay it, will feel the impact of the national debt.

Yet this argument must be qualified. To induce individuals to buy its securities, the government may have paid a high interest rate, causing a credit squeeze because the amount of interest that consumers and business have to pay in order to finance their own purchases may go up. If those higher interest rates reduce personal consumption or business investment, then the current generation will feel the impact of governmental borrowing. When business invests less, it does not buy as many factories and equipment as it would like. As a result, a future generation will not have as many factories as it could have had, which will reduce the level of production that the economy might have had. The condition under which governmental borrowing can reduce the amount of credit available to other sectors of the economy, thereby causing interest rates to rise, is known as "crowding out."

In addition to borrowing in order to finance a deficit, the government can resort to creating new money to meet its spending needs. Most governments have the authority to print money and declare it legal tender, although in the United States this central banking authority has been given to the Federal Reserve System. Increases in the amount of money circulating in a country can, under certain conditions, cause the country to experience a period of rising prices more commonly known as inflation. This inflation will reduce the purchasing power of income just as surely as a tax or higher interest rates.

There are times, however, when it may be necessary for the government to finance some of its deficit through the creation of money. Governmental borrowing and spending can influence the supply of money in the economy. When a government's borrowing plans are likely to have an adverse effect on the money supply, the central bank of the country is called upon to assist the national government in its efforts to manage the national debt. As the government borrows, the central bank may assist it by making sure that sufficient money is available in the banking system to handle the government's needs. In the United States, the function of central banking is performed by the Federal Reserve System. It has the authority to buy or sell Treasury securities through open-market operations, which are part of the policies whereby the Federal Reserve can control the money supply. Under open-market operations, the Federal Reserve enters into the financial markets and buys government securities with new money in order to increase the money supply or sells them in order to decrease it.

The Federal Reserve also uses open-market operations to make it easier for the Treasury to sell securities. In advance of the sale of Treasury securities, the Federal Reserve can purchase other government securities on the open market, providing money to the banking system and making it easier for banks and their customers to buy new government securities. This process is referred to as monetizing the debt, and it is employed to help keep increases in the national debt from causing interest rates to rise. The monetization of a portion of the government's debt leads to increases in the money supply, however, which can cause inflation.

Increases in government spending have an impact on the economy either directly through increased taxes or indirectly through increases in the national debt. Growth of the national debt can have adverse consequences for the economy. If it causes a credit squeeze and higher interest rates, then citizens will find it harder to borrow now and there may be fewer goods available in the future. To the extent that the debt is monetized, its burden may be felt from inflation. In any case, the national debt will have a bearing on both current and future generations.

Context

Until World War II, national debts, while of concern, did not seem to have a great impact on any country's economy. Since then, however, a large national debt has become more common. In the United States, budget surpluses became rare during the 1960's and 1970's, while in the 1980's budget deficits reached levels unheard of in the nation's history. By 1990, the national debt of the United States had grown to more than $3 trillion, about ten times the amount that it had reached at the end of World War II. Most industrialized countries experienced growth in their national debt during this time.

This period of growth in national debt caused concern that the national debt was growing too large. One way of measuring the size of the national debt is to compare it to total income in the economy—that is, the gross national product (GNP). Most individuals can handle more debt if their incomes are rising, so a nation can support more debt when its income is going up. Based on this measure, the national debt of the United States reached a high point of 120 percent of the GNP at the end of World War II. It then declined to 26.8 percent of the GNP in 1975, after which it began rising, reaching a level of about 45 percent in 1990. The time period after World War II was also a period of inflation; if the national debt is adjusted for inflation, its total did not change significantly between 1946 and 1980. During the 1980's, however, even when adjusted for inflation, the national debt of the United States nearly doubled. As might be expected, interest rates were higher in the 1980's than they had been for many years. Because the Federal Reserve monetized a portion of that debt, inflation also became a cause of greater anxiety.

The concern over the consequences of this growth of the national debt in the United States during the 1980's caused many economists and politicians to propose legal measures to slow down its growth. An amendment to the Constitution, requiring the federal government to balance its budget except under certain specified situations, was offered but did not receive sufficient support to pass through Congress. In 1987, Congress did pass the Gramm-Rudman-Hollings Act, which set targets for reduction of the government's budget deficit, although these targets could be avoided in case of a war or recession. As the 1990's began, Congress and the president began meetings to consider ways in which to cut the government's budget deficit, but the Persian Gulf crisis in the Middle East, which caused the armed forces of the United States to be sent to Saudi Arabia in a confrontation with Iraq, made it even harder to reduce spending. If political efforts to reduce the federal government's budget deficits continue to fail, then the national debt of the United States will show further increases.

Bibliography

Anderson, Gary M. "The U.S. Federal Deficit and National Debt: A Political and Economic History." In *Deficits*, edited by James M. Buchanan, Charles K. Rowley, and Robert D. Tollison. New York: Basil Blackwell, 1987. Presents a brief survey of how the national debt has grown over time.

Begg, Iai, and S. G. B. Henry, eds. *Applied Economics and Public Policy*. New York: Cambridge University Press, 1998.

Buchanan, James M., and Marilyn Flowers. *The Public Finances*. 6th ed. Homewood, Ill.: Richard D. Irwin, 1987. One of the classic textbooks in public finance, explaining the economic and political issues involved in government budgetary matters. Suitable for college students.

Eisner, Robert. *How Real Is the Federal Deficit?* New York: Free Press, 1986. Eisner provides several measures of the federal deficit and national debt as a way of showing that their impact on the economy has been minimal. Because so much attention has been paid to the debt as a government liability, he surveys what assets the government holds and finds that they are nearly equal to its debt. Contains numerous tables in its 240 pages, as well as an index and a bibliography.

Fink, Richard H., and Jack C. High, eds. *A Nation in Debt*. Frederick, Md.: University Publications of America, 1987. This collection of essays by noted economists, both past and present, surveys the alternate viewpoints economists have had concerning the impact of the national debt. Included in its three hundred pages are essays by Adam Smith, Karl Marx, and John Maynard Keynes, as well as Nobel laureates James Tobin, James M. Buchanan, Jr., and Milton Friedman.

Heilbroner, Robert, and Peter Bernstein. *The Debt and the Deficit*. New York: W. W. Norton, 1989. This 144-page book provides a description of what the debt and deficit consist of and argues that their impact on the economy has been overstated.

Jha, Raghbendra. *Modern Public Economics*. New York: Routledge, 1998.

Stabile, Donald R., and Jeffrey A. Cantor. *The Public Debt of the United States: An Historical Perspective, 1775-1998*. New York: Praeger, 1991. This 220-page volume presents a comprehensive history of the U.S. national debt and reviews the methods that the government has used to manage and administer it. The authors describe the impact of wars, recessions, and macroeconomic policy on the growth of the debt and trace how government debt policy was linked to the evolution of the banking system. Suitable for a general readership and contains tables, an index, and a bibliography.

Donald R. Stabile

Cross-References

OLIGOPOLIES

Type of economics: Industrial economics
Fields of study: Industrial organization and public policy; industry studies

Oligopoly is distinguished from other market structures by the small number of firms that dominate an industry. The result is that these few firms may exercise market power in the form of higher-than-competitive prices.

Principal terms

CONCENTRATION RATIO: a measure of concentration or market power that is defined as the percentage of industry sales shared by the largest four or eight firms

DEAD-WEIGHT WELFARE MONOPOLY LOSS: social loss to society as the result of higher prices and lower output caused by monopoly power of one or more dominant firms

ECONOMIES OF SCALE: the situation that exists when technology of production causes a firm's long-run average total cost curve to fall over a large range as production increases; mass-production assembly lines are an example

IMPERFECTLY COMPETITIVE MARKET: a market that is not perfectly competitive because of a limited number of firms, product differentiation, or imperfect information

INDUSTRY CONCENTRATION: the situation that exists when a few firms account for most of the output of an industry

MARKET POWER: the extent of control a few firms have over industry price and output

Overview

Oligopoly is a market structure in which a few firms dominate an industry. Public perception is that economic activity is controlled by a few gigantic firms. This perception is valid for a share of the manufacturing sector. In the banking sector, about a dozen banks held nearly 25 percent of all deposits in 1991, while the largest one hundred banks held nearly one-half of all deposits. Overall, a few thousand U.S. corporations held 75 percent of all business assets.

It is no accident, therefore, that the public is concerned about the exercise of oligopoly power by big business. The average person believes that big business can charge higher prices for its products, and that even inflation is caused by the exercise of market power. Big oil firms are thought to be responsible for gasoline shortages and exorbitant profits earned in oligopolistic or imperfectly competitive markets.

In order to measure market power, concentration ratios are helpful. A four-firm concentration ratio measures the market power of the largest four firms, in terms of their sales as a percentage of the total industry sales. According to this measure, the most concentrated industry in the United States in 1981 was the motor vehicle industry with a domestic four-firm concentration ratio of 99 percent. Such a high ratio, however, is misleading because imports are not included. If imports were included, the ratio would have been substantially lower. Such a high ratio also does not imply a lack of competition; in fact, in 1981, most domestic automobile firms were losing money. What it does mean is that factors other than business concentration are responsible for the extraordinarily high concentration ratio. One such factor is the existence of large-scale economies in the mass production of automobiles; thus, small auto producers would be unable to survive because their cost of production would be excessive. The same reasoning applies to the second most-concentrated industry, the household refrigerator producers, with a four-firm concentration ratio of 94 percent. That ratio has increased dramatically since the 1970's because of the technological factors underlying production—economies of scale.

The third and fourth highest four-term concentration ratios in 1981 included cereal breakfast food producers with 86 percent and cigarette producers with 84 percent, followed by the aircraft engine industry with 72 percent; primary aluminum industry with 64 percent; glass container industry with 50 percent; blast furnace and steel mill industries with 42 percent; petroleum and refining with a four-firm ratio of 28 percent; and oil field machines with 27 percent. Economies of scale in mass production are unlikely to explain the high ratios in breakfast foods and cigarettes. There may, however, be economies of scale in marketing, including advertising, in which case advertising expenditures and the power of trademarks may be a barrier to entry.

Chance, mergers, and superior entrepreneurship may also be an explanation of high concentration. International Business Machines Corporation (IBM) is an example. Other large competitors left the computer business because they judged the risk too high and the future profitability insufficient compared to the huge investment necessary for success in this new technology. IBM's superior assessment and heavy spending on research and development in this industry earned it high growth rates and higher-than-competitive profits.

It is incorrect, therefore, to conclude that collusion—the exercise of market power—and concentration are highly related. It is also incorrect to conclude that higher profits are always the result of collusion. Some studies have shown that slightly higher profit rates are earned in more concentrated firms. These correlations, however, are not very meaningful in advocating the deconcentration of industry, since there may be many other explanations in addition to exercised oligopoly or monopoly power.

Oligopolies normally prefer not to engage in price cutting, because rivals will very likely follow the prices down to prevent loss of market share. As a result, everyone loses; if the industry is very capital-intensive (as most manufacturing oligopolies are), then losses may be large and last a long time. Nonprice competition is, therefore, more likely; that is, firms will compete on grounds other than price, such as product design and quality improvements or differences. In the automobile industry, that may mean frequent model changes and competition on warranty, service, performance, mileage, safety, and fewest defects. The number of innovations is infinite and will be used to gain market share.

Advertising is a favored vehicle to convey these and other differences. Consequently, it is often alleged that, as oligopolists overdifferentiate their products and overadvertise to gain a higher market share, they waste resources. For example, the cigarette and breakfast cereal oligopolies have succeeded in maintaining prices well above production cost for years. Inefficiency takes place as a result of monopoly pricing and restricted output. Wealth redistribution from consumers to producers is another side effect. In other cases of oligopoly, the price war between Pepsi and Coca-Cola cola drinks in 1988 became so intense that the supermarket price for a six-pack of cola fell to 59 cents, narrowly covering only the cost of the aluminum cans.

Applications

Large firm size does not necessarily imply monopoly power, as only barriers to competition will maintain high profits. Economies of scale are the most relevant barriers, yet the automobile industry, which is highly concentrated, is also very competitive and does not earn higher-than-competitive profits. The Ford Motor Company is very large, yet few would argue that it has monopoly power; if it raises auto prices, it loses market share. If Ford becomes less innovative than the competition, it also loses sales and profit. Adequate profit is necessary for reinvestment in capital, research, and new technology. Firms that fall behind may never catch up again. These dynamics in changing market shares (such as in the auto and the computer industries) are further evidence of a competitive environment.

The rise of global markets has also diminished oligopoly power. Automobile, aircraft, chemical, and electronic firms now must cope with global competition. Therefore, the domestic four-firm concentration ratio is becoming increasingly obsolete. Once foreign firms are included in the measure of concentration, all concentration ratios decline. Yet, large firms will remain part of the economic landscape because of technological reasons—economies of scale in production—as well as marketing and finance. Concentration ratios are generally higher in foreign countries than in the United States. Furthermore, industries with high concentration in the United States are generally the same industries that have high concentration in foreign countries.

On the other hand, having a low four-firm concentration ratio (such as in fluid milk, lumber, or cement) does not necessarily mean the absence of oligopolistic or market power. The four-firm concentration ratio is a ratio for the national market. Because of the high cost of transportation in these product lines, distant firms are not meaningful competitors. As a result, these firms may have a very high local market four-firm concentration ratio.

In order to evaluate the degree of unwarranted concentration in U.S. industries, one has to construct a measure of society's welfare loss because of the exercise of monopoly power. Oligopolies and monopolies that exercise monopoly power are able to raise prices above the competitive level. Consequently, consumers buy less and output declines. The net social benefit to consumers of added production in a competitive market is lost. Many attempts have been made to measure this dead-weight welfare loss to society because of the exercise of monopoly power in the United States. The average estimate places the welfare loss because of the exercise of monopolistic and oligopolistic power at about 1 percent of gross national product per year.

While such a loss is not negligible, the loss to society from excessive concentration seems rather small and does not warrant a national deconcentration policy as advocated by some. It is more likely, however, that the breakup of most large corporations would result in rising production costs and make U.S. industries less efficient and less able to compete internationally. In other words, there are economic reasons that explain concentration far better than the exercise of oligopolistic and monopolistic power.

Furthermore, large organizations are hard to manage efficiently. Government agencies and General Motors Corporation are fine examples of bureaucracy that reduces performance. The tendency has been in the direction of decentralization for firms, as well as for governments. Competition in the market has created more opportunities for small firms. The computer industry is a good example. Employment patterns confirm this trend. The largest firms (including banks) have reduced employees while the smaller firms have added employees.

Context

Suspicion of big business and concern over the concentration of industry have existed since the era of the "robber barons" following the first merger wave of the late 1800's. Prior to that, the American economy consisted of numerous small farms and small businesses, none of which was large enough to influence price or output. In 1860, there were few incorporated business firms in the urban industrial centers. By 1900, however, the share of manufacturing output increased dramatically as corporations grew internally and via merger.

The Ford Motor Company was such an example. Henry Ford, realizing that he could reduce the price of an automobile by introducing mass-production assembly lines, put many small auto firms out of business and thereby significantly raised the concentration ratio of his industry. Consumers, however, enjoyed the lower prices and bought the cars. Other firms, such as General Motors, followed suit and the concentration of this industry was born. Robber barons in railroad, whiskey, lead, sugar, and cotton industries abused their market power as they fixed prices via collusion, cartels, and trusts and used predatory pricing to drive competitors out of business. The Sherman Antitrust Act of 1890 and the Clayton Act of 1914 broke up many of these collusive arrangements and made monopolization, restraint of trade, or any reduction in competition illegal.

Several other merger waves culminated in the growth of conglomerates (mergers with firms in unrelated businesses) in the 1960's. To the extent that larger firms were more efficient, they survived. As large conglomerates became difficult to manage and lost profitability, they ended in divestiture or bankruptcy. Antitrust policy was an effective halt to anticompetitive mergers and the trend toward concentration. Government regulation, however, particularly in transportation, was counterproductive. Government regulation of the airlines prior to 1978 managed to prohibit entry into the industry and fixed airfares. Thus, the regulated learned how to use the regulatory agency to their advantage as the Civil Aeronautics Board protected the industry from competition, and together, they administered high prices. Airline employees, including the pilots, enjoyed monopoly wages.

Whether the American economy has become more or less concentrated over time and whether large corporations have increased their oligopolistic power are questions considered in a representative study by William Shepherd entitled "Causes of Increased Competition in the U.S. Economy, 1939-1980," in the *Review of Economics and Statistics* (1982). Shepherd found a remarkable growth in the competitiveness of the U.S. economy, particularly after 1958. The share of national income originating in oligopolistic industries held steady from 1939 to 1958 at about 36 percent, but fell dramatically to 18 percent in 1980. Pure monopoly organization fell from 6.2 percent in 1939 to 3.1 percent in 1958 and to 2.5 percent in 1980. Income originating from organizations with a dominant firm fell from 5 percent in 1958 to 2.8 percent in 1980. National income produced under conditions of effective competition picked up market share: In 1939, it was 52.4 percent, growing to 56.3 percent in 1958 and to 76.7 percent in 1980.

Shepherd attributes the reason for at least one-half of the increase in American competition to stricter enforcement of antitrust laws. The other factors are rising import competition as well as deregulation of the transport, communication, and banking industries. The dominance of the large corporation is further eroded by the growth of the service economy, which employs about 70 percent of all workers. Of those service workers, more than two-thirds are employed by firms with less than one hundred employees. If this trend continues, most people will work not for large manufacturing corporations but for hospitals, universities, professional associations, financial services, government agencies, and research institutes.

Bibliography

Brozen, Yale, ed. *The Competitive Economy.* Morristown, N.J.: General Learning Press, 1975. Brozen has edited a fine book of selected readings in imperfect competition, regulation, antitrust, and some applications of antitrust law with contributions from Kenneth J. Arrow, Arthur Laffer, Joseph Schumpeter, George J. Stigler, J. Fred Weston, and others. Excellent for nonspecialists or college students.

Clarkson, Kenneth W., and Roger Miller. *Industrial Organization.* New York: McGraw-Hill, 1982. Provides a good introduction to industrial organization, economic theory, evidence, and public policy, with examples of antitrust cases. Includes numerous graphs, tables, and charts. Excellent for college students as well as nonspecialists.

Douma, Sytse, and Hein Schreuder. *Economic Approaches to Organizations.* 2d ed. London: Prentice Hall, 1998.

Greer, Douglas F. *Industrial Organization and Public Policy.* 2d ed. New York: Macmillan, 1984. A very readable overview of industrial organization, from perfect competition to monopoly, including industry studies and both early and later antitrust cases. Good discussion of advertising, business strategy, and technological change. Suitable for college students.

Hunt, E. K., and Howard J. Sherman. *Economics: An Introduction to Traditional and Radical Views.* 6th ed. New York: Harper & Row, 1990. Written from a Marxist historical perspective, this book is very readable, starting with economic evolution in ancient Greece, moving on to mercantilism, the corporate rise of capitalism, monopoly power, income distribution, and economic theories, and ending with comparative economic systems, such as market socialism and central planning in the Soviet Union. Fine for the general reader.

Scherer, F. M., and David Ross. *Industrial Market Structure and Economic Performance.* 3d ed. Boston: Houghton Mifflin, 1990. Probably the most comprehensive book on industrial organization, touching all topics, with reference to virtually all articles written on this topic. The perspective includes market structure and economic performance in Europe and other countries. Footnotes on antitrust cases and other studies sometimes take half a page. 700 pages. Excellent for graduate students.

Sharp, Ansel, Charles A. Register, and Richard H. Leftwich. *Economics of Social Issues.* 9th ed. Homewood, Ill.: Richard D. Irwin, 1990. Provides the reader with an excellent perspective on the economics of big business and monopoly power. Other topics are also discussed, including the history of airline regulation and deregulation as well as government control of prices, pollution, inflation, and poverty. Suitable for nonspecialists and college students.

Frank Billes

Cross-References

OPPORTUNITY COST

Type of economics: General economics
Field of study: Economic theory

Opportunity cost is a decision maker's valuation of the best alternative. It is inherently subjective and known only to the decision maker at the time of decision. Nevertheless, under certain circumstances, opportunity cost can be estimated. Typically, opportunity cost is estimated as the value of forgone income.

Principal terms

EXPLICIT COSTS: cash (or "out-of-pocket") and barter costs
FIXED COSTS: those costs that do not vary over the relevant range of production
IMPLICIT COSTS: the value of one's own resources, such as one's own time
MARGINAL COST: the cost of the next unit to be produced
OPPORTUNITY COST: a decision maker's valuation of his or her best alternative
SUNK COSTS: unrecoverable costs
VARIABLE COSTS: those costs that vary over the relevant range of production

Overview

To paraphrase James M. Buchanan, Jr.'s preface to his book *Cost and Choice* (1969), the opportunity cost of reading this article is the value that readers place on what they would do instead. This definition presumes that readers have one or more alternatives to reading this article. For example, they might read other articles. Thus, they must make choices, choosing the alternatives they value the most. Once their choices have been made, they must forgo the other alternatives. It is their valuation of the best unchosen alternatives that is the opportunity cost of reading this article.

Notice that opportunity cost is inherently subjective. At the time that a reader chooses, he or she cannot possibly know the actual values of the alternatives. The reader can form only expectations of these actual values. Based on prior knowledge, and with continuous assimilation of new knowledge, the reader chooses among his or her alternatives and continually reconsiders these choices.

Even if the reader has read to this point in this article, there is still a choice to be made. Will the reader go on reading this article or choose some other alternative? This depends on how the reader has revised his or her expectations of the value of this article, which will be based on how valuable it has been so far. The reader might decide, at this time, that continuing to read this article is not as valuable as some alternative. If he or she decides not to finish reading this article, and to do something else, that decision will result from the fact that the reader now thinks that finishing this article is not as valuable as some alternative. If the reader does not finish reading this article, he or she will never be able to judge its true value.

The concept of opportunity cost has become one of the most fundamental concepts in economics, but this was not always the case. The classical school, and Adam Smith (1723-1790) in particular, considered cost to be objective and to be the value of the things that are used up in production. This approach is backward-looking; it defines the value of something as its cost of production. Taken to its logical conclusion, this approach implies a labor theory of value.

The weakness of the classical school approach to value is evident once nonreproducible goods, such as quality paintings of long-deceased artists, are considered. The prices of these paintings are many times their cost of production. The classical economists had one theory of value for reproducible goods—a cost theory of value—and another, quite different, theory of value for nonreproducible goods.

It was for the "marginal revolution" to identify value as the use to which the next unit of a thing is expected to be applied. This is a forward-looking and inherently subjective theory of value. With the marginal utility theory of value, cost—defined as the value of things that are used up in production—became irrelevant. What did the former value of the things that were used up in production matter once an item was produced? Cost, defined in that manner, was considered to be sunk cost and no longer important, except perhaps as information that was useful for future production decisions. With the marginal utility theory of value, a new definition of cost was needed. According to Buchanan, this new definition of cost is opportunity cost, and it involves the following six characteristics: First, it is borne by the decision maker; second, it is subjective and exists only in the mind of the decision maker; third, it is based on anticipations; fourth, it can never be realized because it pertains to forgone alternatives; fifth, it cannot be measured because the decision maker's experience cannot be observed by another; and sixth, it is dated at the time of choice. This definition of cost is very different from most other definitions. Yet, there are relationships between this and other definitions of cost that can be useful.

Applications
There is a set of conditions under which the classical school view of cost is equivalent to opportunity cost. Most important, these conditions include reproducible goods and long-run equilibrium. With these conditions, the cost of a good is, in fact, equal to the value of the goods that are used up in its production, where these values are expressed in the terms of money. The condition of long-run equilibrium implies that decision makers do not make mistakes. Perhaps because they have learned from past mistakes, their valuations of alternatives are correct. Therefore, subjective valuations of alternatives, which exist only in the minds of decision makers, are equal to the actual values which can be observed.

In the abstract world of mathematical economics, the conditions that are necessary for the equivalence between cost in the classical school sense and opportunity cost can be assumed to be true. The degree to which these conditions are approximated in a real-world situation, however, is an empirical question. Price may be thought of as determined by two blades of a pair of scissors (in Alfred Marshall's metaphor), supply and demand, or cost and marginal utility. Yet, both blades are inherently subjective and forward-looking. Under certain conditions, the most important of which is long-run equilibrium, cost—in the sense of the value of the goods that are used up in production—can be brought into alignment with value.

In certain situations, it is difficult for an observer to estimate opportunity costs. Examples include the exploration for natural resources, the research into new technologies, the evaluation of the creditworthiness of would-be borrowers, and the hiring of job applicants.

These are all examples of decisions that involve risk-taking. An observer might be able to estimate actuarial probabilities, but the subjective probabilities of decision makers can be very different.

Another category of situations in which it is difficult for an observer to estimate opportunity costs involves the valuation of a person's time. What is the opportunity cost, for example, of a household consisting of a man and woman choosing to have a baby? Assume that, in order to have the baby, the woman will stop working outside the home for a period of time. In this case, it can be said that the wages that she does not earn during that period of time are the household's opportunity cost of having a baby.

That this particular woman was working outside the home facilitates the estimation of opportunity cost. Assume that the woman is not working outside the home, but instead is working only within the home, doing things such as housekeeping, preparing meals, sewing clothes, or tending a garden. Prior to the massive entry of women into the labor force during the twentieth century, this described the "occupation" of most women. Because this woman is not working outside the home, however, does not mean the household's opportunity cost of having a baby is zero. While it involves a more difficult estimation, an observer should impute a value for her time using the market prices of household services such as house-keeping and preparing meals.

Sometimes, the concept of opportunity cost is incorrectly used to refer only to implicit costs. In the above example, the opportunity cost of having a baby can be incorrectly identified only as forgone wages, as opposed to also including explicit or "out-of-pocket" expenses such as the purchase of diapers. In fact, opportunity cost includes explicit, as well as implicit, costs.

Sunk costs are unrecoverable. As such, they are irrelevant to decision making. Nevertheless, some decision makers will commit themselves to completing a project once the sunk costs of the project are substantial, which has been called "throwing good money after bad." Once a project is under way, all that is relevant is the remaining cost. It is the remaining cost against which the anticipated benefit of the project should be compared.

In a similar way, some decision makers misjudge the nature of fixed costs. Fixed costs do not vary over the relevant range of production. In the long run, in order at least to break even and justify staying in business, a company must sell its products at prices that are sufficiently above its variable costs, so as to cover its fixed costs. In any given short run, however, the company may not be able to cover its fixed costs fully, but it should still continue to produce as long as its prices exceed its variable costs. Even though the company cannot break even, this policy will minimize short-run losses. It should be pointed out that the difference between the short run and the long run is not well measured by clocks or calendars. Rather, it concerns the decision maker's evaluation of the permanency of the fall in demand that is resulting in the company's inability to cover its fixed costs.

Context

The concept of opportunity cost is particularly useful in public policy analysis and in analyzing the behavior of collectives, such as corporations that are owned by many share-holders and representative democracies.

Consider the opportunity cost of a military draft. People who are conscripted into military service are often paid a low wage. This may reduce the explicit cost of the military to the taxpayer, but it may increase the opportunity cost of military service. The opportunity cost of military service is the forgone production of civilian goods. With a volunteer military, many people join because they find the military wage (adjusted for their valuation of the nonpecuniary rewards of military service) to be higher than their civilian wage, which is usually reflective of their civilian productivity. Generally, people with lower civilian wages and productivity join a volunteer military. This minimizes the opportunity cost of military service. With a lottery-style draft, however, people are conscripted into the military without regard to their civilian productivity. Thus, people with higher civilian wages and productivity are among those who are drafted. This increases the opportunity cost of military service.

Public policies tend to be biased because costs such as the high opportunity costs of regulations, as in the case of a military draft, tend to be implicit and borne by persons other than the decision maker and the beneficiary. Deficit spending and special interest legislation likewise tend to shift the actual costs of these policies to persons other than the decision maker and the beneficiary, such as future generations and the general public.

On a larger scale, recognizing the characteristics of opportunity cost questions the possibility of economic calculation in a socialistic economy. Opportunity cost is inherently subjective, involving the internal comparisons of alternative uses. At one level, the possibility of economic calculation in a socialistic economy is doubted for its enormous data and data processing requirements. At another, more fundamental level, this possibility is doubted because of the requirement of finding truly altruistic persons who would make the inevitably subjective choices of a socialistic economy.

The concept of opportunity cost makes clear the nature of scarcity. Scarcity—at least for most people in capitalistic economies—is not so much attributable to a lack of material abundance, but rather to a wealth of alternatives and the inescapable necessity of having to choose from among these alternatives.

When the expression "there is no such thing as a free lunch" is invoked, usually it is to argue that someone must pay for the lunch, such as the taxpayer. Even if the lunch were truly free, however, it would still have an opportunity cost. To partake in the "free lunch" would cost a decision maker the value of the best alternative use of his or her time.

Bibliography

Buchanan, James M. *Cost and Choice.* Chicago: Markham, 1969. The definitive work on opportunity cost.

Eijffinger, Sylvester, and Harry Huizinga, eds. *Positive Political Economy: Theory and Evidence.* New York: Cambridge University Press, 1998.

Kirzner, Israel M. *The Economic Point of View.* Princeton, N.J.: Van Nostrand, 1960. A sympathetic critique and extension of Lionel Robbins' synthesis of the Austrian and English foundations of economics.

Levi, Maurice. *Thinking Economically.* New York: Basic Books, 1985. A series of refreshingly informal applications of economic principles. Chapter 9, "Thinking Opportunistically," is an application of the opportunity cost principle to explain rents and wages.

McCulloch, J. Huston. "The Austrian Theory of the Marginal Use and of Ordinal Marginal Utility." *Zeitschrift für Nationalökonmie* 37, no. 3-4 (1977): 249-280. A technical, but still readable, modern development of the Austrian theory of marginal utility.

Robbins, Lionel. *An Essay on the Nature and Significance of Economic Science.* 2d ed. London: Macmillan, 1933. Integrates Austrian and English contributions to the foundations of economics, including the concept of opportunity cost.

Wicksteed, Philip H. *The Common Sense of Political Economy.* London: Macmillan, 1910. Contains one of the first clear statements of the concept of opportunity cost.

Clifford F. Thies

Cross-References

PARTNERSHIPS

Type of economics: Industrial economics
Field of study: Industry studies

Partnerships are business organizations that are owned by two or more people. The partnership is one of the three major forms of business organization, along with the sole proprietorship and the corporation. Partnerships may be established under varying degrees of formality, ranging from a quite informal, oral partnership agreement to a highly formal, written agreement.

Principal terms

CORPORATION: a type of business firm owned by stockholders that is recognized by law as a legal entity separate from its owners
LIMITED LIABILITY: a characteristic associated with corporations and limited partnerships whereby the owners of these types of businesses are not legally obligated to pay for any debts of the firm beyond an amount equal to their investment in the business
LIMITED PARTNERSHIP: a special kind of partnership in which at least one of the partners possesses a limited liability, usually as a trade-off for reduced opportunities to share in partnership profits or management
PARTNER: a co-owner of a partnership form of business
SOLE PROPRIETORSHIP: a form of business organization in which the firm is owned by a single individual

Overview

Business organizations can be of three different types: sole proprietorship, partnership, or corporation. A sole proprietorship is a business that is owned by one individual. A partnership is an unincorporated business that is owned by two or more people. The co-owners of a partnership are usually referred to as partners. A corporation is a legal entity or artificial "person" that, by enabling laws, is endowed with all of the powers, rights, liabilities, and duties of an individual.

Any time two or more people agree jointly to own their own unincorporated business, a partnership is created. There is a wide degree of diversity in the nature of partnership agreements ranging from a very simple oral agreement, possibly confirmed with a handshake, to a quite complicated written agreement that may be filed with the secretary of the state in which the partnership is to do business. In a legal sense, partnerships are presumed to exist whenever two or more people act in such a way that it can be reasonably inferred they are associated for business purposes.

The two basic types of partnerships are general and limited. The main difference between these two has to do with the distribution of partner rights and liabilities. General partnerships are the most common type. In a general partnership, each partner has the same liabilities as every other partner, even though the individual partners may have contributed different amounts of resources to the business. Each general partner has the authority to serve as an agent representing the partnership; that is, any one partner can commit the partnership to a business deal. All profits and all liabilities in a general partnership are usually shared equally by all of the partners. If the general partnership loses money and the resources of one partner are exhausted, the remaining partners continue to be liable for the debts of the partnership. In an extreme situation, one partner could become responsible for all of the debts of the partnership if no other partner is able to contribute. General partners may agree among themselves not to be treated equally in the delegation of responsibilities or the division of items such as revenues, costs, or profits. Such decisions are often based on differences in job responsibilities or funds invested by the partners. General partnership liabilities, however, cannot be unequally divided among general partners—each general partner remains fully liable for the debts of the partnership.

The other type of partnership is the limited partnership. With a limited partnership, some but not all of the individual partners may be co-owners of the business without incurring the full legal liability of a general partner. Thus, a limited partner has limited liability much like the owners of a corporate business. The amount of liability that a limited partner incurs is generally limited to the amount of money that the individual invested in the partnership. State laws regulating limited partnerships often prohibit limited partners from contributing services to the business or from using their surnames in the business (unless a general partner has the same surname or the business had previously used that name).

Applications

Partnerships are the least common form of business organization. Yet some estimates indicate that partnerships still account for almost 10 percent of all firms and 5 percent of all business volume in the United States. Despite the relatively small percentage of partnership businesses, there are almost two million such businesses in operation in the United States. Most law firms and accounting firms are partnerships, as well as many farming operations and medical clinics.

Partnerships represent the simplest form of business organization that allows two or more people to pool their resources and talents together to their mutual benefit. Partnerships, like the other forms of business organizations, have advantages and disadvantages which should be evaluated by an individual who is considering investing in his or her own business.

What advantages do partnerships have over sole proprietorships? Generally, a partnership can bring together more resources to start up, improve, or expand a business because of the increase in the number of people involved. These additional resources might be additional funds, but they could also be additional talents or skills that different individuals possess and can contribute. More partners are often added as additional money or talents are needed. By forming partnerships, some individuals are able to become involved in a business that might otherwise be unaffordable if they attempted to do so alone. By working together as a team, partners may also increase their motivations to pursue business goals so as not to let their partners down.

What advantages do partnerships have over corporations? Partnerships are much easier and less expensive to start than corporations. Partnerships generally do not face as many business taxes because the net income of a partnership is taxed as individual income to the partners in accordance with their share rather than taxed as corporate income. Corporate profits that are distributed to stockholders as dividends are usually subject to double taxation—before receipt to the corporation and after receipt to the stockholders—while partnership profits are taxed only once to the partners. The managerial decision-making structure in a partnership is often much less complicated than that for a corporation. This situation usually allows an individual partner to have more influence and control over the operation of a partnership than an individual stockholder in a corporation.

Partnerships are not without their disadvantages. When individuals are co-owners of a partnership business, as opposed to the owners of sole proprietorships, they necessarily lose some control over the business by having to participate with others in making decisions. Business profits also must be shared. Relative to owners of corporations, partnership owners must deal with the disadvantages of unlimited liability. Unlike stockholders, general partners must risk all of their personal assets, even those not invested directly in the partnership, although this is not a problem for limited partners. Partnerships also lack continuity and permanence in comparison with corporations. When a partner leaves a partnership because of withdrawal, incapacity, or death, the old partnership must be terminated and a new one must be formed. Calculating the value of a former partner's share can sometimes be difficult. The disadvantages of unlimited liability and the limited life of the organization lead to another disadvantage—the difficulty of raising large amounts of money for the business. Finally, in cases where partners are relatives of one another, there is always the risk that personal or family relationships may become strained, especially if the partnership is not as successful as had been expected.

Some of the disadvantages associated with partnerships emphasize the importance of the partnership agreement. Carefully drafted partnership agreements that are in writing often do more to ensure the success of a partnership than any other factor. When partnerships are started, the partners are all on good terms with one another. Situations change, however, and so do people. Terminating a partnership is easier if the partners had specified in advance the calculation procedure for determining the value of an individual partner's share, as well as the payment method, in the partnership agreement. Written partnership agreements also help partners to recall specific details that were previously agreed on that over time might otherwise be forgotten and become a potential cause of disagreement and dissension.

Context

Households, business firms, and the government represent the three major types of decision makers in an economy. The major role of business firms is to buy resources of land, labor, capital, and managerial ability from households and convert them into goods and services that households want and are willing to pay for. In earlier times, when economies were primarily agricultural, households were primarily self-sufficient and relied much less on firms for goods and services. Households produced most of the food, clothing, and shelter that was needed for members within the household.

The Industrial Revolution which began in Europe during the eighteenth century soon spread to other parts of the world and began to change the household's role in the economy. Technological advancements that were part of the revolutionary process in production agriculture meant that fewer farm households were needed to produce food for the nation because of the development of such items as new seeds, fertilizers, and labor-saving equipment. The Industrial Revolution and the corresponding development of machines also made it more economical for firms to be organized in order to take advantage of labor specialization. The emergence of factories in cities created a market for the surplus of agricultural labor. Thus, over time, more goods and services have been provided by firms through markets.

As off-farm business firms have grown in number and size, the owners of these firms have developed different organizational types. Most farm firms historically and presently are sole proprietorships. Most off-farm firms tend to be much larger, however, making it virtually impossible for one person to own and control such a business. Team effort or group effort through partnerships and even corporations is often necessary to assimilate and manage all the resources involved.

Partnerships have some advantages over both the sole proprietorship and the corporate forms of business. Because of this, the formation of partnerships can be expected to continue. Partnerships also have some major limitations, however, which may result in their playing a lesser role than sole proprietorships and corporations in the U.S. economy in the number of firms and sales.

Bibliography

Douma, Sytse, and Hein Schreuder. *Economic Approaches to Organizations.* 2d ed. London: Prentice Hall, 1998.

Downey, W. David, and Steven P. Erickson. *Agribusiness Management.* New York: McGraw-Hill, 1987. Contains several chapters that provide an excellent overview of managing a business firm that also are relevant to a partnership. The authors present a concise discussion of the advantages and disadvantages of the different forms of business organization. The differences between general and limited partnerships are also explained. Very readable for general audiences and quite practical for anyone involved in management.

Drucker, Peter F. *Concept of the Corporation.* 1946. Reprint. New York: Harper & Row, 1983. Still relevant for managers of corporations and partnerships, as it examines issues related to the structure, organization, power relationships, and social responsibilities of business firms. One of the first books written on management by a leading expert.

Kahn, Sharon, and the Philip Lief Group. *101 Best Businesses to Start.* New York: Doubleday, 1988. Designed for those seriously considering starting their own business, whether it be a sole proprietorship or a partnership. The authors identify the resources required and skills needed, and provide tips for success in 101 different business areas.

Peters, Tom, and Nancy Austin. *A Passion for Excellence.* New York: Warner Books, 1985. This New York Times best-seller presents numerous case studies on how some businesses, both large and small, achieved and sustained success. Managers of all kinds of firms, including partnerships, can learn from the authors' inspiring tales of paying attention to details and pursuing a business dream.

Ross, Stephen A., Randolph W. Westerfield, and Bradford D. Jordan. *Fundamentals of Corporate Finance.* 4th ed. Boston: Irwin/McGraw-Hill, 1998.

Whitmyer, Claude, Salli Rasberry, and Michael Phillips. *Running a One-Person Business.* Berkeley, Calif: Ten Speed Press, 1988. Covers many of the down-to-earth topics that any successful manager of a small business, sole proprietorship, or partnership should understand. The topics discussed include starting the business, bookkeeping, marketing, finance, legal matters, and the support services that are required.

Ron Deiter

Cross-References

POLITICS AND ECONOMICS

Type of economics: General economics
Field of study: History of economic thought

The political system, as the setting for government decision making, depends on the economic system for tax revenues, loan funds, and the supplies of goods and services that are required for the government to operate. The political system generates government policies that define the boundaries of public and private sectors and influence behavior within the private sector of the economy.

Principal terms

DEMAND MANAGEMENT: government policies that influence the level of aggregate expenditure for goods and services throughout an economy
EXTERNALITIES: situations in which significant costs or benefits of an activity are experienced by persons other than the decision makers
FISCAL POLICIES: government policies that relate to tax rates, government expenditures, and the public debt
LOBBYING: efforts to influence government actions in one's favor in close interactions with officials, particularly legislators
POLITICS: important aspects of power and influence in society, particularly relating to identifying who exercises governmental authority and how they obtain and use such power
RENT-SEEKING: efforts to gain income or wealth by the use of political influence, rather than through economic productivity
TRANSFER PAYMENT: a government payment (such as unemployment compensation, welfare benefits, or social security benefits) for which the recipient does not furnish some current goods or services

Overview

The political system consists of networks of individual and group relationships and interactions that generate patterns of power and authority in a society, chiefly in government. In Western democracies such as the United States, the political system involves organized political parties that nominate candidates for public office and promote their election. In less developed societies, the political system is more likely to involve ties of kinship, religion, ethnic identity, personal loyalty, and patronage. These remain important in highly developed countries as well.

Politics involves government. Government involves three major types of roles for individuals. First, some are elected by the public. For them, the political factor is of overriding importance. Candidates for office adapt their promises and actions to what they believe the electorate wants. Because political campaigning is very expensive, candidates will try to cultivate sources of campaign funds in their choice of promises and actions. Second, some persons are appointed to high administrative positions as close allies of elected officials. Such positions are also regarded as intensely political. Third, the vast majority of people who work for government are professional civil service or military people who are hired for their skills and, therefore, may be relatively remote from partisan politics. Where government employs large numbers of professionals, as in the post office, the public school system, or the armed forces, these employee groups can be very powerful special-interest lobbying groups.

Modern economic analysis argues that the people who play these three roles in government will be motivated much like the rest of society—they will pursue their perceived self-interests. A democratic political system in which several parties or candidates must compete in order to win elections is a way of motivating government people to be sensitive to the desires of the public.

Modern governments operate in an environment of buying and selling. Governments buy the goods and services that they need in order to perform their functions. Governments hire people, chiefly through voluntary employment contracts. A military draft is an exception, but in the United States, military service has been voluntary since the early 1970's. Governments buy large quantities of goods from private producers: guns and ammunition, concrete and lumber for public buildings, paper, typewriters, and computers for office work. The availability of these goods and services to the government reflects the level of the economy—whether it is one of high productivity and abundance or one of low productivity and scarcity.

For governments to buy goods and services, they require money. Noncommunist governments rely chiefly on tax revenues. For the individual taxpayer, tax payments are a coerced payment that may be involuntary. In a democratic political environment, however, taxpayers as a group have much influence over the level of tax rates. In the aggregate, the willingness to pay taxes can be a measure of a people's willingness to pay for government services.

Governments can also incur deficits, spending more than their tax revenues by raising money from bond issues and other borrowing or simply by creating money. Financing government by money creation (often by borrowing from a central bank such as the Federal Reserve) may appear a painless mode of financing, but this practice runs the risk of inflation. Issuing bonds imposes on the government the costs of paying interest, which may make the subsequent deficits larger. Large-scale government deficits may signal a situation in which the public is receiving more government than it is willing to pay for, meaning that resources are being misdirected.

The economic system, in turn, is subject to powerful influences from government policy. In a centrally controlled system such as that of the Soviet Union, most major economic decisions were made by the government and, therefore, were political decisions. Soviet political decisions were often dominated by the concern for national power in the international realm and for the power of the communist dictatorship within the national borders.

In Western industrialized countries, most economic activity is carried on by profit seeking private business firms. In all modern countries, the private economy is affected by many layers of government policy. Monetary and fiscal policies exert a major influence on aggregate demand and thus on output, prices, interest rates, and foreign exchange rates. Governments create monopolies in some sectors, such as the postal service, electric power, telephone service, and water supply, but may prosecute monopolies in sectors of the private economy. Taxes not only raise revenue but also may benefit some groups at the expense of others, as in the case of protective tariffs. Governments regulate and inspect many areas of labor relations, reflecting concerns for fairness and protection against health and safety hazards, but also at times favoring some workers at the expense of others. Governments also pay vast sums of money either to their employees or in the form of transfer payments to worthy beneficiaries, such as persons who are retired, sick or disabled, unemployed, or simply poor.

These government policies can greatly affect the economic welfare of each individual or business firm. Thus, people have a strong incentive to try to use the political process in order to win a larger share of government benefits. Much of the political process simply becomes a competition among organized lobbying groups seeking a larger share of the national product. Government is not a neutral, unbiased authority, but rather simply another group of self-interested individuals whose behavior can be influenced by rewards and penalties.

Applications

Because the political process so often appears to be a scramble for money, some observers have viewed politics as a dirty business. One traditional response has been to try to limit the role of government in the economy, thus keeping down the potential "spoils" that can be gained by political success. In much of the world, the Great Depression of the 1930's and World War II led to large increases in the economic role of government and the creation of programs. Once in place, government programs tend to create a politically powerful vested interest of beneficiaries who can usually prevent those programs from being dismantled. Most noncommunist, industrialized countries have developed similar roles for govern-ment—large but not totally dominating—and political systems that have become more or less democratic. For most of them, several considerations have become important, including externalities, coercion, rent-seeking and income redistribution, producer-group bias, and the short-run nature of political life.

Externalities exist when activities or transactions have significant effects on persons who are not directly involved in the decision making about those activities or transactions. The presence of externalities can create gaps between the social and private costs of an activity, or the social and private benefits. Pollution represents a type of externality in which social costs are higher than the private costs on which production decisions are made. Education represents a type of externality in which the activity generates benefits for persons other than the students and their parents. Where externalities are significant, private economic deci-sions are not socially optimal. High-polluting products may be produced to excess, while education may be underproduced. Government action can improve matters by taxing or restricting pollution while subsidizing education, but externalities are very difficult to measure. Consequently, policy decisions concerning externalities are often intensely political.

Coercion is another issue. A government that controls the police force and the military has a great potential for using force, and a major task of the political system is to prevent the use of force by politically powerful people for their own benefit. Politically controversial areas involving the use of government coercion concern taxes, the military draft, the government acquisition of private property, and efforts to prohibit private actions such as abortion or drug or alcohol consumption. Political systems are always exposed to the risk that a majority will use government's coercive powers against a minority.

A third consideration is rent-seeking and income redistribution. In the twentieth century, it has been a widely accepted principle that government can legitimately promote some redistribution of income to the benefit of "disadvantaged" people whose individual earning capacity may be unjustly impaired. Definitions of "fairness," however, can be extremely vague. Powerful lobbies can influence many types of government policies in order to give their constituents direct or indirect economic benefits. Retired people, who have more time for political activity, have been able to secure generous pensions and other old-age benefits. Industries have lobbied successfully for monopoly privileges, subsidies, tax advantages, and favorable government contracts. Such efforts to gain unearned incomes through political privilege have been termed "rent-seeking" behavior.

A market economy generally works best when people's incomes represent rewards for productive activity. The further a political system goes toward rewarding people who are not productive and putting corresponding financial burdens on those who are productive, the greater the risk that the economy will be impaired.

Another issue is producer-group bias. The most effective lobbying activities are often carried on by groups of people who stand to gain or lose much through one particular law or policy. A producer group can be greatly affected by tariffs, taxes, and regulatory policies that relate to their specific industry. In contrast, consumers buy many products and are often not heavily affected by a change in the price of any one item. Tariffs and other import restrictions are a classic area in which producer groups have been able to gain higher prices through policies that are harmful to consumers and may impair the total output of the economy.

The last consideration of industrialized countries is the short-run orientation of political life. Politicians need to be concerned about the next election. In the United States, many officials must run for reelection as frequently as every two years. This time frame puts a premium on actions that give the appearance of quick and popular benefit, even if the long-run consequences may be damaging. Therefore, it is politically expedient to increase government spending on popular programs or reduce tax rates without concern for the resulting deficits. The long-run burdens arising from an increase in the size of the national debt and rising interest payments may be neglected. At times, it has been politically popular to offer lower interest rates or easier credit through monetary expansion. The long-run tendencies toward increased inflation may be neglected. If demand stimulation is timed to coincide with elections, a "political business cycle" may result.

Context

Adam Smith's (1723-1790) great treatise, *An Inquiry into the Nature and Causes of the Wealth of Nations* (1776), was chiefly concerned with the areas in which politics and economics intersect. Smith was alarmed that politically powerful groups in England were able to use government policies to their advantage and to the disadvantage of efficiency and justice, particularly toward the working class. Smith advocated limiting the economic role of government in order to limit the opportunities for such a private capture of public power.

During much of the nineteenth century, writers on economics tended to refer to their subject as "political economy," recognizing that the topics often involved controversial areas of public policy. John Stuart Mill's (1806-1873) *Principles of Political Economy* (1848) attempted to identify the things that the government could and could not do in the economic realm. Mill feared that governments might undertake such extensive responsibilities that

British philosopher John Stuart Mill, whose Principles of Political Economy *(1848) attempted to define the limits of government involvement in economics.* (Library of Congress)

efficiency and democratic accountability would be lost. As he grew older, however, Mill became more concerned about the injustices in society, particularly regarding the status of the working class and of women in general, and thus became more open to the possibility of interventions by government.

Mill's contemporary, Karl Marx (1818-1883), presented a theory of politics in which political power was simply the reflection of whatever economic class was dominant in society—in Marx's time, the capitalists, or "bourgeoisie." While Marx himself never offered a detailed blueprint for an ideal communist society, latter-day Marxists generally used his doctrines to bring about vast extensions of state power in the economy, notably in the Soviet Union after 1917. Marx's notion that revolution could lead to a (benevolent) "dictatorship of the proletariat" (the low-income working class) became a justification for having the Communist Party monopolize political power.

Most industrialized countries, including the United States, experienced large increases in the economic role of government arising from the Great Depression of the 1930's and World War II—a combination of a "welfare state" and a "warfare state." During much of this time, Western economists wrote extensively to identify areas where market failure appeared to afflict the private economy, leaving important opportunities for government. As time went on, however, and as many of the interventionist programs failed to achieve their goals, a more balanced view emerged. Major contributions were made by Nobel Prize-winning economist James M. Buchanan, Jr., whose work helped to develop an entire economic discipline known as "public choice" or "public economics." This type of analysis analyzes government failure as well as market failure, recognizing that people in government are as self-serving as the rest of society and that policies need to be designed accordingly.

In the United States, a waning of enthusiasm for government activism resulted from the failure of such measures as insurance of bank deposits and President Lyndon B. Johnson's War on Poverty program. Internationally, a reassessment of the role of government resulted from the successful disestablishment of communist regimes in much of Eastern Europe in the late 1980's. The communist combination of political dictatorship and government monopolization of economic life produced repressive political systems and economic systems that failed to provide people with the economic abundance that was once promised by Marx and his followers.

Bibliography

Buchanan, James, et al. *The Economics of Politics.* London: Institute of Economic Affairs, 1978. Includes a superb nontechnical overview of public choice economics by Nobel laureate Buchanan, as well as a bibliography. Papers by other contributors explore market failure, the political business cycle, bureaucracy, and related topics.

Buchanan, James, and Gordon Tullock. *The Calculus of Consent.* Ann Arbor: University of Michigan, 1965. A classic analysis by two founders of public choice analysis. Despite some technical material, much is written clearly for nonspecialists.

Dahl, Robert A., and Charles E. Lindblom. *Politics, Economics, and Welfare.* New York: Harper, 1953. A political scientist and an economist collaborated on this comprehensive analysis which stresses such issues as control, organization behavior, and bargaining. Relatively advanced.

Downs, Anthony. *An Economic Theory of Democracy.* New York: Harper, 1957. The ideas are profound, but the exposition is simple. A pioneering effort to apply economic logic to the political process.

Eijffinger, Sylvester, and Harry Huizinga, eds. *Political Economy: Theory and Evidence.* New York: Cambridge University Press, 1998.

Galbraith, John Kenneth. *The Affluent Society.* Boston: Houghton Mifflin, 1958. Galbraith argues that society contains a strong bias against providing adequate resources to the public sector, a view that is opposite to that of James Buchanan. Galbraith's style is entertaining, but his standards of evidence and analysis do not command much respect among professionals.

O'Neill, John. *The Market: Ethics, Knowledge, and Politics.* New York: Routledge, 1998.

Rosen, Harvey S. *Public Finance*, 2d ed. Homewood, Ill.: Irwin, 1988. This comprehensive textbook for university undergraduates provides a good overview of central concepts and gives brief bibliographies. Chapter 6 deals with public choice and chapter 7 with externalities.

Stigler, George J. *The Citizen and the State.* Chicago: University of Chicago Press, 1975. Nobel laureate Stigler writes with wit and style, as well as insight and originality. This volume contains several brief essays dealing with economic policy, particularly analyzing the reasons for programs regulating private industry and their effects.

Tufte, Edward R. *Political Control of the Economy.* Princeton, N.J.: Princeton University Press, 1978. This brief, readable study presents evidence that there has been a macroeconomic political business cycle in the United States and other Western countries, with demand stimulation often occurring a short time before elections.

Paul B. Trescott

Cross-References

Antitrust Policy, 6; Communism, 80; Federal Reserve Bank, 223; Great Depression, 263; History of Economics, 295; Marxist Economics, 412; Monetary Policy, 431; Quotas and Tariffs, 520; Regulation and Deregulation, 526; Tax and Taxation, 569; Welfare Economics, 631.

POPULATION AND ECONOMICS

Type of economics: Labor and population
Field of study: Economic growth, development, and planning

Traditional economics fears that population growth, in the absence of improvements in technology or organization, will lower per-capita output because of diminishing returns. Rapid population growth also can affect the distribution of income by lowering wages and raising the rewards to owners of capital and land.

Principal terms

DEMOGRAPHIC TRANSITION: the idea that, in the process of economic growth and development, there will be a period when the reduction of death rates accelerates population growth, but then birth rates will tend to decline, slowing population growth
DEMOGRAPHY: the scientific study of factors that determine the size, composition, and growth of a population
DEPENDENCY RATIO: the proportion of a population who are not actual or potential producers but are too old, too young, sick or handicapped, students, and homemakers
LAW OF DIMINISHING RETURNS: the economic principle that, if units of a variable input such as labor are added to a fixed input such as land, then the total output tends to increase but proportionately less so than the increase in the variable input
OPTIMUM POPULATION: the number of people which yields the maximum output per capita, taking advantage of specialization and not seriously damaged by diminishing returns
PARTICIPATION RATE: the proportion of a population who are able-bodied people of working age and are actually working or seeking work

Overview

The performance of an economic system can be judged by how much output it produces per person. Other things being equal, the larger the population, the larger the number of workers and the larger the total output. Yet a larger population also means a larger number of consumers. Much of the economic analysis of population growth concerns whether it will increase or decrease the output of that population per capita.

The influence of population size on total output depends in part on the participation rate, that is, the proportion of the working-age population who are working. The participation rate depends on individual preferences and social customs, particularly regarding the employment status of women. Workers' productivity is affected by qualitative factors such as health, education, and work attitudes. If a population is growing rapidly, a large proportion of that population may be too young to be productive; thus, there will be a high dependency ratio. Moreover, if the typical family has a large number of children, it may be difficult to provide them with good education and good medical attention.

If growing population means a growing labor force, this condition can lead to an increased output per worker if people can become more specialized. Yet, there are limits to the potential gains from specialization. Beyond some point, according to traditional thinking, an increase in population and labor force will tend to reduce the output per worker because of the law of diminishing returns. This principle states that if one input (such as land) is fixed in quality and quantity, while increasing amounts of a variable input (such as labor) are added, the total output will increase, but the proportional increases in output will be less than the proportional increases in the variable input. Thus, the output per worker and per capita will tend to decline. The law only holds, however, if all other things are assumed to be equal, notably resource quality and technology. At one time, some economists attempted to identify an "optimum population," one large enough to achieve the gains from specialization but not so large as to experience seriously diminishing returns. Yet, even if population growth does not lower the output per capita, it may worsen the tendencies of that population toward pollution and resource depletion.

Because wage rates move in proportion to the productivity of labor, a country that is experiencing rapid population growth will tend to have downward pressure on wage rates. This process tends to increase the productivity of land and capital and the income that is paid to owners of property.

These considerations have led most economists to believe that rapid population growth is economically undesirable. The problem has appeared most severe in low-income less developed countries. At some point in the past, most societies possessed a relatively static total population, with high birthrates and high death rates. If such a country experiences some economic improvement, and particularly if the medical and sanitary conditions improve, its death rates are likely to decline. Consequently, infant mortality rates decrease and more children survive. If birthrates remain unchanged, that population will grow, and the increase will initially consist of unproductive young people who need to consume but do not produce.

In the United States and other industrialized countries, birthrates have declined in tandem with decreasing death rates, and population growth rates have slowed. The goal of zero population growth, with equal birth and death rates, appeared to be achieved in many industrialized nations by the late twentieth century. Population problems remained, however, in low-income countries in which many people continued to live in rural areas and to retain the traditional values and motivations that led them to desire large families.

One exception to this adverse view of population growth arose in the "stagnation hypothesis," which was widely held during the Great Depression of the 1930's. It was argued that slowing population growth reduced the formation of families, therefore undermining the demand for new housing and contributing to the great decline in aggregate demand in 1929-1933 and the subsequent slow recovery. The modern view is that "demand management" policies by government can overcome such capricious changes in expenditure motivations.

Applications

In the United States, the chief long-standing policies regarding population growth have involved immigration. In the nineteenth century, restrictions on immigration were first imposed on Asians. Immigration from Europe was relatively free, however, and in the early twentieth century, as many as one million immigrants a year were coming to the United States. In 1924, Congress enacted the first of a series of general immigration restrictions, largely in response to political pressure from labor unions that wanted to reduce the competition for jobs. In the 1980's, legal immigration into the United States averaged 600,000 persons per year. The flow of illegal immigrants, however, chiefly across the southern border, may have been as large.

Some countries have tried to conduct national policies regarding birthrates. Governments concerned about their military power have sometimes tried to encourage population increase, as in Adolf Hitler's Germany in the 1930's and 1940's and in Romania under Nicolae Ceausescu in the 1970's and 1980's. Family allowances and other financial inducements were offered.

Until the twentieth century, efforts to bring about lower birthrates were largely of private origin. The recognition that unwanted pregnancies and large families often contributed to poverty, however, gave rise to efforts to encourage family planning and the use of birth control techniques. Margaret Sanger (1879-1966), an American nurse, devoted much of her life to international efforts of this nature. Such efforts encountered many obstacles from people who opposed free discussion of the sensitive subjects, and especially from the Roman Catholic Church, which has consistently opposed contraception and abortion.

Since World War II, many low-income countries have recognized the problems that are posed by rapid population growth. International efforts to eradicate many traditional health hazards brought drastic reductions in death rates but left birthrates high. India, the world's second most populous country, started the world's first national family planning program in 1952. The government attempted to reduce birthrates through education about birth control objectives and techniques and through an extensive network of birth control clinics. In the 1970's, these policies went further, involving pressures for sterilization and for delaying marriage.

In China, with the world's largest population, the communist government adopted a drastic policy to restrict births beginning in the late 1970's. This included strong prohibitions against early marriages. For urban couples, permission prior to having a child was required. Neighborhood family planning staff members have monitored the use of contraceptives and often were able to detect unauthorized pregnancies which were usually terminated by abortion. The official policy of "one couple, one child" was unpopular, mainly because every family wanted to have a son. Such a drastic intrusion into people's private lives is only possible in a strict authoritarian system in which the government controls employment and housing.

Desired birthrates remain high in some low-income countries, because children become an economic asset at a relatively early age in rural areas, because child mortality is still a problem, and because children are seen as the chief source of economic support for parents in their old age. In India, the persistence of these patterns caused the voluntary birth limitation program to be largely unsuccessful. In China, coercive methods were employed to overcome these traditions, resulting in a significant slowing in that country's population growth.

Context

Prior to 1800, much of the discussion of population matters reflected the concerns of national leaders for military security. Mercantilist writers also favored a large population in order to maintain a cheap labor force and to promote exports. In 1798, British clergyman and economist Thomas Robert Malthus (1766-1834) published the first edition of *An Essay on the Principle of Population.* He viewed population growth with alarm, fearing the tendency for population to outrun food supplies. In later writings, Malthus and his friend, David Ricardo (1772-1823), helped to formalize the law of diminishing returns, which has become a central element in the concern of some mainstream economists over population growth.

Malthus and Ricardo feared that any improvement in the economic condition of the mass of the people would be only temporary. A momentary improvement in living conditions would reduce death rates, accelerate population growth, and bring workers' incomes back down to the subsistence level. Many economists of the period opposed poor relief for fear that it would encourage irresponsible childbearing. Critics termed the Malthus-Ricardo labor-market analysis "the iron law of wages."

Both Great Britain and the United States began to conduct systematic population censuses during Malthus's lifetime. As a result, discussions of population became increasingly informed by statistical data. By the end of the nineteenth century, the systematic analysis of population data gave rise to the science of demography. Fortunately, the prognosis that population growth would doom working people to subsistence level did not materialize. One reason was that technological improvement enabled food production, processing, and distribution to keep pace with, and even outrun, population.

As Malthus had predicted, economic improvement during and after the Industrial Revolution lowered death rates. After some delay, however, birthrates began to decline also. Several reasons can be cited. First, urbanization brought crowded living conditions and situations in which children were more of an economic liability than they had been in the countryside. Second, as educational levels improved, more people learned of birth control techniques. Families concerned for their children's education limited their numbers in order to devote more resources to each child. Third, the resulting improvement in women's status gave mothers more influence in decisions about pregnancy and childbearing, as well as more opportunities for employment outside the home. Fourth, declining death rates made it possible to achieve desired family size with fewer births than before. Fifth, and last, contraceptive techniques greatly improved by the twentieth century. This sequence, in which declining death rates were subsequently matched by declining birthrates, has been termed "demographic transition." The great virtue of demographic transition has been that it came about spontaneously, as people's self-interest led them to lower the desired birthrates.

After World War II, the continued presence of poverty and hunger in much of the world led to a strong international concern over the population "explosion" in less developed countries. Many studies were skeptical that the demographic transition could be expected in less developed countries. Paul R. Ehrlich's book *The Population Bomb* (1968) helped to dramatize this issue, leading to increased efforts by public and nonprofit organizations to help to alleviate the effects and causes of these population increases.

There was no population explosion in the United States and the other developed countries in the 1970's and 1980's. Fertility rates were so low that, if continued, they would ultimately produce declining populations. Nevertheless, the U.S. has encountered severe problems arising from teenage pregnancies.

The data in 1990 regarding less developed countries indicated that, in most areas, birthrates and population growth rates were declining, leading to cautious optimism about future prospects. A "medium" forecast by the United Nations indicated that the world's population might reach a maximum and stabilize some time toward the end of the twenty-first century. This equilibrium would entail, however, a world population that is double its size in 1990—10 billion people compared with 5 billion. Even this result might be overturned if desired birthrates remained high in low-income areas. Projections of food availability indicate that the world can support an additional 5 billion people, but the increase is likely to be heavily concentrated in the areas that can least afford it, notably Africa and the Arab Middle East.

Actual experience in the United States with near-zero population growth has revealed some less attractive sides: the self-interest of childless adults and an increase in the political influence of retired elderly persons, which could lead to a diversion of governmental funds toward the support of unproductive consumers at the possible expense of the educational system. In addition, some respected intellectuals, such as Ben J. Wattenberg (*The Birth Dearth*, 1987) and Julian L. Simon (*The Ultimate Resource*, 1981), have argued that population growth is a spur to economic progress and to an invigoration of the quality of life in general. They have been powerful voices urging increased freedom for immigration into the United States.

Bibliography

Bogue, Donald J. *The Population of the United States: Historical Trends and the Future Projections.* New York: Free Press, 1985. Comprehensive, statistically oriented analysis by one of American's top demographic scholars. For the advanced reader.

Easterlin, Richard A. *Birth and Fortune: The Impact of Numbers on Personal Welfare.* 2d ed. Chicago: University of Chicago Press, 1987. A leading economic historian explores the way in which each individual is affected by the number of people who were born at the same time. Brief and written for the nonexpert audience.

Menard, Scott W., and Elizabeth Moen. *Perspective on Population: An Introduction to Concepts and Issues.* New York: Oxford University Press, 1987. A book of forty-seven readings designed for university students. The authors have classified them by their level of difficulty (about half are elementary). Excellently selected, and many items have bibliographies.

Miller, G. Tyler. *Living in the Environment.* 6th ed. Belmont, Calif.: Wadsworth, 1990. In this university textbook, which is designed for an introductory course, chapters 7 and 8 are directly concerned with population. By implication, however, the entire book deals with the subject. Miller is strongly against population growth. Profusely illustrated and contains a good bibliography.

Nickerson, Jane Soames. *Homage to Malthus.* Port Washington, N.Y.: Kennikat Press, 1975. In less than 150 pages, this readable study tells the important things about Thomas Malthus's life and work. For the general reader.

Simon, Julian L. *The Economics of Population Growth.* Princeton, N.J.: Princeton University Press, 1977. A comprehensive scholarly analysis of all aspects of the economics of population. Simon is skeptical of much of the modern argument against population growth; an appendix presents "Common Objections to the Book's Conclusions and Some Simplified Rebuttals." The bibliography is 36 pages long. For the advanced reader.

Weeks, John R. *Population: An Introduction to Concepts and Issues.* Belmont, Calif.: Wadsworth, 1989. A competent college-level textbook.

Paul B. Trescott

Cross-References

Development Theory, 152; Economies and Diseconomies of Scale, 158; Employment Theory, 180; Environmental Economics, 187; Food Economics, 239; Growth Theory, 281; History of Economics, 295; Labor Economics, 353; Poverty, 488; Undeveloped and Underdeveloped Countries, 593; Unemployment Causes, 600; World Economies, 638.

POVERTY

Type of economics: Growth and development
Fields of study: Economic growth, development, and planning; health, education, and
welfare theory

*Poverty is a condition faced by families and individuals that fail to receive sufficient income
to meet their basic needs. It is a condition of material deprivation. The existence of poverty
shows a national economy that is failing to provide adequate incomes for all of its people.*

Principal terms

ABSOLUTE POVERTY: the condition of having an income that is not sufficient to live on for
long periods of time
AID TO FAMILIES WITH DEPENDENT CHILDREN (AFDC): the major federal transfer program
for the nonelderly in the United States, consisting of money payments to dependent
children and their parents
IN-KIND BENEFITS: government assistance to poor families made in the form of goods rather
than money; for example, food stamps and free medical care
POVERTY LINE: the level of income which divides poor families from nonpoor families
POVERTY RATE: the fraction of all families (or all individuals) that fall below the poverty line
RELATIVE POVERTY: a subjective feeling that one lacks adequate income and is poor
compared to others
TRANSFER PAYMENTS: government cash payments made to individuals; for example, social
security, unemployment insurance, and AFDC payments

Overview

The official U.S. definition of poverty was developed by Mollie Orshansky of the Social
Security Administration in the early 1960's. U.S. Agriculture Department studies at the time
had estimated that it would take at minimum $20 a week to feed a family of four during a
temporary financial emergency, or about $1,000 for an entire year. At the same time, surveys
of American households showed that the average family spent about one-third of its income
on food. Orshansky reasoned that if the minimum food requirements for a family were
multiplied by three, this would give the minimum income required by that family. As a
result, the poverty line for a family of four was set at $3,000 in 1964.

Different poverty lines have been set for families of different sizes and for families living
in different locations based on their differing food requirements. Each year these poverty
lines are increased with the rate of inflation, so that the official poverty lines represent a
constant living standard. In 1988, the poverty line for an urban family of four was $12,092.
To calculate whether a particular family or individual is poor requires adding together all
of their money income. This includes government transfer payments such as unemployment insurance, Social Security, and Aid to Families with Dependent Children (AFDC),
but excludes in-kind benefits such as food stamps, free medical assistance, or housing
subsidies. If money income equals or exceeds the poverty line, then the family is not
poor; if it falls below the poverty line (given family size), then it is classified as poor. The

poverty rate is the fraction of families (or individuals) that live below the poverty line. In 1988, the poverty rate for American families was 10.4 percent. This represents a sharp decline from the 1959 family poverty rate of 18.5 percent but is greater than the 8.8 percent poverty rate for families in 1973 and 1974. As these figures indicate, poverty in the United States sharply declined in the 1960's and early 1970's but increased in the late 1970's and in the 1980's.

A number of economists have criticized the Orshansky method of computing poverty. Some have questioned the assumption that families spend one-third of their income on food. Surveys of household expenditures have indicated that families spend closer to one-fourth of their income on food. Other economists have argued that the original decision to use an economy food budget for establishing poverty lines was unwarrantable. This budget was developed for use during emergencies only; as such, it could not provide adequate nutrition for a family over a long period of time. Economists have also questioned the use of an absolute poverty standard. They maintain that people naturally make comparisons with those around them. People will feel poor if they have much less than their fellow citizens. A relative definition of poverty recognizes the fact that poverty is, in part, a subjective feeling. Such a definition would set poverty lines as a certain fraction of the average national income. As a result, when the national standard of living rises, so too will the standard of living deemed necessary for all families.

Planned by the Reverend Martin Luther King, Jr., and carried out shortly after his assassination in 1968, the Poor People's March on Washington was an attempt to dramatize the government's responsibility for addressing the needs of the nation's poor. (Library of Congress)

One implication of these three criticisms is that measured poverty rates are too low, and so poverty in the United States is worse than official statistics would indicate. On the other hand, some economists have argued that the reported poverty rates are too high because in-kind benefits are not counted as part of family income. These goods raise the standard of living of American families, and, from the point of view of the family, are just as good as transfer payments. If in-kind benefits were considered income, family incomes would be higher and the official poverty rate would be lower.

In response to such criticisms, the U.S. Bureau of the Census (which is responsible for calculating U.S. poverty rates) in the 1980's began experimenting with other ways of setting poverty lines and calculating poverty rates. Still, the original Orshansky definition of poverty is cited and used most frequently.

While economists may disagree how best to measure poverty, they agree that poverty is undesirable. Poverty generates humanitarian concern for those deprived of adequate income. The existence of poverty shows a national economy that fails to provide adequately for its citizens. In addition, poverty imposes economic costs on the rest of society. The poor will need to be supported through government programs, and the money for such programs will need to come from the taxes paid by everyone. Poverty also tends to breed crime, which requires that time and money be spent on prevention, insurance against loss, and incarceration. Finally, poverty has deleterious physical effects on those people who must survive on less than an emergency food budget. Workers who live in poverty are less productive workers, and poor children are worse students. Consequently, an economy experiencing high levels of poverty will tend to become economically less competitive.

Applications

Four views have developed about the causes of poverty and the appropriate policies to remedy this problem. Two approaches consider a lack of jobs and inadequate economic growth as the cause of poverty and await greater growth to reduce poverty. Two other approaches view poverty as a result of unequal distribution of income in the market economy and focus on helping those at the bottom portion of the income distribution. One approach looks to government transfer payments to raise the income of the poor to remove them from poverty, while the other works to augment the skills and abilities of low-income workers, thereby making them more productive workers and increasing their wages. Both of these policies are redistributive solutions to poverty.

Economic growth reduces poverty because growth creates jobs and increases incomes, pushing families above the fixed poverty line. Growth can be achieved in either of two fashions. First, greater demand guarantees that jobs will be available for all those seeking employment. Standard Keynesian fiscal and monetary policies call for tax cuts, greater government spending, or the creation of more money in the economy in order to generate this needed demand.

A second means of achieving economic growth works on the supply side of the growth equation. If workers are more productive, their incomes will rise. Supply-side economists advocate increasing incentives for investment and work effort in order to spur worker productivity. These economists call for reducing government regulations and taxes on business and for reducing individual income taxes. While these policies will directly benefit the more affluent, supply-side economists argue that the benefits from having a more productive economy will trickle down to those near or below the poverty line.

Supply-side economists have also severely criticized redistributive antipoverty policies. They argue that such solutions require higher taxes, which discourage the investment needed to end poverty. Supply-side economists also point to the work disincentives associated with transfer payments. Two types of work disincentives operate in transfer programs. First, people may work less because they receive income from the government. Second, because benefits are reduced when income rises, transfer payment recipients may find that they have little or no extra income as a result of working. In addition, work requires additional expenses such as clothing, transportation, and child care. Consequently, working may make a transfer recipient worse off economically.

While supply-side economists have criticized redistributive solutions, other economists have been skeptical that economic growth can reduce poverty. They argue that while growth increases average incomes, those at the bottom of the income distribution will not necessarily benefit. This is most likely to be the case when poverty results from the specific circumstances in which individuals find themselves. For example, single women with young children will not be able to work full time if they must care for their children because no adequate child care is available. Economic growth also cannot help the elderly or the disabled escape poverty, since these individuals cannot be expected to work even if jobs are available. In these cases, programs that rely on government transfer payments are required—Social Security for the elderly, workmen's compensation or disability insurance for the disabled worker, and child care or AFDC payments for the single mother and her children.

Finally, economic growth may not solve the problems of the poor because these individuals lack the ability to earn above-poverty incomes in the market economy. A final approach to reducing poverty tries to counter the deficiencies of low-income individuals. If poverty stems from workers lacking adequate job skills, its solution is a training program to provide them with the necessary skills; if the problem is inadequate schooling, its solution is to increase funding for education; if certain groups start behind in school and cannot catch up, its solution is a Head Start program. When President Lyndon B. Johnson declared his War on Poverty in his 1964 State of the Union address, his main weapons were such above-mentioned policies. The "war" was to be fought with job training programs, with Project Head Start (begun in 1965), and with community development programs. The thrust of these programs was developing the capacity of individuals to earn higher incomes in the private sector of the economy by augmenting their skills and abilities.

During the 1960's and early 1970's, rapid economic growth was accompanied by sharply falling poverty rates. At first, growth was regarded as the cause of falling poverty, but subsequent analysis revealed that redistributive transfer payments had increased in the 1960's and early 1970's and that their growth was responsible for most of the reduction in poverty. In contrast, the causes of rising poverty in the late 1970's and the 1980's are poorly understood. Poverty rates rose despite a rise in transfer payments, despite a record economic expansion, and despite greater incentives for investment and work effort.

Unable to explain these changes in the overall poverty rate, economists in the late 1980's began to focus their attention on different demographic groups. They studied the causes of poverty and proposed antipoverty policies that were designed for each group. Families headed by women and families living in urban ghettos received the greatest attention. These two groups came to constitute a much larger fraction of the total poverty population in the 1970's and 1980's, and their poverty rates have stayed at very high levels.

Context

The earliest economists tried to understand whether wage rates would tend to rise above the subsistence level. This subsistence level of wages is essentially what economists refer to as the "poverty level."

Adam Smith (1723-1790), regarded by most people as the father of economics, argued that economic growth and greater productivity would push incomes above subsistence. Two of his major successors, however, held that humanity was destined to receive poverty level wages. David Ricardo (1772-1823) maintained that there were natural limits to the fruits of the land. Consequently, as the population grew, it would become harder and harder to feed people and living standards would have to fall. Thomas Robert Malthus (1766-1834) maintained that, whenever the condition of the poor improved, it would cause their population to increase. The ensuing competition for jobs would, in turn, exert a downward pressure on wages and push them back to poverty levels.

John Maynard Keynes (1883-1946), writing during the Depression, however, looked forward to the day when poverty would be eliminated from the world. According to Keynes, strong government action was necessary to accomplish this end. Keynes advanced various economic policies to stimulate economic growth, as well as redistributive policies to make sure that the benefits of economic growth reached the entire population.

Most developed countries in the world have come to employ the antipoverty remedies of Keynes. While Keynesian policies have not entirely eliminated poverty, they have succeeded in reducing poverty and in keeping poverty rates down for rather long time periods. This is most true in Western Europe, where generous transfer programs have been very effective remedies for poverty, and where poverty rates are approximately half of those in the United States. It is also true in the United States, where Social Security has reduced poverty for the elderly from 25 percent in the early 1960's to 8 percent in the late 1980's. Keynesian economic policies that have helped to keep the world economy out of another depression have also helped to keep poverty rates relatively low.

The situation facing the less developed nations of the world is less sanguine. These are countries where, in the late twentieth century, poverty has been the predominant experience of the population rather than the exception. These nations lack the resources to implement effective programs of income redistribution. They are also heavily in debt and therefore are unable to borrow the money that would be needed to begin programs of economic growth. Any progress in the fight against poverty is therefore likely to be very slow in the developing world.

Bibliography

Auletta, Ken. *The Underclass.* New York: Random House, 1982. Case studies of the ghetto poor by a New York City journalist. This book is very good when it describes why some people are poor and how difficult it is for them to escape poverty. The book is less satisfactory when it generalizes about the poor and about welfare policy from case studies.

Danziger, Sheldon H., and Daniel H. Weinberg, eds. *Fighting Poverty: What Works and What Doesn't.* Cambridge, Mass.: Harvard University Press, 1986. Essays by both economists and noneconomists from a conference sponsored by the Department of Health and Human Services. The essays examine the causes of poverty and its potential cures. While the essays vary in quality and while some are rather technical, this book contains the thinking of many of the best social scientists who study poverty.

Ellwood, David T. *Poor Support: Poverty in the American Family.* New York: Basic Books, 1988. A readable, thoughtful account of poverty in the 1980's. Ellwood argues that poverty is no longer a single phenomenon with a single cause; rather, different types of families experience different sorts of poverty, and each sort of poverty requires a different solution.

Galbraith, John Kenneth. *The Affluent Society.* 3d ed. Boston: Houghton Mifflin, 1976. A brilliant work which can be read with great profit by everyone. Dismissing the views of other economists, Galbraith proposes much greater government spending to end poverty and argues that the United States is rich enough to afford it. With Harrington's *The Other America*, this book helped to make the public aware of the problem of poverty.

_____. *The Nature of Mass Poverty.* Cambridge, Mass.: Harvard University Press, 1979. This work examines poverty in the developing world. It explains how the mass poverty of less developed nations differs from the poverty experienced by developed nations, and provides some policy solutions. This book is accessible to all readers and is written with the style and wit that have made Galbraith famous. One minor gap in the book is that it addresses only rural poverty in the less developed world and thus ignores urban poverty.

Harrington, Michael. *The New American Poverty.* New York: Holt, Rinehart and Winston, 1984. This work compares the poverty population in the early 1980's with the poverty population that existed in the early 1960's. While possessing neither the brilliance nor the impact of *The Other America*, this work provides a good description and analysis of the changing nature of poverty over a two-decade period.

_____. *The Other America.* New York: Macmillan, 1962. This classic has been one of the most influential books of the twentieth century. More than anything else, this work inspired President Lyndon B. Johnson to declare his War on Poverty in 1964 and is responsible for much of the antipoverty legislation of the 1960's and early 1970's.

Haveman, Robert. *Starting Even.* New York: Simon & Schuster, 1988. Haveman argues that poverty can be reduced without any negative economic consequences if current antipoverty policies are radically redesigned. Haveman's analysis of past successes and failures in reducing poverty, and his policy proposals, are generally very good.

Murray, Charles. *Losing Ground: American Social Policy, 1950-1980.* New York: Basic Books, 1984. A supply-side economist looks at redistributive antipoverty policies and argues that they make it profitable for the poor to have children and go on welfare. This book influenced President Ronald Reagan and was partly responsible for his attempts to reduce welfare spending. Although Murray overstates his case and his use of data is questionable throughout, the value of this book is its sensitivity to the potential negative effects of antipoverty policies.

Rodgers, Harrell R., Jr. *Poor Women, Poor Families.* Armonk, N.Y.: M. E. Sharpe, 1986. This book documents the rising number of female-headed families among the poor, and then discusses some consequences and possible cures. A flaw in this book is its failure to look into the causes of the rising incidence of female-headed families among the poor.

Steven Pressman

Cross-References

Economists, 164; Employment Theory, 180; Food Economics, 239; Great Depression, 263; Growth Theory, 281; Income, 301; Labor Economics, 353; Undeveloped and Under-developed Countries, 593; Unemployment Causes, 600; Wealth, 626; Welfare Economics, 631.

PRICE FIXING

Type of economics: Industrial economics
Field of study: Industrial organization and public policy

Price fixing is the process by which one or more firms in a particular industry attempt to avoid unprofitable price competition by establishing and maintaining some mutually beneficial price level.

Principal terms

ANTITRUST LAWS: the body of law designed to ensure the maintenance of competitive market forces

CARTEL: a consortium of firms whose primary purpose is to thwart competition in an industry

COMPETITIVE MARKET FORCES: the forces that are generated through the efforts of producers and consumers to obtain the best possible terms when engaging in the exchange of goods and services

COMPETITIVE PRICE: the price that results when firms independently compete against one another in an attempt to maximize their profits

CONTESTABLE MARKET: a market in which it is easy for new firms to enter and contest existing firms for a share of the profits

PRODUCT DIFFERENTIATION: the process by which firms make their products appear as different from their competitors'

Overview

Price fixing refers to the process by which a firm or group of firms is able to manipulate the price of a good by either preventing or reducing price competition in an industry. When more than one firm is involved, the process is referred to as collusive price fixing (although the term "collusive" or "collusion" by itself may refer to a much broader range of interfirm coordination). As a result, price fixing may be viewed as similar to the fixing of a sporting event, since in both cases the outcome is artificially influenced by participants' failure to compete to the fullest of their abilities. The incentives to participate in price-fixing arrangements are derived from the fact that under certain circumstances it is the most profitable option. More bluntly, under certain circumstances firms can ensure for themselves higher profits by not competing, because under certain circumstances the profit-maximizing efforts by one firm (competition) are neutralized by the profit-maximizing efforts of its opponents. The net result of these opposing efforts is a decrease in industry or per-firm profits.

In the absence of a price-fixing arrangement, individual firms compete aggressively among themselves for a share of the industry profits. This competition not only provides a strong incentive for firms in the industry to refrain from setting too high a price but also encourages firms to cut their own prices if they believe that their revenues will increase significantly as a result. The reason for this is that, other factors being equal, consumers will migrate to the firms with the lowest prices, causing firms with relatively higher prices to sell little if any of their product. Therefore, in an effort to gain sales or prevent themselves from losing sales, firms have a strong incentive to cut prices until their per-unit profit margins are so small that further cuts would do more harm than good. This type of competition is most likely to take place when there is not a significant difference among the competing firms' products: The more similar the products of competing firms are, the more likely consumers are to substitute one product for another on the basis of price alone.

Different participants in the market have different views regarding this uninhibited price competition. For consumers, the price competition is a real boon, because it causes market prices to exceed costs by relatively small margins. Firms, however, have a different view. Firms recognize that competition results in lower prices, which in turn give rise to lower profits. As a result, firms experience strong and natural incentives to try to increase their profit margins by reducing the level of competition. One way of reducing competition is for firms to strike some type of price-fixing agreement, either formally or informally, thereby preventing or discouraging competition in the form of continued price cuts.

Although price fixing is one method of reducing competition, it is not the only method by which competition may be reduced. Price fixing makes sense only when, in the absence of a price-fixing arrangement, firms are likely to engage in aggressive price competition. Such price competition, in turn, will only make sense when competing firms' products are reasonably close substitutes. Therefore, firms may be able to isolate themselves from competition by making their products appear as different from competing products as is practical, thereby reducing the degree of substitutability between the products. This type of nonprice competition is referred to as product differentiation. When the nature of the product is such that significant nonprice differences are possible, such as may be the case for automobiles or home appliances, there may be little incentive to enter into any price-fixing agreement.

Another factor which may provide a disincentive for price fixing lies in firms' perceptions about their abilities to sustain such an agreement. If firms believe that other firms will not stick to the agreement or that new firms will continually enter the market and disrupt the agreement, then there will be little incentive to enter into such an agreement.

Finally, and perhaps most important, firms may decide not to enter into price-fixing agreements because, under many circumstances in the United States and other countries, price fixing is illegal. These governments believe that the natural competitive market forces produce important beneficial results. Specifically, these governments recognize the way in which such forces keep prices down. Although firms continue to break the law and attempt to fix prices, the law serves as an additional and substantial deterrent.

Applications

In a classic market scenario, prices are determined by competition. In a town in which there is a single gasoline station, the price at which the owner will sell her gasoline will initially be based on her experience and understanding of the consumers in the market; she will select a price that maximizes profits. Assuming that the station operator is able to sell gasoline at a price of $1.25 per gallon, even though it costs her only $1.00 per gallon (including overhead and other operational expenses), if these profits are significantly larger than those being obtained by gasoline stations in the surrounding communities, some other station operator will have a strong incentive to come to the town and open a gasoline station of his own. If that were to happen, then the new station might have to start out with a price lower than $1.25 per gallon, such as $1.22 per gallon, in order to draw customers away from the existing station. To prevent the loss of all of her customers, the operator of the old station will have to lower her price as well, presumably to $1.22. This price cutting will continue to take place until neither station has an incentive to mark down its price further, because of shrinking profits. Thus, in the end, the two different gasoline stations will split the market, but at a very low profit level.

When firms compete for sales as in the above example, the final price that is formed is referred to as the competitive price, because that final price is the result of firms' competing against one another until no one has an incentive to make further price cuts. The consequences of this type of competition are a reduction in the profits of competing firms, while goods and services are made less expensive for consumers. Aggressive price competition, however, is not the only option available to the gasoline station operators. An alternative strategy would be for the operators to strike an agreement to split the market, with each firm charging $1.25 per gallon rather than splitting the market at the much lower competitive price. By agreeing to avoid price competition, the operators fix the price of gasoline, thereby securing profits over and above those that could be obtained by accepting the competitive price.

Are there any factors which might serve as a deterrent to price fixing? In this example, the station operators are more than happy to strike an agreement that will keep the price of gasoline at $1.25 per gallon. As was demonstrated when the second station entered into this market, however, this relatively high price may well attract additional competitors. If more operators were to set up stations in this market and if the firms wanted to maintain the $1.25 price, then the new operators would have to be brought into the agreement. Continually bringing new operators into the market will result in each station's serving a smaller share of the market, until the original two firms are no better off than if they were selling the gasoline at the competitive price and sharing the market among themselves. If the two original operators anticipate this problem, they probably will not decide to fix prices, as there would be no real benefit from the exercise. A market in which new firms can easily enter and begin to compete is said to be contestable. In other words, a market is said to be contestable when new firms can easily enter the market and contest existing firms for their sales. As a result, firms are not expected to concern themselves with price-fixing agreements when markets are contestable, as there is no apparent gain from such an agreement.

Several cases similar to this gasoline station example have taken place in the real world. One of the more celebrated examples took place in the electrical supplies industry in the late 1950's. This case involved as many as twenty-nine different firms that illegally conspired to fix prices on a wide range of products in the industry. In 1982, Robert Crandall, then president and chief executive of American Airlines, placed a phone call to Howard Putnam, then president and chief executive of Braniff Airways, in an effort to persuade his competitor that the present price competition was unprofitable and could be avoided. Much to Crandall's surprise, the telephone conversation had been tape-recorded and the justice department filed a suit against American Airlines. The airline was able to have the case dismissed on a technicality, but not before promising not to engage in such an act again.

The establishment of an agreement among competing firms may not be the only way in which prices are fixed. Another form of price fixing involves a process that is more frequently referred to as "retail price maintenance." This practice involves a wholesaler that prevents its retail customers from selling the wholesaler's products below some predetermined price. This practice reduces price competition at the retail level and prevents the wholesaler's customers from being driven out of the market. Although this practice is widespread, its legality is on rather tenuous ground, with decisions being passed down on a case-by-case basis.

Context

Records dating back hundreds of years provide documentation of firms explicitly engaging in efforts to fix prices. Oftentimes, such circumstances involved firms formally banding together and forming a consortium whose sole purpose was to thwart competition by fixing the price in the particular market. Such consortiums were, and still are, referred to as cartels, and although cartels did not always engage in price fixing, that was frequently their objective. British common law attempted to deal with these types of circumstances as early as 1552.

Market forces may provide both strong incentives to restrict competition and fix prices and disincentives to fix prices. Therefore, when disincentives do not naturally occur in a market, governments many times see fit to introduce their own. In the United States, the laws that have been produced to protect against price fixing as well as other anticompetitive actions fall under the umbrella title of antitrust law. The primary enforcers of these laws in the United States are the Department of Justice and the Federal Trade Commission. The enforcement of these laws unfortunately is not as straightforward as it might appear. For example, in the absence of any evidence aside from behavior, if two or more firms simultaneously raise their prices are they guilty of price fixing? Does this not seem to run contrary to how firms should respond to competitive market forces? These are the issues which the enforcers, as well as the courts, must address.

The difficulty in dealing with these issues stems from the vagueness of antitrust law. The major elements of United States antitrust law are contained in two pieces of legislation, the Sherman Antitrust Act (passed in 1890) and the Clayton Act (passed in 1914). Combined, these two pieces of legislation are designed to outlaw any practices which restrain free and competitive trade—such as price fixing. These laws were intentionally vaguely written with the hope that the courts could uphold the spirit of the law on a case-by-case basis. As history has demonstrated, however, interpreting the evidence in a wide and varied range of cases has been a difficult and sometimes impossible task for the courts to accomplish.

Bibliography

Porter, Michael E. *Competitive Strategy: Techniques for Analyzing Industries and Competitors.* New York: Free Press, 1980. An excellent book for gaining an understanding into the way in which firms compete and respond to competitive pressures. Although price fixing is not the focus of the text, its potential as a strategy is made apparent by the author's straightforward presentation.

Posner, Richard A., and Frank H. Easterbrook. *Antitrust Cases, Economic Notes, and Other Materials.* St. Paul, Minn.: West, 1982. The authors, two well-known judges and legal scholars, provide strong insights into the nature of competition among firms, the incentives to fix prices, and the objectives of antitrust law in the United States. Provides particularly interesting insights into the historical evolution of practices such as price fixing.

Scherer, F. M., and David Ross. *Industrial Market Structure and Economic Performance.* 3d ed. Boston: Houghton Mifflin, 1990. Chapters 7 through 9 provide probably the most complete discussion of price fixing and its legal implications to be found. A thorough listing of more detailed materials is also provided.

Shepard, William G. *The Economics of Industrial Organization.* 3d ed. Englewood Cliffs, N.J.: Prentice-Hall, 1990. A straightforward analysis of markets and the competition that takes place within them. Probably the most readily accessible book for the reader untrained in this area. Part 5 provides particularly important insights into the process of price fixing.

Sloman, John. *Essentials of Economics.* New York: Prentice Hall, 1998.

Stocking, George W., and Myron W. Watkins. *Cartels in Action.* New York: Twentieth Century Fund, 1946. An in-depth analysis of cartel formation and objectives, establishing important historical evidence as to when and why certain cartels have pursued price-fixing objectives.

Robert Lee

Cross-References

PRODUCTION AND COST FUNCTIONS

Type of economics: Quantitative methods
Fields of study: Econometrics and mathematical models; economic theory

Individuals in an economy engage in production, either directly or indirectly, in order to enhance their economic advantage and well-being. Output usually can be produced in manifold ways, as technological forces normally do not impose a unique input combination. Consequently, there are different costs that are associated with alternative activities. Economic choice criteria must be employed in order to select the most beneficial production for consumption.

Principal terms

COST MINIMIZATION: the ability of a producer to save resources and to achieve a higher realization of the ends of economic activity

EFFICIENT PRODUCTION: production that creates the maximum possible and desirable output of goods and services that available resources and know-how permit

MARGINAL COST FUNCTION: the relationship between changes in a firm's total cost and variations in its volume of production

OUTPUT GROWTH: growth that is limited by resource constraints and by how much output can be produced per extra unit of a resource

POTENTIAL OUTPUT: output that depends on the resources that are at an economy's disposal and the existing state of knowledge about efficient production

PRODUCTION FUNCTION: a function that depicts the maximum amount of output that can be obtained from each combination of inputs at a specified point in time

Overview

The problem of production is the transformation of inputs into outputs, that is, the process of transforming various kinds of labor; capital (such as plant, machinery, equipment, and tools); stocks of finished or intermediate goods (goods that have undergone some processing but have not yet been converted into final products); and natural resources (such as land, fuels, minerals, and forests) into economic goods and services. Economic goods and services are those that are scarce relative to the demand for them. The problem of scarcity arises because most things that economic actors need and desire are available only in limited supply. Therefore, production is constrained in relation to competing wants. For example, more and better food and leisure goods are desired, rather than a combination that would have more of one but less of the other.

Because all the goods or services that are desired cannot be obtained, the basic fact of economic life must be faced: the choice between alternative courses of action or satisfaction. When a choice must be made between scarce goods and services, the opportunity cost of a decision is necessarily being incurred. Opportunity cost is the cost of the things that are forgone by making one particular decision rather than selecting other available alternatives.

The prevalence of scarcity makes choices for all economic actors (consumers, producers, investors, government, exporters, and importers) the necessity of economic life.

Discussions of the economic theory of production usually begin with specific technological or engineering constraints and information. Nature imposes technological limitations on acts of transforming labor, materials, and energy into products, that is, making the various goods and services that people ultimately want or need. Usually, products can be produced in manifold different ways, as technological forces normally do not impose a unique input combination. At any given time, however, only certain combinations of inputs are technologically possible to produce a given quantity of products. In other words, technology limits and prescribes the feasible production alternatives.

If all available inputs are used, at any time, then there will be a maximum attainable amount of product (output) that can be produced by each and every combination of inputs. The technological (technical) relationship between outputs and inputs—that is, the maximum amount of product that can be attained from any specified combination of inputs that existing technology (know-how) permits—is called the production function. Clearly, decisions on inputs and outputs cannot be made independently. A knowledge of the relationship or mathematical function that determines and specifies the balance between the amount of output that can be produced and the quantities of various inputs that are used is essential to the economist. Economic decisions involve the characteristics and specification of relevant production functions (best engineering know-how), input prices, and the different costs that are associated with alternative activities. Thus, economic decisions select economic choice criteria for the most valuable or beneficial production for individual or collective consumption in the present and future. The underpinnings of the various cost-output relations are the production relations that are portrayed by and derived from the production function.

Technically, the growth of an economy's capacity to produce is limited by the quantity of its resources, the qualitative improvements of its labor force, and productivity (the amount of output that is produced by a unit of input). Thus, growth of output is limited by resource constraints and by how much output can be squeezed out per extra unit of resource that is used. Productivity, in turn, is determined in part by improvements in technology and organizational know-how, which itself depends on the allocation of resources to those activities and measures that facilitate a diffusion of knowledge and the mobility of resources. Productivity is also influenced by labor skills, education, motivation, the quantity and quality of capital, the supplies and quality of natural resources, and the incentives and working arrangements for resource utilization.

Efficient production means that an economy combines the inputs (factors of production such as labor, capital, land, and entrepreneurship) that are used by firms in their production process in such a way as to produce the maximum possible and desirable output of goods and services (for current consumption or for further production) that the available resources and know-how permit, in the light of alternative employments of resources. In other words, production efficiency means that it is impossible to reshuffle or redirect resources or to reorganize the production process—given the existing know-how and techniques of production—in order to produce a larger quantity of any one product without reducing the quantity of another product.

Production efficiency occurs when, under existing conditions, all the feasible exploitable opportunities for improvement have been exhausted. Society cannot have more of one product without having less of another: For example, it can only produce more military hardware by sacrificing some consumer goods. Note that the constrained choice of "more of one product means to have less of another" assumes the full utilization of existing resources and given know-how. If resources are unemployed, then society can (within limits) have more of both products. Also, if new resources are discovered or new inventions result in improvements in production techniques, then more of one product can be had without cutting back on the production of another product. Therefore, improvements in production techniques (technical and organizational progress) somewhat relax the production possibility constraints. When society's production possibility frontier is enhanced, however, new wants multiply. Thus, the fundamental problem of scarcity and choice remains.

Mathematical and economic analysis deals with variable quantities—quantities that can assume different values. The problem of production is a manifestation of the general economic problem—the transformation of economic quantities, such as inputs into outputs. It is necessary to discover the dependence or functional relationships between variables: How one variable depends on others and the way in which different variables are related to one another. One wants to discern whether quantities and associated variables merely change independently of one another or whether there is a functional connection between corresponding values, a dependence of one variable on another (in contrast to coincidental, disparate, and spurious relations or occurrences). A case in point is the production function that relates inputs to outputs.

The production function is a starting point for economic theory of production and cost price, national output and income, and growth. It portrays essential and specific technical (technological) and engineering data and relations. Note the need to introduce purely economic dimensions or coefficients of economic choice (such as prices) into an economic theory of production and cost.

Applications

The production function depicts the maximum amount of output that can be obtained from each and every combination of inputs (factors of production), at a specified point of time. The last stipulation is necessary because it delimits a given state of technical and organizational know-how. Each production function is defined for a given level of technology and, once technological innovations and technical progress are introduced, the production function changes (or shifts). Dynamic economies are characterized by rapid and significant changes and advances in production techniques (shifting production functions, or the rapid displacement of old production functions by new ones). A production technique is constant (unchanged) as long as the functional relations that express the dependence of product quantities on input quantities remain the same.

A production function does not merely show every quantity of inputs that technology prescribes in order to obtain a certain output. Production functions confine themselves to those combinations of inputs that are technically efficient. Methods or alternative sets of inputs that use more of any input than is technically indispensable simply waste resources. It is not necessary to know what the specific prices are in order to eliminate production processes that use more than the minimum amount of inputs that is needed to support a certain level of output.

When alternative production processes are considered, it is of interest to know how a given output can alternatively be produced by using "more cloth and less labor" or "more labor and less cloth." In economics, it is usually postulated that the decision maker aims to minimize the cost of production of whatever volume of production is produced, but this is not so only for the profit-maximizing producer. Cost minimization enables any producer, or even a nonprofit-oriented economy, to save resources and to achieve a higher realization of the ends of economic activity, however these ends are determined. The cost-minimizing (least-cost) producer can lower its cost by substituting labor for material. For example, the same output could be produced by using less material and more labor. Suppose that a tailor decides to economize on cloth, which costs $10 per unit, by cutting it more carefully, which entails an extra hour of labor at a wage of $6 per hour. If one less unit of cloth is needed by using one more hour of work, then a cost reduction of $4 has been achieved.

Note that, as far as the technologist and engineer see it, each of the alternative technical ways (combination of inputs, such as labor and material) is equally satisfactory for producing a specific output. Production theory usually postulates that many alternative ways of producing exist, each of which entails an alternative combination of resources use, which in turn, involves different associated costs. The economist, who is interested in containing costs, would select the method among the various technically equivalent production methods that would reduce the cost to its very minimum. This minimum will depend on the relative prices of inputs (wages and cloth in the above example).

In order to understand cost functions from a more familiar perspective, examine the case of a profit-maximizing firm. A firm would increase its profit as long as the additional revenue that it can realize from an extra unit sold is larger than what it costs to produce that extra unit. The economist examines the information that is needed for such a decision. The required data include a knowledge of the difference that the transaction would make to revenue and cost, as compared to a situation in which the transaction had not taken place. If the extra revenue (one unit of output × the price of output, such as $100) exceeds the extra or differential cost—what economists call marginal cost (such as $80)—then the execution of the transaction would enhance the firm's profit by $20.

Marginal cost is the increase in total cost that is required if the firm increases its output by one additional unit. The marginal cost function shows the relations between changes in the firm's total cost and variations in the volume of production. In other words, marginal cost is defined as the increment of total cost that comes from producing an extra unit of output. Usually, costs do not vary in equal proportion to the variations of output; that is, marginal costs do not remain constant irrespective of whether output is increased from 50 to 51 units or from 100 to 101 units. Underlying the cost relations are the production relations that are portrayed by and derived from the production function. An extra unit of output can be accomplished by using more labor, holding all other inputs constant (land or plant are the staple examples). The marginal (physical) product is the increase to total output that results from a one-unit increase in the input (labor), holding the amount of all other inputs (land) unchanged. Because of variable proportions, varying one input in successive small increments will eventually yield smaller and smaller increases in output. Diminishing returns implies decreasing marginal physical product if cooperating inputs are held constant. Consequently, the successive employment of labor, for example, results in a falling (smaller) marginal product of labor and generates smaller and smaller extra revenue than the employment of an additional unit of labor costs (one unit of labor × wage).

The behavior of costs in relation to variations of the volume of output (or the shapes of cost curves, if graphically depicted) is a matter of great importance in economics. An extra unit of output can also be accomplished by varying all inputs (such as both labor and land) proportionately. Doubling all inputs (both labor and land), however, might or might not result in a doubling of output. Economists call such situations "constant returns to scale" if the doubling of output occurs, "increasing returns to scale" when the output is more than doubled, and "decreasing returns to scale" when the output is less than doubled. Thus, an important characteristic of the production function is the nature of the return to scale—the rate at which output rises as all inputs are increased together.

A firm may respond to an increasing demand by merely intensifying the utilization of existing capacity. According to the law of diminishing returns, successive increases in inputs produce less and less incremental output. Thus, larger and larger quantities of inputs will be required in order to produce an extra unit of output. Productivity per unit of output then decreases and marginal cost rises. The implication is that, in order to enjoy extra quantities of one product, society must give up ever-increasing quantities of another product.

Note that, in production and related cost (and price decision) analysis, it is useful to distinguish between the short run (given capacity), the long run (all factors of production variable—a constant production function), and the very long run (when innovation, inventions, technical and organizational progress, and changing production functions determine production).

Context

Theories regarding the relationship between production and cost are the center of economic analysis. They have implications for almost the whole spectrum of economics, and indeed, motivations for the development of these theories stem from a variety of sources.

The Industrial Revolution released great productive powers. Adam Smith (1723-1790) and his followers—classical economists such as David Ricardo (1772-1823), John Stuart Mill (1806-1873), and arguably, Karl Marx (1818-1883)—tried to explain production growth and its propellers and mechanism. The classical economists, particularly Ricardo, presented cogent and strong arguments in favor of indirect production through foreign trade. The classical economists held that a nation's welfare increases necessarily in proportion to an increase in production—a view challenged by the marginal or neoclassical revolution in the 1870's.

Post-1870's economists stressed that in no sense is mere production as such a proper measure of well-being. Rather, it must be production for the ends that individuals want. Early neoclassical economists shifted the emphasis from the growth of production to exchange, to the allocation of given resources between competing uses, and to the logic of and criteria for choice. Much of the material that is found in economic principles and microeconomics textbooks reflects this trend. It can be best understood not as a separate topic but as part and parcel of the neoclassical theory of a profit-maximizing firm and of a neoclassical approach to the study of economics.

The resumption of interest in some of the great classical themes, such as growth and income distribution, in the post-World War II period shifted the attention of economists to questions of growth. The theoretical growth model-building industry became one of the most prestigious in economics. Despite the intrinsic value of that literature, some economists believed that it failed to address or deal satisfactorily with some fundamental issues. Ambitious work was also done on aggregate production functions for the U.S. economy and others. The empirical findings shed light on the sources of growth and gave rise to controversies about the extent to which the work corroborates neoclassical production theory (marginal productivity theory). Disputes arose about the proximate role of labor, capital, technical progress, and other components of economic growth. Textbooks on macroeconomics increasingly include chapters on economic growth and on policy measures to affect potential output (aggregate supply).

John Maynard Keynes (1883-1946) had great insight into the critical role of aggregate effective demand—the problem of finding enough buyers to ensure the remunerative sale of the goods and services that can be produced. Keynes determined that aggregate effective demand was a factor determining the degree to which an economy's productive potential is used. A vast literature on opportunities and limits to demand management followed, and fruitful work has been done on the integration of aggregate demand and aggregate supply approaches.

Bibliography

Ahiakpor, James C. W., ed. *Keynes and the Classics Reconsidered.* Boston: Kluwer Academic Publishers, 1998.

Feiwel, George R., ed. *Arrow and the Ascent of Modern Economic Theory.* London: Macmillan, 1987. An anthology that presents developments in modern economic theory, including advances in production theory at the frontiers of economics.

_____, ed. *The Economics of Imperfect Competition and Employment.* New York: New York University Press, 1989. A survey and critical analysis of developments in price and income theories.

_____, ed. *Issues in Contemporary Microeconomics and Welfare.* London: Macmillan, 1985. This compilation surveys major topics in microeconomics, including alternative theories of the firm.

Frisch, Ragnar. *Theory of Production.* Chicago: Rand McNally, 1965. A leading economist examines the fundamentals of production theory.

Kalecki, Michal. *Selected Essays on the Dynamics of the Capitalist Economy.* Cambridge, England: Cambridge University Press, 1971. Contains the essentials of Kalecki's theory of effective demand and income distribution and his novel theory of the firm.

Palley, Thomas I. *Plenty of Nothing: The Downsizing of the American Dream and the Case for Structural Keynesianism.* Princeton, N.J.: Princeton University Press, 1998.

Samuelson, Paul A., and William D. Nordhaus. *Economics.* 12th ed. New York: McGraw-Hill, 1985. An authoritative survey of major developments in a leading textbook. Part 1 explains basic economic concepts and how to read graphs. Part 4 examines the essentials of microeconomics. Part 5, chapter 26 discusses the theories of production and marginal products.

Scott, Allen John. *Regions and the World Economy: The Coming Shape of Global Production, Competition, and Political Order.* New York: Oxford University Press, 1998.

George R. Feiwel
Ida Feiwel

Cross-References

Business Organization, 57; Classical Economics, 74; Economists, 164; Elasticity, 175; Growth Theory, 281; History of Economics, 295; Law of Diminishing Returns, 372; Marginal Principle, 390; Production Theory, 507; Substitution, 558; Welfare Economics, 631.

PRODUCTION THEORY

Type of economics: General economics
Fields of study: Economic theory; industrial organization and public policy

The theory of production lies at the very foundation of the neoclassical theory of the firm. Firms are presumed to maximize profits, which involves producing their output in the most efficient manner. Production theory examines the relationships between inputs or factors of production and outputs. Specific quantitative input-output relationships are referred to as production functions.

Principal terms

INPUT-OUTPUT ANALYSIS: a specialized approach used in examining the interdependencies between the various sectors of an economy, typically assuming fixed technology

INPUTS: factors of production, such as physical capital or labor, that are utilized in the process of output generation

ISOQUANTS: graphical representations of those combinations of inputs that produce the same level of output

LONG RUN: the span of time over which a firm is able to alter freely the use of every input

MARGINAL PRODUCT: the additional output that is derived from the employment of one additional unit of an input

PRODUCTION FUNCTION: the explicit quantitative relationship indicating the maximum output obtainable from any given set of inputs

RETURNS TO SCALE: a measure of the relative change in output resulting from a change in the scale of a firm's operation, as determined by its input usage

SHORT RUN: the span of time over which at least one input is fixed at a particular level

STAGES OF PRODUCTION: the demarcations of input levels relating marginal product and average product

TECHNOLOGY: the current scientific state of the art of production

Overview

Economics has been defined as the study of the production and distribution of wealth. Certainly production is central to the resource allocation that is studied by economists. Microeconomics is typically divided into the study of households and the study of firms, which corresponds to the demand side and the supply side, respectively, of standard market analysis. The theory of the firm has production at its very core; supply requires production.

Production refers to the process by which inputs or factors of production are transformed into outputs or products. Production theory addresses the manner in which firms produce. Note that production is not an economic phenomenon, but rather a scientific or engineering activity. In order to produce a particular output or product, such as light bulbs, an engineer or scientist would be far more capable of identifying the necessary inputs and possible processes of production than an economist. Economists' interest in production stems from the intimate relationship between production and costs, the latter of which is an economic phenomenon.

In economics, firms are assumed to pursue the objective of maximum profits. Profits are the difference between the firm's revenues and its costs. Revenues are obtained by the production and sale of commodities, goods, or services; costs reflect payments to the factors of production or inputs that were used in the process of creating that output. If a firm is to maximize its profits, then it must produce efficiently. A firm is producing efficiently if its costs are minimized for any given output level. Efficiency can also be defined in a reciprocal fashion: A firm acts efficiently if it maximizes output for any given cost outlay.

Technological efficiency is embodied in the production function, the primary construct of production theory. A production function is a precise quantitative or mathematical representation of an input-to-output relationship. The production function specifies the maximum amount of output that can be produced with any given set or combination of inputs. When a production function is written, it is understood that the relationship is specified for a particular state of the art of production or technology. With an improvement in the production process, a new production function will result.

Production functions are categorized as short-run or long-run relationships. A short-run production function specifies an input-output relationship in which at least one input is fixed at some level. For example, if a manufacturer is unable to alter freely the number of machines in a shop (because of order delays or firm-specific installation adjustments), then that manufacturer's production function will reflect the fact that the number of machines in use is fixed at the current level. If a manufacturer is able to freely alter the use of every input, then this time horizon is defined as the long run. A long-run production function includes all inputs as variables.

Although most businesses use a wide range of inputs, there have traditionally been references to three factors of production: land, labor, and capital (or machines). It is standard to speak of a short-run production function relating output to labor input (all other variables being held constant). The long-run production function usually specifies output as a function of labor and capital.

Therefore, in the short run, there is a unique labor-output relationship. Holding other factors constant, increases in labor generally raise output, but by shrinking increments. For agricultural production on a single farm, the first farmer would work the most fertile land and would generate a certain amount of output. The next farmer would work less favorable land, and, while output will rise, it will generally increase by a smaller amount than from the application of the original worker. The change in output resulting from the application of one additional worker is called the marginal product or marginal physical product of labor.

This generally observed empirical phenomenon is known as the law of diminishing marginal productivity. Holding all inputs constant but one, increases in the variable input will raise output, but the marginal product of the variable input will eventually fall. This theory is also referred to as the law of diminishing returns.

As an extreme example, if more and more farmers were applied to the single farm, then there would be a point at which the last worker adds nothing to the farm's output. Additional laborers might actually begin to trample the crops; at this point, marginal product would become negative.

There are stages of production that are defined in the terms of the marginal product and the average product of the variable factor. The average product of an input is simply the number of units of output per unit of input. In the first stage of production, marginal product exceeds average product. The second stage is characterized by a marginal product which is below the average product, but which is still positive. In the third stage, the marginal product becomes negative. No competitive optimizing firm would ever produce in the first stage or the third stage, but a firm with monopoly power might produce in the first stage.

In the long run, there is no longer a single input-output relationship. There are generally many ways to produce any given level of output; one factor can typically be substituted for another in production. A given quantity of an agricultural product, for example, can be produced using many laborers and little capital (a labor-intensive approach) or using few workers and a large amount of farm machinery (a capital-intensive approach). The rate at which capital can be substituted for labor, holding output constant, is defined as the marginal rate of technical substitution.

The graphical representation of those input combinations that yield the same level of output are called isoquants. The firm, producing efficiently, will select that lowest-cost input combination that is capable of producing the target output level. The degree of input substitutability is seen in the curvature of the isoquants; a formal measure of the response in the use of inputs to changes in factor prices is the elasticity of substitution.

One of the most important characteristics of production is known as returns to scale. Returns to scale indicate the proportional change in output or production that results from expanding or contracting the size of a firm's operation. The scale of operation refers to the level of a firm's input usage. If a firm employs 20 percent more of every factor next year, and it experiences a 20 percent increase in output, then that firm will be said to exhibit constant returns to scale. If output were to increase by less than 20 percent, however, then that firm would display decreasing returns to scale. An increase in output greater than 20 percent would indicate increasing returns to scale.

Most firms experience increasing returns to scale at first, but decreasing returns to scale are encountered eventually. Increasing returns are readily seen with the use of specialized equipment, such as assembly-line processes, and task-specific labor. One rationale for businesspeople to organize production under one roof is to take advantage of these increasing returns. Decreasing returns appear when the business becomes too large and difficult to manage, which explains why one firm generally does not dominate an entire industry.

Applications

The primary employment of production theory has been to assist the firm, or other productive agencies, in utilizing its resources or inputs in the most efficient fashion. Production is a technological phenomenon, but knowledge of a firm's production function yields insight into costs and, therefore, optimal input use and output production. A firm which has estimated its production function can employ that knowledge to minimize its costs of production, which ensures that the firm will receive the highest possible profit.

The close association between production functions—the engineering entity—and cost functions—the economic entity—is known as a dual relationship. Duality allows for the determination of one of these functions from a knowledge of the other function. It may be easier to calculate a cost function than a production function, but given the estimated cost relationship, the associated production function can be derived. This ability has both practical applications and theoretical value.

Nobel Prize-winning economist Kenneth J. Arrow, who helped define the concept of "constant elasticity of substitution." (Nobel Foundation)

The econometric estimation of production functions, for large-scale operations, is fairly common, and a variety of functional specifications can be used. One of the most frequently employed production functions is the Cobb-Douglas function, which has several attractive features. A more general form named the "constant elasticity of substitution" (CES) production function was introduced by Kenneth J. Arrow, Hollis Chenery, Bagicha Singh Minhas, and Robert M. Solow in 1961. There has been an increasing use of what are known as flexible functional forms in production function estimation; these leave open to investigation the properties that the production function will exhibit.

While the role of production in microeconomics has been stressed, the ubiquitous nature of production is reflected in the fact that almost every area of economics hinges in one way or another on production theory. Since production theory is at the heart of the theory of the firm, it is crucial to the study of industrial organization and regulation. Empirical evidence on production functions has been used increasingly in antitrust and regulatory review cases. A natural monopoly would manifest itself in its production figures. Growth theory also builds on a country's production possibilities frontier. The theory of production underlies the production possibilities frontier, which indicates the feasible combinations of various outputs that a country could produce. The theory of international trade and the doctrine of comparative advantage center on the reality of different countries having different production functions.

Technological progress at the microeconomic level generates a new production function for the firm being studied and typically presents itself in a volatile and erratic way. At the macroeconomic level, though, economists can identify trends in the level of technology. Sir John R. Hicks and Roy Harrod provided the fundamental research in this important area.

Input-output analysis is a very specialized model of production relations. It examines the links between the different sectors of the economy based on a simple linear productivity model. With this approach, a fixed coefficient technology is assumed, which means that the inputs must be combined in an exactly determined fashion with no possibility of substitution. One of the more useful applications of this approach was in the avoidance of bottlenecks in production in command (or nonmarket-oriented) economies.

Production theory has even filtered over to the theory of household behavior. Gary S. Becker's theory of the family views many household activities as (nonmarket) production. For example, a home-cooked meal includes as inputs the necessary groceries, kitchen utilities and utensils, and the time and labor of the family members involved in the preparation and cleanup.

Context

The classical economists, such as Adam Smith, Thomas Robert Malthus, and David Ricardo, had poorly developed theories of production. Because it was unclear how the various inputs (land, labor, and capital) contributed to the production of the society's output, a fully developed theory of distribution was not derived. John Stuart Mill actually denied a link between production and distribution.

Smith did perceive the gains from organizing production within one firm. His example of the pin factory is considered to be classic. Smith relates that one man producing pins could make, at most, twenty in a day. He also observed that a pin factory of ten men, each doing specialized tasks, could make forty-eight thousand pins in one day. This situation is a case of increasing returns to scale and justifies the existence of firms.

While several classical economists offered insights into the production process, the marginal productivity theory did not evolve until after the marginal revolution of the 1870's which immediately affected the theory of value. The leading contributors to the development of modern production theory include Johann Heinrich von Thünen, Arthur Berry, Philip H. Wicksteed, John Bates Clark, Alfred Marshall, and Knut Wicksell.

The marginal productivity theory indicates that firms will hire a factor of production as long as the value of the output that the factor generates exceeds the additional cost of hiring the factor. From this observation, the theory of distribution follows rather directly. Clark was so convinced of this theory's correctness that he lent it normative support.

Once a standard production function is written, the entire corpus of neoclassical economic theory follows. There was a debate in the 1960's regarding the appropriateness of the specification of production functions and their behavior; it has come to be known as the Cambridge controversy because the primary proponents were located in Cambridge, England, and Cambridge, Massachusetts. The possibility of pathological behavior in production, termed "reswitching," appeared to the British economists to compromise some of the basic neoclassical results. The American economists questioned the specialized instances that might generate the unusual results, labeling them as highly unlikely.

Although there have been alternative representations of production relationships, including input-output models, multivalued production correspondences, and set-theoretic models, production remains paramount to much of modern economics. To quote C. E. Ferguson: "Neoclassical theory turns upon production functions; and it has been shown that when a model contains a production function, neoclassical results are obtained. That is just to say, so long as production functions are explicitly used in models of economic behavior, there are no 'alternative' theories. The models are essentially neoclassical and so are the results."

Bibliography
Ahiakpor, James C. W., ed. *Keynes and the Classics Reconsidered*. Boston: Kluwer Academic Publishers, 1998.

Carlson, Sune. *A Study on the Pure Theory of Production.* London: P. S. King, 1939. This seminal work is an early survey of the main principles of production theory that are typically found in modern textbook presentations.

Douglas, Paul H. "Are There Laws of Production?" *American Economic Review* 38 (1948): 1-41. An excellent discourse on classical production and distribution theory, the development and generalization of the Cobb-Douglas production function, and the empirical results prior to 1948. Douglas was one of the codiscoverers of the production specification bearing his name and that of Cobb.

Ferguson, C. E. *The Neoclassical Theory of Production and Distribution.* New York: Cambridge University Press, 1969. An encyclopedic treatment of neoclassical production theory, this book covers some topics typically circumvented by other works on production. These subjects include multiproduct firms, vintage capital models, a taxonomy of technological change, and the learning-by-doing approach.

Kemp, Murray C., ed. *Production Sets.* New York: Academic Press, 1982. This collection of essays offers a modern look at production theory using a set-theoretic approach, methods which have dominated general equilibrium analysis.

Nerlove, Mark. *Estimation and Identification of Cobb-Douglas Production Functions.* Chicago: Rand McNally, 1965. The main thrust of this work is to apply modern production theory empirically. Focusing on the Cobb-Douglas production function, Nerlove demonstrates how this production formula has been, and can be, statistically estimated.

Palley, Thomas I. *Plenty of Nothing: The Downsizing of the American Dream and the Case for Structural Keynesianism.* Princeton, N.J.: Princeton University Press, 1998.

Salvatore, Dominick. *Microeconomics.* New York: HarperCollins, 1991. An outstanding text which gives an extremely lucid presentation of production theory, both in the short run and in the long run. The stages of production, as well as the relationship between production functions and cost curves, are discussed. A very accessible and highly recommended reference.

Sato, Kazuo. *Production Functions and Aggregation.* Amsterdam: North-Holland, 1975. While the microeconomic theory of production is well understood, the study of macroeconomic or aggregate production is less established. This monograph is an examination of the nature, properties, and statistical estimation of aggregate production functions.

Shephard, Ronald W. *Theory of Cost and Production Functions.* Princeton, N.J.: Princeton University Press, 1970. The classic treatment of the duality relationships between production functions and cost functions. This book is necessarily rather technical, and it presumes some mathematical sophistication.

Stigler, George J. *Production and Distribution Theories: The Formative Period.* New York: Macmillan, 1941. Developed from Stigler's Ph.D. thesis, this critical survey chronicles the development of the marginal productivity theory and its relationship to a cohesive theory of distribution. The coverage spans the work of ten primary economists from 1870 to 1895.

Walters, A. A. "A Survey of Cost and Production Functions." *Econometrica* 31 (1963): 1-66. The definitive article on production functions. Walters begins with the theoretical basis for the set-theoretic approach to production, continues on to functional specifications, covers the production-cost relationship, and critiques the existing econometric literature.

He presents a comparison of previous empirical studies and concludes with an extensive reference compilation.

Timothy M. Weithers

Cross-References

Business Organization, 57; Classical Economics, 74; Economists, 164; Elasticity, 175; History of Economics, 295; Law of Diminishing Returns, 372; Production and Cost Functions, 500; Substitution, 558; Technology, 581; Welfare Economics, 631.

PROFIT AND PROFIT THEORY

Type of economics: General economics
Field of study: Economic theory

At the microeconomic level, profit consists of the net revenue that is received by the firm after it pays its production costs. At the macroeconomic level, profit equals the surplus that remains after the consumption needs of workers have been met. In other words, profit is the portion of production that is available to be accumulated as capital.

Principal terms

AGGREGATE: refers to the level of the economy as a whole

CAPITALIST: one who owns the means of production (capital, or plant and equipment); an entrepreneur

FACTORS OF PRODUCTION: the major inputs into the production process, which are land (including raw materials), labor, and capital (plant and equipment)

MACROECONOMICS: a branch of economics that is concerned with the economy as a whole

MARGINAL PRODUCTIVITY THEORY: the neoclassical theory that the return to a factor of production is determined by its contribution to the production process; these returns are rent (which goes to land), wages (to labor), and profit (to capital)

MICROECONOMICS: a branch of economics that is concerned with the level of the individual firm or household

OLIGOPOLIZED INDUSTRY: an industry in which a few firms account for most production; characterized by market power (the ability of firms to set prices) and barriers to entry

PERFECTLY COMPETITIVE INDUSTRY: an industry in which there are so many buyers and so many sellers that none can influence prices; characterized by the absence of barriers to entry to new firms

WORKER: one who works for wages

Overview

Economists do not agree on the approach that should be taken in defining profit. For example, profit can be defined at the microeconomic level or at the macroeconomic level. Furthermore, each school of thought in economics defines profit differently. Finally, theoretical definitions of profit may diverge greatly from the definitions that are used by businesspeople (and tax collectors) in the real world.

At the microeconomic level, in a perfectly competitive industry, competition will push the price of a product down to the level at which only "normal" profits are earned. The price of the good would be just high enough to include all the costs of production, including labor costs, raw materials costs, and overhead costs, with a net revenue (profit) that is just high enough to compensate the firm's capitalist owner for the amount that he or she has invested in the firm. Whether the owner invested his or her own funds or borrowed them, the profit that is earned from production must be as high as that which the owner could have earned in other possible investment projects that have a similar risk. If the price of the product were lower, then profits would be below normal. Consequently, firms would leave the industry and move to others with higher (normal) profits, which would cause the price of this good to rise and allow the remaining firms to earn the normal profit.

On the other hand, if the price were too high, then firms would earn above normal profits (called "economic profits" or "economic rent"), attracting new firms into the industry. This would push prices back down, so that only normal profits could be earned. Thus, in neoclassical theory, competition ensures that profits will tend toward "normal" levels because new firms would enter any industry which earned extra profits. If an industry is monopolized (one firm) or oligopolized (several firms), however, then extra profits may be maintained even in the long run because of barriers to entry of new firms.

There has been a long-running controversy regarding the source of profit. Karl Marx (1818-1883) argued in *Das Kapital* (1867) that profits arise because workers are exploited. By this, Marx meant that labor is paid less than the full value of its product. This is most easily explained through the use of an example. Assume that one worker in a hat factory produces five hats per day, each of which sells for $20. Thus, the worker produces a total value of $100 per day (five hats multiplied by $20). Assume that the going wage (which is competitively established) for a worker of average skill in the hat industry is $55 per day. Therefore, this factory will pay the worker the competitive wage, or $55. The worker has produced a total value of $100, however, which means that the owner of the firm "appropri-ates" (in Marx's terminology) $45. Marx called this $45 the "surplus value," that is, the value that was produced, but not received, by labor. Out of this surplus value, the owner of the firm may have to pay taxes to the government, interest to banks (if the owner had borrowed funds to start the production process), overhead (such as management and advertising), and other costs. Whatever remains out of the surplus value would be profit for the owner.

In neoclassical theory, it was long believed that profits arise because of "round-about" production and the "pain of waiting." The entrepreneur must advance accumulated savings to workers and raw materials suppliers in order to undertake the production process. Because production takes time, the entrepreneur incurs a hardship between the time the workers are hired and the time at which finished products are sold. The more complicated the production process (which would be partially determined by the sophistication and quantity of the machines that are used), the longer the wait. Thus, the capitalist would have to be rewarded for the "pain of waiting" during the "roundabout" production process in order to induce him or her to advance funds. This reward for waiting would be profit.

Later, after the development of marginal productivity theory, neoclassical economists adopted the view that profit merely represents a payment to one of the factors of production. According to this approach, there are three factors of production: land, labor, and capital. Each of these earns a return (rent, wage, and profit, respectively) because each contributes to the production process. In equilibrium, a competitive economy is supposed to produce the result that each factor is paid exactly according to its contribution. Thus, the neoclassical approach is very different from Marx's approach, in which labor is the only factor of production and, thus, produces all value.

Unfortunately, it was proven later that neither the neoclassical "pain of waiting" model nor the marginal productivity theory can explain profit; that is, it is not possible to construct an internally consistent theory in which profit is equal to the contribution that capital makes to the production process, nor is it possible to link profits to the length of the production process. Much literature has been written on this subject, which has become known as the "capital debate" or the "Cambridge controversy." As a result, neoclassical theory has been left without a rigorous and consistent theory of profit.

Some economists have tried to formulate a theory of profit that can apply to an economy that is not perfectly competitive. If a firm has market power and is able to prevent the entry of new firms into its industry, then it is able to set its price high enough to maintain profits even in the long run. Some economists (and many entrepreneurs) argue that firms simply calculate costs of production and then add a "markup" over costs when they set the price. For example, a firm might use a rule of thumb in which prices are set 25 percent above costs. This allows the firm to cover all costs and retain profits. Again, the assumption of market power is essential—in a perfectly competitive industry, new entrants would lower the markup until prices just covered costs and normal profits. Yet, an oligopoly firm can maintain its markup through price leadership, product differentiation, and intensified advertising.

Applications

Profit theory also can be applied at the macroeconomic level, with very interesting results. At the microeconomic level, profit refers to a situation in which revenue exceeds costs. At the macroeconomic level, profit theory is necessarily concerned with the distribution of national income between workers and capitalists.

National income may be divided into three main categories: wage income (W), profit income (P), and taxes, or government income (T). Similarly, national spending (the gross national product, or GNP) may be divided among consumption out of wage income (Cw), consumption out of profit income (Cp), government spending (G), investment spending (I), and net exports (NX). Each dollar that is spent must be received as income by someone, so national income must be equal to national spending. Using this identity, an equation may be formed that shows that the sum of the various categories of income equals the sum of the components of spending: $W + P + T = Cw + Cp + G + I + NX$.

Michal Kalecki (1899-1970) rearranged this equation to create an identity for aggregate profit. His profit equation, which is one of the most important macroeconomic relations in economic theory, is: $P = Cp + I + Def + NX - Sw$, where Def is the government's deficit (government spending, minus taxes) and Sw is saving out of wages. Kalecki argued that aggregate profits are determined by consumption out of profit income, plus investment spending, plus government deficit spending, plus net exports, minus saving out of wages. An increase of consumption out of profits, investment, government deficit spending, or net exports must increase profit at the aggregate level. On the other hand, an increase of saving out of wages would lower profits.

Kalecki argued that saving out of wage income would be almost insignificant because worker's wages tend to be so low that workers are forced to spend all their income on necessities. If workers do save a portion of their income, however, then capitalist profits are diminished because fewer goods and services are sold to workers. Similarly, Kalecki argued that net exports could be ignored for many countries simply because they are small relative to the size of the GNP. This assumption clearly would not be valid for a country such as Japan in 1990, which exported far more than it imported. In this case, the profits that would be received by Japanese capitalists would be large.

Kalecki also believed that consumption out of profit would be small simply because capitalists are primarily interested in accumulating capital, rather than in high levels of consumption. If capitalists do consume, however, profit income will be higher because more goods and services can be sold. Finally, prior to World War II, most governments tended to run balanced budgets. Thus, Kalecki believed that it is safe to assume that the government's deficit can be ignored. If, however, the government does run a deficit, profit income will be higher because goods and services can be sold to the government.

If Kalecki's various simplifying assumptions are combined, then it is assumed that saving out of wages, consumption out of profits, government deficits, and net exports are all equal to zero. In this case, aggregate profits exactly equal investment spending. If investment rises, profits rise; if investment falls, profits fall. Kalecki's theory is frequently summarized in the statement that "workers spend what they get; capitalists get what they spend." By this, he meant that workers consume all their income (saving out of wages is zero) and that capitalist spending on investment goods determines profit (the income that is received by capitalists).

This result may seem to be mysterious—why would investment spending create profits? This can be clarified through an analysis of a hypothetical economy. Assume that there are only two industries, one which produces consumption goods (food) and one which produces investment goods (machines). Assume also that there are workers in both industries who receive wage incomes and that each worker spends all of his or her income on consumption goods. The wages that are paid to workers in the consumption goods industry will equal the cost of producing food, while the wages that are paid to workers who are producing machines will represent spending on investment. Assume that the capitalist owners of the two industries do not consume, as well as Kalecki's other simplifying assumptions: The government budget is balanced and there are no net exports.

Given these assumptions, the total spending on food will be equal to the wages that are received by workers in both the consumption goods industry and the investment goods industry. Yet, the cost of producing food is equal to the wages that are paid to workers only in the consumption goods industry. Thus, the wages that are paid to workers in the investment goods industry are the source of profits that are received by the capitalist owners of the food industry. This is because, while the workers in the investment goods industry spend their wages on food, and this income is received by capitalists in the consumption goods industry, these wages were not a cost that was incurred by these capitalists.

The key, then, to Kalecki's profit equation is the notion that profit income is generated when there is spending on consumption goods out of income that does not represent a cost that is incurred by capitalists in the consumption goods industry. Economists have extended this model in order to relax Kalecki's restrictive assumptions and allow for saving out of wages, capitalist consumption, net exports, and government deficits. For example, net exports represent spending by foreigners out of their income. Because the income of foreigners does not represent a cost that is incurred by domestic capitalists, net exports must generate profit income. Similarly, deficit spending by the government represents spending that is not based on income that is provided by capitalists; that is, no capitalist had to give the government income.

It is best to think of Kalecki's equation in terms of gross profit rather than net profit. Clearly, wages are not the only expense that is faced by the capitalist owners of the consumption goods industry. Out of the gross profit that is received by these capitalists, there are a variety of other costs that must be paid, such as interest costs on loans and overhead expenses. After these payments, the owners are left with net profit.

Finally, it is important to note that Kalecki's equation applies only to aggregate profits. There is no reason to believe that an increase in the investment spending by an individual firm will raise its profits. While its investment spending will generate more profits at the aggregate level, the individual firm may not receive any additional profit. Similarly, an increase in deficit spending by the government will raise aggregate profits, but there is no guarantee that a particular firm will receive any of the increase.

Context

Profits are essential for the functioning of capitalist economies. In a capitalist society, most production is undertaken by the owners of firms in the expectation that profits will be generated. If owners believed that sales revenues would just cover costs, then they would not begin the production process. It is the expectation of profit that drives capitalist production.

This does not mean, however, that every capitalist is always successful in obtaining profit. In the real world, many expectations will not be fulfilled—some capitalists will find that revenues just cover costs, while others will find that revenues are below costs. If a sufficiently large number of capitalists do not receive profits and become discouraged, then they might decide to cut production. This can make matters worse; if a large number of capitalists reduce production, employment and wages fall, sales to workers fall, and profits will decline.

As Kalecki's equation makes clear, spending on investment goods is an important determinant of the aggregate level of profits. When capitalists are optimistic about the future, they will increase investment spending in order to buy more plant and equipment so that they may increase future output. This investment spending will simultaneously increase aggregate profits and reinforce optimism. On the other hand, when capitalists are pessimistic and reduce investment, aggregate profits fall and make the pessimism appear justified.

Fortunately, investment spending is not the only source of profits. If a country can increase its net exports, its profits can rise and help to raise the expectations of capitalists. Similarly, deficit spending by the government can increase profits and help to generate optimism. Thus, Kalecki's equation supports the policy recommendations which came out of John Maynard Keynes's *The General Theory of Employment, Interest and Money* (1936): If an economy is in a depression, the government should use deficit spending to lift it out.

Bibliography

Clark, John Bates. *The Distribution of Wealth.* New York: Macmillan, 1899. One of the first expositions of the marginal productivity theory of distribution, by the economist who is usually cited as the "father" of the theory.

Dobb, Maurice. *Theories of Value and Distribution Since Adam Smith.* Cambridge, England: Cambridge University Press, 1973. Dobb traces the development of the two competing theories of value (the labor theory of value and the utility theory of value). Primarily designed for specialists.

Hamouda, O. F., ed. *Controversies in Political Economy: Selected Essays of G. C. Harcourt.* New York: New York University Press, 1986. A collection of essays written by Harcourt, a famous economist who is quite good at summarizing and explaining difficult theories for general audiences. In part 3, three essays on the "capital debate" or "Cambridge controversy" examine the problems that are faced by neoclassical theory in dealing with the determination of profit. While Harcourt has probably written the simplest and clearest exposition of this topic that is available, nonspecialists will find these essays difficult.

Kalecki, Michal. *Theory of Economic Dynamics.* London: Allen & Unwin, 1954. Contains an exposition of Kalecki's profit equation, as well as his theory of the business cycle. While much of the analysis concerns profit at the macroeconomic level, Kalecki also explains the markup theory of the determination of micro level profits. Nonspecialists will find this book moderately difficult.

Kregel, J. A. *Rate of Profit, Distribution, and Growth: Two Views.* London: Macmillan, 1971. Kregel examines the neoclassical theory of profit, the "Cambridge controversy," the Cambridge (or post-Keynesian) approach to profit, and the relation between profit and economic growth. Probably the best single source on profit theory, covering a wide range of viewpoints and topics.

Marx, Karl. *Capital.* Translated by Ernest Mandel. 3 vols. New York: Vintage Books, 1977-1981. Marx's classic work on his theory of the functioning of capitalist economies. Contains his labor theory of value, which explains the source of profit as the ability of labor to produce surplus value. While this is a difficult book, it is rewarding.

Palley, Thomas I. *Plenty of Nothing: The Downsizing of the American Dream and the Case for Structural Keynesianism.* Princeton, N.J.: Princeton University Press, 1998.

Panico, Carlo. *Interest and Profit in the Theories of Value and Distribution.* New York: St. Martin's Press, 1988. Examines various theoretical approaches to profit, including the neoclassical approach and Karl Marx's approach, at a fairly advanced level.

Samuelson, Paul A. *Economics.* 9th ed. New York: McGraw-Hill, 1973. A traditional textbook with sections devoted to both microeconomics and macroeconomics. Samuelson was one of the famous economists involved in the "Cambridge controversy." He at first tried to defend the neoclassical theory of profit, but later admitted that it is flawed.

Skousen, Mark, and Kenna C. Taylor. *Puzzles and Paradoxes in Economics.* Brookfield, Vt.: Edward Elgar, 1997.

L. Randall Wray

Cross-References

Quotas and Tariffs

Type of economics: International economics
Field of study: Commercial policy

Quotas and tariffs are two of the methods that governments use to protect domestic industry from import competition. Their functions are to create a scarcity of import products and raise the prices of imported products, so that consumers will be induced to buy domestic products instead. In developing countries, tariffs are also an important source of tax revenue. Governments have agreed that tariffs are the most acceptable way to regulate international trade; however, they continue to employ nontariff barriers such as quotas because of pressures from domestic industry groups and concerns about the direction of the world economy.

Principal terms

AD VALOREM TAX: a tax imposed on goods as a percentage of the invoice value
INFANT INDUSTRY: a new industry that cannot grow without protection from established foreign competitors
NONTARIFF BARRIER: a trade barrier other than a tariff, such as a quota, restrictive import licensing system, or restrictive standards and quality import inspection procedure
PROTECTIONISM: efforts made by governments to protect domestic industry from foreign competition
TARIFF STRUCTURE: the relationship between tariffs on products in a given industrial sector
TRADE MANAGEMENT: the intervention of governments in trade flows between nations
VOLUNTARY EXPORT RESTRAINT: an agreement between an exporting country and an importing country under which the exporter agrees to limit exports through a quota

Overview

Quotas and tariffs are two methods that governments use to regulate imports. A tariff, or duty, is a tax levied on merchandise that crosses national borders. The tax is paid by the importer and is passed to the consumer in the price of the merchandise. The majority of tariffs are levied against imports, although a few countries charge export duties on certain products. A quota is a quantitative restriction on the amount of a product that the importing country will accept within a given period, usually one year. A tariff quota is a restriction under which a specified amount of the product may enter the country duty free or at reduced rates, but once that amount is exceeded, a higher tariff applies.

Quotas may be global, applying to a specific product regardless of the country of origin, or unilateral, affecting only products from certain countries. In the case of a product that undergoes manufacturing in more than one country (for example, shirts cut in Hong Kong and sewn in Taiwan), the importing government will use a formula based on the percentages of manufacturing done in each country. The majority percentage determines which country that the product came from; if 80 percent of the manufacturing activity for the shirts took place in Taiwan, the imports will be counted against Taiwan's quota share.

Governments usually administer their quotas through a licensing system. Licenses are issued to importers on fractions of the quota. In fact, many unofficial quotas are hidden inside licensing systems; once the limit on imports has been reached, the government simply stops issuing licenses.

Tariffs may be either ad valorem or specific. An ad valorem tariff is a duty calculated as a percentage of the value of the imported product, such as 5 percent of a $10 million shipment. The value of the shipment may be subject to negotiation with customs officials, depending on how much of the freight, transportation, and insurance costs they decide to include in the valuation. A specific duty is a specific amount charged per physical unit of the shipment, such as $3.00 per pair or $18.00 per ton—it is not negotiable. Both types of duties may be charged on the same shipment—for example, 5 percent plus $3.00 per pair—which are called compound duties.

Specific duties are easy for customs officials to calculate, as the only information necessary is the number of units in the shipment. Importers also find specific duties easier to manage because there is no disagreement over valuation; however, a specific duty may result in a proportionately higher price increase than an ad valorem duty. For example, suppose that the ad valorem tariff on leather shoes is 10 percent. Shoes imported from Italy may be valued at $40.00 per pair, for a duty of $4.00, costing the importer $44.00. The duty on shoes from Taiwan at $10.00 per pair would be $1.00, a cost of $11.00 to the importer. If a specific duty of $4.00 per pair were applied instead of an ad valorem duty, the Italian shoes would still cost $44.00, but the price of the Taiwanese shoes would rise to $14.00. Thus, the actual duty rate on the Taiwanese shoes would be 10 percent under the ad valorem tariff, but 40 percent under the specific duty.

Tariff rates are published in national tariff schedules, which are revised periodically as the tariffs change. Because there is a very large number of products traded internationally, with new products added frequently, tariff rates are assigned to numerically coded groups and subgroups of products rather than individual products. The tariff schedule may have one or more columns. In a single-column schedule, the tariff is the same for a specific product regardless of the country of origin. In a multi-column schedule, the product will have different duty rates depending on which exporting country it came from. The lowest rates apply to exporting countries with which tariff treaties have been negotiated.

In developed countries, tariffs are used primarily to raise the cost of imports. In developing countries, tariffs also function as revenue collection mechanisms. Tariffs provide 20 percent to 60 percent of the government revenue of developing countries, compared to 5 percent in industrial countries. The average tariff rate for manufactured products in industrial countries is about 7 percent, with a large number of items entering duty free, but for some sensitive products, rates are still over 30 percent. Average rates in developing countries are much higher, sometimes more than 100 percent.

Tariffs and quotas are regarded by economists and exporters as barriers to trade. A tariff barrier is a situation in which the tariff rate on a particular product is so high that the product cannot be price competitive in the domestic market. Quotas are one of a group of trade barriers known as nontariff barriers, that is, mechanisms that restrict imports by means other than high tariffs.

Applications

The purpose of quotas and tariffs is to protect domestic producers from import competition. Quotas provide a greater degree of protection, since there is only a certain amount of the import product available regardless of how much consumers are willing to pay for it. When the permitted amount is gone, consumers must buy domestic products. Agricultural products are the items most frequently protected by quotas because of government farm price support policies. Other products subject to quota protection include steel, textiles and apparel, and Japanese automobiles. About twenty-five countries have official quotas (quotas that are not disguised in licensing systems). For example, the United States has quotas on milk, butter, cheese, chocolate, peanuts, cotton, some types of steel, and several other products. Canada has a quota on leather footwear. Imports of Japanese cars are restricted by quota to 3 percent of the market in France, and thirty-five hundred units per year in Italy. Developing countries also have quotas on various products. Governments usually base quota ceilings on the amount of imports of the product in a selected past year (sometimes several years back). They will often allow small incremental increases in the quota each year, such as a 1 percent increase over the previous year's imports.

Quotas are the major feature of voluntary export restraints (VERs), agreements under which producing countries limit their exports of specific products. The products are usually low-priced items which, if exported in unlimited amounts, would flood the market and present a serious threat to domestic industry. The agreements are not really voluntary; the exporting countries, under pressure from the importing countries, set quotas of their own in order to avoid retaliatory protectionist legislation in the import markets. The most wide-ranging VER is the Multifiber Arrangement (MFA), a system of bilateral agreements regulating trade in textiles and apparel. The MFA sets quotas on textile and apparel exports from more than forty developing countries (such as Hong Kong and Taiwan) and to the United States, the European Community, and other developed countries. Another large-scale VER is Japan's quota on exports of automobiles to the United States. There are more than two hundred fifty VER's in effect worldwide. Voluntary export quota ceilings are usually based on market share.

Tariffs are designed to protect domestic industry by increasing the prices of imported products relative to domestic products; this gives consumers an incentive to buy domestic products, rather than compelling them to buy domestically when the quota supply of foreign goods runs out. The degree of protection provided by tariffs can vary greatly; sometimes there is no protection at all. Imported products from low-wage countries may be so inexpensive that they can be priced far below competing domestic products, even with high tariffs plus retail markup; this is often the case with textiles, apparel, rubber footwear, plastic ware, and small electronics. In other cases, exporters with excess inventory or idle production capacity may be willing to lower the prices of their products enough to negate the cost of the tariff. Tariffs also tend to be negligible on products that a country both imports and exports, since the domestic producers of those products are able to compete internationally.

Tariff structures, the relationships among tariffs in industrial sectors, are more useful for understanding the protection that tariffs can provide. Each input for a product has a nominal tariff rate, that is, a numeric rate for that input alone. Tariff rates, however, usually rise as a product goes through successive stages of production; duty rates are low on raw materials, higher on semifinished products, and highest on finished products. Tariffs that increase during production are called cascading tariffs. Domestic manufacturers can remain competitive by importing raw materials and components at low rates and then add value by producing the finished products. For example, if the tariff on imported mahogany wood is 3 percent and the tariff on finished mahogany tables is 7 percent, an American furniture manufacturer could take advantage of the cascading tariff structure by importing the wood and making the tables, which would retail for less than the finished imported tables. The percentage derived from calculating the cost difference between a value-added product made from imported materials and a finished imported product is called the effective rate of tariff protection; this rate will be higher than the nominal rate.

The most restrictive use of tariffs is for infant industry protection. An infant industry is a new industry that cannot develop in a given country without protection from established producers in other countries. High tariffs protect the infant industry until it is large enough to compete with foreign producers. Theoretically, the tariffs are supposed to be reduced as the industry grows, but in practice, the high rates often remain unchanged, even when the industry becomes mature. Infant industry tariff protection is most often used by developing countries. Brazil has used the infant industry concept to protect its computer industry and aircraft industry. Some of the other countries that have used the concept are India, the Philippines, Thailand, and Peru.

Context

Quotas and tariffs are part of the international system of trade management, the intervention of governments in trade flows between countries. A certain amount of trade has always been managed trade; tariffs, for example, have been used since antiquity by virtually all countries. In modern times, trade management peaked in the 1930's, when there was a worldwide economic depression. Tariffs reached such high levels that countries could barely afford to trade with each other; the European tariff on wheat, for example, reached 350 percent in 1931.

The United States levied prohibitive tariffs, averaging 53 percent, on many products through the Hawley-Smoot Tariff Act of 1930. After World War II, trade management began to decline through cooperation of the major countries in trade liberalization efforts such as the General Agreement on Tariffs and Trade (GATT). The dual forces of increasing amounts of low-priced exports from developing countries and recessions caused by oil price increases during the 1970's and 1980's created new pressures for trade management. The United Nations has estimated that 50 percent to 80 percent of all trade was managed to some extent by the mid-1980's. Tariffs are no longer the main instrument of trade management; quotas and other nontariff barriers have emerged as the major regulatory mechanisms.

Although economists regard the tariff as a trade barrier, under GATT rules, the tariff is the accepted device for regulating import competition and is not considered "trade management." Countries have negotiated their tariffs through the GATT approximately every five years since 1947. Tariff concessions are extended to the entire GATT membership (more than one hundred countries) under the most-favored nation (MFN) principle, under which each country agrees to grant the same market access to all GATT contracting parties that it grants to its most-favored trading partner. Developing countries receive nonreciprocal tariff privileges, such as the Generalized System of Preferences (GSP), under which industrial countries allow many products from developing countries to enter duty free. The GATT prohibits quantitative restrictions and other nontariff barriers, except in certain narrowly defined circumstances; the MFA, for example, is allowed under the "market disruption" concept.

The GATT's success in tariff reduction has unfortunately led to an increase in nontariff barriers, as countries search for new methods of protection from import competition. Since the GATT has no legal enforcement powers, countries can use quotas and other unauthorized arrangements to restrict imports. Continued negotiations may eventually reduce these trade barriers; however, the elimination of barriers is contingent upon sustained improvement in the world economy.

Bibliography

Baldwin, Robert E. *Trade Policy in a Changing World*. Chicago: University of Chicago Press, 1989. This book is a 273-page collection of essays on the problems of U.S. trade policy and other international trade issues. Included is a critical analysis of the forces behind the decisions made by the General Agreement on Tariffs and Trade, and a discussion of infant industry protection. Suitable for college students.

Bhagwati, Jagdish. *Protectionism*. Cambridge, Mass.: MIT Press, 1988. This 147-page book is a collection of lectures delivered by one of the foremost experts on international trade policies and practices. Includes analyses of the evolution of free trade practices and the General Agreement on Tariffs and Trade, as well as important current economic issues such as voluntary export restraints. Suitable for college students.

International Monetary Fund. *Annual Report on Exchange Arrangements and Exchange Restrictions*. Washington, D.C.: Author, 1979-   . This report is a useful reference for identifying trade practices by country. In addition to information on monetary exchange arrangements and restrictions, it provides information on quotas and other trade restrictions, tariffs, other taxes, and licensing. Information is provided alphabetically by country for all IMF member countries.

Staudt, Kathleen A. *Free Trade? Informal Economies at the U.S.-Mexico Border*. Philadelphia: Temple University Press, 1998.

Stern, Robert M., ed. *U.S. Trade Policies in a Changing World Economy*. Cambridge, Mass.: MIT Press, 1987. This book is a 437-page collection of essays by notable economists on a range of trade policy issues confronting the United States. Topics discussed include protectionism, trade wars, and negotiation procedures of the General Agreement on Tariffs and Trade.

U.S. Department of the Treasury. Customs Service. *Importing into the United States*. Washington, D.C.: Government Printing Office, 1989. This 90-page manual is designed for businesspeople who import products into the United States. It provides detailed information on import regulations, documentation, and procedures, including information on tariffs and quotas. All items subject to quotas are listed. There are also brief, simple explanations of trade agreements in which the United States participates, such as the Generalized System of Preferences.

Yarbrough, Beth V., and Robert M. Yarbrough. *The World Economy: Trade and Finance*. New York: Dryden Press, 1988. This detailed, 666-page introduction to the world economy provides discussions of economic theory with examples and cases. There is an extensive discussion of tariffs in chapter 7 and of quotas and voluntary export restraints in chapter 8. Although there is a heavy emphasis on mathematical equations, overall the book is written clearly enough for persons without a background in economics. Suitable for college students.

C. G. Alexandrides

Cross-References

Balance of Payments, 23; Barter and Exchange, 36; Comparative Advantage, 86; European Economic Community, 199; Exports and Imports, 212; Food Economics, 239; Free Trade and Protection, 251; International Trade, 343; Trade Deficits, International Debt, and Budget Deficits, 587.

REGULATION AND DEREGULATION

Type of economics: Industrial economics
Field of study: Industrial organization and public policy

Regulation is a form of public policy that institutes government controls over (but not government ownership of) economic behavior. Adversarial legal proceedings, rather than unfettered market forces, mediate economic controversies arising in the modern industrial economy. Deregulation is an attempt to lessen legal restrictions and increase reliance on market forces to shape industrial activity.

Principal terms

COMMISSION: an agency "independent" of the three main branches of government (executive, legislative, and judicial) devised to control business behavior in one or more industries

COMMISSIONER: usually appointed by the executive branch, an individual who, typically with two or more other commissioners, administrates regulatory laws through quasi-executive, quasi-legislative, and quasi-judicial actions.

ECONOMIC REGULATION: government control over entry and exit, prices, and financing within an industry

MARKET THEORY: a return to emphasis on natural supply-demand relations, which formed the intellectual basis for the deregulation movement of the 1970's and 1980's

SOCIETAL REGULATION: government control over business actions affecting the environment, consumers, and labor-management relations (including safety and minority issues)

THEORIES OF REGULATION: economic, bureaucratic, political, and behavioral approaches to explaining the consequences of regulation

Overview

Regulation and deregulation are approaches to social control that fit on a spectrum between the extremes of government ownership and the free market. Regulation occurs when lawmakers are persuaded that a market failure has occurred; resulting legal controls attempt to shape market forces to bring about economically and socially desired consequences. Deregulation occurs when lawmakers are persuaded that regulation has altered competition drastically; legal controls are reduced and private-sector decision making is increased in order to stimulate competition and innovation.

Regulation and deregulation appear in societies marked by capitalistic, market-driven economies. Both reflect a "mixed economy," in which economic decisions are made in part by private businesses and in part by public officials. Generally, regulation involves more public intervention in the market, while deregulation involves more private input. The goal of both policy approaches is to shape economic growth and development.

Regulation includes both economic and societal controls over business behavior. In economic regulation, the government grants franchises and licenses that allow individuals and firms to engage in business, controls prices, sanctions investment decisions, and enforces insurance and safety rules. In societal regulations, the government protects entities that hold weak bargaining positions in the political economy. Such controls attempt to protect consumers from dangerous products, the environment from harmful industrial activity, and minority groups from discriminatory business practices.

Public utilities or natural monopolies have long been regulated, for the concentrated economic power of such firms clearly affects the public interest. Competitive industries are also sometimes regulated, often because businesspeople have requested relief from undesirable consequences of market forces, such as too-low prices and too many firm failures. Regulation occurs in all business enterprises, including manufacturing, agriculture, transportation, wholesale and retail, and service industries. While taking an essentially microeconomic perspective (one commission regulates one industry), some aspects of regulation, such as interest-rate controls, embrace macroeconomic concerns.

The most confusing system of regulation has emerged in the United States; nevertheless, the history of regulation in the United States reflects the general controversies that regulation has attempted to solve in modern capitalist societies. American policymakers developed a unique blend of control systems—and antitrust—to shape economic activity. Both regulation and antitrust, however, have often resulted in undesirable and unintended consequences, such as concentrating business power, raising prices, restricting growth, and stifling innovation.

Development of regulation in the United States has centered on the independent regulatory commission, and several trends have accompanied that institution's evolution. One is the state-to-federal pattern. The states were the first to use commissions to control business enterprise. As the Industrial Revolution gave rise to a national economy in the late nineteenth and early twentieth centuries, however, Congress had to act to control business activity that crossed state lines. A second pattern involved the transition from a "sunshine" to a "strong" approach to controlling business activity. Initially, commissioners used publicity of discriminatory behavior in an attempt to persuade businesses to change. When publicity failed to elicit change, regulators were given "strong" powers, such as licensing and price setting, with which to shape industrial behavior.

A third pattern was the development of quasi-executive, quasi-legislative, and quasi-judicial powers for the commissioners. These powers, while suggesting that the agency was "independent," were nevertheless checked, for all government branches contributed to the making and sustaining of the commission: The legislature created the agency and gave it its powers; the executive appointed the commissioners; and the judiciary monitored its activities. A fourth pattern involved the substitution of legal procedure for economic thinking in deciding controversies. Instead of economic competition shaping an industry, more and more it was the ability to argue one's case before a commission that determined winners and losers in the market. It was the evolution of the third and fourth trends that led to calls for deregulation. Concentration on the details and procedures of regulation led regulators to become more concerned with legal issues than with understanding the economic forces they were supposed to be shaping.

Legal issues surmounted economic wisdom in part because commissioners were not educated in economics (most were lawyers). By the mid-twentieth century, critics of regulation, educated in new economic thinking, argued that commission regulation had perverted natural market forces to such an extent that important sectors of the economy were threatened with stagnation. Political scientists and economists developed theories of regulation to show that commissioners had not given sufficient attention to the desired consequences that unfettered market forces could bring. The so-called Chicago School of market theorists, especially, promoted the idea of deregulation. Practitioners of deregulation incorporated cost-benefit analyses to determine if the economic costs of a proposed or existing regulation outweighed the intended benefits.

Economic deregulation, ironically, appeared just as a new movement to impose more stringent societal controls over business actions also emerged. Lawmakers enacted regulations that detailed how businesses must protect the environment and serve the interests of consumers and minority groups, endeavors not subject to clear-cut cost-benefit analyses. In sum, regulation and deregulation never occur as purely economic phenomena, but exist necessarily within the usual societal tensions between economics and politics.

Applications

Railroads were the first big businesses and the first to be regulated. That story not only explains much about why modern regulation developed but also furnishes examples in the application of regulatory controls. Generally, results of unfettered railway competition—too-high rates in some areas, too-low rates elsewhere, and poor service and discriminatory practices (charging two shippers different rates for similar hauls)—led lawmakers to establish controls, first in the states, then on the federal level. In both, the pattern from sunshine to strong control appeared; and in both, an adversarial relationship between government and business anchored regulatory proceedings. This adversarial relationship generally distinguishes business-government relations and regulation in the United States from that found in other capitalist countries.

The first federal regulatory commission was the Interstate Commerce Commission (ICC), established in 1887 to eliminate discriminatory railway practices. Regulatory decisions were made at the ICC (and in other commissions) in a quasi-judicial atmosphere. Regular monthly hearings were scheduled, but, over time, more and more special hearings crowded the commissioners' dockets. Sometimes the commissioners left Washington, D.C., where the ICC was located, to make personal inspections of controversies or to hold public hearings in cities and towns where complaints had surfaced. Lawyers for the railroads presented the commissioners with charts, graphs, and accounting material to argue their client's side of an issue. Sometimes shippers countered with their own lawyers, but more often than not the commissioners assumed the shippers' point of view. Each case was decided separately; few general rules were ever promulgated, for it seemed as if each railway transaction included a detail that prevented general rule making.

The particularistic, case-by-case approach prevented the commissioners from seeing the bigger picture. For example, between 1910 and 1917, regulators, affected more by shippers' ideological fears of concentrated powers than by economic principles, refused to grant the railroads needed rate increases. Expansion and improvements of railway systems did not occur; thus, paralysis of the national railroad network early in U.S. participation in World War I forced the federal government to assume direct control for the duration of the war.

Two other national regulatory commissions, the Federal Reserve Board (1913) and the Federal Trade Commission (1914), followed the ICC. The former attempted to control the national banking system, while the latter attempted to eliminate "unfair" business practices (a combination of regulation and antitrust) in all industries in the United States. Each of these regulatory agencies, however, differed from the ICC in scope of operations. The Federal Reserve Board attempted a macroeconomic approach to decide how much the money supply should be contracted or expanded to shape economic prosperity. While the FTC followed the case-by-case method, its scope of activities included all industries not regulated by another commission. The FTC tended to prosecute cases of business misconduct that its lawyers were sure to win; thus, some questionable business activity went uncontrolled.

An example of a deregulation movement that preceded the more recognizable one of the 1970's and 1980's occurred in the 1920's, but its fate reflects the problems Americans have faced in applying regulatory and antitrust forms of social control of business. In this era of "associationalism" Americans tried to duplicate the success of business-government cooperation during World War I, but without the direct government interference that had marked the war experiment. Government officials encouraged industries plagued by overproduction to elect representatives to industry-wide associations. These leaders would establish fair trading rules and plan industry activity through agreements to control supplies, prices, and growth. Associationalism, however, clearly violated antitrust laws that prohibited businesses from colluding to shape the market. In the late 1920's and early 1930's, antitrust proceedings stopped the associational movement.

Until the 1980's, the Securities and Exchange Commission, established in 1934, reigned as the best example of effective commission regulation. This developed in part because industry leaders recognized that regulation would help their industry; rather than engage in adversarial tactics, they worked with the regulators to improve accounting techniques and to stabilize the business of selling stocks and bonds.

Throughout the 1940's, 1950's, and 1960's, most commissions were bogged down in bureaucratic inefficiencies, legal restraints, and regulatory lag. Economists and lawyers, relying on new theories of regulation, concluded that commission controls, based heavily on adversarial legalistic approaches, had perverted the natural workings of market forces to such an extent that the overall economic performance of the nation was being retarded. Significantly, new competitors—not subject to commission control—took advantage of new technologies and regulatory loopholes to take market share from regulated firms.

In the 1970's, the critics and the injured firms persuaded Congress to roll back economic regulation. Restrictions on entry and exit, on pricing, and on financing were loosened in an attempt to reintroduce competitive thinking, along with the new marginal price theory, into American business decision making. Deregulation of the telecommunications, transportation, and banking industries proceeded throughout the 1980's. (In Great Britain, a "privatization" program attempted to achieve similar results.)

A final application of regulation needs to be noted. Even as lawmakers removed economic controls, they imposed new societal regulations. Federal agencies monitored business activity affecting the environment (through the Environmental Protection Agency), consumer and worker welfare (through the FTC and the Occupational Safety and Health Administration), and minority rights (through the Equal Employment Opportunity Commission). The adversarial approach to regulation reemerged as business challenged the regulations for being too expensive to implement and representing too much interference in private affairs. Nevertheless, implementation of the societal regulations improved the environment, afforded consumers some protections, and helped minorities achieve better bargaining positions.

Context

Regulation during ancient and medieval times usually involved local controls over business activity. By the seventeenth and eighteenth centuries, mercantilism, a system through which government controlled business enterprise to maintain the nation's comparative advantage over its colonies and competing nation-states, shaped the Atlantic trading world.

With the appearance of the democratic experiment in the United States in the late eighteenth century, the growing acceptance of the emerging system of capitalism, the recognition of private rights, and the appearance of industrialism, regulation took on new, more complicated tasks. Now the government acted to enhance the wealth of the individual, rather than the wealth of the nation. This meant, theoretically, that the government would be less restrictive of business affairs. Yet the undesired consequences of industrial capitalism in the late nineteenth and early twentieth centuries, concentrated economic power especially but unstable business conditions generally, gave rise to government regulations.

The coexistence of democracy and capitalism in the United States led to a system of regulation different from that found anywhere else in the world. Unlike European societies, the United States did not have a legacy of nation-state bureaucracy with which to implement regulation. Thus, Americans had to develop new institutions of regulation. Regulation and deregulation policies have been most prominent in the United States in large measure because Americans were less receptive than citizens of other capitalist countries to the rise of big business. Because such fears of bigness rested on ideological and political beliefs, regulators faced a difficult task in reconciling economic reality (the efficiencies of big business) with American politics (demands to be free of potential concentrated economic power.

On the state level and national levels, lawmakers established "independent" commissions whose members were supposed to decide controversies between businesses and consumers and between competing businesses. Commissioners had to accommodate their decisions not only to industrial economic structures but also to constitutional restraints. Regulatory responses to the economic and political upheavals of the Great Depression of the 1930's constituted the highwater mark of public support for regulation. By the mid-twentieth century, however, the bureaucratic and legalistic workings of the regulatory commissions had restrained market forces so much that economic growth was slipping. Court delays and bureaucratic inefficiencies had supplanted the natural forces of the market.

Consequently, deregulation would underscore policy actions in the last thirty years of the twentieth century. Deregulation was in part a reaction against the perceived failures of the regulatory commissions and in part a general reaction against too much government interference in the economy. Deregulation did not repudiate regulation completely but instead attempted to shape government controls to conform more closely to natural industrial and market forces and less to artificial legal constraints. Unintended consequences of deregulation, however (fraudulent behavior, rising prices, and growing concentration), in the banking, airline, and telecommunications industries led to calls for "re-regulation" in the 1980's and 1990's. In conflict with the economic deregulation movement was the modern movement to control business impact on the environment and business power over consumers and minority groups. Thus, regulation and deregulation would reflect the ongoing tensions involved when a nation tries to shore up the positive and eliminate the undesirable consequences of business enterprise in a capitalist economy.

Bibliography

Armstrong, Christopher, and H. V. Nelles. *Monopoly's Moment: The Organization and Regulation of Canadian Utilities, 1830-1930*. Philadelphia: Temple University Press, 1986. Furnishes a well-written comparison to the better-known story in the United States. Focused on utility regulation, the book does not deal very much with other businesses regulated in Canada.

Breyer, Stephen. *Regulation and Its Reform*. Cambridge, Mass.: Harvard University Press, 1982. Provides the theoretical underpinnings of and case studies for the deregulation movement. Breyer worked closely with Senator Edward M. Kennedy to bring about deregulation of the airline industry in the late 1970's. While not as clearly written as the Alfred E. Kahn and Thomas K. McGraw volumes cited below, the work is well worth the reader's extra effort.

Derthick, Martha, and Paul J. Quirk. *The Politics of Deregulation*. Washington, D.C.: Brookings Institution, 1985. The authors downplay the notion that economic self-interests mostly motivate politics. Covering the airline, trucking, and telecommunications industries, the authors argue instead that, even though industry interests opposed deregulation, they failed because the new economic thinking, the abilities of politicians to use publicity to bolster their positions, and new legal doctrines worked against continuation and extension of regulation. While a useful study, it ignores too much the effects of technological and economic change over time on regulation.

Kahn, Alfred E. *The Economics of Regulation*. 2 vols. New York: John Wiley & Sons, 1970-1971. Volume 1 analyzes the reasons for and the theories of regulation. Volume 2 discusses the principles and institutions of regulation. Kahn describes complicated economic theories in terms clearly accessible to the general reader. These volumes reflect the intellectual connections between regulation and deregulation and formed the basis for Kahn's application of deregulation while chair of the Civil Aeronautics Board in the late 1970's.

Khoury, Sarkis J. *U.S. Banking and Its Regulation in the Political Context*. Lanham, Md.: University Press of America, 1997.

McCraw, Thomas K. *Prophets of Regulation: Charles Francis Adams, Louis D. Brandeis, James M. Landis, Alfred E. Kahn*. Cambridge, Mass.: The Belknap Press of Harvard Press, 1984. Using a creative biographical approach, McCraw introduces the reader to the reasons for, the thinking about, and the changes in regulatory policy in the United States. Awarded the Pulitzer Prize in History, this book is based on copious research, furnishes the broader reform context in which regulation and deregulation materialized, and is the most accessible work to the general reader listed in this bibliography.

Roussakis, Emmanuel N. *Commercial Banking in an Era of Deregulation*. 3d ed. Westport, Conn.: Praeger, 1997.

Wilson, James Q., ed. *The Politics of Regulation*. New York: Basic Books, 1980. The essays in this book suggest in clear prose that regulation is as much a political phenomenon as an economic one. This work is cited often in studies of regulation and deregulation and is especially illuminating on the politics within regulatory commissions.

William R. Childs

Cross-References

Antitrust Policy, 6; Banks, 29; Business Organization, 57; Capitalism, 69; Federal Reserve Bank, 223; Free Trade and Protection, 251; Laissez-Faire, 366; Market Structure, 406; Politics and Economics, 476; Price Fixing, 495.

RESOURCES

Type of economics: Growth and development
Fields of study: Economic growth, development, and planning; natural resources

Resources are the factors of production that are normally derived from the natural environment and are used to produce goods and services. Land and capital are generally referred to as physical resources and labor as a human resource. Renewable resources are environmental resources that can be reused without diminution, so that their usage through time is not fixed. Nonrenewable resources are environmental resources that are transformed in use, so that they become a less usable form.

Principal terms

CRUSTAL ABUNDANCE: the amount of an element or a mineral that is estimated to be in the earth's crust

ECONOMIC RESOURCES: proved reserves at a location and with an infrastructure that would allow them to be exploited at a cost that is competitive with other producing sources of that resource

FACTORS OF PRODUCTION: the inputs that are required to produce a good or service, such as land, labor, and capital

NEW PARADIGM: the often-stated or recognized claim that existing paradigms or theories are inadequate as a framework for addressing emerging problems; an interpretation that implies an instant solution to all problems rather than a framework or mechanism for the difficult research task of addressing problems

PARADIGM: a coherent theory or body of ideas that shape or define humanity's interpretation of the world around it and actions in it

POTENTIAL RESOURCES: the estimated reserves of a resource at a grade that is economic at current technology and resource prices; these estimates are the result of careful scientific inquiry, not guesses

PROVED RESOURCES: the actual three-dimensional measured volume of a resource at a grade that is economic at current technology and resources prices

SECOND LAW OF THERMODYNAMICS: also known as the law of entropy, the principle in physics and engineering that energy or material is used in a system

SUSTAINABILITY: the characteristic of an economic productive activity that will allow it to be carried out indefinitely into the future; contrasted with practices that are destructive or exhaustive of some essential inputs and will no longer be able to support human life in the future

TECHNOLOGY: the total of humans' problem-solving capability, including ideas, knowledge, and skills; generally uses the resources that it has created by finding a human use for preexisting raw materials or nonmaterials

Overview

The distinction between renewable and nonrenewable resources is useful but not precise. Renewable resources are essentially what the term says—they are resources for which, if used intelligently, there are operative forces that recreate them. In some instances, these operative forces require direct human intervention for sustainability. Thus, forestry as a renewable resource requires a variety of human actions for its sustainability, including replanting trees when they are cut. Ocean fishing, if not done to excess, is self-sustaining, as the fish will repropagate. The category of nonrenewable resources generally includes most minerals and energy sources such as the hydrocarbons. The basis for their nonrenewability is that there is a fixed amount of them in the earth's crust. Consequently, as they are extracted and used, they are also being depleted. Some nonrenewable resources such as the minerals can be recycled. The second law of thermodynamics states, however, that energy is used in a system and, therefore, recycling can never be 100 percent; some energy is always lost in the process. This interpretation of an initially fixed supply of nonrenewable resources that diminishes through time has been the historic basis of many theories in political economy which argued that, at some future time, economic growth must cease, with the economy reaching what was called a stationary state.

This distinction between renewable and nonrenewable is not as firm as these definitions might imply. Though there may be a fixed quantity of iron, aluminum, copper, or other minerals in the earth's crust, the human ability to use them has increased through time and has not yet diminished. Consequently, the accessible available supply of economically usable resources has been expanding through time so far. Most of these minerals are part of various compounds and in different grades of purity. The various forms of some minerals or their grades of purity, which caused them not to be an economic resource at one period in history, allowed them to become economic resources at a later time with the development of new technology for extraction and processing. The net result is that, in technologically advancing societies, not only have these nonrenewable resources been sustained but, in most cases, their reserves of economically useful resources have actually been increasing and their real price has been falling as well.

Both renewable and nonrenewable resources are created with technology. A number of the renewable resources, such as soil, receive their resource character by continually working in a complementary fashion with technology. The domestication of plants and animals greatly intensified the amount of food that humans could harvest from a particular area and therefore can be said to increase the resource character of the soil. As humans developed improved varieties of crops or adapted crops to new areas, they were transforming the renewable aspect and enhancing the resource character of these soils.

Once people begin to use land intensively to grow food and once that food is exported to another area, however, the renewability of the resource of soil is threatened. Sustainability or renewability through time has depended on human beings developing technologies that allow for the amending of the soil to replace the nutrient that is taken out through agriculture. Some of what are now the finest agricultural lands in the world were once nutrient poor for human purposes and required both modifying the plants and amending soil with nutrients. These soils required technology in order to become a resource and required other technology in order to become a renewable resource.

What transformed land, soil, and all other materials and nonmaterials into resources was human ideas translated through skills and behavior. Arable land, said to be the fixed factor of production, was only a limited resource for gatherers and hunters until humans transformed its potential with the domestication of plants and animals, known as the fields of agriculture and animal husbandry. Various forms of earth that are called ores became resources following the development of a variety of technologies from the construction of ovens to the control of fire and the drafts of oxygen.

The creation of some resources, such as metal, that largely replaced earlier resources shows that technology not only creates resources but also, in effect, destroys others by superceding them with new improved means of problem solving. This function defines the essence of a resource. A resource is basically an anthropomorphic concept that involves the use of material or nonmaterial stuff for human purposes. Resources then are truly human capital and are only limited by the ability of humans to find new and creative ways of using the raw material of the universe. Resources are not finite, though in strict mathematical terms it cannot be said that they are infinite. It can be said, however, that they are nonfinite, in the sense that the historical record indicates that humans have transformed the environment into resources faster than they have used them thus far. Using resources is not the same as depleting them if they are used in an imaginative and intelligent way in a process that creates more resources.

The anthropomorphic definition of resources ultimately involves a practice of using the essence of a resource. In a market economy, the use of a resource would constitute an economic demand for that resource, which means that the resource commands a price. The role of price in defining an economic resource is often overlooked by the noneconomist. Changes in price can sometimes alter dramatically the proved reserves of a resource just as technology does. In the 1950's, a 50 percent increase in the price of coal would have brought a twenty-fold increase in the proved economic reserves. For most minerals, the increases in reserves are not of this magnitude but are, nevertheless, significant.

Applications

Between 1950 and 1990, the world's population more than doubled. The food supply grew at an even faster rate than the population, allowing per-capita food production to reach new records. The technologies of the green revolution have therefore allowed for what amounts to a dramatic continuous increase in what was considered the most fixed and finite of all resources, land, and that renewable aspect of it, the soil.

Sometimes the distinction between renewable and nonrenewable resources involves the element of biology as the major component of the renewable resources. Human intervention has been continuously transforming various forms of plant and animal life, making them more productive for human usage. It is frequently noted that as yet unanalyzed, and in some cases undiscovered, species of plants and some varieties of microorganisms are potential resources that humans may be destroying, as biological diversity is being diminished with the continued encroachment of agricultural lands into other habitats, particularly rain forests. It could also be argued that these biological resources have become resources or are potential resources because humans have developed a variety of technologies to utilize them for human purposes. Some people have used this distinction between renewable and nonrenewable resources in order to argue for a restructuring of modern economies from a dependence on nonrenewable resources to one of dependence on renewable resources. For these people, sustainability implies a fundamental reconceptualization of the nature of human economic life. Many are seeking what is called "new paradigm," which incorporates a dualism between renewable and nonrenewable resources and a philosophy of living within limits.

Others claim that these arguments are ironic and that the resources that are in the most jeopardy have been and continue to be renewable resources, particularly biological ones. Further, these people argue that many of these plans for sustainability, such as for agriculture, essentially involve recycling and, because it is impossible to recycle that which is not there, sustainability involves an initial transformation that is generally the result of the addition of some product of industry, such as fertilizer. This second group states that sustainability in resources, be it in agriculture or minerals, is dependent on the continued advance of technological knowledge.

Mineral rich should not be confused with resource rich. Economically, minerals may not be resources because the same materials can be found at other places at lower prices. Similarly, there are rich deposits on the surface of the moon and in asteroids which have a mineral content and purity that is higher than any known on Earth. Though these are not economically worthwhile to exploit, their existence reveals that there are potential mineral resources in excess of humanity's current usage. Moreover, there is an understood pathway of technologies that may allow humans to gain access to these resources should they become necessary. Because humans are not close to exhausting the crustal abundance of any minerals, however, technological change offers a continued long-term opportunity for expanding proved economic reserves of resources. In addition, as recent discoveries have demonstrated, there are still undiscovered sources of high-grade minerals. In addition, there are those minerals that are known about that have recently become or will eventually become resources with changes in technology.

With greater efficiency in use of resources, the "natural resource" content of the gross national product (GNP) has been steadily declining. There has been, in the latter part of the twentieth century, a trend in technology which has allowed humanity to use an array of basic elements and minerals. In addition, some of the most abundant of these elements, such as silicon or basic constituents of a variety of clays, have become increasingly significant as resources in the development of silicon chips and the very rapid development of ceramic technologies.

Context

The classical and neoclassical factors of production—land, labor, capital, and entrepreneurship—involve what are called renewable and nonrenewable resources. Land was defined as the nonhuman, nonman-made fixed factor of production. Labor was the human factor of production, and the units of labor were often conceived of in terms of some raw labor power that was untransformed by skill or knowledge, and thus fixed and limited except in numbers. Capital was the nonhuman man-made factor of production, which could be accumulated through time by a societal process of savings. The combination of these three factors in the classical system was the source of growth and development. The growth of population (labor), however, placed pressure on land that would eventually bring diminishing returns to agriculture. Diminishing returns to agriculture meant increases in the price of food and, therefore, increases in the costs of subsistence for labor. Increased subsistence costs meant that wages would have to increase so that labor could continue to be a renewable and reusable resource. Increased labor costs contributed, along with other forces, to a long-term decline in the return to capital. This mechanism was worked out in classical economic theory before it became a pillar of Marxist economics.

Entrepreneurship became the fourth factor of production in the neoclassical system. It was the factor that brought the other factors together in a productive process. Entrepreneurship was the driving force for invention and innovation. Though economists became less concerned about the theory of the decline of the long-term rate of profit or the eventual reaching of a stationary state at which economic growth and development ceased, land as a fixed factor of production and the theory of diminishing returns still remained beneath the surface as a long-term restraint on sustained economic development.

In the 1950's and 1960's, there were a number of studies of the historical process of growth of the then industrialized countries and the extent to which growth in one or more of the factors of production could serve as an explanation for this growth. It was argued that the traditional factors of production were insufficient as causal forces to explain the economic growth that had taken place. Stated differently, the growth in the factors of production could account for only a small fraction of the growth that had taken place. The unexplained variable was called technology. This proposed deficiency in explanatory powers of the traditional factors of production led some economists to expand the original definition of these factors. Both labor and capital came to include knowledge, skills, and other characteristics that are associated with technology.

Thus, there is a term "human capital," which to some is the most critical resource of any community. This idea of human capital had its antecedents in economics, but largely in dissenting schools of thought. Early in the twentieth century, the American economist Thorstein Veblen (1857-1929) had spoken of human knowledge and capability as the most important capital asset of a community. Several decades later, Wesley C. Mitchell (1874-1948), who had links to both dissenting and mainstream economics, asserted that knowledge is the most important of all resources because it is the "mother of other resources."

If resources are considered to be the creation of human ingenuity and problem-solving capability, then the entire economic system is open to possibilities that would not be allowed in classical and neoclassical theories. Although the perspective that resource creation is in the hands of humans would not justify the squandering of resources, it might stir people to use their creativity in order to find new technologies and institutional arrangements to use resources more constructively.

Bibliography

Abelson, Philip H., and Allan L. Hammond, eds. *Materials: Renewable and Non-Renewable.* Washington, D.C.: American Association for the Advancement of Science, 1976. An excellent compilation of articles that detail the role of technology in defining and creating the resources for modern economies.

Adam, Barbara. *Timescapes of Modernity: The Environment and Invisible Hazards.* New York: Routledge, 1998.

Boserup, Ester. *Population and Technological Change.* Chicago: University of Chicago Press, 1981. A major work by seminal author that argues that population growth has facilitated technological change in agriculture and allowed for more intensive use and greater food production. Attempts to demonstrate that land is not a fixed factor of production.

DeGregori, Thomas R. *A Theory of Technology: Continuity and Change in Human Development.* Ames: Iowa State University Press, 1985. Argues that natural resources are a function of technology. A comprehensive theory of the nature of technology is offered as a framework for defining resources and how they are created.

Gottinger, Hans-Werner. *Global Environmental Economics*. Boston: Kluwer Academic Publishers, 1998.

McLaren, Digby, and Brian Skinner, eds. *Resources and World Development*. New York: John Wiley & Sons, 1987. A large, comprehensive collection of articles on virtually every aspect of resources and what defines and creates them by outstanding authors in science, engineering, and economics.

Simon, Julian L., and Herman Kahn, eds. *The Resourceful Earth: A Response to Global 2000*. New York: Basil Blackwell, 1984. An optimistic rebuttal to the Global 2000 Report that argues that the world is not in dire straits and that human creativity can be applied to the environmental and resource challenges that lie ahead.

United States. Global 2000 Study. *The Global 2000 Report to the President: Entering the Twenty-first Century*. 3 vols. Washington, D.C.: Government Printing Office, 1980-1981. A pessimistic assessment of the possibility that available resources would sustain continued economic growth.

World Resources Institute Staff. *World Resources, 1990-1991*. New York: Oxford University Press, 1990. An annual survey of the current state and prospects of the world's resources that is organized and presented from the perspective that resources are being threatened.

Thomas R. DeGregori
Randal Joy Thompson

Cross-References

Capital Goods, 63; Classical Economics, 74; Comparative Advantage, 86; Environmental Economics, 187; Labor Economics, 353; Population and Economics, 482; Technology, 581; Wealth, 626.

SAVING

Type of economics: Monetary and fiscal theory
Field of study: Monetary theory

Saving represents income that is received but not spent on consumption goods or services. Saving may be used to accumulate money hoards, or it may be used to purchase financial and real assets. In the aggregate, savings equals spending on investment goods plus the government's deficit and net exports.

Principal terms

CONSUMPTION: the purchase of goods and services by the final consumer over any period
DEFICIT: expenditure in excess of income over any given period by issuing debt
HOARD: a stock of cash held
INTERMEDIATION: the purchase of long-term debt by a financial institution so that savers may hold the short-term debt of the financial institution
INVESTMENT: the purchase of capital goods (plant and equipment) to be used as instruments of production
SAVING: after-tax income that is not spent on consumption goods or services

Overview

For the individual household, saving equals the after-tax income that is not spent on currently produced consumption goods and services. Saving may take a variety of forms. Some savers prefer to hide their cash in their houses, while others are willing to hold deposit accounts at a bank. Those who are willing to take risks might use their savings to purchase stocks and bonds, to play in the lottery, or even to purchase plant and equipment in order to start a new business. Finally, some individual savers may prefer to purchase old cars, works of art, or real estate.

While the noneconomist frequently refers to any form of saving other than a cash hoard as an "investment," the economist narrowly defines investment to include only the purchase of newly produced capital goods (such as plant and equipment). Thus, very little of the saving which is done by households represents investment as defined by economists. The only exception to this rule is owner-occupied housing, which is treated by economists as an investment because it will provide a stream of housing services to the owner.

Firms and governments may also save. A government that receives more in tax revenues than it spends will run a budget surplus as it "saves." For example, many state and local governments in the United States do run budget surpluses, which may be saved in the form of purchases of federal government bonds. On the other hand, the federal government usually runs a deficit budget and must issue debt (some of which is purchased by savers), which can be called "negative saving" or "dissaving." Firms may also save if sales receipts exceed expenditures. The savings of a firm are called "retained earnings" and may be accumulated in anticipation of purchasing new plant and equipment in the next period. In this case, the savings of the firm are invested. On the other hand, retained earnings may be used to purchase financial assets—in which case the savings are not invested.

While the savings of the individual saver may not be directly invested, they may be indirectly invested by a financial intermediary. For example, if the saver purchases a certificate of deposit from a bank, the bank may then make a loan to a firm that is purchasing plant and equipment. In this way, the bank intermediates between the saver and the investor; there is, however, no guarantee that savings will be intermediated in that manner. For example, cash savings hidden in one's house cannot fund investment, and even if savings are deposited in banks, there is still no guarantee that the banks will make loans to investors. Banks purchase government bonds and finance corporate mergers, neither of which adds directly to investment.

There is, however, a link between saving and investment, although it can be allusive if one considers only individual saving behavior. In the aggregate, all income must come from someone's spending; that is, spending determines income. Thus, it is the spending of firms, households, and the government that generates the income that is received by firms, households, and the government. The various components of aggregate spending are consumption, investment, government purchases, and exports less imports (or net exports). Each type of spending must be received by some economic agent as income. Income may then be used to finance consumption, saving, or tax payments.

Consumption spending must be equal to the portion of income that is spent on consumption; that is, investment, plus government spending, plus net exports must equal the portion of income that is saved, plus the portion that is used to pay taxes. Government spending, less taxes, is the government's deficit. Thus, investment, plus government deficit spending, plus net exports equals saving. That portion of income that is saved can only be generated by spending on items other than consumption goods.

Applications

For the individual, some saving will be directly invested, while other saving will indirectly finance investment through an intermediary; other saving will never, even indirectly, finance investment. In the aggregate, causation must always run from investment to saving: Investment spending generates the income that can be saved. Some of this saving may then directly or indirectly fund the investment that has already occurred. Thus, there must be a way of temporarily financing investment that does not rely on saving, as the saving can only be generated by the investment spending. The key to investment finance must be short-term credit created by the financial system, as short-term credit can finance investment projects until investment spending has created saving. At this point, investors can sell long-term debt to savers and use these proceeds to retire the short-term credit provided by the financial system. If savers refuse to buy this long-term debt (for example, because they prefer to keep hoards of cash stuffed in mattresses), then the long-term debt will have to be sold to financial institutions.

Government deficit spending and net exports must also generate income that is not consumed—that is, income that is saved. While the government deficits must generate equivalent saving, savers may not wish to buy government bonds. A country that runs a large trade surplus (net exports are positive because exports exceed imports) will receive income that is not spent on consumption goods, because the goods that are exported cannot be consumed by the domestic population.

While an individual may choose to increase saving by reducing expenditures, this option is not available to society as a whole: Society may increase saving only by increasing spending on categories other than consumption. This paradox, "the paradox of thrift," is probably the most surprising and difficult concept in macroeconomics. Assuming that a population, on average, consumes 90 percent of its income and saves 10 percent, and that a portion of the population (which will be called the "thrifty" portion) decides to reduce consumption to 80 percent of its income and increase saving to 20 percent, then expenditures would fall and the income of those who formerly received the consumption spending would have to be reduced. This situation forces those who experience falling income to cut back on consumption (by 90 percent of the fall of income) and on saving (by 10 percent of the fall of income) as well.

Yet, as this group also cuts back on consumption, other groups also experience falling income and are forced to reduce consumption and saving; the initial reduction of consumption has a "multiplier" effect on the economy as a whole. The final result will be that aggregate income will fall so much that the reduction of saving by those experiencing a fall of income will exactly offset the initial increase of saving by the "thrifty" group. Thus, one reaches the surprising result that an attempt to increase saving by reducing spending will not result in an increase of aggregate saving. Any individual may increase his or her saving, as long as he or she does not experience falling income. In the aggregate, however, more thrifty behavior cannot increase saving because it reduces spending and income.

Saving can increase only if there is a rise of spending in areas other than consumption. Returning to the original "thrifty" group, if its reduction of consumption is exactly offset by an increase of investment, government deficits, or net exports, then income will not fall. In this case, the rise of saving by the thrifty group will not cause a fall in income of other groups, so others are not forced to reduce their saving.

The paradox of thrift also works in reverse: If a group decides to save less and consume more, more income and more saving will be generated by other groups. Thus, any attempt to reduce thriftiness will not reduce aggregate saving; the only way to reduce aggregate saving is to reduce investment, government deficits, or net exports. Individual decisions over consumption and saving have no impact on the aggregate level of saving, even if all consumers behave the same way.

A rise of thriftiness that is not matched by a rise of investment, government deficits, or net exports will depress an economy and lead to lower levels of spending and income. Such a society might be said to be "oversaving," even though its level of saving will not increase because of the paradox of thrift. This society will experience high levels of unemployment and low capacity utilization rates for which there are two possible routes of escape: Either consumers could become less thrifty and consume more (which will not affect the aggregate level of saving, but will increase consumption spending, employment, and income), or investment, government spending, and net exports could be increased (which will increase income and saving).

A society in which consumers are just thrifty enough to provide a level of consumption that, when added to investment, government deficit spending, and net exports, generates sufficient aggregate demand to operate the economy at full employment of labor and at full capacity utilization, might be said to exhibit "optimal saving." In reality, this happy state of affairs seems to be achieved rarely. Given that each saving decision, consumption decision, and investment decision is individually made, it is not surprising that the sum of these decisions is rarely at the optimal level.

Context

Economists formerly were concerned about the possibility that saving might exceed or fall short of investment. After John Maynard Keynes's *The General Theory of Employment, Interest, and Money* (1936) was published, however, economists recognized that investment must create an equivalent amount of saving. Some economists were then concerned that some of this created saving might be "forced," rather than "desired." For example, a firm might increase spending on investment, which takes resources out of the production of consumption goods. Thus, although the investment spending will generate income received by households, these households are forced to increase saving, not because they want to, but because fewer consumption goods are available.

Forced saving may be likely during a major war when all resources are fully employed and the government is redirecting resources toward the production of war goods. Economies usually do not operate so close to full employment that additional investment or government spending will cause a reduction of output in the consumption goods industry. Instead, a rise of such spending will generate more income, some of which will be spent on consumption and thereby will encourage additional production of consumption goods. Furthermore, even if investment did lead to "forced saving" by removing resources from the production of consumption goods, this effect would probably be temporary because the additional production of investment goods would raise the productive capacity of the economy and would lead to greater production of consumption goods—even with fewer resources involved in their production.

Concern about the aggregate level of saving is focused on two areas: First, rather than worrying about saving as such, economists try to determine whether the level of aggregate demand (consumption plus investment plus government spending plus net exports) is sufficient to generate full employment. Second, economists are concerned about the form in which savings are held. If savers prefer to retain all savings as hoards of cash, it becomes difficult for firms that undertake investment projects to obtain long-term finance. In this case, funding may be available only at interest rates which are so high that firms decide not to invest. This decision can cause high levels of unemployment, a stagnant economy, and a slow productivity growth.

An investor might have to save for years in order to accumulate sufficient capital goods to undertake production. The development of credit, however, enables an investor to undertake a project on the basis of short-term loans. As investment expenditure occurs, it creates income and generates saving. The investor could then sell stock in his or her firm to savers and use the proceeds to retire the short-term loans. Many savers, however, might not be willing to take the risks associated with stock ownership. Thus, intermediaries have been developed that can issue short-term debt (such as savings deposits) to be held by savers; the financial intermediary can then hold the long-term debt issued by investors. Financial intermediaries work with savers and investors, reducing the risk to the saver and encouraging investment by offering the investor a lower interest rate than is possible in the absence of intermediation. Thus, investment can be stimulated to increase income and generate saving.

Bibliography

Adams, F. Gerard, and Susan M. Wachter. *Savings and Capital Formation.* Lexington,

Mass.: Lexington Books, 1986. An orthodox examination of the relation between savings and investment, with special focus on capital accumulation.

Blecker, Robert A. *Are Americans on a Consumption Binge? The Evidence Reconsidered.* Washington, D.C.: Economic Policy Institute, 1990. The most complete examination of saving in the United States for the two decades prior to 1990. The author finds that the national saving rate did decline, but he attributes most of the decline to accelerated depreciation of plant and equipment by firms and to the trade deficit.

Bosworth, Barry P. "There's No Simple Explanation for the Collapse in Saving." *Challenge* 32 (July/August, 1989): 27-32. One of a series of articles in *Challenge* that examine the fall of the U.S. saving rate during the 1980's. Unfortunately, Bosworth (like most noneconomists) falls into the trap of confusing individual behavior with that of the economy (the "fallacy of composition") and so blames the lack of saving on "overspending."

Chernow, Ron. *The Death of the Banker: The Decline and Fall of the Great Financial Dynasties and the Triumph of the Small Investor.* New York: Vintage Books, 1997.

Hendershott, Patric H., ed. *The Level and Composition of Household Saving.* Cambridge, Mass.: Ballinger, 1985. A collection of articles which analyzes trends regarding household saving by various demographic groups. Some of these articles would be appropriate for the nonspecialist.

Keynes, John Maynard. *The General Theory of Employment, Interest, and Money.* New York: Harcourt Brace Jovanovich, 1964. The classic exposition of Keynesian theory, which explains why spending determines income and investment determines saving. May be difficult for the nonspecialist.

_____. "The Process of Capital Formation." In *The Collected Writings.* Vol. 15. 2d ed. London: Macmillan, 1987. In this brief article, Keynes explains why saving and investment must be identical, why investment must determine saving, and how investment is financed.

Lipsey, Robert E., and Helen Stone Tice, eds. *The Measurement of Saving, Investment, and Wealth.* National Bureau of Economic Research Conference on Research in Income and Wealth 52. Chicago: University of Chicago Press, 1989. Part of a technical series which examines various aspects of the measurement of income and wealth. While this volume analyzes some of the problems encountered in measuring saving, it will appeal primarily to those interested in technical details.

Nordhaus, William D. "What's Wrong with a Declining National Savings Rate?" *Challenge* 32 (July/August, 1989): 22-26. One article from a series in *Challenge* which examines the low saving rate of the United States during the 1980's. Nordhaus argues that consumption must be lowered to promote economic growth and higher future living standards through more investment.

Schor, Juliet. *The Overspent American: Upscaling, Downshifting, and the New Consumer.* New York: Basic Books, 1998.

L. Randall Wray

Cross-References

SOCIALISM

Type of economics: General economics
Fields of study: Economic systems and history of economic thought

Socialism refers both to a set of doctrines and to political movements that advocate the transformation of capitalism, which is based on private ownership of wealth and the means of production, into a political-economic system that is based on public or community control over the means of production and social resources.

Principal terms

ANARCHISM: a set of doctrines that stresses that authority, particularly governmental, is oppressive and that advocates a cooperative society of freely associating producers

CAPITALISM: an economic system that is based on private ownership of the means of production, labor markets, and production for the purpose of profits

CLASS: the fundamental social grouping, according to Marxists, that consists of people who have a common position in the relations of production and, consequently, similar interests

COMMUNISM: a late stage of socialism in which goods have become so plentiful and human behavior so cooperative that social resources can be distributed according to need, not effort

EVOLUTIONARY SOCIALISM: a version of socialism that advocates the gradual transformation of capitalism through reforms that are brought about by the political process

MARKET SOCIALISM: a version of socialism that advocates combining market mechanisms for distribution and production with socialist planning and control over social resources

NATIONAL SOCIALISM: a form of Fascism (not socialism) that is associated with the Nazi movement in Germany and emphasized duty, discipline, and unquestioned obedience to the state

Overview

Socialism refers both to a set of doctrines and to political movements that advocate the transformation of the capitalist political-economic system to one that is based on public or community control over the resources, means of production, and wealth of a society. As an economic system, socialism is fundamentally distinguished from capitalism. Capitalism is characterized by private ownership of productive property (the means of production), individuals working for others and being paid in wages (labor markets), and production on the basis of opportunities for profit. Advocates of capitalism see the pursuit of self-interest as the driving force behind economic production, growth, and development. Capitalists, striving to improve their own lives, are seen as the major source of increased wealth and resources for a society.

Socialists, in contrast, advocate public or community ownership of the productive resources of society. They believe that the production of goods should be based on need (use value), not profit opportunities, through some form of public planning. They advocate the redistribution of societal resources in order to guarantee all individuals a basic standard of living instead of relying on individual participation in labor markets to do so. Socialists have a cooperative vision of humans and believe in the wide and efficient use of resources for the benefit of all members of the community instead of stressing economic growth as the solution to social conflicts. They see labor as the source of all societal wealth. In socialists' view, the ability of capitalists to buy the power of workers allows them to utilize the labor of others in order to enhance their own wealth, rather than using it in a socially effective manner. Thus, socialists advocate some form of public economic planning, as opposed to what they see as the "trickle down" variety of economic theory that is associated with capitalism.

Some socialists have advocated nationalization of the means of production and central-ized planning as necessary to develop societal resources to a level that makes the transfor-mation to socialism possible. Others have proposed forms of mixed economies or market socialism that call for the selective nationalization of key industries and guidance by socialist planning while retaining some degree of private ownership of the remainder of the economy. These versions of socialism stress decentralization and democratic planning and call for delegating decision-making authority to community planning boards, quasi-public agencies, and workers' councils.

Although all socialists are committed to a more egalitarian distribution of national resources, they disagree over the degree of quality and the means of bringing it about. Some call for a basically equal distribution of national income with only a limited degree of income differentials for different occupations or different amounts of effort. Others would be satisfied with a society that permitted greater income differentials as long as all citizens were first assured minimum levels of food, clothing, shelter, and basic services such as education, health, recreation, and transportation.

Socialists share a vision of a new society that is based on the principles of equality, democracy, and human solidarity. Socialists also argue that, in order to understand and change society, the political, economic, social, and cultural must be seen as interconnected parts of a whole, not as segmented spheres of life as under liberal-capitalist doctrine. Like other major political concepts such as democracy, liberalism, or equality, socialism encom-passes a wide diversity of ideas and political practices.

The word "socialism" is often mistakenly used interchangeably with the word "commu-nism." Karl Marx (1818-1883) and Friedrich Engels (1820-1895) initially used the two words to mean the same thing in the famous *The Communist Manifesto* (1848). They and most Marxists, however, subsequently used the term "communism" to mean a late stage of socialism in which goods had become so plentiful and social patterns of behavior had so developed that social resources would be distributed on the basis of need, not effort. Therefore, at the doctrinal level, socialism should be distinguished from communism, which is a late stage of socialism. At the level of political movements and doctrines, communist parties or movements are only one type of a broader range of political movements that see themselves as part of the socialist tradition. These include formal political parties, such as the French Socialist Party, the Swedish Social Democratic Party, and the Socialist Party of Japan; revolutionary political organizations such as the Sandinista National Liberation Front (FSLN) in Nicaragua or the Southwest Africa People's Organization (SWAPO) in Namibia; as well as various socialist-feminist, ecological-socialist, and democratic-socialist political movements.

Anarchism, which also is sometimes confused with socialism, encompasses a diverse range of beliefs and attitudes. Its unifying feature is the belief that government is a form of organized oppression that is the major obstacle to a good society. Anarchists believe that power corrupts, that property is a form of power incompatible with freedom, that authority and property are the source of most social problems, and that human nature is fundamentally cooperative. They offer a vision of an alternative libertarian society, without rulers, where work and goods are shared and individuals are truly happy and free because they act on the basis of their consciences, not because of laws that are imposed by authorities. Socialists disagree with the anarchists' complete distrust of all power and with their view of an inherently cooperative human nature.

Socialists also stress class as a fundamental source of social conflict and as a basis for the transformation of capitalism. As political movements, these differences primarily have been reflected in the issue of how to transform capitalist society, with socialists emphasizing the need to use political power and to plan on a transitional stage to a socialist society in which government and community power will be a necessity.

Finally, National Socialism is sometimes mistakenly equated with socialism. National Socialism refers to the doctrines and political movement that were associated with Adolf Hitler's Nazi Party in Germany between the 1920's and the 1940's. Its fundamental principles emphasized the nation (race or state) as the center of life and the embodiment of the unfolding of the meaning of history. People were expected to obey the indisputable authority of the leader of the state. Discipline and complete devotion to duty were emphasized, with the fighting spirit and action stressed. National Socialism rejected individualism and scientific skepticism and, in their place, stressed the coordination of political and intellectual activities in the service of the state. These values, beliefs, and doctrines contrast sharply with those of socialism, which stress equality, human solidarity, individual dignity, and cooperation. Economically, under National Socialism, the economy remained fundamentally capitalistic, not socialistic, with private ownership, labor markets, and production based on the profit principle. Thus, fundamental differences exist between socialism and the National Socialism of Germany at the level of doctrine, economic practice, and political movement.

Additionally, socialists also disagree on the issue of whether socialism was established in the Soviet Union or other countries that have been routinely labeled as communist countries. Some socialists have considered the Soviet-style societies to be a particular, but not a universal, model of socialism. Others have argued that they are not socialist but state-capitalist. Still others have seen them as postcapitalist societies.

Applications

Various political movements and governments have laid claim to the socialist tradition in the twentieth century. Three areas of the world that have done so are the Soviet Union and Eastern Europe, Western Europe, and the Third World

In the Soviet Union, the Bolshevik Revolution did not resolve the issue of how to restructure the Soviet economy. Debate has continued over the kind of socialist economy that Vladimir Ilyich Lenin (1870-1924) envisioned after the revolution was consolidated and the kind of political system that he favored. Some believed that Lenin's New Economic Policy (NEP) was an attempt to create a form of market socialism in which socialist planning at the level of production would be combined with markets in order to aid in the distribution of goods and to motivate workers. Others see in Lenin a precursor of Joseph Stalin (1879-1953), who advocated a system of five-year plans, bureaucratic control of the economy, and industrialization as the road to development.

Not only Stalin's political system, but his centralized command economy as well, became associated with the concept of socialism, especially after World War II when Eastern European states adopted similar political-economic systems. While this economic model of socialism was quite successful in raising living standards and building an infrastructure, the problems that are associated with its rigidity and control led to economic stagnation in the 1970's. Consequently, a reform movement in the Soviet Union developed under Mikhail Gorbachev in the mid-1980's. Initially, Gorbachev advocated a form of economic reform that was similar to Lenin's NEP, blending socialist planning with the market as a means of

economic motivation and as a device for allocating goods and resources. By the end of the 1980's, however, Gorbachev called for the privatization of the means of production and a transition to capitalist markets. In Eastern Europe, especially Poland and Czechoslovakia, the transformation of bureaucratic socialism into capitalism moved forward at a faster pace than in the Soviet Union. These developments raise significant questions about the future of both Soviet-style bureaucratic socialism and socialism in general.

In Western Europe, many socialists gave up not only the idea of revolution but also the idea of transforming capitalism. The socialist political parties of Western Europe chose to emphasize the social welfare state as their vision of the good society. Their platforms emphasized a mixed economy in which a certain degree of public planning and control of social resources, combined with private ownership of the means of production and capitalistic labor markets, would bring enough social benefits for all. These parties successfully chose the parliamentary road to power, sometimes ruling by themselves, and at other times participating in coalition governments with liberal and conservative parties. For example, by 1959,

Vladimir Ilyich Lenin's long-term goals for Soviet socialism have been obscured by the heavy-handed control of the economy exercised by his successor, Joseph Stalin. (National Archives)

the program of principles of the German Social Democratic Party no longer used the words "class" or "class struggle" and advocated private property and a competitive free market. Similarly, most other Western European socialist or social-democratic parties sought quiet reform rather than the radical transformation of capitalism.

The Scandinavian countries are often seen as the most successful examples of this nonrevolutionary reform of capitalism. They have a large degree of social planning and government regulation of the economy but retain private ownership of the means of production and capitalist control over basic investment and management decisions. These social welfare states were very successful between the end of World War II and the late 1970's in combining economic growth with low unemployment and extensive social services, and they served as a model for some of the Eastern European reformers of the 1980's. Nevertheless, these countries suffered the same economic stagnation during the 1980's as did most other countries of the world.

In comparison to the United States, these social-democratic countries of Europe have had much larger social welfare components to their economies, higher and more progressive tax structures, a more equitable distribution of incomes, and lower unemployment. Their growth rates and standards of living have been comparable to or have exceeded those in the United States. Their combination of some of the elements that are associated with socialism with a basically capitalist economy is seen by some as the future for both the former countries of the Soviet bloc and the United States. The economic problems of these mixed economy countries in the 1980's, however, lead others to see a more "pure" form of capitalism as desirable, while more traditional socialists retain a vision and commitment to the transformation of capitalism, not its modification.

In much of Asia and Africa, the conditions for building socialism were very different from those that were envisioned by Marx or those existing in Western Europe or the Soviet Union. Many of these countries were not industrialized, had large peasant populations, and had been colonies of European powers for a long period. Under those conditions, socialism or communism often became the ideology of industrialization or modernization. To their leaders, it seemed that meaningful national independence could be achieved only through state direction of the economy. To varying degrees, many of these countries chose the Soviet model of economic development, channeling national resources into building productive facilities and restricting consumption. Many of these countries also adopted the Soviet model of a one-party state. The hostility of the former colonial powers and the United States to new revolutionary states also influenced the choices that were made by these countries in terms of their economic and political policies.

In Latin America, Cuba is the outstanding example of a revolutionary movement that was based in the socialist tradition and that succeeded in acquiring political power. Despite the long-standing opposition of the United States, Cuba has remained under the control of its Communist Party and has served as an alternative model of national development for a wide variety of Third World countries. While initially basing their economy on the bureaucratic socialist model, Cuba was rather innovative in the 1970's and 1980's in experimenting with new ways of trying to motivate workers and distribute economic rewards while retaining its basic socialist emphasis on public ownership and social planning.

Overall, until the 1980's, a significant number of countries in Asia, Africa, and Eastern Europe had established political systems that were based on some version of the socialist tradition. Yet, the momentous changes that occurred in Eastern Europe and the Soviet Union in the late 1980's raised major questions about the future of the socialist movements in those countries.

Meanwhile, in much of the world, the original democratic-socialist vision of Marx continued to serve as an inspiration to variety of progressive movements and political organizations, ranging from trade unions to feminist movements to new environmental organizations. Marxism also remains a significant influence in intellectual circles.

Context

Modern or scientific socialism, both as a set of principles, doctrines, and beliefs, and as a series of political movements, was grounded in the writing and theories of Marx. Marx saw societies as dynamic sets of social relations with conflict between classes as the moving force of historical development. To Marx, a fundamental fact of human existence was the material need to make a living. In the process of doing so, humans entered into social relations with one another, and those social relations changed over time as the forces of production developed. At a certain stage in human social development, a division of labor emerged that led to the formation of antagonistic classes.

Classes were groupings of people who shared a common position in the relations of production and consequently shared a similar outlook and recognition of their mutual interests. The types of classes and the nature of the class struggle varied over time. Marx also considered societies to be structured wholes, not composed of separate spheres. Therefore, a society's laws, art, religion, and educational system were related to one another and to the system of economic production. Marx argued that, in the final analysis, a society's mode of production was the foundation on which the other elements of society rested.

In modern society, the primary, though not exclusive, classes were capitalists and workers. Marx believed that the struggle between them would eventually lead to the overthrow of capitalism by the new majority class of workers and, after a transitional period, to the establishment of a socialist society. Once this occurred, the class struggle would end because the source of class conflict would have ended.

Within the socialist movement, socialists have primarily disagreed on the means of transforming the capitalist system and on the organization of the postcapitalist or socialist society. One school of socialism has argued that, ultimately, the only way to overthrow capitalism is through revolutionary action. The power and class consciousness of capitalists is so strong, they argue, that capitalists will never yield power except to force.

Within this revolutionary tradition, some socialists such as Rosa Luxemburg (1870-1919) emphasized the need for mass, popular action to overthrow capitalism and build a postrevolutionary society that is based on principles of democracy and equality. A variant on this approach was the syndicalist movement, which grew out of French trade unionism. Syndicalists argued that only direct action by workers, organized in their unions, would bring about the socialist transformation. The general strike would paralyze the country and deliver power into the hands of the organized workers, who would then use their unions as the basis of organizing and administering the society. Lenin, on the other hand, stressed the need for a militant, disciplined organization of professional revolutionaries to mobilize the masses of workers and peasants into action. Once power was seized, this disciplined organization, the vanguard of the proletariat, would serve as the basis for organizing the new society during its transitional phase to socialism.

The second major tradition within socialism is associated with those who advocated the evolutionary road to socialism. Marx himself suggested in the 1860's that a peaceful transition to socialism might be possible in some countries such as England and the United States. Writing forty years later in very different conditions, Eduard Bernstein (1850-1932), a leader of the German Social Democratic Party, urged his party to reject its revolutionary principles. He argued that capitalism could be gradually transformed into socialism through reforms that were brought through the parliamentary political process. While his ideas were officially rejected in 1903, by the end of World War II almost all the European Democratic Socialist parties had sought to become popular parties pursuing the parliamentary road to power and advocating a social welfare state instead of a postcapitalist one.

Socialists have also disagreed about the particular way to structure a socialist economy and society. While socialists agree on the need for equal political rights for all citizens and the leveling of status differences, which can be transformed into political power, they have disagreed on the possibility or desirability of allowing such rights in the immediate postrevolutionary state, especially to supporters of the former regime. Socialists also disagree on the particular economic structure for a socialist economy and the degree to which status differences should be leveled in the future socialist society.

While socialism has been the major challenge to capitalism in the twentieth century, its future development will be worked out in response to the growing internationalization of the world economy; the dramatic changes of the 1980's in the Soviet Union, China, and Eastern Europe; and the developing global political agenda of a new world order.

Bibliography

Bell, Daniel. "Socialism." In *International Encyclopedia of the Social Sciences.* Vol. 14, edited by David L. Sills. New York: Macmillan, 1968. One of the best available short surveys of socialism. Bell discusses the formulation of early socialist doctrines, the development of and differences in socialist political movements, the role of socialist political parties, and the variations in socialist thought since Karl Marx.

Bellofiore, Riccardo, ed. *Marxian Economics—A Reappraisal: Essays on Volume Three of "Capital."* New York: St. Martin's Press, 1998.

Cabral, Amilcar. *Revolution in Guinea: An African People's Struggle.* London: Stage 1, 1969. A book by one of the most original of Africa's socialist thinkers and political activists and a leading influence on Third World political thought. Describes the struggle for independence from Portuguese colonialism and offers a realistic and self-critical assessment of the nature of revolutionary struggle in the Third World.

Cole, G. D. H. *A History of Socialist Thought.* 5 vols. London: Macmillan, 1953-1960. A classic general study of the development of socialist movements throughout the world and of the development of socialist thought. An accessible, clear, well-researched survey that is particularly strong on the growth of socialism and laborism in Great Britain and on socialist political thought in Western Europe.

Kolakowski, Leszek. *Main Currents of Marxism.* 3 vols. New York: Oxford University Press, 1978. Considered by many a modern classic in the critical exposition of the development of Marxist thought. Surveys the origins of Marxism, distinguishes it from other forms of socialism, examines the controversies among various Marxist theorists, and traces the developments in socialism and Marxism since World War II.

Marx, Karl. *Capital.* 3 vols. Moscow: Foreign Languages Publishing House, 1957-1959. The major economic work of Marx in which he presents his analyses of capitalism as a mode of production and of the contradictions, inherent in the social relations of capitalism, which he argues will lead to its transformation by socialism.

Marx, Karl, and Friedrich Engels. *The Communist Manifesto.* 1848. Reprint. New York: W. W. Norton, 1988. The most famous document in the history of the socialist movement. It announced to the world, in brief and brilliant prose, the new synthesis of socialist ideas that was worked out by Marx and Engels in the early 1840's.

Miliband, Ralph. *Marxism and Politics.* New York: Oxford University Press, 1977. An excellent, very readable, nonsectarian introduction to the politics of Marxism. Reconstructs the main elements of the political theory and actual politics that are specific to Marxism. Also discusses some of the problems and contradictions that are found in the Marxist political tradition.

Carl Swidorski

Cross-References

Capitalism, 69; Communism, 80; Economists, 164; History of Economics, 295; Labor Economics, 353; Labor Theory of Value, 358; Marxist Economics, 412; Unions, 613; Welfare Economics, 631; World Economies, 638.

STOCKS AND THE STOCK MARKET

Type of economics: Monetary and fiscal theory
Fields of study: Business finance and investment; monetary theory

The modern stock market was organized as a marketplace in which a corporation could sell its stocks in order to raise money that was external to the firm. In addition, the stock market is a place where brokers can buy and sell securities for their customers and themselves. The above two functions of the stock market help to support the general economy and capitalism.

Principal terms

CAPITAL: a resource that aids in the generation of income for a business enterprise

COMMERCIAL BANK: a financial institution that makes retail loans to private and government agencies

COMMON STOCK: a certificate issued as ownership shares in a publicly held corporation; shareholders have voting rights and may receive dividends based on proportionate ownership

DIVIDENDS: the income, in the form of cash or additional stock, that stockholders receive on their investment in a company's stock

INVESTMENT BANKER: a middleman between the investing public and companies or government units that need funds for expansion and development

PREFERRED STOCK: a certificate that provides ownership but not voting rights in a corporation and pays a fixed or variable stream of dividends

SELLING GROUP: several retail brokerage firms that get together and share the risk and rewards of selling a new issue of corporate stocks to the general public

Overview

The stock market is an organized marketplace in which buyers and sellers come together in order to exchange stocks. Prices or quotes for shares are determined at the exchange. There are generally two types of stocks that investors can buy or sell: common stock and preferred stock. Many corporations issue both preferred stock and common stock.

Common stock represents the basic ownership of a company. As legal owners of a corporation, shareholders participate in the financial risks and rewards of the firm. Each share of stock is interchangeable with every other share and carries with it the rights to income, property, and control that every other share does.

The second type of stock that is available to investors is preferred stock. The primary investor advantages of preferred stock are that it has larger fixed-rate returns than bonds and that it has greater financial safety than common stock. Legally, preferred stock also provides an ownership interest. In addition, preferred shareholders enjoy prior claim to company income. As a rule, preferred shareholders do not have voting rights, as do common stockholders. Preferred stock is sold with the understanding that there is a trade-off between having a prior claim to dividends, but no voice in management through voting rights.

When a corporation is organized, its founders often agree to authorize more stock than is initially offered for sale. This is done because some issues are held back for future sale. Once stock is sold, it is called "outstanding stock," which means that issues are held by owners other than the corporation itself. A company can and does buy and hold part of its own stock, thus reducing the number of outstanding shares. Furthermore, the amount of outstanding stock may be reduced through the return by some stockholders of part of their stock to the corporation. This returned stock is called "treasury stock." If the company sells its treasury stock, the stock again becomes outstanding, or the company may choose to cancel the stock and thus reduce the issued amount.

The par value of stock has little practical significance to modern investors. Historically, par value was equal to the amount of money that was originally paid in to a company for each share of stock. Par value no longer reflects the corporation's original paid-in investment because, as a company grows, the price of its outstanding shares reflects the firm's profits and has little relationship to par. Thus, the trend has been for the par value of stocks to have some arbitrarily low value, such as one dollar per share.

Investors are often attracted to a stock because of its dividend, which is a distribution of corporate earnings among the stockholders. A dividend is usually paid in cash or property, or it may be in the form of additional shares of stock. It is the responsibility of the board of directors of the firm to authorize the payment of a dividend. Cash dividends are typically paid on a quarterly basis. The payment of a stock dividend does not alter the company's net worth, as instead each share of outstanding stock from that day forward represents a smaller proportion of the total net worth. Therefore, a cut in dividends can be particularly harmful for a company's financial position in the industry. A disruptive dividend stream often causes a decline in the financial faith that investors have in that firm.

Once the decision to buy or sell stocks has been made, the investor contacts a retail stockbroker. The broker completes the transaction by relaying the order to the floor of the appropriate stock exchange. The majority of stocks of publicly traded U.S. corporations are traded on the New York, American, and Over-the-Counter Exchanges, the former being the dominant exchange in the terms of transaction volume.

These exchanges are formally organized membership institutions. Membership on the New York Stock Exchange (NYSE) is called a "seat," which may only be bought and sold with the approval of the board of governors of the exchange. Members must comply with certain requirements, and the board of governors also enforces the requirements for corporations to be listed or have their shares traded on the exchange. To be considered for listing, a company must meet specific requirements, such as being in a growth industry, demonstrating sufficient profit potential, and satisfying certain net worth requirements. Finally, a listed corporation must have at least one million common shares that are outstanding and held by no less than two thousand stockholders.

In addition to the NYSE, there are many other exchanges at which stocks are traded. Besides other national exchanges, there are also regional exchanges, such as the Pacific Coast Stock Exchange. The structure of the exchange may vary as well. Buyers and sellers dealing on the NYSE find that the prices that they receive for their stocks are determined by a type of auction method on the floor of the exchange. In contrast, transactions on the Over-the-Counter Exchange are completed between offices of brokerage houses, where prices are established by individual negotiation. Regardless of the structure

Traders working on the floor of the New York Stock Exchange shortly after an opening bell in late 1996. (Reuters/Peter Morgan/Archive Photos)

or method, all exchanges are charged with the responsibility of maintaining a fair and orderly marketplace.

Applications

The purpose of the stock market is twofold. First, it functions as an organized exchange where the business sector can sell its stock with the intent of raising money for the expansion of plant and equipment. Secondly, the stock market provides a marketplace where investors can buy and sell outstanding corporate shares and participate in the financial growth of business. Most individual and group retirement portfolios contain stocks that are issued by the corporate sector.

The initial issuance of stock is an involved procedure. The decision for corporations to issue stock (preferred or common) is a financial one. Once the company has decided on the type and amount of stock to sell, it contacts an investment banker, which is a private firm or a part of a larger brokerage house. These "bankers" act as financial intermediaries by bringing the sellers (corporations) and buyers (investors) of stock together.

The investment banking process of bringing stock to public investors is often called issue underwriting. The procedure begins when a firm decides that it wants to sell authorized stocks for business expansion. An investment banker is contracted for financial consultation. The initial meetings are concerned with how much money the corporation is trying to raise, the number of shares to be issued, and the price of these shares. The price is sometimes difficult to arrive at because the company often wants an initial price per share that may be unrealistically high. It is the job of the investment banker to recommend a price for the newly offered stock that is practical and one that will be attractive to the initial investors. The process that is used in order to determine price is to fit the corporation into an industry and then to calculate the price-earnings ratio for that industry. For example, if an industry is earning $1 in profits and investors are willing to pay $10 (the price of the stock per share) for that $1 in earnings, the price-earnings ratio is 10 to 1.

With the help of an investment banker, the corporation determines its forecasted earnings with the anticipated infusion of new financing from the stock offering. If the earnings forecast for the company are $2 per share, and the public is willing to pay $10 for every dollar of industry earnings, then the estimated price for this newly issued stock would be $20 ($10 \times 2). Once an initial price has been agreed on by the corporate management, other details, such as complying with legal and financial disclosures and the filing of a prospectus for potential investors, need to be done. While the investment banker guides the company through these decisions, they simultaneously put a "selling group" together. A selling group is made up of several retail brokerage houses (stockbrokers) that help the investment banker sell the company's authorized stock to the public.

Once the administrative details have been completed, the investment banker purchases the total amount of stock (at a wholesale price of $20 per share, for example) from the issuing corporation. They do so with the intent of distributing the stock at retail through the selling group with a sales commission for the efforts of all concerned. The investment banker borrows the money that is necessary to purchase the stock issue, at wholesale cost, from commercial banks. The investment banker is charged interest for the loan and is also required to put up the unsold stock as temporary collateral for the loan from the commercial bank. The money that is borrowed from the commercial bank is used to pay the company for its newly issued stock. The company has what it wanted—money for plant expansion. Meanwhile, the investment banker and the selling group work hard to find buyers (investors) for the new stock issue. Once the total issue is sold, the investment banker pays off the commercial bank loan, plus the accrued interest. Assuming that no unforeseen problems occur, all parties that are involved in the underwriting are better off. The corporation has money for business expansion and the investment banker, selling group, and commercial bank have earned commissions and interest, respectively. Finally, the investors also are better off, assuming that the corporation grows and distributes earnings to shareholders.

Once the above process is completed, the newly issued stock become publicly traded on a stock exchange. All newly issued stock initially trades on the Over-the-Counter Exchange and continues to do so until the corporation qualifies for a listing on another exchange. Investors can now buy, hold, or sell this stock as part of their personal or group investment portfolios.

Context

Businesses often have found it necessary to raise money that was outside the corporation. The process of selling newly issued stock has been a large part of that fund-raising activity. Prior to 1934, the stock market was not formally organized. During 1934, however, the Securities Exchange Act was passed, which marked the beginning of the modern period in the exchange's history. This legislation allowed for an orderly process by which investment banking could take place.

Modern stock exchanges have not only filled an important need in the capitalistic system but also played a vital role in the growth of the economy. Economic growth is dependent on two distinct functions. First, aggregate demand must exist; that is, the willingness and ability of consumers to purchase the economy's total output of goods and services (the gross national product, or GNP) must be present. Secondly, the productive base on which the GNP is created must grow. This expansion process is called capital formation. The daily function of the stock market directly and indirectly perpetuates both aggregate demand and capital formation.

Aggregate demand requires both the willingness and the ability of consumers to spend on final economic output. This willingness comes from an optimistic consumer attitude and confidence to spend, while the ability requires income. A bullish or rising stock market generates profits (income), which in turn fosters the ability to purchase the nation's output.

Capital formation, on the other hand, occurs when the business sector invests money in the expansion of plant and equipment, which encourages a greater future output in the GNP. For several years following World War II, the business sector obtained a portion of the investment dollars for capital formation from retained income (internal financing). In more recent times, however, as corporations found the demand for their output exceeding their ability to finance expansion internally, many corporations turned to external sources of financing. Thus, an important function of the stock market is to act as a type of clearinghouse where money is created for the purpose of forming capital, which is a vital part of the growth of a capitalistic economy. The market also provides an opportunity for individual investors to participate in the growth of business, as well as a dividend income stream that provides the potential for further consumer spending.

The future role of the stock market, as it pertains to the needs of the business sector and the individual investor, will be of even greater importance than it has been in the past. In the case of the business sector, the need to expand the domestic and international marketing of products and services will continue to make capital formation a high priority. Finally, as society ages, the need to procure stock portfolios for financial appreciation and income in preparation for retirement will continue to expand. Therefore, the stock market will play a very significant and important role in the economy's future.

Bibliography

Auerbach, Robert D. *Financial Markets and Institutions.* New York: Collier Macmillan, 1983. A text that is devoted to financial markets and the theory and application that are behind them. Excellent background reading for understanding the economics of general investments. Provides excellent charts, tables, and graphs and also contains a good glossary of terms.

Casey, John L. *Values Added: Making Ethical Decisions in the Financial Marketplace.* Lanham, Md.: University Press of America, 1997.

Chernow, Ron. *The Death of the Banker: The Decline and Fall of the Great Financial Dynasties and the Triumph of the Small Investor.* New York: Vintage Books, 1997.

Fabozzi, Frank J., and Irving M. Pollack. *Fixed Income Securities.* Homewood, Ill.: Dow Jones-Irwin, 1983. Designed as a complete and detailed collection of readings, the chapters of particular concern are 1, 6, and 13 on interest rates and preferred stock investment. Although this book is over one thousand pages in length, the above chapters are most appropriate for a general background on the stock market. Graphs and charts are included.

Lehmann, Michael B. *The Dow Jones-Irwin Guide to Using the Wall Street Journal.* 3d ed. Homewood, Ill.: Dow Jones-Irwin, 1990. This outstanding book integrates economics, financial markets, and investments. Lehmann explains how monetary and fiscal policies are used to influence business cycles and investment behavior. Very well written, concise, and well suited for the lay reader. Highly recommended.

Maginn, John L., and Donald L. Tuttle. *Managing Investment Portfolios.* Boston: Warren, Gorham & Lamont, 1983. Although this book is a collection of excellent works, Chapters 5 and 10 are the most relevant to a study of stock markets. Well written and concise, but lacks sufficient graphs or charts. Chapter 10 is of particular interest and is concerned with individual stock portfolio construction.

O'Neil, William J. *How to Make Money in Stocks.* New York: McGraw-Hill, 1991. An excellent book for those interested in how to select stocks. A very well-prepared introduction to individual stock portfolio selection and management. Clear and very well written, with outstanding examples and graphs that apply the concepts.

Marshall D. Nickles

Cross-References

Banks, 29; Business Cycles, 51; Business Organization, 57; Capitalism, 69; Corporations, 106; Financing, 228; Growth Theory, 281.

SUBSTITUTION

Type of economics: General economics
Field of study: Economic theory

Substitution is the rational act of choosing a good, service, or asset in the place of another good, service, or asset. A change in the price, quality, desirability, or affordability of an item, relative to another, causes substitution among the various choices that are available.

Principal terms

COMMODITY: a good that is durable, divisible, and easily standardized as to grade or quality
COMPLEMENT: a good or service that is used in conjunction with a given good or service
DEMAND: the quantities of a good or service that buyers are willing and able to purchase at various prices
INPUTS: factors of production, usually categorized as belonging to the major classes of land, labor, capital, or enterprise
LAW OF ONE PRICE: a law that states that, in different markets, the prices of commodities will differ only by the cost of transportation from one market to the other
SUBSTITUTE: a good or service that is similar in nature to a given good or service
SUPPLY: the quantities of a good or service that owners offer for sale at various prices
UTILITY: a subjective measure of the satisfaction, enjoyment, or pleasure that the user of a good or service obtains

Overview

Substitution is at the heart of the central economic problem: making proper choices among competing alternatives under conditions of scarcity. In order for a choice to be made, substitutes or competing goods and services must be available. The act of substitution, therefore, is the embodiment of choice. Substitution is what affects many economic laws and principles, such as arbitrage, the law of demand, the principle of diminishing marginal rates of substitution and diminishing marginal utility, and the law of one price.

In arbitrage, for example, a commodity or asset is sold in one market and simultaneously purchased in another for a sure and certain profit. Rarely, however, is the commodity that is sold and repurchased in the other market identical. More often, arbitrage involves two items which are very close substitutes, but not, strictly speaking, identical. For example, in currency substitution, German marks might possibly be sold in New York and used to acquire British pounds. The pounds are simultaneously sold in London and used to acquire U.S. dollars, the currency that the trader started with. If a profit occurs, then arbitrage opportunity is said to have existed, but this profitable arbitrage depends on the exchange of very close substitutes—marks, pounds, and dollars—and not the simultaneous purchase and sale of identical items.

In financial markets, the exchange of very close but not perfect substitutes is often what keeps interest rates the same among competing bonds. For example, if the yield to maturity on a twenty-year, 8 percent coupon government bond exceeds that of a twenty-one-year, 9 percent coupon government bond, then investors are more likely to purchase the higher yielding bond and dispose of the lower yielding bond. In this way, the prices of the bonds are changed and the yields to maturity are brought very closely into line. This is the finance version of the law of one price. It should be recognized, however, that a twenty-year, 8 percent government bond is not the same item as a twenty-one-year, 9 percent government bond: They are close substitutes. Thus, it is substitution that yields the law of one price and not arbitrage, strictly defined.

In production and cost theories, productive inputs, such as labor and capital goods, are subject to substitution. The degree of substitution can be limited by the amount of time available, by the nature of the productive process, and by other factors. Those limits aside, an increase in the unit cost of one input, other things being equal, can be expected to result in a decrease in that input's use, as substitution in favor of other inputs occurs.

It is the ability to substitute that underlies the familiar law of demand, which states that, other things being equal, a higher price of an item results in a lower quantity that is demanded of that item. This law works because, as the price of item A increases, the relative desirability of other items with similar attributes (that is, substitutes) becomes greater. Consequently, the purchaser substitutes other items in order to replace the original item whose price has increased. This substitution effect, as it is called, is always negative. If the consumer is compensated for the loss in purchasing power that results from the increase in price of item A, then the consumer will always be observed to purchase less of the commodity as substitution for relatively less expensive items occurs. If income is not compensated, then one can never be sure whether the consumer will buy more or less of an item whose price is increased. If the income effect is counteracted by an income replacement, however, so that real purchasing power is held constant when the price of an item is increased, then the substitution effect can always be relied on to decrease purchases.

Thus, the law of demand depends crucially on the substitution effect. As Sir Robert Giffen (1837-1910) is said to have demonstrated, it is always possible that the increase in the price of the necessity or good that most cheaply satisfies the consumer's basic desire for survival, and that requires a large proportion of income, may so depress purchasing power that more, not less, of the now more expensive good is consumed. Although such a good has not yet been found, its hypothetical name is a Giffen good. As the great British economist Alfred Marshall (1842-1924) showed, however, this result could only occur because of the income effect operating on a so-called inferior good, one whose demanded quantity increases as income drops. Only if the income effect is stronger than the substitution effect will a Giffen good be observed. So far, an example of a Giffen good has not been found.

Applications

The substitutability of two goods has been quantified by using two methods. First, the cross-price elasticity of demand measures the degree of substitutability by calculating the percentage change in the quantity that is demanded of one good when other things are held constant except a price change of a competing good. For example, if a 1 percent increase in the price of beef results in a 1 percent increase in the quantity that is demanded of pork, then pork is said to be a substitute for beef because the cross-price elasticity of demand is equal to + 1. Goods are classified as to their substitute or complementary nature vis-à-vis another good by observing whether the cross-price elasticity coefficient is positive (substitutes) or negative (complements). Therefore, the higher the positive cross-price elasticity of demand coefficient, the more substitutable are the two goods. In the case of perfect substitutes or identical goods, the cross-price elasticity of demand would equal the ordinary price elasticity of demand. The divergence then of the cross-price elasticity from the ordinary demand elasticity tells the degree of substitutability of the two goods.

Another calculation of the degree of substitutability between two goods occurs with the marginal rate of substitution, which underlies the modern indifference analysis approach to demand theory. Suppose that there are two goods, X and Y. Hold the amount of Y constant and give the consumer more of good X. The consumer will be better off. Now assume that just enough of good Y is taken away from the consumer, along with the increase in the amount of good X, so that the consumer's welfare (utility) is neither improved nor diminished. The consumer is said to be "indifferent" between the two positions, one of which contains more Y but less X, the other which contains more X but less Y.

This ability or willingness of the consumer to substitute a certain amount of good Y in order to gain additional good X and not become better or worse off is called the marginal rate of substitution of X for Y. For example, suppose that a consumer was willing to give up five units of good Y in order to attain one additional unit of good X and not become better or worse off in the process. Then, the marginal rate of substitution of Y for X is five; that is, the consumer is willing to substitute five units of Y for one additional unit of X. Although this calculation is not ascertained in practice, as to do so requires the comparison and aggregation of subjective data, its relevance has been proven in psychological experiments not only with humans but also with animals. The marginal rate of substitution, part of indifference analysis, is also used to explain the demand curve and consumer preference in modern demand theory.

As more and more X (and less and less Y) is given to the consumer, the amount of Y that the consumer can forgo in order to obtain an additional unit of X, without changing the level of satisfaction, necessarily becomes smaller and smaller. After all, the consumer sooner or later has a great amount of X and just a small amount of Y. X is relatively abundant, while Y is, relatively, a rarity. This implication is formally stated as the principle of the diminishing marginal rate of substitution: As more and more of a good is consumed, the marginal rate of substitution of other goods for that good must diminish.

The degree of substitution in the use of inputs has been quantified in the elasticity of technical substitution, which is the quotient of the percentage change in the input-usage ratio divided by the percentage change in the marginal rate of technical substitution. An example is useful to make the marginal rate of technical substitution clear. Suppose that two inputs, labor and capital, are used to produce one hundred units of a product. If more labor is used, then production will increase—unless the amount of capital is, at the same time, reduced. Suppose that it is just enough to keep production at one hundred units. The marginal rate of technical substitution (of capital for labor) is the amount of capital that can be forgone, per unit of added labor, while output remains constant. As more and more labor is added, the amount of capital that can be forgone while leaving production constant necessarily becomes smaller and smaller because of the superabundance of labor working with the decreased quantity of capital. Thus, the marginal rate of technical substitution must diminish as more labor (and less capital) is employed. This is the productive corollary to the principle of diminishing rate of substitution in consumption, called the principle of diminishing marginal rate of technical substitution: As more and more of a productive input is employed, the marginal rate of technical substitution of other inputs for it must diminish.

Context

The concept of substitution is, and for the foreseeable future will remain, firmly embedded in the structure of economic science because it is basic to an understanding of what economics is about. Resources have never been abundant enough to be valueless; predictions of limitless (and therefore free) supplies of energy or food remain the dreams of science-fiction writers. The goals for these resources to accomplish have expanded along with increases in living standards.

Optimal choice under conditions of scarcity is at once the basis and the goal of economic understanding. The concept of substitution necessarily intrudes whenever the conditions of choice change. When relative prices of goods change, consumers choose different amounts by substituting away from dearer goods in favor of their less costly alternatives. When the yields to maturity of different bonds change, for example, investors choose different amounts of bonds to hold by substituting away from lower yielding bonds in favor of their higher yielding alternatives. When the unit costs of resources change, producers choose different amounts by substituting away from more costly resources in favor of their less costly alternatives. When the productivities of inputs change, managers choose different amounts by substituting away from less productive inputs in favor of their more productive alternatives.

Three economists are generally credited with the visualization of substitution. During the 1930's, Vilfredo Pareto (1848-1923), Francis Ysidro Edgeworth (1845-1926), and Irving Fisher (1867-1947) began to use indifference curves in microeconomic analysis as a replacement for the marginal utility approach of their predecessors. The utility approach required economic agents to be aware of the individual contribution to welfare or output of each specific quantity of good or input. Indifference analysis, however, only requires that the consumer or producer be aware of a potential improvement in welfare or output. The assignment of numerical values to welfare, or the prediction of output that is obtained, is not a requirement. Because the theory's assumptions are much less restrictive, indifference analysis has progressively been the tool of choice for the analysis of problems in demand, production, exchange, and value. Also bound up in indifference analysis is the concept of substitution—of consumers, producers, traders, and prices that respond to changes in conditions by substituting from among competing alternatives.

Economic analysis is continually being extended to new areas of inquiry. Some, such as the choice of marriage partner or the number of children to bear, may appear to have little to do with economic life. Yet, virtually all human activity is affected by incentives and when incentives change, so too does the optimal choice. The change in optimal choice in response to changing incentives is another way of saying "substitution" and is the basis for the economic analysis of social phenomena.

Bibliography

Becker, Gary S. *The Economic Approach to Human Behavior.* Chicago, Ill.: University of Chicago Press, 1976. Gives a unique viewpoint to the choice-among-substitutes problems that are faced by humanity. Becker has spent most of his professional career applying economic methods and models to a wide range of noneconomic applications, from the choice of a spouse to crime. This book is a condensation of Becker's previous work, rewritten for the general reader.

Glahe, Fred R., and Dwight R. Lee. *Microeconomics Theory and Applications.* New York: Harcourt Brace Jovanovich, 1989. A popular textbook at the intermediate level in college economics courses. Like other texts that are used in intermediate microeconomics courses, major portions are devoted to indifference analysis and isoquant-isocost analysis. Those topics are founded on substitution, which is well treated here. This book shines in the application of marginal rate of substitution tools to specific cases, such as leisure-income substitution and food subsidies.

Heilbroner, Robert, and Lester Thurow. *Economics Explained.* Englewood Cliffs, N.J.: Prentice-Hall, 1982. For years, Heilbroner has written a series of books that popularize economic topics. All are well written, and all are aimed toward clear, nontechnical exposition. This book is no exception and is highly readable and accessible. Substitution and consumer choice are illustrated in a few well-chosen words and simple graphs, with no equations. Although Heilbroner reveals his bias toward socialist thought, this book is a good first study.

Heyne, Paul. *Microeconomics.* New York: Macmillan, 1991. Chapter 2 is especially relevant because it develops the concept of demand by considering substitutes. This is one of the more basic undergraduate economics texts. Noteworthy is the clarity of language and the large number of questions for discussion: There are at least thirty at the end of each chapter.

McEachern, William A. *Economics: A Contemporary Introduction.* Cincinnati: South-Western, 1991. A college-level introductory text that explains substitution effects and the marginal rates of substitution, in both consumption and production, clearly and well in separate appendices. Supports the words with excellent graphical aids, printed in color. Especially good is the appendix to chapter 20. For readers who are interested in a clear explanation of the marginal rate of technical substitution.

Riddell, Tom, Jean Shackelford, and Steve Stamos. *Economics: A Tool for Critically Understanding Society.* 5th ed. Reading, Mass.: Addison-Wesley, 1998.

Skousen, Mark, and Kenna C. Taylor. *Puzzles and Paradoxes in Economics.* Brookfield, Vt.: Edward Elgar, 1997.

Sloman, John. *Essentials of Economics.* New York: Prentice Hall, 1998.

Ralph C. Gamble, Jr.

Cross-References

Competition, 91; Demand Function, 140; Elasticity, 175; Marginal Principle, 390; Marginal Utility, 396; Market Price, 401; Production and Cost Functions, 500.

SUPPLY FUNCTION

Type of economics: General economics
Fields of study: Econometrics and mathematical models; economic theory

A supply function is a mathematical expression that specifies the quantity of a good that will be produced and offered for sale under the various conditions that influence firm behavior in that market. A supply function typically identifies the direct or positive relationship between the quantity supplied of a good and its price. The theory of supply constitutes one of the cornerstones of modern economic analysis.

Principal terms

AGGREGATION: the process of combining the supply functions of many businesses into a single market or industry supply function
CETERIS PARIBUS: an expression meaning "everything else remaining the same"
ELASTICITY: a measure of responsiveness or sensitivity in the quantity that is supplied of a good to a change in one of its determinants, typically price
EXTERNALITIES: the spillover effects by which the production of one firm influences the costs, and therefore the supply, of another firm
LAW OF SUPPLY: the empirical observation that the quantity that is supplied of a good and its relative price are directly or positively related, *ceteris paribus*
MARGINAL COST: the minimum additional cost that is incurred as a result of increasing the output level by one unit
PROFIT MAXIMIZATION: the hypothesized goal of the typical firm or business, which ultimately explains the supply behavior of producers
SUPPLY CURVE: the graphical depiction of a supply function, which records quantity along the horizontal axis and price along the vertical axis by convention

Overview

The primary presumption about businesses or firms is that they produce a commodity, a good or a service, in the hope of selling it and obtaining a profit. In that respect, individual firms are the fundamental producers or suppliers, and a microeconomic study of market or industry supply must be built up from these disaggregated production units.

Two points of terminology warrant clarification. First, all of the firms that produce the same (type of) output are collectively referred to as an "industry." Each industry has its own supply curve or function, and it is the industry or market supply functions that are of the greatest interest to economists. Second, the expression "supply" is used ambiguously, indicating more than one referent. When one speaks of the supply of gasoline, one typically refers to the quantity that is currently being offered at the going market price; a more definite way to indicate this is by the use of the term the "quantity supplied." Supply also is used to indicate the relationship between the quantity that is supplied of a commodity and its various determining variables. At an elementary level, a supply curve or function highlights the relationship between price and quantity supplied; this is the standard textbook case. In general, supply will depend on several factors, including the price of the good in question, the prices of the resources or factors that are used to produce that good, the level of technology, the number of firms producing the good, and the interdependencies between the firms.

Supply, in conjunction with demand, will determine the market price and the quantity of the good that will trade hands. Alfred Marshall (1842-1924) likened supply and demand to the two blades of a scissors; only together do they interact to determine market equilibrium.

The focus on individual markets, as advocated by Marshall, is labelled partial equilibrium analysis. The problems that are associated with the set of all markets and the aggregate economy are eschewed in lieu of the more tractable study of specific commodity markets. Because partial equilibrium analysis abstracts from the many complex interconnections in a modern economy, this approach requires an eclectic delineation of the relevant determining variables. Building on the groundwork of the theory of the firm, the standard determinants of supply are identified.

The quantity that is supplied over time is a flow and, as such, it entails a time component. Marshall found it useful to distinguish between two time frames of reference: the long run and the short run. These are commonly defined in the terms of the underlying production relationships. The short run refers to that time period over which at least one input or factor of production is fixed. Typically, one thinks of physical capital (machinery) as a fixed or invariant factor over a short time horizon, while the amount of labor that is employed may be varied. Associated with any fixed factor is a fixed or unavoidable cost. The long run refers to that time period over which all factors are variable (or can be freely adapted) and, therefore, over which there are no fixed costs.

The theory of individual firm supply is founded on the premise of profit maximization. Businesses are presumed to take those actions that yield the highest level of profits, where profits are defined as revenues net of all costs (both explicit and implicit). Therefore, business behavior, as characterized by the choice of an optimal output level, will depend on the firm's production function (reflecting the firm's level of technology), resource prices or the prices for the factors of production, and the obtainable output price. Output price, in turn, will depend on the structure of the market under consideration, the defining character of which revolves around the number of firms in the industry.

In the case of a competitive economy in which every firm is small relative to the industry, firms are essentially price takers. Because of their insignificant size, they have no illusions about their ability to affect the market, and they simply respond optimally to the going market price.

If the additional revenue from selling an additional unit of output (that is, the marginal revenue) exceeds the additional cost that is associated with the production of an additional unit of output (that is, the marginal cost), then it is in the firm's interest to increase production; such action will increase the firm's profits. If the marginal revenue is less than the marginal cost, however, then the firm has produced too large an output level. Therefore, the optimal production level is determined by locating that output at which the market price is equal to the firm's marginal cost of production. In a sense, then, the firm's marginal cost curve is the firm's supply function.

There is one caveat with respect to the aforementioned rule. A firm will not produce at the output level at which price equals marginal cost if it is better for the firm to shut down and cease production. In the long run, because all factors and costs are variable, a firm will close if it is unprofitable. Too low an output price could bring about such action. In the short run, a similar case could arise, but it may actually involve a firm remaining in business even though it is losing money; this would occur if the losses are smaller than the payout on the unavoidable short-run fixed costs. This exception is to rule out the marginal cost curve as the firm supply curve at lower prices (in which case, firm supply will be zero).

The market or industry supply function is, in the absence of externalities, simply the summation of every firm's supply function. It specifies the unique output level for the market as a whole (which is simply the sum of output levels for all of the individual firms) that is associated with each price. While the stated rule is generally correct, it should be noted that, given a sufficiently long time horizon, the supply function will reflect the entry of new firms into the industry and the exit of preexisting firms from the industry.

The reason that the market supply is not tautologically the sum of the individual firm supply functions is because of the possible presence of spillover effects. If one firm's actions affect another firm's costs (and therefore, that other firm's supply function), then an externality is said to exist. Externalities may be either good or bad. An externality that lowers another firm's costs is called an external economy, while one that raises another firm's costs is called an external diseconomy. The influence may come about because of the first firm's influence on factor prices (a pecuniary externality) or because of its influence on the inputs that are necessary to produce any given level of output (a technological externality). The factor price effect, in which one firm's expansion drives up the value of scarce inputs for the entire industry and therefore raises the other firm's costs, is an example of an external pecuniary diseconomy.

An industry with a supply function that is positively or directly related to price is known as an increasing cost industry, which is the most common case. If the market supply is negatively related to price, then it is said to reveal a declining cost industry. A horizontal industry supply curve reflects a constant cost industry. Economists have observed increasing cost industries with such frequency that they have formulated the "law" of supply. This law states that, *ceteris paribus*, price and the quantity that is supplied are positively related. While the law of demand is stated with the utmost confidence, the law of supply is simply intended to reflect the typical case.

The supply function is represented in two standard ways. The classic textbook supply function reduces to a two-dimensional graph in which quantity is measured along the horizontal axis and price along the vertical axis, and the other relevant variables are suppressed. The law of supply corresponds to a supply curve with a positive slope. A more general supply function is the mathematical expression or formula that links the quantity that is supplied with its several determinants, which is generally derived using statistical methods of estimation.

Supply defines a unique price-quantity relationship. While equilibrium price and quantity depend on both demand and supply, one can find the supply function independently of the demand side of the market. Such is not the case with a monopoly; the output behavior of a monopolist does depend on the demand side of the market. Therefore, a monopolist does not have a supply function.

Applications
Every partial equilibrium study necessarily involves the identification of the associated supply and demand function. Through the collection of historical data and subsequent

statistical, or econometric, analysis, an estimate of the supply function can be deduced. The accuracy of this estimate can also be examined in order to ascertain the extent of the confidence that is to be placed in the derived supply formula. Supply estimation and forecasting are central to any industrial study.

A statistic that is of great practical importance is the elasticity of supply. This is a measure of the responsiveness or sensitivity in supply to changes in the commodity's price. It is defined as the ratio of the percentage change in the quantity that is supplied to the percentage change in price that brought about the change in supply. The elasticity of supply links supply theory to the actual economy, and it is more easily obtained than a full supply function estimation.

Supply elasticities are important tools for businesspeople, economists, and policy-makers. If supply is very inelastic—that is, if the quantity that is supplied does not respond significantly to large changes in the price of the good—then a tax that is placed on that good will be borne mainly by the sellers. If a good is supplied elastically, then a tax will be borne largely by the consumers of that good.

Supply elasticity depends on the time frame that is under review. Consider a large price increase for hiking boots. The day after the price changes, there will probably be little change in the quantity that is supplied. After a short period of time, however, such as a week, the existing hiking boot companies will step up production and supply will respond. If the price increase remains in effect, then there will not only be more hiking boots produced by the existing firms but new firms will be attracted into the hiking boot industry as well. The longer the period of adjustment, the more elastic will be the supply curve.

The majority of empirical studies are based on partial equilibrium analysis. Therefore, supply figures largely in the scheme of empirical economic research. Studies have ranged from the supply of agricultural products and their dependence on the weather to the supply of money in a complex banking system.

While emphasis has been placed on the derivation of commodity supply functions that are based on the profit-maximizing behavior of firms, the same general properties of supply functions will hold in the case of factor or input supply. The fundamental distinction is that, in the latter case, the supply derives from the resource owners, typically households. The supplies of labor in various employments have been extensively studied. In one unusual case, a backward-bending supply curve for physician services was reported. The interpretation is that, as is typically the case, as the wage (the price of physician services) rises, so too does the amount of labor that is supplied, but only to a point. Once the wage reaches a sufficiently high level, further wage hikes are met by labor withdrawals; the physician chooses to withhold labor, presumably in order to enjoy his or her higher income.

Context

The importance of supply and demand in determining market outcomes is not a modern revelation. Adam Smith (1723-1790) noted that "the market price of every particular commodity is regulated by the proportion between the quantity which is actually brought to market, and the demand of those who are willing to pay the natural price of the commodity," but these lines were far from the incipient recognition of this fact.

In 1838, Antoine Augustin Cournot (1801-1877) was the first economist to model a supply function formally. The quantity that was supplied of a good was written as a mathematical function of the good's price. The first graphical analyses of supply and demand were carried out by Fleeming Jenkin (1833-1885) in 1870. The next year saw William Stanley Jevons (1835-1882) present a theory of labor supply in *The Theory of Political Economy*. His argument states that people will supply their labor up to the point where the utility they receive from the consumption of goods which their marginal labor affords just balances with the disutility of working an additional amount.

The precise connections between production, costs, and supply were initially spelled out in Marshall's *Principles of Economics* (1890). Although Marshall wrote for the lay reader, avoiding technical detail, the full extent of his understanding of the subject is clear. Marshall is credited with several of the fundamental contributions to supply theory (such as the short-run/long-run distinction and the recognition of the role of externalities), as well as with establishing the graphical convention of placing price on the vertical axis and quantity on the horizontal axis in the case of a simple single market depiction of supply.

The step from theoretical analysis to empirical study was undertaken in the 1920's and 1930's. The identification problem of separating the supply function from the demand function through the use of observable data was solved by H. L. Moore and E. J. Working. In addition, the possibility of specifying the supply curve in markets that involve a production lag was addressed. The typical dynamic cobweb models also were studied in relation to the latter topic.

With the seminal paper of Jacob Viner (1892-1970) on cost curves and supply curves in 1931, the formal study of the production-cost-supply relationship was initiated. The firm's supply function can be derived, in theory, through the process of constrained optimization. The constraints involve the output price, factor prices, and the technology (as summarized by the production function).

The relationship between a production and a cost function is one of "duality," which denotes the intimate reciprocity between the two. The cost function can be ascertained from an estimated production function, or the cost function can be estimated directly. Given a firm's cost function, its marginal cost function can be immediately obtained. Because the firm's marginal cost function (over the relevant range) is the firm's supply function, the market supply can be found by simply aggregating the individual firms' marginal cost functions (taking into account, if necessary, any external effects).

A knowledge of the industry supply function is essential before any policy prescriptions are undertaken which impact on that market, such as taxes, tariffs, or other regulations. Henry Schultz (1893-1938) wrote that empirical "investigations, if they are to have theoretical as well as practical significance, should have for their object the determination of the production functions, the cost functions, and the supply functions of the more important commodities and industries."

Bibliography

Coase, Ronald H. "The Nature of the Firm." *Economica* 4 (1937): 396-405. Reprinted in *American Economic Association Readings in Price Theory*, edited by George J. Stigler and Kenneth E. Boulding. Chicago: Richard D. Irwin, 1952. A historically important contribution to the fundamental notion of the firm and its behavior, which is crucial to a proper understanding of supply.

Friedman, Milton. *Price Theory*. Chicago: Aldine, 1976. Chapter 5, entitled "The Relationships Between Supply Curves and Cost Curves," is a classic reference on industry supply curves and their derivation from individual firm cost curves.

Marshall, Alfred. *Principles of Economics*. 1890. 8th ed. London: Macmillan, 1920. In book 5, chapters 3 through 5, Marshall first sets forth what has come to be understood as the modern neoclassical theory of supply. Also see appendix H.

Nerlove, Marc. *The Dynamics of Supply: Estimation of Farmers' Response to Price.* Baltimore: The John Hopkins University Press, 1958. For those with an interest in applied analysis, Nerlove's classic study provides an economic approach to supply.

Pigou, A. C. *The Economics of Welfare*. 4th ed. London: Macmillan, 1932. Appendix 3 builds on Pigou's earlier work on supply analysis and addresses the important issue of externalities or spillover effects in production and their implications for the industry supply relationship.

Robinson, Joan. *The Economics of Imperfect Competition*. 2d ed. London: Macmillan, 1969. Robinson initiates the analysis of imperfect competition by giving a penetrating, and somewhat critical, presentation of the standard supply theory. Especially relevant are chapters 6, 7, 9, and 10. This sets the stage for noncompetitive market analysis in which the supply curve, by the usual construction, is not well defined.

Salvatore, Dominick. *Microeconomics*. New York: HarperCollins, 1991. An outstanding text that gives a particularly insightful presentation of supply theory, as based on the profit-maximizing (cost-minimizing) behavior of firms. A graphical derivation of market supply from firm cost curves lends greatly to the understanding of the nature of supply. The short-run and long-run distinction is carefully analyzed. A most thorough and highly recommended reference, quite accessible to those with very little background.

Sloman, John. *Essentials of Economics*. New York: Prentice Hall, 1998.

Stigler, George J. *The Theory of Price*. 4th ed. New York: Macmillan, 1987. Stigler has contributed in an integral way to modern economists' perceptions of supply. In chapters 10 and 11, costs, externalities, and supply are discussed. The market supply for a factor of production, such as labor, is examined in chapter 6.

Varian, Hal R. *Macroeconomic Analysis*. 2d ed. New York: W. W. Norton, 1984. A popular first-year graduate textbook that provides a formal mathematical presentation of the derivation of supply functions.

Viner, Jacob T. "Cost Curves and Supply Curves." *Zeitschrift für Nationalökonomie* 3 (1931): 23-46. Reprinted in *American Economic Association Readings in Price Theory*, edited by George J. Stigler and Kenneth E. Boulding. Chicago: Richard D. Irwin, 1952. The classic reference on the derivation of supply curves from cost curves.

Timothy M. Weithers

Cross-References

TAX AND TAXATION

Type of economics: Monetary and fiscal theory
Field of study: Fiscal theory and public finance

Taxation is the process used by governments to raise revenue in order to pay for public services such as schools, highways, and national defense. The total amount of taxes collected in the United States at all levels of government is nearly a trillion dollars per year as of 1991.

Principal terms

AD VALOREM TAX: a tax on a good or service in which the amount of the tax depends on the value of the good or service taxed

EFFICIENCY: in one sense, the situation that prevails when a tax raises revenue without affecting the decisions of consumers or firms

EXCISE TAX: a tax levied on a specific commodity, such as gasoline

EXTERNALITIES: the actions of one economic agent (firm or consumer) that have external effects on other economic agents

FREE-RIDER: a person who uses a public good, such as defense, but is not required to pay for it

HORIZONTAL EQUITY: a concept of fairness in taxation in which similar individuals pay similar amounts of tax

PROGRESSIVE TAX: a tax that is borne more heavily by the rich than by the poor

PUBLIC GOODS: goods which cannot be provided properly by the private market mechanism because of their nonexclusive and nonrivalrous nature

REGRESSIVE TAX: a tax that is borne more heavily by the poor than by the rich

TAX INCIDENCE: a measure of who really pays the tax

UNIT TAX: a tax on a good or service in which the amount of the tax depends on the number of units of the good or service purchased

VERTICAL EQUITY: a concept of fairness in taxation in which dissimilar individuals pay dissimilar amounts of tax

Overview

Taxes are collected by all levels of government—federal, state, and local—for the purpose of paying for the services provided by those governments. Governments must intervene in the marketplace when either private markets fail to allocate resources properly or the distribution of wealth provided by the market mechanism is judged unacceptable to society. In either case, there is a role for taxes to pay in solving the problem.

Private markets tend to misallocate resources in the cases of externalities, public goods, and monopoly. Externalities are actions of one economic agent (a firm or a consumer) that have an impact on other economic agents, in either a negative or a positive manner. An example of a negative externality is air pollution produced by a manufacturing firm that makes automobiles. The air pollution negatively affects the health of residents near the factory, but the market for automobiles functions regardless of that impact; people buy and use cars regardless of how their actions affect the health of residents near the factory.

Producers and consumers of automobiles are not required to compensate those affected by the air pollution of the factory, and as a result, they face artificially low prices and produce and consume too many cars. Thus, the private market for cars fails because it provides a quantity that is too large relative to the proper quantity that would be produced if all the costs associated with the air pollution were included. Because of this private market failure, it becomes the government's role to tax automobiles in order to cause the price to reflect accurately the real costs involved—private costs to the drivers of the cars and social costs arising from the health risks posed by the pollution.

A second reason that government intervention may be needed arises from the need to produce public goods Public goods have two distinctive characteristics: nonrivalry and nonexclusion. Nonrivalry means that when one person consumes the good, there is just as much left of the good for others to consume. Nonexclusion means that if the good is provided, it cannot be provided for some people and not for others; if it is available for anyone, it is available for all. A classic example of a public good is a lighthouse. The navigational service provided by a lighthouse is both nonrivalrous and nonexcludable. If one additional sailor wants to use the beacon to navigate a channel, there is just as much of the beacon left for other sailors. Hence, the beacon is nonrivalrous. In addition, it is nonexcludable since if the beacon is there for any sailor to see to navigate by, it is there for all sailors to use; in other words, it is impossible to exclude some sailors from use of the beacon because (for example) they have failed to pay for the service. This nonexclusion characteristic leads to the problem of the free-rider. All sailors have an incentive to understate their willingness to pay for the services provided by the lighthouse, since they cannot be excluded from using it. Consequently, they all want to free-ride—to use the lighthouse but not pay for it. As a result of these characteristics, public goods must be provided by the government, since the private market cannot provide the service. No private entrepreneur can operate a lighthouse profitably given the nature of the service, even though society values the service and would be willing to pay for it (although they do not want to admit it).

A final reason that governments may levy taxes arises from an unequal distribution of wealth. If the wealth generated by the economic system is distributed in an uneven way between many poor in society and some very wealthy, a tax structure can be fashioned to redistribute that wealth more equally. Taxes are sometimes applied in order to take wealth from the rich and give it to the poor in order to correct an unacceptable distribution of wealth. This process of redistributing wealth to provide more equity may, however, cause the economic system to become less efficient. There is a fundamental trade-off between equity and efficiency: Having more of one means having less of the other.

Issues of fairness, or equity, are crucial in taxation. In order to judge the fairness of taxes, there are several equity measures. Horizontal equity is a concept of equity which can be applied to check that similar individuals are paying similar amounts in tax. For example, if Mr. Smith and Ms. Jones both have annual incomes of $30,000, an income tax is said to be horizontally equitable if they both pay the same amount in tax. Tax loopholes are problematic because they violate the concept of horizontal equity. If Mr. Smith is able to use a loophole unavailable to Ms. Jones to avoid paying tax on $10,000 of his income, then the tax system is unfair in the sense that his tax is one-third less than Ms. Jones's.

A second concept of fairness in taxation is vertical equity. This concept is used to check whether taxpayers with higher income are paying higher taxes, as a fair tax system would require. Vertical equity can be achieved with either a flat rate tax or a progressive tax. In either case, taxes rise with income assuring that dissimilar individuals pay dissimilar amounts in tax.

A final important concept in tax equity is known as the ability-to-pay criterion. This concept is applied in taxation to assure that those individuals or firms having the ability to pay taxes are the ones being taxed.

Applications

The U.S. federal tax that generates the greatest revenue is the personal income tax. Each year, taxpayers report their income, including wages, salaries, interest, royalties, and other forms of income. After making several adjustments to that income total, a figure called "adjusted gross income" is calculated. Personal exemptions and deductions are permitted from that figure to arrive at taxable income. The tax owed is then calculated as a percentage of the taxable income. The precise percentage depends on the level of taxable income. At the lowest levels of income, no tax is due. At increasing levels of income, the tax rate rises from 15 percent to 28 percent to 33 percent according to tax schedules for 1990.

The corporate income tax is applied only to businesses that are incorporated. (Partnerships and proprietors pay individual income taxes on the money they earn.) This tax is a tax on corporate profits. Businesses calculate their total sales, subtract all business expenses, and pay a tax on the remaining business income. The tax rates range from 15 percent to 34 percent of taxable income.

Both the personal and corporate income taxes underwent historic change with the Tax Reform Act of 1986, which changed the structure of both taxes by expanding the definition of taxable income and lowering tax rates. In addition, there was a nominal shift of tax burden from individuals to corporations. (Whether there has been an actual change in the incidence of either tax awaits further investigation.)

Property taxes are the main source of tax revenue for local governments (cities, counties, and school districts, for example), accounting for about three-fourths of their tax revenue. Property owners, both homeowners and businesses, must pay a tax on the value of all real estate (both land and structures) they own. The assessor has the job of establishing the official value of the property for tax purposes. The tax bill is then calculated by applying the combined tax rate for all the units of local government to the assessed value of the property. For example, a homeowner's property may have market value of $100,000. The assessed value of that property is typically defined as some percentage of that market value, for example 50 percent, making the assessed value of the home $50,000. If the combined tax rate is 2 percent, the property tax bill is $1,000. That $1,000 in taxes is then divided among the units of local government to pay for police protection, fire protection, schools, libraries, parks, and a host of other services. Property taxes are a form of ad valorem taxation. The incidence of the property tax has traditionally been thought to be regressive, with the percentage of income paid in tax falling as income rises.

State and local governments also rely on sales taxes for a major portion of their tax revenue. The typical state sales tax of 5 percent is applied to all purchases of goods. Many states exempt purchases of food to reduce the regressivity of the sales tax. Some states allow local units of government, cities, or counties, to add an additional sales tax of 1 percent or so to that of the state.

VOL. XXXVII. No. 949.   PUCK BUILDING, New York, May 15th, 1895.   PRICE 10 CENTS.

Copyright, 1895, by Keppler & Schwarzmann.

Entered at N. Y. P. O. as Second-class Mail Matter.

Puck

WITHOUT A FRIEND.

After the U.S. Supreme Court ruled a federal income tax law unconstitutional in 1895, Puck *magazine published this cartoon calling attention to the tax's universal unpopularity.* (Library of Congress)

Excise taxes are collected by federal and state governments on commodities such as cigarettes, beer, wine, spirits, gasoline, tires, telephone services, airline tickets, and other commodities.

The issue of who really pays a given tax is crucial to understanding the way taxes affect society. It is often the case that the person who initially pays the tax to the government is not the person who ultimately pays the tax. For example, federal law specifies that the approximate 15 percent Social Security payroll tax be borne equally by employer and employee. Consequently, employers send 7.5 percent of their payroll to the government while employees do the same. On the surface, it appears that the incidence of the tax is equally shared. The true incidence of the tax is quite different, however, since the employer has an ability to shift part of his tax burden back to the employee in the form of lower wages than would otherwise have been paid. As a result, the employee bears nearly all of the burden of the payroll tax. In taxation, as in many other aspects of life, things are not always as they appear.

Context

U.S. Supreme Court Justice Oliver Wendell Holmes (1841-1935) said that taxes are the price paid for civilization; if one wishes to have a society which assures justice, enforces property rights, provides economic opportunities, and offers a host of other benefits, one must be willing to support those efforts with taxes. Society must, however, be vigilant in keeping a watchful eye on government to assure that the services it provides are provided with a minimum of waste and fraud. Benjamin Franklin (1706-1790) is credited with saying that there are only two certainties in life: death and taxes. His point was that there is certainty in taxation; while one might like to think that he or she can avoid taxes, he or she must at some point pay them. This point of view acknowledges the economist's axiom that there is no such thing as a free lunch and that no one can expect to receive valuable services from the government (or anyone else) without having to pay for those services in some way. For example, if people want better roads, they must be willing to raise gasoline excise taxes to fund that road improvement; they might get the road improvement without raising gasoline excise taxes, but only if they give up some other service provided by the government. That forgone service is the price they pay.

Most citizens are willing to pay a reasonable tax in order to receive services they find useful; but they will only support that tax structure if they believe it to be fair. The classic characterization of a fair tax system is contained in Adam Smith's tax canon, *An Inquiry into the Nature and Causes of the Wealth of Nations* (1776). He suggested four maxims which should guide tax system design: taxes should be fair, based on ability to pay; taxes should be predictable and noncapricious; taxes should be convenient to pay; and the tax system should be efficient in the economy of collection. This canon, more than two hundred years old, remains a high standard by which any tax or tax system can be judged.

The U.S. Constitution specifically provides that "the Congress shall have power to levy and collect Taxes, Duties, Imposts, and Excises, to pay the Debts and provide for the Common Defense and General Welfare of the United States." Yet the power of Congress to levy taxes is limited by the Constitution in three specific ways. First, taxes cannot be levied on exports. Second, all duties, imposts, and excises must be uniform (the uniformity clause). Third, any direct tax paid by each individual must be a uniform tax, the total collected in each state to be proportional to the state's population (the apportionment clause). This third limitation has since been altered with the Sixteenth Amendment to the U.S. Constitution, adopted in 1913, which permits a federal income tax.

Bibliography

Advisory Commission on Intergovernmental Relations. *Significant Features of Fiscal Federalism.* Vols. 1-2. Washington, D.C.: Author, 1989. These volumes are the best source of tax data for federal, state, and local governments. They provide information on tax rates, tax revenues, and interstate comparisons. Published annually.

Begg, Iai, and S. G. B. Henry, eds. *Applied Economics and Public Policy.* New York: Cambridge University Press, 1998.

Musgrave, Richard A., and Peggy B. Musgrave. *Public Finance in Theory and Practice.* 5th ed. New York: McGraw-Hill, 1989. This text is the traditional bible of public finance, including theory and applications of taxation and government expenditure programs as well.

Pechman, Joseph A. *Federal Tax Policy.* 5th ed. Washington, D.C.: Brookings Institution, 1987. For information on U.S. federal taxes, this is the definitive source. It not only includes numerical information on all the federal taxes but also describes the process of making federal tax laws.

Sloman, John. *Essentials of Economics.* New York: Prentice Hall, 1998.

Smith, Adam. *An Inquiry into the Nature and Causes of the Wealth of Nations.* 1776. New York: Random House, 1937. This is Smith's 1776 classic, with a modern introduction, notes, marginal summary, and an enlarged index. Contains Smith's tax canon.

Stiglitz, Joseph E. *Economics of the Public Sector.* 2d ed. New York: W. W. Norton, 1988. A modern undergraduate text which teaches both tax and expenditure sides of public finance. Provides a very good historical background on the U.S. tax system, as well as excellent treatment of both tax theory and policy issues.

Weber, Carolyn, and Aaron Wildavsky. *A History of Taxation and Expenditure in the Western World.* New York: Simon & Schuster, 1986. An excellent history of the role of the public sector, including both tax and expenditure issues. In 734 pages, covers the history of Western civilization and the role of taxes within that history. Includes an index and an exhaustive bibliography.

John E. Anderson

Cross-References

Elasticity, 175; Financing, 228; Income, 301; Investment Decisions, 348; National Debt, 455; Politics and Economics, 476; Quotas and Tariffs, 520; Tax Systems, 575.

TAX SYSTEMS

Type of economics: Monetary and fiscal theory
Field of study: Fiscal theory and public finance

The structuring of tax systems tends to reflect the values and objectives that various societies either tolerate or encourage their governments to maintain or achieve for them over long periods of time.

Principal terms

DIRECT TAXES: taxes that are intended to stay on the object of taxation and not be shifted

GRANTS-IN-AID: payments made by superior and richer governmental units to equalize tax burdens by allocating funds to poorer governments

INCIDENCE: an estimation of who pays a tax's burden, which may or may not be the intended object of taxation

INDIRECT TAXES: taxes, such as those on alcohol, tobacco, and other products, that are expected to be shifted through higher manufacturers' prices

PROGRESSIVE TAXES: taxes that rise with the ability to pay or with income, ostensibly in the interests of equity and fairness

PROPERTY TAXES: direct taxes that are levied on land or buildings and, less often, on personal belongings

REGRESSIVE TAXES: taxes, such as sales taxes, that bear most heavily on people who are the least able to pay

USER TAXES: taxes that are paid for benefits that are presumably enjoyed for the use of highways or other public facilities

Overview

While the structure and purpose of tax systems have varied widely among nations over time, nearly all have been justified by the governments that imposed them, on several of the same self-evident principles. Thus, the operations of all tax systems, it is almost universally agreed, should produce results that are equal or fair, certain rather than arbitrary, as well as convenient and necessary. Tax systems have been judged from within and from outside of governments by their proximate realization of these ideals. In reality, however, bridging the gaps between stated principles and actual practices has proved to be an immensely complex task, not only because governments must have sufficient revenues to ensure their functioning but also because those taxed must be satisfied that the services that governments are expected to render comport with the tax burdens that people must bear. The perceived failure to align these popular expectations closely with mandated tax burdens has been a significant cause of most major revolutions—the American, French, Russian, and Chinese Revolutions, for example—along with innumerable minor rebellions. Tax systems also have proven to be important factors in the collapse of political parties and of governmental administrations.

Since the late nineteenth century, throughout the Western world and more developed nations, several broadly shared features have come to characterize tax systems. First, the most revenue-abundant direct taxes (for example, those taxes on personal and corporate income, as well as Social Security taxes) have been imposed principally by national and, in smaller measure, by state or provincial governments. The less flexible direct taxes (for example, general property taxes), as well as indirect and regressive taxes, have been imposed chiefly by local and municipal governments, although state and provincial governments in the United States and Western Europe still impose some of these taxes. The ideal has been for various levels of government to cooperate in achieving a fair balance of taxation overall, with direct progressive taxation predominating.

These characteristics in the tax structures of economically developed countries have been associated with the expanding roles and changing functions of governments themselves. Popular sentiments either have accepted or demanded that governments, in varying degrees, undertake a redistribution of national wealth—often in the cause of egalitarianism. More-over, the notion that governments have a moral and financial responsibility to institute and maintain a variety of welfare programs has also been closely linked to this general insistence on reallocations of private income, including corporate income. In addition, whether consciously following Keynesian economics or not, nearly all of the world's major govern-ments, by the 1990's, were expected to tax, spend, and borrow in order to moderate excessive swings in the business cycle. Thus, one of the chief objectives sought in restruc-turing national tax systems has been to introduce a substantial measure of progressive taxation, the largest part of which goes to national or central government for their decisions about its allocation.

The attainment of these governmental objectives has meant that modern nations' taxation, computed by any previous standards, has been extremely high since 1939. Even discounting various forms of hidden taxation, manifested by inflation and by government-sponsored gambling and lotteries, about 33 percent of U.S. gross domestic product (GDP) during the 1980's was siphoned off by federal, state, and local taxes. In Great Britain, as well as in most Western European countries, governments taxed from 40 to 50 percent of their people's incomes. None of these estimates included the hidden consequences of inflation—which, for example, was at a rate of 10 percent a year in Great Britain in 1988 and never fell below 4 percent during the 1980's—or the influence of revenues from gambling. Because the impact of a nation's taxation must be judged politically, that is, in terms of popular satisfaction with the services that governments are expected to render and the perceived results of the obligations that they shoulder, the effectiveness of the principle of progressive taxation has been under review continuously.

The principle of progressive taxation—in the form of graduated personal income and corporate taxes—has been the keystone of the federal and most state tax systems in the United States. Personal and corporate income taxes, however, fit into a still broader structure of federal taxes. In order of importance, in 1990, came sales or excise taxes (on alcohol, tobacco, and manufactures), employment or payroll taxes (such as Social Security), and death and gift taxes.

In theory, graduated personal income and death taxes bore most heavily on those persons enjoying higher incomes, including corporations. To the extent that is true, they are equitable and progressive taxes. Corporate income taxes—if other influences such as federal subsi-dies, the ability of corporations to pass taxes on to consumers by raising prices, the influences of lobbyists, or the use of legal loopholes, are waived—have been deemed by economists to be mostly progressive in nature. Federal payroll and sales taxes, however, are clearly regressive. Overall, even after the 1987 reforms in income taxation, the U.S. federal tax system is only arguably progressive.

Despite the U.S. federal government's vastly greater fiscal role, the fifty states and their county and municipal subdivisions have also enlarged their taxing authority since the 1920's. By 1983, for example, twenty-five states had income taxes (as did a few municipalities, such as New York City). Some of these were progressive, graduated income taxes, while others were set at flat rates and based on payments that were made on federal income taxes. Most other state taxes, such as property taxes, highway (gasoline) and other user taxes, and sales or excise taxes, either remain more burdensome for small property holders than for larger ones or are clearly regressive. Adding these and several other state taxes to those imposed by the federal government, it appeared during the 1980's that just under one-third of an American's personal income—33 percent of the GDP—passed to the government in one kind of taxation or another.

Nevertheless, American taxation was comparatively lighter than in other highly developed world economies during this same period. In the 1960's, for example, West Germany was taking nearly 34 percent of its GDP in taxation, much of which fell most heavily on its working and middle classes, mainly because of income and sales taxes. By 1981, this figure had risen to over 37 percent, almost exactly the amount taken from the GDP in Great Britain by a Conservative government. Similarly, in Austria, Belgium, Denmark, France, the Netherlands, Norway, and Sweden during the 1980's, from 42 to 51 percent of the GDP went to taxes. In Japan, during the same period, however, taxes absorbed only 26 percent of the GDP, rising to only 30 percent by 1987.

Applications

The heavy reliance on graduated personal and corporate income taxes in most highly developed economies in order to provide revenues for expanded governmental functions—economic planning, redistributing wealth, moderating the business cycle, managing welfare and social service programs, and paying for wars and defense—has raised questions about how the principle of progressivity has worked in practice. At one extreme, the Swedish government was taxing so heavily in 1990 that some of its professional population were engaged in forms of barter that circumvented the tax system—one sign that taxes were decreasing incentives or were flatly regarded as inequitable in the light of the services that the government supplied. At another extreme, involving an American government that has been much less interventionist than Sweden's, the effects and effectiveness of purportedly progressive personal and corporate taxes have been debated continuously.

In the 1940's, for example, corporate taxes yielded 35 percent of U.S. federal revenues. Thereafter, while rising absolutely, corporate taxes began falling behind those of individuals—the corporate share declining to less than 25 percent in the 1960's, to 15 percent in the 1970's, and to 8.1 percent in 1987. In addition, corporate profits, which between the 1940's and 1970's had been taxed at a flat 50 percent, by the mid-1980's were being taxed at an average effective rate of 16 percent. In order to stimulate investment, the federal government permitted a further 10 percent reduction in corporate taxes against the value of new plants and equipment. Unlike personal income taxes, corporate income taxes—despite complaints from business and industry—have never been significantly progressive.

Progressivity in practice appears to have fared better in respect to personal income taxes. By the 1990's, these U.S. federal taxes had come to bear more heavily on the relatively wealthy than was the case in the 1950's and before. Some of this shift resulted from inflation, which steadily pushed many families into higher tax brackets, although the maximum rate applicable fell from 70 percent during the 1960's and 1970's to 50 percent by the 1980's. Still, personal income taxes, which had furnished $28 billion to the Treasury in 1950, were supplying $315 billion in 1980: 36 percent of federal revenues. Complaints about such taxes abounded, however, leading to legislative reforms in 1987. Even before the changes of 1987, 9.5 million couples and individuals, or one in ten of those paying federal income taxes, paid 48 percent of all personal income taxes, their average federal tax bill amounting to $14,500.

Social Security taxes have also become important contributors to federal revenues in the United States since the passage of the Social Security Act in 1935. Constituting only 5 percent of federal revenues in the late 1930's, they increased to furnish 16 percent in the 1950's, 24 percent in the 1960's, 33 percent in the 1970's, and 27 percent by 1987. Sixteen percent of Social Security levies came from employers (and therefore can be regarded as a mandated corporation tax) and slightly more than 11 percent from employees in 1987. Social Security taxes have often been described as going into a trust fund, when, in fact, they have not. Basically, younger workers have paid for retired workers drawing Social Security benefits. Consequently, serious problems developed in this connection by the end of the 1970's and into the 1980's, as the proportion of retired persons to American society as a whole increased and the number of younger workers decreased, opening the prospects of an insufficient "trust fund" in the future.

Like the United States, other advanced industrial and postindustrial economies, in which national governments have assumed even more extensive social obligations, have also come to count Social Security taxes as very significant components of their national revenues. Thus, through the 1980's, more than 39 percent of Canada's national tax receipts came from such sources, nearly 27 percent in Sweden, 25 percent in Japan, 35 percent in West Germany, 31 percent in Italy, and roughly 40 percent in the Netherlands and in France.

In these countries, public opinion and organized business and trade union groups influence their governments' tax structures. Yet, substantial portions of their national tax receipts derive from regressive taxation, notably, taxes on goods and services—from the production, sale, transfer, or leasing of goods and services. These include narrow-based sales taxes and general consumption taxes (that is, value-added or sales taxes), as well as taxes on specific goods and services (such as on alcohol, tobacco, and gasoline). Therefore, the progressivity of their systems of personal and corporate income taxation tends to be significantly diluted. Roughly 19 percent of U.S. federal taxes and 15 percent of Japan's taxes flow from such sources of regressive taxation, but compared to other major economies during the 1980's, those are modest figures. In Canada, for example, the comparable figure was more than 29 percent; in West Germany and the Netherlands, 27 percent; in Sweden and Great Britain, 24 and 31 percent, respectively; in France, 30 percent; and in Italy, 26 percent. The justifications for taxes in this form are that they take only small bites at a time from the pocketbook, are obscured in consumers purchases, and are easily collected.

Because of the variability of many national taxes and the difficulties in computing them, the 1980's witnessed demands in most tax systems for the introduction of a flat rate charged against everyone. Such suggestions emerged in the United States during congressional debates over tax reform in 1987 both on grounds of the simplification of taxation and the maintenance of equity. A number of states had instituted such plans in regard to their income taxes by the early 1980's, among them Indiana, Illinois, Nebraska, Massachusetts, Pennsylvania, Rhode Island, and Vermont. In the flourishing economy of the British Crown Colony of Hong Kong, a flat rate of 15 percent has been successfully in effect for many years. Therefore, dissatisfaction with the implementation of progressive taxation continues.

Context

The transitions from the national tax systems of the nineteenth century to those of the twentieth were striking in their ranges and complexities. Prior to 1900, the principal tax revenues in Great Britain and the United States, for example, came chiefly from customs collections and from landed or commercial property. Although Great Britain made its income tax permanent in 1842 and the United States followed suit during its Civil War (1861-1865), both enactments, each exceedingly unpopular, remained ineffectual. In the American case, the U.S. Supreme Court, long after the tax was inoperable, rejected attempts to revive it in 1895 as unconstitutional.

Nevertheless, the principle of progressive taxation had many advocates among reformers, including some leading economists, such as Edwin Robert A. Seligman (1861-1939) in the United States. These reformers applauded the successes of progressive taxation in a number of American states by 1900, as well as in Germany. Yet, the resistance to such taxation was tenacious. Deeply rooted beliefs in the tenets of laissez-faire capitalism, in noninterventionist states, and in the expansion of the government's role in social, economic, or political life, delayed such tax reforms. Not until 1916, with ratification of the Sixteenth Amendment to the U.S. Constitution, was even the principle of progressive taxation included in law, and only prospective American involvement in World War II gave some meaningful effect to the national income tax.

Still, industrialization had so altered the dominant forms of property, making old tax structures glaringly inequitable, that change in democratic societies was inevitable. Tangible, or corporeal, property—mostly in the form of land, livestock, buildings, and machinery—was giving way to the intangible, or noncorporeal, property—stocks, bonds, bills of exchange, business paper, and easily concealed personal property—that is characteristic of financial-industrial societies. Furthermore, the demands by reformers and social democrats for various types of tax equalization and for unemployment or welfare benefits in return for their taxes led to growing government intervention in economic life.

First, under Germany's Chancellor Otto von Bismarck, such expensive benefits were provided by the government beginning in the 1870's and 1880's to quell complaints by the working classes. Then, by 1909, similar welfare legislation was initiated by the British government. More stubbornly anti-interventionist, the U.S. government, under the influence of President Franklin D. Roosevelt's New Deal during the 1930's and the general guidance of Keynesian economics, launched its own interventionist social programs in order to remedy unemployment and other inequities. Such rapidly changing responsibilities, charged to government by popularly rising expectations, drastically altered traditional tax systems so as to make the restructured ones conform to the requirements of a more active—and purportedly more equitable—state.

Bibliography

Begg, Iai, and S. G. B. Henry, eds. *Applied Economics and Public Policy*. New York: Cambridge University Press, 1998.

Friedman, Milton, and Rose Friedman. *Free to Choose*. New York: Avon Books, 1980. Two distinguished economists place the increased fiscal and monetary roles of modern states in a conservative perspective. Popularly written and provocative, but well based factually. Particularly good, if brief, on specific tax systems. Contains few illustrative materials and endnotes, but an excellent index.

Galbraith, John Kenneth. *Money: Whence It Came and Where It Went*. Boston: Houghton Mifflin, 1975. Popularly written by an economist and public servant, this liberal interpretation treats tax changes during the twentieth century in the context of expanding government responsibilities. Contains good notes and a full and excellent index. Makes for informative and thoughtful reading.

Kolko, Gabriel. *Wealth and Power in America*. New York: Praeger, 1962. A challenging assertion that neither alterations in the tax structure nor other government policies have redistributed wealth in the twentieth century United States. Overall, a provocative thesis. The notes are full, the select bibliography is adequate, and the index is helpful.

Musgrave, Richard A. *The Theory of Public Finance*. New York: McGraw-Hill, 1959. A distinguished contribution to the subject, although a difficult book for beginners. While taxation is treated throughout, chapters 1, 5, 8, 10, and 11 are especially pertinent. The notes are full and there is an excellent index of names and subjects that aids selective reading. Required reading for serious students.

Shonfield, Andrew. *Modern Capitalism*. New York: Oxford University Press, 1965. Though it requires some updating, this is an ambitious, authoritative, and easily read survey of the changing balance between public and private power. Excellent on the restructurings of tax systems in France, Great Britain, the United States, West Germany, and other capitalist states of Western Europe. The closing essay on the political implications of active governments is splendid. Required reading for substance as well as context. Liberally footnoted, and contains five appendices and a fine index.

Sloman, John. *Essentials of Economics*. New York: Prentice Hall, 1998.

Clifton K. Yearley

Cross-References

Business Cycles, 51; Capitalism, 69; Elasticity, 175; Financing, 228; History of Economics, 295; Income, 301; Investment Decisions, 348; Laissez-Faire, 366; National Debt, 455; Politics and Economics, 476; Quotas and Tariffs, 520; Tax and Taxation, 569.

TECHNOLOGY

Type of economics: Industrial economics
Field of study: Technological change

Technology is a critical catalyst to growth and development, especially economic develop-
ment. It radically affects the lives of communities and individuals, producing diverse benefits
but also costs. Many assume technological change to be an irreversible trend, though not
everyone is pleased with its outcome.

Principal terms

DEVELOPMENT: the process through which a society becomes increasingly able to meet its
    human needs and ensure a higher standard of living and quality of life for its members
ENGINEERING: the application of objective knowledge to the creation of plans, designs, and
    means for achieving desired goals
INNOVATION: the conception of a new or improved product, process, or system and the
    application of these with resulting commercial success
INVENTION: the usually purposeful discovery of knowledge which may yield a useful result
KNOW-HOW: the skill and capability necessary to convert technological knowledge into an
    economic reality, usually smoothly and efficiently
SCIENCE: the understanding of both the nature and the properties of the universe and the laws
    or theories that govern or explain physical phenomena
TECHNOLOGICAL MULTIPLIER: the induced or consequential effects flowing from an innova-
    tion and having broad impact on the economy
TECHNOLOGY: the systematic knowledge and action applicable to any recurrent activity
    closely related to science and engineering and viewed as providing the means to do
    something desirable
TECHNOLOGY DIFFUSION: the generally nondeliberate spread, emulation, and replication of
    a technical innovation
TECHNOLOGY TRANSFER: the generally deliberate moving of research and development
    results into a different setting in the same society or another for private or public use

Overview

Technology—which the Spanish philosopher José Ortega y Gasset facetiously described as
the production of the superfluous (since mankind can do without any of it and probably did
in a state of nature)—is in fact the application of knowledge and science to the production
of goods and services. It is one of the most powerful agents of economic, social, cultural,
political, military, and other change—indeed, of civilization itself. In the twentieth century
alone, the generalization of automobiles, jet airplanes, washing machines, air conditioners,
television sets, computers, and wonder drugs has made it possible for humans to live longer,
more comfortable lives with less strenuous physical labor and more leisure time. Yet
technology has also made life more dangerous, with the possibilities of industrial and
transportation accidents, toxic spills, and radiation, not to mention nuclear war. In the
economic field, technology is associated with technological unemployment, as automation

and robotization replace human labor; in the public health field, with asbestos and other poisons, carcinogens of all kinds, noise, and especially psychological disturbances that flow from boredom and stress related to the high division of labor and specialization that technology has entailed. Too, there is erosion of individual privacy facilitated by computerized data banks and surveillance equipment.

Still, technology was an important condition underlying the rise of the industrial system of modern capitalist production, whose material benefits are shared by most social strata, however unevenly. Similarly, outside the industrial process, no one has remained completely untouched by technology, as any office worker or housewife can testify.

Technology may be native or imported, whether deliberately transferred or incidentally diffused. While much technology—such as the mechanical clock, the navigational compass, and gunpowder—reached the West from the East, a particularly fortunate mix of conditions favorable to the expansion of technology and its application to mining, production, and transportation occurred beginning in mid-eighteenth century Great Britain, providing a powerful stimulus to one of the more significant technological cycles in history: the Industrial Revolution. Innovations such as the flying shuttle, the power loom, the spinning jenny, and the cotton gin followed in quick succession. First steam and later electric power underlay the exponential technological step that eventually allowed human beings to begin to conquer space.

The many dislocations consequent on such rapid technology-led change included the regimentation and exploitation of labor, urbanization and its attendant social ills, and, more recently, pollution, but also rising living standards, thanks to the explosive multiplication of goods and services on the heels of assembly-line production techniques and generally affordable mass-production prices.

Microelectronics, informatics, computer-aided design (CAD), three-dimensional computerized screen displays, and computer-integrated manufacturing with physical tasks performed by programmable robots are among the more recent fields of technological progress, as are advanced materials entailing new compositions or microstructures with improved characteristics, such as specialty polymers and fine ceramics. Biotechnology has produced innovations that have uses in agricultural production, waste recycling, pollution control, and medical treatment.

Equipment, processes, and systems embodying technological change are rarely entirely new but are normally evolutionary, with every novel artifact having some antecedent. Invention, usually deliberate, and its accidental counterpart, discovery, often involve a combination of known elements—for example, an automobile's internal combustion engine adapted to create an airplane power plant. Similarly, there are linkages among, for example, steam engines (one of the major advances of the Industrial Revolution), railroad locomotives, and power-driven textile equipment. Such cumulation in technology has enabled humankind to evolve from the horse-and-buggy era in the nineteenth century to space travel and exploration of the cosmos in the twentieth.

What the full impact of these technological changes will be in terms of costs and benefits is hard to project, but some are evident. Thanks to instantaneous global communications via international telephone hookups, teletype, telefax, or satellite-relayed radio or television signals, multinational corporations can take advantage of differentials in various capital and foreign exchange markets by effecting arbitrage operations. It is possible to fly around the world at supersonic speeds, not in eighty days, as the French writer Jules Verne fantasized in the nineteenth century, but in less than one. In contrast, the various fears involving technology now tend to revolve around environmental concerns—global warming and the depletion of the ozone layer—even more than such economic concerns as higher unemployment and loss of skills.

Applications

Technology was described by French historian Fernand Braudel as the queen that changes the economy and hence changes the world. The purpose of technology is to enable workers to transform things better, faster, and more cheaply or to make it possible for consumers to live more easily, comfortably, safely, or pleasurably. It was hoped that repetitive, boring, or backbreaking tasks could be performed by machines, as lampooned in Charles Chaplin's well-known motion picture *Modern Times* (1936). Sound scientific knowledge and good technological skills are basic to technological development, without which progress and well-being are not generally possible. Such knowledge and skills are, in turn, a function of good education and of how the hard sciences and engineering are regarded in a particular society. They are also dependent on private or public technology policy.

In the application of some newer fields of technology, such as genetic engineering, superconductivity, optical fiber technology, and robotics, the United States is still leading the field, although by diminishing margins. In a few older sectors, such as consumer electronics, the United States has lost its earlier predominance, while Japan, South Korea, and others have forged ahead, especially in the application (as against theoretical research) of these technologies. Such technological cycles involving the changed ranking of societies are not unfamiliar. Indeed, for a long time, much American industrial success consisted in adopting foreign innovations—such as automatic automobile transmissions—and turning them into viable, practical products. Indeed, innovation and its uses are closely linked, since applications often prompt changes in the prototype itself. The acquisition of technology through innovation, transfer, or diffusion is not an ultimate guarantee of development. For example, under British rule, the Indians were introduced to Western technology (such as railroads, steamships, and telegraphs) before other Asian societies. Yet, some of these societies, such as those of Japan and China, developed faster.

Common fallacies in predicting future technological applications have included extravagant projections of the universal use of nuclear energy, which was supposed to supplant all other forms of power, even in automobiles. In fact, both optimism and pessimism are evident regarding the technological fix which the "cornucopians" foresee as solving all major human problems, including overpopulation, resource shortages, and pollution. On their part, the "realists" stress the negative effects of technology, likening it to Dr. Frankenstein's monster, which ultimately destroyed both the scientist and itself.

The general applications of technology and technological change have had an immense impact on workers, especially the very high division of labor and specialization that the former have experienced: the deskilling of much ordinary labor, the weakening and even disappearance of crafts and special skills, and the loss of a sense of job autonomy and pride in one's work. Accordingly, managerial supervision over the production process has increased greatly, and an entire organizational revolution has followed in the wake of new technical ways of turning out the escalating variety of new products of all kinds. Some believe that all social institutions, even the church (and "televangelism"), have become the captives of a technological society.

These events have led, among others, to the creation of a Western minority ideology of antitechnology, which advocates the use of simple, inexpensive, labor-intensive "intermediate" or "appropriate" technology optimizing local resources—especially for the Third World—and to a worldwide antinuclear movement. Thus, the major question regarding technology still remains to be answered: How far should technology be permitted to advance, and subject to what controls? How, in other words, should it be applied? The question became especially pertinent after such devastating accidents as the nonnuclear toxic fumes catastrophe at Bhopal, India (1984) and the nuclear disaster at Chernobyl, in the Soviet Ukraine (1986).

Context

Humans are physically ill-endowed for survival in most environments. They soon learned to cooperate with one another and to use tools and techniques—that is, technology—at first to provide the bare necessities of life and then to go beyond essentials all the way to the absolutely trivial. Thus, social organization and technology together yielded improved chances of survival in the face of hostile nature, and later, provided better living conditions. In sum, technology has shaped the contours of society since the beginning.

The combined deployment of technical and commercial resources is the essence of industrial success, that is, of market penetration and economic growth, with all of their repercussions on economic aggregates such as output, employment, and balances of trade and payments. In this interacting process, technology underlies productivity, that is, efficiency, or a high output-input ratio. In turn, productivity gains translate into a rising real income and the relative well-being of the entire producing economy, as a result of the multiplier effect. Conversely, failure to keep equipment, processes, or systems up to date foretells lesser competitiveness for that economy compared to others, and thus stagnation or even a slide in its standard of living. To compete in international markets in the modern integrated global economy, products must incorporate the latest techniques yet be cheap enough and of comparable quality.

That, at least, is the mainstream view. There is a minority, however, that is opposed to the concept that technological advance is irreversible and feeds on itself, or is essential and that therefore there is no choice because all that is possible is also necessary. Most, however, concede that technological process is indispensable to economic growth and thus to higher output and productivity, lower prices, greater diversity, and perhaps even better quality.

In the meantime, there is ambivalence about the feared employment effect of technology. While, on one hand, the invention and production of new hardware and software generate more economic activity and call for higher employment, the increasing number of manufacturing and control functions performed by robotics and microelectronics, respectively—the outcome of some of these same technological innovations—tends to make human labor redundant. At the very least, changes in technology cause shifts in skill requirements, as well as geographic and other dislocations in the labor market.

While there have always been fluctuations in aggregate and sectoral employment because of business or technological cycles, with labor consequently "excessed," if technology greatly increases efficiency in both industry and services, as it has already done in agriculture, there will no longer be any sector left to absorb the surplus labor, as there was when agriculture became mechanized and large-scale and when millions of farmers were driven off the land.

The saving feature is that most human needs in goods and services seem to be insatiable for anything "new and improved" regardless of merit, so that manufacturing employment may in fact increase. Indeed, public policy may shorten the workweek and lengthen leisure time, both of which would stimulate employment. Technology may also reduce the competitive disadvantage of high labor costs in industrialized countries or in specific sectors. There are many imbalances, rigidities, and tradeoffs involved in this assessment, however, so that the net impact of technology on employment is uncertain.

It should be recalled, nevertheless, that technology is only one of several factors that determine employment levels. Indeed, the state of the world economy, aggregate demand, price levels, the availability of capital, training in technical and managerial skills, and the economic, cultural, and political features of a particular society all play a part.

Bibliography

Adam, Barbara. *Timescapes of Modernity: The Environment and Invisible Hazards*. New York: Routledge, 1998.

Basalla, George. *The Evolution of Technology*. Cambridge, England: Cambridge University Press, 1988. A historian describes the evolution of technology from the perspective of some of its characteristics, such as diversity, necessity, continuity and discontinuity, novelty, and selection. This relatively short but clearly written paperback (248 pages) includes illustrations together with a good bibliography and index.

Braun, Ernst. *Wayward Technology*. Westport, Conn.: Greenwood Press, 1984. A very good description of the rise and future of industrial society from the perspective of its technical, social, economic, and political aspects, with specific references mostly to the British case. Helpful tables and diagrams, but a skimpy one-page index.

Colton, Joel, and Stuart Bruchey, eds. *Technology, the Economy, and Society*. New York: Columbia University Press, 1987. A collection of papers by distinguished academics examines the question of how technological, economic, and social changes interrelate, with specific reference to the American experience.

Corn, Joseph J., ed. *Imagining Tomorrow: History, Technology, and the American Future*. Cambridge, Mass.: MIT Press, 1986. A series of essays by academics and specialists about the American technological culture in various areas, the reasons behind some predictions of technological utopias, and why many of these failed to materialize. This short work (237 pages) is clearly, tantalizingly written and attractively illustrated to depict various, not-so-accurate visions of the future.

Cyert, Richard M., and David C. Mowery, eds. *The Impact of Technological Change on Employment and Economic Growth*. Cambridge, Mass.: Ballinger, 1988. A collection of papers by a panel of experts on technology and employment examining the effects of technological change on worker displacement, job creation and loss, the intersectoral flows of jobs and workers within the U.S. economy, skill requirements, and the distribution of incomes in the United States.

Flynn, Patricia M. *Facilitating Technological Change: The Human Resource Challenge*. Cambridge, Mass.: Ballinger, 1988. On the basis of some two hundred microenterpriselevel case studies detailed in an annotated bibliography, the book surveys how employers adjust to technical change. It develops the concept of skills-training life cycle—the human resource equivalent of the traditional product and technology life cycle—over the course of development of a technology.

Metcalfe, J. Stanley. *Evolutionary Economics and Creative Destruction*. New York: Routledge, 1998.

Susskind, Charles. *Understanding Technology*. Baltimore: The Johns Hopkins University Press, 1973. Still a very fundamental and simple but comprehensive account of the topic. It covers the history of technology as well as its relationship to ideologies, values, and social and ethical problems. Barely but attractively illustrated. Informative indexes.

Williams, Trevor I. *A Short History of Twentieth-Century Technology c. 1900-c. 1950*. New York: Oxford University Press, 1982. An excellent, easy-to-understand, sector-by-sector survey of the topic's technological aspects ranging from agriculture, fishing, and mining to medicine and warfare. Generously illustrated with mostly period photographs.

Peter B. Heller

Cross-References

TRADE DEFICITS, INTERNATIONAL DEBT, AND BUDGET DEFICITS

Type of economics: International economics
Field of study: International finance

A trade deficit indicates that a nation is consuming more than it produces. In the intermediate term, persistent overconsumption can be funded by ever-deepening international debt. Yet, chronic trade deficits and mounting national debt unfortunately inhibit new capital investment. The consequent depressed economic productivity entails lowered tax revenues and, as government revenues lag spending, budget deficits.

Principal terms

BALANCE OF PAYMENTS: a summary statement of all economic transactions between a nation and the rest of the world during a specific time period, usually a year
FISCAL POLICY: the use of governmental taxation and expenditure for the purpose of stimulating or contracting economic activity
NET EXPORTS: the value of a country's exports minus the value of its imports
PREBISCH THESIS: the proposition that the terms of trade move against developing countries
PRIMARY PRODUCER: any producer of a primary product, that is, a product of any extractive industry, including farming, fishing, lumbering, mining, and quarrying
TERMS OF TRADE: the ratio of the average price of a country's exports to the average price of its imports at a specific reference time

Overview

Economics is vitally concerned with the analysis of "deficits" or "surpluses" in a nation's international trade position or in a government's annual budget, and especially with the implementation of mechanisms or processes through which such disequilibrium may be remedied. To understand the United States economy, for example, it is essential to obtain a clear understanding of the "twin deficits"—namely, the trade deficit and the federal budget deficit. In the simplest terms, deficits involve outflows that exceed inflows.

Most references to a nation's exports and imports are to its merchandise-trade account, also called its trade in goods or trade in "visibles." Merchandise trade consists of all the trade in primary products, processed goods, and manufactured products. The trade balance of a nation, which is one element of its balance of payments, is its net balance on merchandise trade only: Specifically excluded are exports and imports of other goods and services, as well as all international payments of money. If, during a particular year, the value of all the merchandise that is exported by the nation exceeds the value of all the merchandise that it imports, then the nation enjoys a trade surplus in the amount of the excess. If the value of all the merchandise that is exported is less than the value of all the merchandise that is imported, however, then the nation suffers a trade deficit in the amount of the deficiency.

Economists also analyze bilateral trade balances, surpluses, and deficits—the net trade relations between two nations during a specific time period. The potential volatility of bilateral trade balances is vividly illustrated by the dramatic exchange of net supplier/recipient roles between the United States and Japan in the mid-twentieth century. During the 1950's, Japan's trade deficits with the United States were enormous and chronic, but by the 1980's, U.S. trade deficits with Japan were greater than those that had plagued Japan three decades earlier.

International debt is created when a nation consumes more than it earns. Such a nation must either receive credit from vendors or borrow money in order to make up its shortfall of income. A nation's net balance of international indebtedness at any particular time is determined by the difference between the total value of its foreign assets and the total value of its liabilities to foreign debt-holders. The nation's balance of international indebtedness, also called its international investment position, is in surplus if foreign assets exceed foreign liabilities, but in deficit if foreign liabilities exceed foreign assets.

Moderate, purposeful international debt is manageable. A large, chronically worsening international debt, however, such as the United States incurred during the 1980's, creates an international debt load that burdens every sector of a nation's domestic economy. When, in 1990, the United States, by then the world's largest debtor nation, owed approximately as much to other nations as was owed by all the developing countries of the world combined, the domestic economy increasingly evidenced consequent strains, demonstrating the limits of the use of international credit as an instrument of national policy. Another accompanying effect of mushrooming international debt is an increase in the ownership of the debtor nation's domestic assets by foreign investors. By 1990, for example, Arab oil holdings in the United States, already valued in the hundreds of billions of dollars, continued to increase.

Whereas trade deficits and international debt arise out of economic transactions among nations, budget deficits are a matter of domestic national fiscal policy. A budget deficit arises when total governmental spending exceeds a government's total revenue during a specific time period, usually one year. The cumulative harm that is caused by chronic budget deficits is dramatized by the effects on the United States economy of its government's massive budget deficits from the 1970's to 1990. Governments that receive more income than they spend enjoy a budget surplus, and governments that spend exactly the amount of their income, no more and no less, maintain a balanced budget. In practical fiscal operations, an exactly balanced annual budget is rare.

Trade deficits, international debt, and budget deficits are integrally related—through obvious linkages and through certain, less apparent, processes. A nation that is slipping into ever-deepening trade deficits must either increase the value of its exports in order to balance the cost of its imports, curtail its imports, or go into debt in order to finance its continuing deficits. Whereas the first two of these responses are predicated on balancing the nation's trade account, the third response manages the nation's international trade disequilibrium by shifting the burden of payment for excess present consumption to future generations through the mechanism of increased international debt.

Countries that run chronic trade deficits face a pragmatic limit to their ability to sustain their trade imbalance: Ultimately, they will run out of reserves and creditworthiness. Trade deficits also produce major negative impacts on the domestic economy and the welfare of the deficit nation's population, ultimately contributing to governmental budget deficits. A chronic lag in exports is an indicator of stagnating national productivity and an omen of an eroding tax base. National economic development and productivity are further impeded as a debtor nation's growing international debt frightens away foreign investors, cutting off the capital investment necessary to promote economic growth and government revenues. Moreover, trade deficits weaken the value of the deficit nation's currency, which (among numerous other adverse effects) increases the real cost of that government's purchases abroad, thereby further draining its treasury and aggravating its serious budget-deficit problem.

Applications

A clear understanding of the policy applications of trade deficits, international debt, and budget deficits can follow only from an analytic, nonemotive approach. "Deficit" and "debt" commonly are perceived pejoratively. In fact, however, the effects of deficits and debts depend on their magnitudes and the uses to which they are put. Trade deficits, international debt, and budget deficits are potential instruments of national policy that are available for manipulation by the nation's decision makers. These devices can be used to accomplish desirable ends or, if mishandled, to bring about disastrous consequences.

Running a trade deficit can prove to be a productive policy expedient for a nation that temporarily needs to import more than it exports—for consumption purposes, for investment purposes, or for both. If a country indefinitely continues to consume more than it produces, however, then it must start borrowing in order to pay for its excess purchases.

During the 1980's, the United States and most of the less developed countries of the world used increasingly deep trade deficits in order to pursue the politically comfortable policy of consuming more than they supplied to the rest of the world. Unfortunately, however, this calculated application of trade-deficit policy produced increasingly severe hardships. In addition, the Third World primary-producer nations that ran trade deficits encountered forces beyond their control: As applied, trade-deficit policy can prove to be an unwieldy instrument. Unpredictable Middle East crises increased the price of oil to oil-importing countries, stacking an unplanned tier of contingent costs upon an already burdensome bill for national imports. Moreover, many Third World spokespeople asserted that international trade favors industrialized nations at the expense of primary-producer nations—the thesis of the Prebisch model of the terms of trade. Thus, the notion that nations can use trade deficits in order to pursue a long-term policy of consuming more than they supply to the world is complicated by real-world constraints. Trade deficits are not merely a tool at the command of the deficit nation but are, to a significant extent, a force driven by exogenous factors which may be beyond that nation's control.

For every trade deficit, there are—in certain other nations' trade accounts—offsetting surpluses. During the 1980's, economically prosperous nations—including Canada, France, Japan, the Netherlands, Saudi Arabia, South Africa, Sweden, Taiwan, and West Germany—implemented measures that were designed to accumulate trade surpluses, in order to achieve such policy objectives as a growing domestic economy and a strong currency unit. On balance, a nation that is able to pursue a trade surplus policy rather than a trade deficit policy is enabled to offer its population a higher standard of living and to operate from a stronger bargaining position in the international economic system. Above all, the nation with a strong trade surplus generates cash flow, enabling it to avoid incurring new international debt.

Like the deliberate use of trade deficits, international borrowing is a normal, and even potentially productive, activity. Particularly in anticipation of long-term international infla- tion, in which hard money can be borrowed in the present and paid back in the future in softer currency (as in the case of "soft" loans to developing nations by wealthy developed nations and cash-rich international lending agencies), the incurring of international debt to promote domestic development and enhance economic productivity often has proved to be a wise policy. International credit mechanisms have enabled countries that lack adequate capital to borrow and to use the proceeds of these loans in order to expand their productive capacities. As in the case of the trade-deficit policy application, what is important is the amount of debt and the purposes to which the borrowed funds are applied.

Debt is cumulative, however, and unpaid interest on principal compounds. The interna- tional debt problems of the United States and many Third World nations have severely inhibited their national economic growth and development. Mounting international debt, entailing significant redistributions of resources and capital, radically restructures the debtor nation's international economic relationships and reduces the present and future welfare of its population. Eventually, foreign-debt principal and interest payments must be met by radically curtailed spending and Spartan saving—necessitating sharp reductions in the debtor nation's standard of living.

Modern governments utilize fiscal policy as an instrument that is capable of minimizing fluctuations in the domestic economy. Budget deficits, created by increasing purchases and reducing taxes, promote expansionary fiscal policy, which governments implement when the economy is operating below its potential output. Fine tuning, or annual changes in the budget to accomplish fiscal policy goals, is designed to adjust for minor fluctuations in economic activity.

For a nation that is encountering economic difficulties, huge deficits—imports in excess of exports and federal expenditures in excess of government receipts—generate increased international debt, including burdensome interest payments. Large trade and budget deficits and mounting international debt in turn feed inflation, push up interest rates, destabilize the financially embattled country's currency unit, and ultimately thwart national economic growth and stability. Although there is no direct cause-and-effect relationship between a nation's trade and budget deficits, the effects tend to correlate because each is adversely affected by common factors, including substandard agricultural and industrial productivity, slow economic growth, and a consequent reduction in tax receipts. Conversely, improve- ments in these common factors can reduce the trade and budget deficits and, ultimately, the international debt.

Context

Trade and financial transactions between cities and empires date from the beginnings of civilization. Economic relations between political entities have invariably entailed trade deficits and surpluses, and credit and debt have been used to lubricate international trade. Paper transactions between countries were facilitated by the credit mechanisms that were instituted by banks, which developed in the late medieval period.

Trade deficits, international indebtedness, and budget deficits took on historically un- precedented dimensions, however, in the twentieth century. From the time of the Great Depression of the 1930's, governments viewed the creation of a budget deficit as a

sophisticated device for stimulating a sluggish economy. The late twentieth century witnessed sensational, record-setting instances of chronic trade deficits, international indebtedness, and budget deficits. Historical records were established by many nations and, in the
prevailing climate of international economic turmoil, were soon exceeded. In 1984, for the
first time since World War II, the United States ran a net trade deficit, with imports exceeding
exports by more than $188 billion.

Throughout history, nations occasionally have been unable or unwilling to pay their
international debts. Militant countries sometimes declared debt repudiations out of mixed
economic and ideological reasons. Revolutionary regimes, for example, typically will not
honor the debts that were incurred by the ousted government for the purchase of armaments
that have been used against them. Among twentieth century revolutionary regimes which
repudiated the international debts that were incurred by the prior, overthrown government
were the Soviet Union, the People's Republic of China, and Fidel Castro's Cuba. Yet, on the
whole, debt repudiation has been the exception.

In addition, until the 1980's, debt rescheduling was unusual. An international-debt crisis
began in 1981. The steep rise in oil prices that had begun in 1973 resulted in a rapid buildup
of debt in Third World nations that were dependent on petroleum imports, especially
Argentina, Brazil, and Mexico. These already serious debt problems were aggravated in the
1980's, when interest rates rose sharply and worldwide recession depressed the debtor
nations' exports. First Poland, then Mexico, Brazil, and Argentina, followed by a host of
lesser borrowers among the Eastern European, Latin American, African, and Asian nations,
declared their inability to retire scheduled international debt obligations when due, necessitating the negotiation of complex rescheduling plans.

Throughout the 1980's, the debt-repayment problems encountered by a number of debtor
countries, heavily concentrated in Latin America and Africa, profoundly threatened not only
the economies of the creditor nations but also the international economic system. Most
heavily involved in loans to developing countries were the giant United States money-center
banks, which played a central role in the world economy, so that the loan-default threat to
their solvency threatened the stability of the world financial structure.

The "debt shock" (world debt crisis) of the 1980's, aggravated by serious trade deficits
and out-of-balance budgets, severely limited future economic development and depressed
the standard of living of much of the world's population.

Bibliography

Bonker, Don. *America's Trade Crisis: The Making of the U.S. Trade Deficit.* Boston:
    Houghton Mifflin, 1988. A concrete, well-written account of the United States trade
    deficit, authored by Congressman Bonker of the state of Washington. Features a com-
    prehensive glossary of technical terms, documentary notes, and suggested readings. A
    knowledgeable introduction, written by a congressional insider.
Carvounis, Chris. *The United States Trade Deficit of the 1980s: Origins, Meanings, and
    Policy Responses.* New York: Quorum Books, 1987. This 190-page analysis hinges on a
    sustained contrast of the monetarist and the structuralist explanations of chronic United
    States trade deficits. Within this analytic framework, separate chapters are devoted to the
    origins of the deficit, its meanings, and appropriate policy responses.
Gilmour, John. *Reconcilable Differences? Congress, the Budget Process, and the Deficit.*

Berkeley: University of California Press, 1990. An authoritative critique of the United States congressional budget process, emphasizing the "reconciliation" phase. Picks up the history in 1966 and carries the account through the implementation of the Gramm-Rudman-Hollings Act. An index provides access to a wealth of concrete details.

MacEwan, Arthur. *Debt and Disorder: International Economic Instability and U.S. Imperial Decline.* New York: Monthly Review Press, 1990. A narrative of international debt and disorder from 1970 to 1990, identifying factors that disrupted the international financial system. Analyzes Third World reliance on foreign capital, and demonstrates close ties between the United States trade deficit and foreign debt. Concludes with a two-chapter examination of the political questions that are implied by foreign debt.

Minarik, Joseph. *Making America's Budget Policy: From the 1980s to the 1990s.* Armonk, N.Y.: M. E. Sharpe, 1990. Overviews the making of United States budget policy in the 1980's, describing the budget-policy environment and analyzing the economic and political issues implicated by budget reform. Assesses the short-term risks that are associated with the nation's reliance on foreign credit. Contains a preface by Senator Bill Bradley of New Jersey.

Santow, Leonard Jay. *The Budget Deficit: The Causes, the Costs, the Outlook.* New York: New York Institute of Finance, 1988. Provides basic knowledge of budget realities in a readily accessible question-and-answer format. Traces the massive increase in the United States budget deficit from 1974 to 1986, explaining its timing, causes, and costs, and even assessing blame. Each of the fifty questions are answered within one to ten pages. Quantitatively based.

Staudt, Kathleen A. *Free Trade? Informal Economies at the U.S.-Mexico Border.* Philadelphia: Temple University Press, 1998.

Kazi Golam Mohiuddin

Cross-References

Undeveloped and Underdeveloped Countries

Type of economics: Growth and development
Field of study: Economic growth, development, and planning

Undeveloped and underdeveloped countries are those that lack the institutional structure to foster the use of modern technology and in which there are persistent low levels of per-capita income and living, as defined by a number of economic, social, and political indicators that are related to the quality of life. These countries have had a significant impact on the shaping of the post-World War II world economic order and the allocation of international resources.

Principal terms

ABSOLUTE POVERTY: a condition in which a group of people is able to meet only its bare subsistence needs of food, clothing, and shelter and to maintain a minimum level of living

GROSS NATIONAL PRODUCT (GNP): the total domestic and foreign output that is claimed by residents of a country, usually for one year

INSTITUTIONS: customary beliefs and practices in a society that affect people's interaction with technology and the material and nonmaterial world

LESS DEVELOPED COUNTRIES (LDCs): the poorest group of developing countries that the United Nations defines as those having an average GNP per capita of $200 or less

LEVEL OF LIVING: the extent to which an individual or a social group can satisfy material (food, shelter, clothing) or spiritual wants

NEWLY INDUSTRIALIZED COUNTRIES (NICs): a group of countries that is at a relatively advanced level of economic development, with dynamic industrial sectors that are well integrated into the system of international trade, finance, and investment

PER-CAPITA INCOME: the total gross national product of a country divided by total population; generally used as an economic indicator of development and the levels of living

PHYSICAL QUALITY OF LIFE INDEX (PQLI): a standard that attempts to measure the performance of developing countries in meeting the most basic needs of people, including indicators of infant mortality, life expectancy, and basic literacy; considered as important as per-capita income in defining developing countries

TECHNOLOGY: a human problem-solving capability and the use of ideas in order to transform the material and nonmaterial world

Overview

Undeveloped and underdeveloped countries are those countries that lack the institutional structures and the intellectual framework to foster the creation and use of modern technology. In these countries, there are persistent low levels of living (as compared to the so-called developed countries) in conjunction with absolute poverty, low per-capita incomes, low rates of economic growth, low consumption levels, poor health services, high death rates, high birthrates, vulnerability to and dependence on foreign economies, and limited freedom to act in order to satisfy basic human needs and wants. Undeveloped and underdeveloped countries encompass a large group of countries—in 1990, they numbered 143—and their identification has played a key role in the delineation of the post-World War II global economy and in the expression of what social, cultural, economic, and political values are emphasized in the world order.

The concept of undeveloped and underdeveloped countries has gone through radical shifts since the late 1940's, as the notion of development has evolved and as the consciousness and position of poor nations vis-à-vis rich ones have been formalized and strengthened. The majority of countries that are categorized as undeveloped and underdeveloped were the former colonies of Western imperial powers, and many of them did not acquire an identity as countries until colonial domination or after their independence. The international recognition that these countries were undeveloped and underdeveloped did not occur until the sweep of independence movements began in the 1940's and the major world powers needed to find another basis on which to interact with their former colonies. At that time, it was apparent to postwar international organizations that these new nations lacked the infrastructure, institutions, and level of living needed to compete in the changing world order.

The classical economic concept of undeveloped and underdeveloped countries can be traced to economic growth theories that were posited in the 1950's and 1960's. These theories, fostered by such economists as Sir Arthur Lewis, Gustav Ranis, and John C. H. Fei, among others, equated development with growth in per-capita income and characterized economies as dualistic, composed of modern and traditional-informal sectors (or capitalist and noncapitalist sectors, enclave and hinterland, or industry and agriculture, depending on the author). In this model, undeveloped and underdeveloped countries were those countries which had weak modern sectors, low total output, and limited capital accumulation. Two differing cultural traditions were manifested by the sectors, according to this theory.

The modern sector was built by a rational outlook, whereas the traditional sector was limited by nonscientific values and approaches. Hence, undeveloped and underdeveloped countries, initially called "backward," were considered culturally as well as economically inferior. Underdeveloped countries, according to the economic growth model, were those that had not yet traversed the development path that was followed by Western nations, implying a unilinear theory of history and one universal pathway which the West had blazed. Modernization, in short, was equated with Westernization.

Institutional economists, such as Clarence Ayres (1891-1972), argued that development, and therefore the concept of underdeveloped countries, could not be understood outside the institutional framework and technological sophistication of countries. According to institutional economists, modernization is an institutional structure that allows a nation to use technology. A large number of people that are involved in development have tried to create indicators for the scientific and technological capability of countries, which would facilitate the categorization of developing countries. The institutional economists, like the latter schools of evolutionary anthropologists, believed that development was an evolutionary process but that countries could leap to higher levels of technological sophistication rather than traverse all the steps. In addition, these economists made it clear that modernization, as related to the use of technology, was not culturally biased and that undeveloped and underdeveloped countries were in no sense culturally inferior. They argued that science and technology are transcendent universals and their application can be explained without ethnocentric biases.

In the 1970's, the purely growth-oriented concept of development, and therefore the characterization of undeveloped and underdeveloped countries only in terms of per-capita income, evolved. Both mainstream economists and political economists argued that growth theory failed to incorporate knowledge about the broad historical forces that are associated with underdevelopment and ignored the institutions, behavior responses, and ways of life of the largest sector within the underdeveloped countries—the rural areas. These economists believed that the concept of underdevelopment could not be understood without looking at the relationships between rich and poor countries and the dependency of these latter countries on their colonial rulers, historically, and on the major economic superpowers, in the modern milieu. Underdeveloped countries, according to these theorists, were defined by sociological, political, and administrative factors, in addition to purely economic ones.

As the debate regarding underdevelopment heightened and the political consciousness of the underdeveloped countries strengthened, the terms "undeveloped and underdeveloped countries" were replaced by "developing countries" and "less developed countries" (LDCs) to account for the fact that they were dynamic and evolving and did not lack in basic qualities, which the previous terms had implied.

The term "Third World" also became popular in the 1970's in order to emphasize the geopolitical nature of development and the fact that the undeveloped countries were, by virtue of their historical and modern position, forced into disenfranchisement. The Third World, in this view, was juxtaposed with the "First World" of Western democratic industrial powers and the "Second World" of communist bloc industrialized nations. In addition, as an expression of the growing realization that the developing nations shared a common political relationship to the rich nations in the new global economy, the term "North-South" became popular. This term, derived from systems theorists who view the world as divided into the center (the rich northern countries) and the periphery (the poor southern countries), attempts to capture the idea that the developing countries are literally cut off from the system resources that are required to improve their level of living.

In the light of the growing criticism of the opponents to mainstream economics, growth theory began to include criteria other than per-capita income in order to identify developing countries. "Growth with equity" became the commonly accepted terminology and other measures of underdevelopment such as income distribution, absolute poverty, the minimum level of consumption, certain composition to the consumption stream, unemployment levels, the diversification of economy, and social indicators such as infant mortality, health status, life expectancy, and literacy rate became essential in the identification process. The physical quality of life index (PQLI), which attempts to measure the performance of LDCs in meeting the most basic needs of their people and which includes indicators of infant mortality, life expectancy, and basic literacy, became a widely accepted criterion. Countries such as Sri Lanka, which scored high on the PQLI in spite of low per-capita income levels, were held up as examples of countries that had shown great strides without focusing only on growth.

An international movement, stimulated in part by the 1987 report of the United Nations' Brundtland Commission, "Our Common Future," and initiatives by futurist Hazel Henderson, began in the late 1980's in order to establish a new set of broader criteria of developed and developing countries, taking into consideration the concepts of sustainability, the economic contribution of the informal sector, democratic and pluralistic values, and the self-determination of the poor.

Applications

Developing countries are generally identified and categorized by international organizations such as the United Nations, the Organization for Economic Cooperation and Development (OECD), and the International Bank for Reconstruction and Development (the World Bank). The categorization of developing countries plays a significant role in the world economic and political order. This categorization is employed in order to determine official foreign assistance allocation and the qualifications for special "soft" loan windows, to influence alliances in international organizations such as the United Nations, to establish trade agreements and concessions, to provide special incentives to investors such as the Overseas Private Investment Corporation's (OPIC) investment insurance, and to influence global politics.

In the mid-1980's, there were 143 member countries of the United Nations that constituted the Third World. In 1984, although the total national product of all nations in the world was valued in excess of U.S. $12,500 billion, less than $2,750 billion (or 22 percent of total world output) were generated by countries in the Third World, although they had 76 percent of the world's population. Developing countries have been identified by a number of indexes, though the GNP per capita remains the most widely accepted criterion internationally. Based on this criterion, the United Nations classifies the Third World into three groups: the "least developed," who are the poorest; the "developing nations," who are the nonoil-exporting countries; and the rich Organization of Petroleum Exporting Countries (OPEC).

The OECD divides the Third World into the low-income countries (LICs)—those with a 1980 per-capita income of less than $600, including the least developed countries or LLDCs; the middle-income countries (MICs); the newly industrialized countries (NICs); and the members of OPEC. The World Bank categorizes developing countries into "low-income economies," "middle-income economies," and "upper middle-income economies." Low-income economies are those whose GNP per capita equals $400 or less in 1985 dollars. Middle-income economies are those whose GNP per capita equals $1,600 or less in 1985 dollars. Upper middle-income countries are those whose GNP per capita is above $1,600 but below $8,000 in 1985 dollars.

In 1987, thirty-seven countries were categorized as low-income economies by the World Bank. These included China, India, Ethiopia, Bangladesh, Burkina Faso, Mali, Bhutan, Mozambique, Nepal, Malawi, Zaire, Burma, Burundi, Togo, Madagascar, Niger, Benin, Central African Republic, Rwanda, Somalia, Kenya, Tanzania, Sudan, Haiti, Guinea, Sierra Leone, Senegal, Ghana, Pakistan, Sri Lanka, Zambia, Afghanistan, Chad, Kampuchea, Laos, Uganda, and Vietnam.

According to the World Bank, thirty-six countries comprised the middle-income countries in the same year, including Mauritania, Bolivia, Lesotho, Liberia, Indonesia, the People's Democratic Republic of the Yemen, the Yemen Arab Republic, Morocco, the Philippines, Egypt, the Ivory Coast, Papua New Guinea, Zimbabwe, Honduras, Nicaragua, the Dominican Republic, Nigeria, Thailand, Cameroon, El Salvador, Botswana, Paraguay,

Jamaica, Peru, Turkey, Mauritius, the People's Republic of the Congo, Ecuador, Tunisia, Guatemala, Costa Rica, Colombia, Chile, Jordan, Syria, and Lebanon.

The twenty-three upper middle-income countries in 1987, as defined by the World Bank, consisted of Brazil, Uruguay, Hungary, Portugal, Malaysia, South Africa, Poland, Yugoslavia, Mexico, Panama, Argentina, the Republic of Korea, Algeria, Venezuela, Greece, Israel, Trinidad and Tobago, Hong Kong, Oman, Singapore, Iran, Iraq, and Romania. Out of this group, Brazil, Greece, Mexico, and Singapore are also categorized as newly industrialized countries (NICs).

In spite of the variety in the classification systems, developing countries share common problems, such as widespread and chronic absolute poverty, lower GNP growth rates than the developed countries, inadequate housing, high rising levels of unemployment and underemployment, and wide disparities in the distribution of income. They also have low and even stagnating levels of agricultural productivity, sizable and growing imbalances between urban and rural sectors, and inadequate health and educational systems.

In these countries, there are low life and work expectancy levels (in 1984, life expectancy in the least developed countries averaged forty-nine years, in developing countries fifty-seven years, and in developed countries seventy-two years); high infant mortality rates (in 1984, about 124 children out of every 1,000 live births died before their first birthday in the least developed countries, compared to 18 in developing countries); and high rates of population growth. In addition, developing countries face debt problems which are exacerbated by balance of payment crises and a dependence on foreign economies, technologies, and values. The majority of developing countries are agrarian, with agriculture being the principal economic activity in the terms of the labor force and generally also in the terms of contribution to gross national product. Moreover, most of these nations are oriented toward the production of primary products which were developed by their colonial rulers, as opposed to secondary (manufacturing) and tertiary (service) activities.

Context

By tracing the concepts and values that have underlaid the definition of undeveloped and underdeveloped countries as it has evolved over time, one can see the evolution of the economic order and the emergence of countries which were historically subjugated to Western imperial rule. One can see a decline in the values that were inherent in the colonial and postcolonial period, such as the idea that the developing countries are resource and political pawns in the game of powerful nations, and an ascendancy of the idea that developing countries can unite to have a significant economic and social impact in the world.

An understanding of the concept of undeveloped and underdeveloped countries has required an interdisciplinary approach which blends economics, history, politics, anthropology, and other disciplines, breaking down the dominance of the traditional growth theory approach to development. In addition, an effort to understand this concept has stimulated Third World thinkers to begin to formulate their own theories of their relationship to rich nations.

In the late 1980's, a shift in orientation occurred in the relationship of the industrial to the developing nations as it became apparent and openly stated that all countries shared common global problems of population, environmental degradation, economic decline, and disease, and that all countries had to work together to find common technological solutions.

This shift in orientation will open up technical cooperation and technology transfer and may transform the relationship between the rich and the poor countries to one of increasing partnership.

Bibliography

Adjibolosoo, Senyo B-S. K. *Global Development the Human Factor Way.* Westport, Conn.: Praeger, 1998.

Agarwala, A. N., and S. P. Singh, eds. *The Economics of Underdevelopment.* New York: Oxford University Press, 1963. This book, although outdated, provides an excellent overview of the early thought on underdeveloped countries within classical growth theory. Papers by all the major economists who set the foundation for the theory of underdevelopment are included.

Bingham, Richard D., and Edward W. Hill, eds. *Global Perspectives on Economic Development: Government and Business Finance.* New Brunswick, N.J.: Center for Urban Policy Research, 1997.

DeGregori, Thomas R. *A Theory of Technology: Continuity and Change in Human Development.* Ames: Iowa University Press, 1985. Examines the issue of underdeveloped countries from the point of view of the level of technological sophistication and underlying institutional framework, instead of per-capita income.

Dorn, James A., Steve H. Hanke, and Alan A. Walters, eds. *The Revolution in Development Economics.* Washington, D.C.: Cato Institute, 1998.

English, E. Philip, and Harris M. Mule. *The African Development Bank.* Boulder, Colo.: L. Rienner, 1996.

Maxfield, Sylvia. *Gatekeepers of Growth: The International Political Economy of Central Banking in Developing Countries.* Princeton, N.J.: Princeton University Press, 1997.

Meier, Gerald. *Leading Issues in Economic Development.* 5th ed. New York: Oxford University Press, 1989. This prominent, almost standard text on development discusses undeveloped and underdeveloped countries from the point of view of traditional growth theory.

Mishkin, Frederic S. *Understanding Financial Crises: A Developing Country Perspective.* Cambridge, Mass.: National Bureau of Economic Research, 1996.

Pearson, Lester, et al. *Partners in Development: Report of the Commission on International Development.* New York: Praeger, 1969. The first annex contains an exhaustive summary of the diverse structures and the major economic characteristics of developing countries.

Todaro, Michael P. *Economic Development in the Third World.* 3d ed. New York: Longman, 1985. Todaro has organized a comprehensive, basic text on economic development and presents a concise chapter on the characteristics of developing countries. He goes beyond classic economic theory and includes a social systems theory to account for the major issues.

United Nations. Conference on Trade and Development. *The Least Developed Countries: 1988 Report.* New York: United Nations, 1989. This annual publication contains statistical information on the forty-two LDCs and highlights issues of the efficiency of resource use and allocation, women's role in development, policies regarding production sectors, social development, transport and communications, measures to improve the institutional capabilities in LDCs, and the world of international support.

Wilber, Charles K. *The Political Economy of Development and Underdevelopment.* 2d ed. New York: Random House, 1979. Contains articles from traditional economics and the political economy school which challenge the characterization of developing countries by their per-capita gross national product and assert that development should be concerned with the reduction of poverty, unemployment, and inequality.

World Bank. *Social Indicators of Development, 1989.* Baltimore: The Johns Hopkins University Press, 1989. This annual publication includes social statistics on the developing countries, such as human resources, natural resources, income and poverty, expenditure, and investment in human capital.

_____. *Trends in Developing Economies.* Washington, D.C.: Author, 1989. This annual publication provides extensive information on developing countries on a country-by-country basis and provides the reader with a good overview on the major economic and social issues which the countries are dealing with.

_____. *World Tables.* 6th ed. Baltimore: The Johns Hopkins University Press, 1989-1990. This annual report includes detailed statistical information on developing countries which allows them to be compared with each other and the industrialized world on the basis of a number of criteria.

Thomas R. DeGregori
Randal Joy Thompson

Cross-References

Development Theory, 152; Employment Theory, 180; Food Economics, 239; Gross National Product: Actual and Potential, 270; Gross National Product: Real and Nominal, 275; Growth Theory, 281; International Monetary Fund, 336; International Trade, 343; Population and Economics, 482; Poverty, 488; Trade Deficits, International Debt, and Budget Deficits, 587; World Economies, 638.

UNEMPLOYMENT CAUSES

Type of economics: Monetary and fiscal theory
Fields of study: Fiscal theory and public finance; monetary theory

Unemployment, or joblessness, is a problem of the utmost social importance. An understanding of the reasons for unemployment is a major first step in designing programs and policies to reduce joblessness.

Principal terms

FULL EMPLOYMENT: the absence of nonfrictional unemployment; in the United States, the full employment unemployment rate has traditionally been 4 percent

GROSS NATIONAL PRODUCT: the total value of all goods and services that are produced by an economy during one year

MONEY WAGE: the wage that is actually received by workers

OKUN'S LAW: a mathematical relationship between the rate of economic growth and a change in the rate of unemployment

POTENTIAL GROSS NATIONAL PRODUCT: the total value of aggregate production when all physical and human resources are fully utilized

REAL WAGE: the actual or money wage rate, adjusted for the cost of living

RECESSION: a sustained decline in economic activity

Overview

The largest single cause of unemployment is a decline in economic activity. These cyclical fluctuations are termed recessions or depressions. When production is falling, workers are laid off and the overall unemployment rate sharply increases. Most of the unemployment during recessions or depressions is called cyclical unemployment. Wage rigidity prevents workers from readily finding new jobs at lower wage rates.

The burden of cyclical unemployment is not spread evenly. Some industries and occupations suffer major declines in employment, while others are essentially insulated from variations in overall economic activity. Employment in manufacturing, especially durable goods manufacturing, is quite sensitive to business fluctuations. Employment in service industries, however, is relatively unaffected by changes in economic conditions. Because developed economies have gradually shifted from goods producing to services, variations in economic conditions have smaller effects on employment levels than had previously been the case.

A second reason for joblessness is a lack of congruence between the skills and abilities of some workers and the employment requirements of industry. This mismatch is generally attributed to various changes in the occupational structure of an economy, and the resultant joblessness is called structural unemployment. For example, workers in Appalachia may remain unemployed because they are unable or unwilling to accept employment outside that region. Poorly educated workers continue to be jobless because many available jobs require a high school diploma. Automation may lead to layoffs of production workers whose specialized skills are obsolete and not necessarily transferable to other jobs. While most economists would accept the fact that there is some structural unemployment, there is considerable disagreement about its magnitude and social significance.

In a swiftly changing economy such as that of the United States, technological progress, growth in the stock of both physical and human capital, and additions to the total labor force make possible progressively higher levels of output. Unemployment will increase, however, if economic growth has been insufficient to provide jobs for both the new entrants into the labor force and those who are displaced because of technological change. Thus, even if an economy were able to avoid recession or depression, the rate of unemployment could increase if the level of economic growth was below what is required for full employment.

Even during a period of business prosperity, some unemployment is unavoidable given the dynamic nature of an economy. These jobless workers are considered to be frictionally unemployed. Frictional unemployment consists of unemployed new entrants and re-entrants to the labor force, the seasonally unemployed as well as those presently unemployed because they have quit one job and have not been able to find another position. Thus, much frictional unemployment is independent of the movement of the general business cycle.

The volume of frictional unemployment partly reflects the ability of workers to withstand some unemployment while they are looking for a job. The relatively high earnings of U.S. workers, for example, permit many families to build up sufficient savings so that economic pressure does not force an individual to take the first position that is available. Programs that improve the mobility of labor, however, such as employment exchanges, aptitude testing, and the collection of adequate job vacancy information, will tend to reduce the volume of frictional unemployment. This is the case because workers will be better informed about labor market conditions and will be less likely to quit one job before they have obtained another.

Seasonal unemployment results from changes in business activity during the year that are caused by climatic or other seasonal changes in supply. The agricultural industry, for example, reflects the direct influence of the weather and is therefore strongly susceptible to seasonal variations in output and employment. Moreover, a number of industries that are involved in agricultural processing are likewise subject to the availability or nonavailability of the raw material on which their enterprise depends.

Seasonal unemployment also reflects variations in demand that are attributable to custom, habit, or religious observances. This is particularly evident in those industries that produce consumption goods for sale at a particular time of the year, of which Christmas decorations and Easter clothes are two examples. Many retail establishments account for nearly 50 percent of their total sales in the four weeks between Thanksgiving and Christmas and, as a result, must have extra sales personnel on a temporary basis.

Applications

Slow economic growth is an important cause of unemployment. There is a quantitative relationship between economic growth and the change in the unemployment rate. This association is known as Okun's law, which states that, for every 2 percent that the gross national product (GNP) declines relative to the potential GNP, the unemployment rate rises one percentage point. Thus, if the GNP begins at 100 percent of its potential and falls to 98 percent of the potential GNP, then the unemployment rate would rise from 4 to 5 percent. Assuming that the potential GNP grows at 3 percent annually—which was the approximate U.S. rate for the decade 1975-1985—the real GNP would have to grow at 3 percent each year merely to keep the unemployment rate constant.

During the period from 1979 to 1982, actual output in the United States remained unchanged but the potential GNP grew at 3 percent per annum. Thus, from 1979 to 1982, the potential GNP increased by over 9 percent. Under the circumstances, what should have happened to the unemployment rate? According to Okun's law, each 2 percent gap between actual and potential output adds one percentage point to the overall unemployment rate. Therefore a 9 percent gap in the GNP should have led to a rise in the unemployment rate of 4.5 percentage points. Because the unemployment rate in 1979 was 5.8 percent, Okun's law would predict a 10.3 percent unemployment rate in 1982. The official statistics show the actual unemployment rate for 1982 was 9.7 percent. In this case, the discrepancy between actual and predicted unemployment was relatively small.

The reasons for unemployment vary considerably from boom to recession. In both situations, less than 1 percent of the labor force are unemployed because they left their jobs, and another 2 to 3 percent are jobless new entrants or reentrants into the labor force. The group of unemployed new labor force entrants are primarily composed of recent high school and college graduates who have not yet obtained employment. The major change from boom to recession is found in the percentage of job losers. In the United States from 1973 to 1982 (a recession year) the fraction of the labor force that was unemployed because of lost jobs tripled. Moreover, during recession, the breadwinner or primary earner may become unemployed. In order to prevent a major decline in living standards, other family members (secondary earners) may enter or reenter the labor force.

The composition of unemployment changes as an economy moves between boom and recession, with certain industries or occupational groups of workers being the most adversely affected by cyclical unemployment. A very large fraction of unemployment is usually of short duration. Thus, in the boom year of 1973, less than one-fifth of U.S. unemployment lasted more than fourteen weeks. In recessions, however, it takes considerably longer to find jobs, and long-term unemployment becomes a serious economic problem. The number of U.S. workers out of a job for more than six months rose from 340,000 in 1973 to 2,600,000 at the end of 1982. In Europe, with lower geographical and social mobility and greater labor market rigidity, long-term unemployment in the early 1980's reached 50 percent of the total unemployed.

In November, 1982, the U.S. unemployment rate for men was 10.1 percent, up 4.1 percentage points from the third quarter of 1981. This increase was larger than that recorded in all postwar recessions except the 1948-1949 downturn. For women, the unemployment rate was 9.1 percent, up 2.4 points, which is about the average increase during a recession. The U.S. unemployment rate for men increases more than for women in most recessions, but it is unusual for the rate for men to increase so much that it exceeds the rate for women.

Blue-collar workers in the United States experienced a very sharp increase in their unemployment rate during the 1981-1982 recession. The blue-collar rate was up 6.8 percentage points to 16.5 percent from July, 1981, to November, 1982. Over the same time period, the rate for white-collar workers increased modestly—up only 1.6 points to 5.6 percent.

The sharp increase in the unemployment rates for men and blue-collar workers can be traced to the industries that are most affected by the weakness in economic activity. Among nonagricultural private wage and salary workers, the highest November, 1982, U.S. unemployment rates, were for construction workers (21.9 percent), miners (18.0 percent), and durable goods manufacturing employees (17.1 percent). In construction, the increase was 6.0 percentage points. For mining and durable goods manufacturing, the increases were 12.1 and 10.0 points, respectively. These three goods-producing industries had a predominantly male labor force in 1982.

Context

According to classical economics, labor market equilibrium, which was determined by the intersection of the demand and supply schedules for labor, had to be at the full employment level. Classical economists indicated that, if nonfrictional unemployment occurred, it must be because some workers were demanding wages in excess of the marginal productivity of labor. If these workers were unemployed because of their refusal to accept lower money wages, then their unemployment had to be regarded as voluntary. Had they accepted a reduction in money wages, the real wage would have declined, other things being equal, and more workers would have been employed.

The classical full employment theory was accepted by practically all economists from 1820 to 1930. Few economists of the modern day, however, believe there is any automatic tendency for an economic system to reach equilibrium at the level of full employment. The demise of the classical theory of employment can be attributed to two major factors: the experience of the Great Depression of the 1930's and the appearance of a more feasible explanation of the level of employment.

From 1929 to 1939, serious and prolonged unemployment was experienced on a continuous basis. Under these circumstances, not even the strongest defender of classical analysis could seriously maintain that there existed forces within the economy that would automatically generate continuous full employment. The Great Depression was a social catastrophe without previous parallel in economic history, and classical employment theory simply proved incapable of explaining this phenomenon.

The second reason for the collapse of the classical employment theory was the appearance in 1936 of *The General Theory of Employment, Interest, and Money* by John Maynard Keynes (1883-1946). This volume provided the intellectual foundation of all modern theories of the aggregate labor market.

In attacking the classical doctrine that the supply and demand for labor determine both the real wage and the employment level, Keynes made two points. First, he criticized the idea that the supply of labor is a function of the real wage by pointing out that workers do not normally leave the labor force if there has been a fall in real wages. Secondly, he refuted the notion that workers are in a position to determine the real wage and volume of employment as a result of the money wage agreements that they make with employers. Workers cannot do this, according to Keynes, because money wages cannot move independently of the general level of prices. Thus, a change in the money wage will not necessarily bring about any variation in the real wage and employment level. Keynes demonstrated that a lack of demand in the private economy could prevent a return to full employment. He advocated large-scale public works expenditures by governments in order to reduce cyclical unemployment.

After World War II, the idea that full employment was a proper and desirable objective of public policy gained widespread acceptance in the United States. Even though modern economists rejected the classical notion of an automatic tendency for the economy to be in full employment equilibrium, modern economists believed that it was the responsibility of the government to attempt to achieve full employment. Partly as a result, Congress passed the Employment Act of 1946, which indicated the responsibility of government "to promote maximum employment, production and purchasing power."

The Employment Act did not precisely define full employment. A 4 percent unemployment rate, however, has come to be accepted as a measure of full employment in the U.S. economy. Full employment not only means that frictional unemployment is at a minimum but also implies that the economy can attain the former without considerable inflation. Unfortunately, in the forty-four years since the passage of the Employment Act, full employment has seldom been attained.

Bibliography

Bernstein, Michael A. *The Great Depression.* New York: Cambridge University Press, 1987. This excellent book focuses primarily on the reasons that the Great Depression and accompanying cyclical unemployment lasted during the entire decade of the 1930's. Also considers modern problems of unemployment and economic growth from a historical perspective. Written for a varied audience.

Blau, Francine D., Marianne A. Ferber, and Anne E. Winkler. *The Economics of Women, Men, and Work.* 3d ed. Upper Saddle River, N.J.: Prentice Hall, 1998. The authors explore in some detail the different experiences at work, in terms of wages and occupations, of men and women. They also explore the changing structure of the American family and how it has affected the employment situation.

Gilpatrick, Eleanor C. *Structural Unemployment and Aggregate Demand.* Baltimore: The Johns Hopkins University Press, 1966. Considers whether structural unemployment or lack of sufficient aggregate demand were primarily responsible for the persistently high unemployment rates in the United States from 1948-66. Gilpatrick demonstrates that both reasons for unemployment were important. The main strength of this book, from a modern perspective, is the method of analysis that is used to determine the causes of joblessness.

Hughes, James J., and Richard Perlman. *The Economics of Unemployment.* New York: Cambridge University Press, 1984. This study develops a comprehensive analysis of unemployment in the United States and Great Britain. The authors observe substantial differences in the measurement, explanation, and treatment of unemployment in the two countries. Presents a good synthesis of the literature on the economics of joblessness.

Keynes, John Maynard. *The General Theory of Employment, Interest, and Money.* New York: Harcourt, Brace, 1936. This treatise effectively demolishes the classical theory of employment and income determination. Keynes demonstrates that cyclical unemployment may persist for some time in the absence of government programs to stimulate the economy.

Peterson, Wallace C. *Income, Employment, and Economic Growth.* 4th ed. New York: W. W,
    Norton, 1978. This volume presents an excellent discussion and comparison of the
    classical and Keynesian theories of employment. The discussion is basically nontechni-
    cal, with little use of mathematics. Well written.

Alan Sorkin

Cross-References

Business Cycles, 51; Classical Economics, 74; Great Depression, 263; Gross National
Product: Actual and Potential, 270; Growth Theory, 281; Labor Economics, 353; Technology, 581; Unemployment Types, 606; Wages, 620.

UNEMPLOYMENT TYPES

Type of economics: Monetary and fiscal theory
Fields of study: Fiscal theory and public finance; monetary theory

Economists distinguish between three main types of unemployment: cyclical, structural, and frictional. The purpose of this categorization is to help economists better understand the causes of unemployment and to help them develop better economic policies to reduce unemployment.

Principal terms

CYCLICAL UNEMPLOYMENT: unemployment that results from insufficient spending in the economy; sometimes called demand-deficient unemployment

DEINDUSTRIALIZATION: the loss of manufacturing or industrial jobs in a developed economy

ENTERPRISE ZONE: a depressed area in which governments attempt to create jobs by giving economic incentives to businesses that locate there

EXPANSIONARY MACROECONOMIC POLICIES: fiscal and monetary policies that are designed to increase spending in the economy and to reduce cyclical unemployment

FRICTIONAL UNEMPLOYMENT: short-term unemployment that results when individuals are between jobs and searching for new employment

JOB SEARCH POLICIES: government programs that are designed to reduce frictional unemployment by helping individuals to find new jobs

MANPOWER POLICIES: government programs that are designed to reduce structural unemployment by attempting to improve the job skills of workers

STRUCTURAL UNEMPLOYMENT: unemployment that results from a mismatch between the characteristics and skills of those looking for work and the characteristics and skills that employers seek from workers

Overview

The unemployed are those individuals who are looking for work but who have not succeeded in finding a job. There are many different reasons why people may not be able to find work. To understand these reasons better, economists have attempted to classify the basic causes, or types, of unemployment. Three main types of unemployment are usually singled out: cyclical or demand-deficient unemployment, structural unemployment, and frictional unemployment.

Cyclical unemployment occurs when the national level of production is less than the level that is necessary in order to employ all those who want jobs, which occurs when spending or demand in the economy is too low. With little spending taking place, businesses sell few goods and services, their inventories pile up, and they need fewer workers. Those workers who get laid off because of falling sales, and those new labor market entrants who cannot find a job because businesses are not hiring, are considered to be cyclically unemployed.

Nations periodically undergo changes in their levels of economic activity. During recessions and depressions, cyclical unemployment grows dramatically. A 5 percent unemployment rate—the sum of frictional and structural employment—has been regarded as full employment by some economists. Anything above this percentage is taken to be cyclical unemployment. Thus, during the 1980-1982 recession when the U.S. unemployment rate exceeded 10 percent, more than half of all unemployment was of the cyclical variety. In addition, the very high levels of unemployment that were experienced during the Great Depression of the 1930's, reaching 25 percent in some years, represented primarily cyclical unemployment.

Structural unemployment results when there is a mismatch between the needs of employers and the characteristics of those who are looking for work. This mismatch can have several sources. There can be a mismatch of skills, there can be a geographic mismatch, or there can be a mismatch in the terms of personal characteristics.

Much of the unemployment in urban ghettos is the result of a mismatch between the jobs that are available in urban areas and the skills of those who live there. Many jobs in inner cities are service-sector jobs that require a knowledge of advanced communication technology, computing skills, and facility in communicating with others. In contrast, many residents of urban ghettos are high school dropouts who possess few or none of these skills. Consequently, businesses are unwilling to hire these people, and structural unemployment runs very high in inner cities.

One important type of structural unemployment occurs when automation, or a technological improvement in production, reduces the number of workers that a firm needs in order to produce the goods and services that it can sell. Another important type of structural unemployment occurs when a domestic industry moves its production facilities to foreign countries. Workers who are laid off because of automation or deindustrialization are typically skilled and experienced workers. Yet, the specific skills and experiences that they have accumulated over time are no longer in demand by domestic business firms; hence, they are structurally unemployed.

Geographic mismatches can occur because employers are not in the same area as job seekers. For example, in the United States during the 1970's and 1980's, businesses expanded in the West and the South and shut down operations in the North and the Midwest. Some of those who were laid off in the Snowbelt did not want to leave their friends and relatives in order to search for new jobs in the Sunbelt. Because they did not move to where jobs existed, they became structurally unemployed.

Mismatches can also occur within one geographic region. If businesses are moving from inner cities to suburban districts and people cannot follow because they do not own cars, there is inadequate mass transit, or housing in the suburbs is too expensive, then the workers who are laid off in the inner cities become structurally unemployed.

Finally, there can be a mismatch between the personal characteristics of job seekers and the characteristics of workers who are demanded by businesses. If businesses are looking for younger workers, men, or whites, while those who are seeking jobs are older workers, women, or minorities, then these latter individuals will not be hired. Discrimination in employment based on age, sex, or race, therefore, can lead to structural unemployment.

Frictional unemployment results from people being in between jobs and is a very short-term phenomenon, experienced by someone who is actively seeking out the best possible position. For example, a high school or college graduate may not accept the first job offer, deciding instead to wait for something better. It may also take a few months to

Michigan autoworkers line up to receive unemployment insurance benefits in 1996, when a parts shortage idled their plant. (AP/Wide World Photos)

receive a job offer following graduation. During this time, this graduate is frictionally unemployed.

In addition, people who are employed but desire a different job may quit their present job while they look for another, better position. Sometimes they do this because they dislike their current job and expect to find a new position quickly. Sometimes they quit their present job in order to put more time and energy into looking for other work.

Finally, the frictionally unemployed individual may have been laid off recently but has yet to find another job. This case is similar to cyclical unemployment; however, if jobs are available and the individual who is laid off has the necessary skills in order to obtain one of these jobs, then it will only be a short time before this individual finds new employment. While looking for work, he or she is classified as frictionally unemployed.

Applications

Just as each type of unemployment is associated with a different cause, each type of unemployment requires a different policy solution.

Two different schools of thought have developed about how to remedy cyclical unemployment. The classical school to macroeconomics has argued that, when the demand for labor falls in the economy, workers must accept lower wages. If they do not, then businesses will not hire them. Unions, minimum wage laws, and the psychological resistance of workers to wage cuts all explain cyclical unemployment, according to classical economists. Its solution requires eliminating unions and minimum wage legislation that keeps wages too high.

In contrast, the Keynesian school of macroeconomics argues that the classical solution will only worsen matters because lower wages reduce spending by workers. This reduction, in turn, will reduce business sales and increase layoffs. The only viable solution to the problem of cyclical unemployment, according to Keynesian economists, can be expansionary macroeconomic policies. The federal government must increase its spending and reduce taxes, and the central bank must lower interest rates, making it easier to borrow money. In the former case, consumers and government spend more. Businesses will then hire workers to produce those goods that are demanded by individuals and the government. In the latter case, businesses that borrow more money will need more workers in order to expand their operations.

Economists have formulated several policies to deal with the problem of structural unemployment. If structural unemployment is the result of individuals who lack adequate skills, then the solution is a manpower or training program that helps these individuals to develop the skills that are required in order to obtain jobs. Similarly, if structural unemployment results from workers being replaced by advanced technology, then the solution is to retrain workers so that they can operate and service the new machinery. In the United States, the Manpower Development and Training Act of 1962 was designed to provide federal financial support for training and work programs to upgrade the skills of the structurally unemployed. Its replacement, the Job Training Partnership Act of 1982, shifted the administration of the program to state and local governments and to the private sector. Yet, it retained the essential features of the remedial training programs from the 1960's and 1970's.

On the other hand, if structural unemployment results from deindustrialization, then its solution is to revive the basic manufacturing industries of a nation. Plant closing legislation, which requires advance notice for all plant closing and layoffs, and an industrial policy, in which government provides assistance to growing manufacturing industries, have been suggested as two means of reversing deindustrialization in the United States.

If structural unemployment results from locational mismatches, then workers can be provided with assistance in moving to areas where jobs are more available. Federal income tax deductions for moving expenses are one type of government assistance of this variety. Improved mass transit between inner cities and metropolitan suburbs can also help alleviate locational mismatches.

Alternatively, the government can give tax breaks, low-interest loans, or regulatory concessions to businesses that locate in urban areas that contain a large number of unemployed workers. By creating these urban enterprise zones, jobs come to the unemployed, rather than forcing people to move to areas where jobs exist. The Enterprise Zone Employment and Development Act of 1983 allowed the Secretary of Housing and Urban Development to designate up to fifty urban enterprise zones in the United States.

Some poorly thought-out government policies actually discourage movement among different areas and thus may contribute to structural unemployment. For example, state residency requirements for individuals to become eligible for unemployment insurance or other social benefits may keep people from moving to states where jobs are more readily available. Therefore, one solution to structural unemployment that is attributable to locational mismatches could be to eliminate state residency requirements for unemployment insurance and other income support programs.

Structural unemployment that results from discrimination against women, minorities, or the elderly can be remedied by prohibiting discrimination in hiring. In 1964, the Civil Rights Act that was designed by President John F. Kennedy created the Equal Employment Opportunity Commission, which barred firms with federal government contracts from discriminating against job applicants on the basis of race, creed, or national origin. Evidence of discrimination in employment can result in the loss of government business. Extending this principle, title VII of the Civil Rights Act made it unlawful for any firm to discriminate in employment on account of race or sex.

Frictional unemployment has always been regarded as the least undesirable type of unemployment and part of the normal turnover of labor. If jobs exist and if unemployed individuals have job skills, then these workers will soon find employment. Nevertheless, all developed nations provide some assistance to help the frictionally unemployed find jobs. Job search policies can reduce this type of unemployment by faster or better dissemination of job information and by subsidizing job search costs. Job information in the United States is provided by local unemployment offices. Federal income tax deductions for job hunting expenses are another way that job search is subsidized in the United States. Countries such as Sweden and Great Britain also offer the services of employment agencies without charge in order to help with job searches.

Context

Unemployment has been a relatively unknown phenomenon in economies without a significant industrial base. In fact, the term "unemployment" did not come into general usage until the late nineteenth century, when joblessness first became a major economic problem.

One early solution to the unemployment problem was the workhouse, which provided shelter and sustenance to those without jobs in exchange for their labor. The problem with the workhouse system, and the reason that it failed to accomplish its purpose, was that it treated symptoms rather than causes; it provided make-work jobs rather than a solution to the labor market problems causing unemployment in the first place.

The classification of unemployment by type attempts to get at the root causes of unemployment. This classification is important because different types of unemployment have different cures, and applying a particular cure to the wrong type of unemployment will have detrimental, rather than beneficial, effects. For example, expansionary macroeconomic policies will not create jobs in an economy that is suffering from structural unemployment. In fact, such policies would create worse problems. Because the structurally unemployed lack the necessary skills to be hired, increasing demand will not result in more employment. Rather, the increase in demand will only create inflation. Conversely, if unemployment is primarily cyclical, then job search or manpower policies that are used in order to train workers and help them find jobs will inevitably fail. Because employers are not hiring as the result of bad economic conditions and insufficient sales, there will be no jobs for newly trained workers and no jobs for those who are helped with their job search.

The search for types, or causes, of unemployment is also important because economists agree that unemployment is undesirable and that it has severe and significant costs. The nation loses the output that unemployed individuals could have produced. The government loses tax receipts because people are unemployed, and it will likely have to pay out more in unemployment benefits and other types of social spending. Unemployed workers are also more likely to resort to crime in order to support themselves and their families.

For the unemployed individual, however, the costs are even greater. The loss of income that is associated with unemployment greatly reduces one's standard of living and presages financial disaster if employment is not found soon. Employment can also bring non-economic rewards, such as friendships with coworkers, prestige, power, and feelings of accomplishment. These rewards are lost when workers lose their jobs, and the result is often an overwhelming feeling of depression. Moreover, numerous studies have found that, as the rate of unemployment grows, suicides rise, marital disputes increase, more families break up, and alcohol consumption and alcohol-related deaths both increase. Because unemployment has such negative consequences, economists have attempted to classify different types of unemployment and to devise policies that focus on reducing each specific type of unemployment.

Bibliography

Bawden, D. Lee, and Felicity Skidmore, eds. *Rethinking Employment Policy.* Washington, D.C.: Urban Institute Press, 1989. A series of papers by distinguished labor economists that were presented at the Urban Institute, a Washington think tank. Each paper focuses on possible policy solutions to unemployment. Although written primarily for a professional audience, the papers remain worthwhile to educated lay readers and undergraduate students.

Blau, Francine D., Marianne A. Ferber, and Anne E. Winkler. *The Economics of Women, Men, and Work.* 3d ed. Upper Saddle River, N.J.: Prentice Hall, 1998. The authors explore in some detail the different experiences at work, in terms of wages and occupations, of men and women. They also explore the changing structure of the American family and how it has affected the employment situation.

Bluestone, Barry, and Bennett Harrison. *The Deindustrialization of America.* New York: Basic Books, 1982. The authors argue that, because U.S. business has focused on mergers and foreign investment rather than on production, cyclical and structural unemployment in the United States has increased. They then discuss numerous policy solutions. Many have quibbled with the analysis and policy assessments that are contained in this work; however, it remains a thought-provoking and compelling account of U.S. labor market problems at the end of the twentieth century.

Garraty, John A. *Unemployment in History: Economic Thought and Public Policy.* New York: Harper & Row, 1978. A historical account of public perceptions and the views of economists about the unemployed, beginning in ancient and medieval times and continuing up to the 1970's. Also discusses the different economic policies that have been designed over time in order to deal with the problem of joblessness.

Perry, Charles R., Bernard E. Anderson, Richard L. Rowan, and Herbert R. Northrop. *The Impact of Government Manpower Programs.* Philadelphia: University of Pennsylvania Press, 1975. A thorough, detailed analysis of the manpower programs that were put into effect during the 1960's. Summarizes the main provisions of each manpower policy, surveys research on its impact, and provides an overall assessment of each program. This book will appeal most to those who enjoy facts and figures.

Tobin, James. *The New Economics One Decade Older.* Princeton, N.J.: Princeton University Press, 1974. A Nobel Prize-winning Keynesian economist, Tobin describes, in simple and clear language, how the ideas of Keynesian economics came to the United

States and how they were used in the 1960's in order to fight cyclical unemployment.

Weiner, Stuart E. "Enterprise Zones as a Means of Reducing Structural Unemployment." *Economic Review* 6 (March, 1984): 3-16. This excellent short article provides a history of enterprise zones, an explanation of how they are supposed to reduce structural unemployment, and an assessment of this policy tool. The article can be obtained free of charge by writing to the Federal Reserve Bank of Kansas City at 925 Grand Avenue, Kansas City, Mo., 64198.

Wolfbein, Seymour L. *Employment, Unemployment, and Public Policy.* New York: Random House, 1965. Describes in simple, easy-to-understand terms how unemployment is calculated, gives concrete examples of the different types of unemployment, and discusses how expansionary macroeconomic policies and manpower policies can remedy the problems of cyclical and structural unemployment. Unfortunately, the book is somewhat out of date. Nevertheless, it is the best simple and general introduction to unemployment and unemployment policy that is available.

Steven Pressman

Cross-References

Business Cycles, 51; Classical Economics, 74; Great Depression, 263; Gross National Product: Actual and Potential, 270; Growth Theory, 281; Labor Economics, 353; Technology, 581; Unemployment Causes, 600; Wages, 620.

UNIONS

Type of economics: Labor and population
Field of study: Trade unions

Labor unions are organizations of workers that are formed for purposes of collective action. Typically, improvements in wages and working conditions are the objective of unions, although broader social goals may be union objectives as well. Unions throughout the world are organized in a variety of ways and play differing roles in their economies.

Principal terms

BUSINESS UNIONISM: an orientation by a union toward maximization of economic benefits to members without any broader social goal

COLLECTIVE BARGAINING: the negotiation of wages, other compensation, and conditions of employment with an employer, resulting in an agreement, binding on the union membership

CORPORATISM: a system of societal management in which major interest groups, such as union federations and employers' associations, resolve important national issues through negotiation

CRAFT UNIONS: unions organized on the basis of shared skills or professions; examples include carpenters and electricians

INDUSTRIAL UNIONS: unions organized on the basis of shared employment in specific industries; examples include automobile and steel industry workers

PATTERN BARGAINING: a practice of industrial unions in which an agreement with one major national employer becomes the model for agreements with other major employers

SOCIAL UNIONISM: the tendency of a union to work for broader social goals as well as direct benefits to members

Overview

The many types of labor unions throughout the world can be classified by their purpose and organizational structure. Unions are the most common forum for workers in various industries to act collectively to advance their direct interests and other social goals that could not be met through individual action. Collective bargaining between unions and employers over wages and other compensation, working conditions, and other aspects of working life are the primary functions of most unions, while others place more of an emphasis on political activism to achieve the goals of their membership.

Unions are led by elected officials and financed by dues payments, which may be voluntary or mandatory. Collective bargaining takes place between unions and individual employers or employers' associations. In the event of a failure to reach agreement with employers, the tool most widely used by unions is to go on strike, which is the collective withholding of the labor of the union membership. A variety of organizational structures is found in labor unions throughout the world. Workers may be organized by their trades or profession in craft unions; the production workers of mass-production industries may be organized into industrial unions; the employees of individual companies may be organized into enterprise or company unions.

The earliest organizational type is the craft union, which is composed of members of the same skilled trade. Craft unions became common in Europe and North America during the nineteenth century. Craft unions typically exert some degree of control over the transmission of their skills and the entry of new workers into their trades through union-administered apprenticeship programs. They are most common in industries that rely on skilled workers to create products without a high degree of coordination or mechanization (such as the construction industry) rather than in mass-production industries.

Mass-production industries are the home of the industrial unions, which typically attempt to include all production workers within an industry. They are the largest, most influential, and most politically active unions in North America and Western Europe, and they represent the economic interests of workers of a wide variety of skill and wage levels. Industrial unions typically engage in pattern bargaining, in which the union attempts to set industry-wide wage standards and to avoid giving competitive advantages to individual firms within the industry. In some cases, most frequently in Scandinavian unions, a "solidarity wage policy" is followed, in which the union attempts to achieve some degree of wage equality among different types of workers within the industry. This may mean that some workers receive much more pay than they would under competitive market conditions, while other workers whose skills are in greater demand are paid at or below competitive market rates. In the United States, while some degree of wage equalization takes place in industrial unions, considerable wage differentials among workers reflect varying levels of skills.

Enterprise or company unions consist of the employees of single companies. This limitation distinguishes them from industrial unions, which they otherwise resemble. The most prominent enterprise unions are found in the large export industries of Japan, such as automobiles, steel, and electronics. The bargaining strategies of enterprise unions are more likely to take the interests and the competitive position of the employer into account than are industry-wide unions. Enterprise unions, however, are criticized by adherents of industrial unions as being dominated by the companies whose workers they represent. In Japan, white-collar workers and production workers are frequently members of the enterprise unions.

National union confederations, which exercise varying degrees of control over the actions of individual labor unions, are found throughout the world. The United States and Great Britain have examples of decentralized labor movements in which individual unions have virtually complete freedom from the national confederation. Sweden and Austria have examples of more centralized labor movements in which union strategy is coordinated at the national level, and individual unions tend not to deviate from national strategies. In some countries, such as France and Italy, there are rival union confederations that are engaged in political or ideological conflict with one another. In these countries, the role of unions in collective bargaining is less important, and unions are closely linked to political parties.

While the fundamental purpose of labor unions is to advance the economic interests of their members, there have always been other purposes as well. The early years of labor movements in the industrialized world were marked by intense political and ideological struggle with employers, and frequently, the political order. In many countries, unions are closely linked with political movements. There are also cases in which unions have aimed at the overthrow of the existing social and political order and the construction of a new society.

Labor movements which have no direct ties to political parties and limit their actions to furthering the direct economic self-interest of their members are engaging in business unionism. This style of union activity is quite rare in a pure form. Most unions throughout the world engage in some degree of social activism. Craft unions in the United States and enterprise unions in Japan are the purest examples of business unionism.

Attempts by labor unions to achieve broader social goals are described as social unionism. Almost all labor movements engage in some degree of social unionism. Western European unions are the best example of socially active labor movements. The European labor movements had to fight from the start for basic citizenship rights, as well as for improved wages and working conditions. American labor unions became involved in social unionism with the successful organization of mass-production industry in the 1930's. American unions, however, have never had the high degree of distinct political identity found in Europe.

Revolutionary unions attempt to realize economic and political goals by the overthrow of the existing social order and arise in desperate circumstances. Most frequently, these are small and unsuccessful movements. There have, however, been some successful revolutionary unions. The Histadrut Labor Confederation in British-administered Palestine was an integral part of the Labor Zionist movement to establish a Jewish state, forming businesses and cooperatives as well as organizing workers. Histadrut cooperatives and businesses became the economic foundation of the new state of Israel, which owes its existence, in many respects, to its labor movement. The Solidarity labor movement in Poland in the 1980's was able to overcome peacefully the communist dictatorship by enduring severe repression under martial law.

Applications

Unions pursue their goals in widely varying environments. The strongest and most influential labor movements are found in the capitalist democracies of North America, Western Europe, and Japan, where they are influential actors on the national economic stage, although they have lost some of their influence during the 1980's. Unions in the communist and post-communist countries and unions in the developing countries face much more difficult situations.

In the capitalist democracies, unions had won a widely acknowledged role in the organization of industry by the middle of the twentieth century. The macroeconomic policies of the capitalist democracies followed policies in which the consumer spending of well-paid union workers contributed to economic growth. A strong union role was common, especially in the mass-production industries. This postwar economic order began to come unraveled in the 1970's, leading to a period of increased insecurity in the mass-production industries and a diminished role for unions.

Unions in the United States differ from union movements in the other capitalist democracies in several ways. First, American unions lack the strong ties to larger political movements that are common in Western Europe. American unions are highly active in plant-level issues, unlike their European counterparts. American union locals, which are typically organized at the plant level for industrial unions, are deeply involved in handling local grievances and administering work rules and seniority issues. The range of issues that are subject to collective bargaining is broader in the United States, with highly detailed work rules and shop floor procedure issues negotiated between labor and management. The union shop, in which union dues payment is mandatory, is much more frequent in the United States than in Europe. Unions in the United States are concentrated in the durable goods manufacturing, transportation, and communications industries, as well as among state and local public employees. The American Federation of Labor and Congress of Industrial Organizations (AFL-CIO) is a national union confederation containing almost all unions as members. The AFL-CIO is a decentralized confederation, with very little coordination of the activities of individual unions. The AFL-CIO is not associated with any political or ideological movement, although it has tended to support the Democratic Party in national politics.

Modern labor unions had their beginnings in Western Europe. European unions are among the most successful and influential in the world. In general, European unions differ from American unions by having much stronger links to political movements, most of which are some variant of social democracy. The first modern labor movement arose in Great Britain. Great Britain's labor movement is similar to that of the United States in the presence of both craft and industrial unions, the highly decentralized structure, and the application of collective bargaining to issues of shop floor procedure and work rules. The national trade union confederation is closely associated with the Labour Party.

The labor movement in West Germany was completely reconstructed following World War II into a small number of industrial unions. German unions are not heavily involved in plant-level issues; rather, workers' councils at individual plants, established by federal law, are responsible for plant-level issues and negotiate supplement agreements to the industry-wide labor agreements. In large employers, the federal law of codetermination provides for equal representation of union representatives and stockholders on the boards of directors for firms.

Sweden, Norway, and Austria have the most centralized and powerful union movements in the world. These are small, homogeneous countries with highly skilled labor forces geared to the capital-intensive production of high-quality producer and consumer goods for export. Their economies rely on corporatist decision-making procedures, relying heavily on negotiations between highly centralized union movements and employers' associations. The national trade union federations in these countries exercise considerable control over wage bargaining by member unions. The union federations, closely allied with the social democratic parties which have been dominant since World War II in these countries, routinely place goals such as overall economic efficiency, stability, and income equalization higher than maximization of wage increases. This style of collective bargaining, which is an integral part of the management of the national economy, has been successful because of centralization, the high proportions of union membership, and high degrees of social consensus.

The Japanese labor movement was rebuilt following World War II. There are several national labor federations that are politically active without playing a major role in collective bargaining. Enterprise level or company unions are responsible for collective bargaining in the major industries. These unions include most company employees, including white-collar workers. They are advocates for the interest of employees within a context of avoiding demands that could be harmful to the competitive position of their companies. The major industries in Japan are well known for building strong ties with their employees, with extensive company-provided social benefits and lifetime employment as the norm. This model of employee relations is limited to the major export industries of Japan.

Labor unions under communism fulfilled a different social function from that of labor movements elsewhere. These state-dominated organizations served to mobilize and control workers ideologically, as well as to provide a variety of social welfare functions. They were rarely seen as effective advocates for the interests of their members. With the collapse of communism in Central Europe in 1989 and 1990, these widely discredited unions were left adrift in a rapidly changing economic environment. One of the unanswered questions of the collapse of communism was whether these unions or newly created unions would be able to advance effectively the interests of workers in countries attempting the difficult transition from centrally planned to market economies. The success of the democratic oppositionist Solidarity labor movement in Poland, in an attempt to resolve Poland's severe economic crisis, placed it in the position of supporting measures which, in the short run, were harmful to its members.

Unions in the developing countries typically face difficult circumstances. The relative surplus of labor in such countries gives unions little leverage. Authoritarian governments frequently persecute union activists and prevent union organization from gaining a foothold. In some cases, unions are able to win enclaves of influence in key export industries. This occurs frequently in miners' unions, which are among the most successful unions in South America, as well as in South Africa. There are long traditions of union activity in many South American countries such as Argentina, Bolivia, Brazil, and Chile. Authoritarian governments and economic collapse have weakened labor movements, although organized labor played an important role in the reestablishment of democracy in Brazil and Chile during the 1980's.

Context

Labor unions have developed as the predominant institutions of the workers in mass-production industries. Unions advance the interests of workers to achieve goals that could not be met through individual action.

There are many economists who believe that the overall role of unions is harmful. Microeconomic theory tends to look askance at unions, viewing them as harmful to the overall welfare of society. From this perspective, unions distort the functioning of labor markets by using their monopoly power to force wage levels above what a competitive market would set, thus reducing employment and increasing wage inequality. Many employers complain that an extensive union voice in shop floor control detracts from the efficient deployment of labor. Analysts of the role of interest groups in setting economic policy believe that unions, by furthering their interests, may cause harm to the interests of society as a whole.

In response to such criticism, others argue that unions are more than a labor market cartel; rather, they are a collective voice, enabling workers to shape their work environments. From this perspective, collective action influences wage and benefit determination in socially beneficial ways that would not occur through individual bargaining. The criticism of the special interest characteristics of union behavior may only apply to fragmented and decentralized labor movements such as American and British unions. In contrast, the highly centralized unions of northern Europe are exemplary in paying attention to the interests of society as a whole.

During the 1980's, labor unions grew weaker in many parts of the world, including the United States. Job growth in the mass-production industries was stagnant or declining. At the same time, most job creation was in sectors traditionally averse to unions. The expansion of competitive export industries in many of the developing countries has substantially decreased the bargaining power of labor unions in the capitalist democracies. Unions have become much weaker in the United States than in Europe or Japan. Union membership in the United States fell by half from the peak of 35 percent of the work force in 1945 to 17 percent in 1988.

It has been suggested that as mass-production industry is reshaped by technological change that points in the direction of more specialized and flexible production, unions will be forced to change their role. Unions may evolve from the industrial union model into a more collaborative relationship with employers. Many believe that international union cooperation is necessary to provide a counterweight to the ability of corporations to shift jobs around the world, placing downward pressure on wages in the developed countries. Although the union's future evolution is undetermined, it seems clear that workers will continue to organize for collective action and that unions will play a part in social and economic life.

Bibliography

Aronowitz, Stanley. *Working Class Hero: A New Strategy for Labor.* New York: Pilgrim Press, 1983. A critique of American union history and current orientation by a well-known labor historian and former union official. Aronowitz describes how unique aspects of American unionism came about that now pose problems, and advocates changes in union strategy and orientation.

Edwards, Richard, Paolo Garonna, and Franz Toedtling. *Unions in Crisis and Beyond: Perspectives from Six Countries.* Dover, Mass.: Auburn House, 1986. A collection of articles on the impact of changes in the world economy on unions in the United States and Western Europe. Concise, readable essays show how differences in union structure and strategy have led to varying degrees of success in coping with a less favorable climate.

Freeman, Richard B., and James L. Medoff. *What Do Unions Do?* New York: Basic Books, 1984. This widely recognized and influential assessment of the role of unions in the United States interprets a major empirical research undertaking for the general reader. The study found that negative economic impacts of unions were outweighed by positive economic and social impacts.

Kuttner, Robert. *The Economic Illusion.* Boston: Houghton Mifflin, 1984. A stimulating and iconoclastic critique of the "conventional wisdom" on the relationship between equality and economic growth by *Business Week* and National Public Radio commentator Kuttner. A wide range of topics includes an extensive discussion of the role that trade unions play in the capitalist democracies, contrasting American and European unions.

Larsen, Simeon, and Bruce Nissen, eds. *Theories of the Labor Movement.* Detroit: Wayne State University Press, 1987. An anthology of classic and modern writings on labor movement theory designed for an undergraduate audience. This comprehensive and highly diverse sourcebook discusses everyone from Karl Marx to Milton Friedman to Pope John Paul II.

Sturmthal, Adolf, and James G. Scovine, eds. *The International Labor Movement in Transition*. Urbana: University of Illinois Press, 1973. This collection of essays covers the evolution of labor movements in the United States, Europe, Japan, Africa, and South America. Highly readable essays focus on the relative importance of collective bargaining and political action in unions throughout the world.

Michael Duncan

Cross-References

Communism, 80; Labor Economics, 353; Labor Theory of Value, 358; Socialism, 544; Undeveloped and Underdeveloped Countries, 593; Wages, 620.

WAGES

Type of economics: Labor and population
Field of study: Labor markets

Wages, the price of labor, are one of the principal topics of economic analysis; the differences among the major competing economic theories often center on the explanation that each gives of the concept of wages. The effects of changes in wages on unemployment and inflation have occasioned controversy.

Principal terms

LABOR THEORY OF VALUE: the view, held in classical and Marxist economics, that the value of a commodity is determined by the labor that is necessary to produce it

MARGINAL PRODUCT: the value that is added to production by the last unit that is employed of a factor of production

RICARDO EFFECT: the claim that an increase in wages may cause entrepreneurs to substitute machinery for labor in order to increase productivity

RIGIDITY OF WAGES: the doctrine, held by Keynesian economists, that downward shifts in wages will not increase employment during a depression

SURPLUS VALUE: according to the labor theory of value, the uncompensated time during which workers labor for capitalists, accounting for the existence of profit

UTILITY: the value of a good or service, as rated by the preferences of economic actors

ZONE OF INDETERMINACY: the area, allowed by the interaction of the demand and supply curves for labor, within which bargaining over wages can take place

Overview

A principal topic in economics is the explanation of wages, which is understandable considering that almost all goods are produced by means of labor. Three competing schools of thought dominate the discussion of wage determination: the marginal productivity theory, the labor theory of value, and the neo-Ricardianism of Piero Sraffa. The first of these is, by far, the most widely accepted by economists in the United States and Western Europe.

Marginalist economics subsumes the explanation of wages within the general theory of price. In this view, consumers' relative preferences ultimately determine the value of all goods. For example, if A and B exchange apples for oranges, then the price—the ratio at which the goods are exchanged—will be determined by the relative preferences of A and B for apples and oranges. For each good, a demand and a supply curve can be constructed. The demand curve indicates what quantity of the good will be demanded at each price, and the supply curve indicates how much will be supplied at each price. The point of intersection determines the price that will clear the market. At this price, no surpluses or shortages exist.

The question arises, however, as to how production goods can be valued. These are goods, such as capital and labor, that are not directly consumed but are used to manufacture consumption goods. According to the marginalist school, the values of consumption goods are imputed to the goods that are used in their production. A capitalist who produces consumer goods can use their anticipated prices to determine his or her demand schedule for the means of production that are used. Similarly, the demanders and suppliers of goods at higher stages of production—such as goods that are used in the manufacture of production goods—can determine their prices by reference to anticipated prices of the next lower stage to their own.

Labor, in this view, is a factor of production whose price is determined in the same manner as that of inanimate goods. The wage of a unit of labor will be determined by the amount of value that it adds to the finished product. Labor receives its marginal value product, under conditions of perfect competition. Wages can vary from this optimum under other market structures, such as monopoly and oligopoly, but no more so than the prices of other factors of production under these structures. Because the capitalist advances the prices of the factors of production in anticipation of sales, the marginal value products must be discounted by the rate of interest in order to obtain the actual price of the factor. Applied to labor, marginalism thus maintains that wages are the discounted marginal value product of the worker.

Although this theory of wages is a description or model of how part of the economy works, not a prescription for how it should work, the marginalist account has been used in defense of the justice of market wages. The American economist John Bates Clark (1847-1938) argued in *The Distribution of Wealth* (1899) that, because labor obtains in wages what it produces, the free market does not exploit labor. Clark's views have been influential in mainstream American economics.

Partisans of the labor theory of value, most of whom are Marxist economists, vigorously reject this account. In their view, the values of economic goods are not determined by the preferences of consumers. Quite the contrary, what ultimately accounts for the price of a commodity is the labor time that is socially necessary to produce it. Karl Marx (1818-1883) held that the determination of wages provides the key to the origins of interest and rent.

The wages of labor are determined by the socially necessary time that is required to produce labor. Marx took this to mean that wages are fixed by the cost of the commodities that are required for a laborer's subsistence. In exchange for the money that he or she needs to purchase goods, the worker supplies the capitalist with labor-power for the working day. The capitalist, having thus secured control of the laborer, obtains more work from him or her than the hours that are required to produce the worker's subsistence. This extra time constitutes surplus value, and its extraction by the capi-

British economist David Ricardo, whose ideas on labor costs have had a profound impact on theories about wages. (Library of Congress)

talist lies at the origin of interest and rent. Theorists who accept this position tend to hold that capitalist wage policy is unjust.

A third school, the neo-Ricardian, maintains that prices are determined by the cost of production of a standard commodity. In the model of Sraffa, the founder of this view, the standard commodity was grain. Given the price of the standard commodity and the production functions of each capital good, the price of each of the factors of production can be determined. Labor is an exception in this system: Its price is not fixed by the value equations but must be determined by circumstances that are outside the economic system. Supporters of this view see it as offering a place for labor union activity and governmental efforts to increase wages. Because wages are fixed outside the economic system, an increase in wages need not upset the price mechanism. Marginalists strongly repudiate this conclusion.

Applications

Wage determination is much more than a mere theoretical issue. In the marginalist view, efforts to increase wages above market rates will have undesirable consequences. Because workers receive marginal value products, a minimum wage—if it exceeds the market rate—will require employers to pay workers more than they add to the value of the product. Rather than do so, it is in the employer's interest to discharge workers whose costs exceed the value their labor produces. The result of increases in wages above the market rate is the unemployment of the submarginal worker. It does not follow from this argument that these wage increases ought not to be granted—this would be a matter of ethics rather than of economics. Nevertheless, this claim is often used by opponents of non-market-generated wage increases, which appear to be obtained only at the expense of other workers.

Economists who are sympathetic to labor unions usually try to meet this argument by an appeal to a zone of indeterminacy in labor contracts. Because of the peculiar shapes of the demand and supply curves for labor, the market price may not be determined at a fixed point. Instead, a number of market-clearing prices may exist, which allows room for labor unions or governments to raise wages without causing unemployment. The critics of this argument deny that a case has been made for irregular demand and supply curves of labor. Wages, its critics allege, are no more undetermined than any other price.

Some labor economists meet the claim that nonmarket wage increases cause unemployment with a demurrer: Granted that wage increases have this effect, what will follow? Employers will tend to substitute machinery for workers, as the price of machinery has gone down relative to that of labor. The result will be increased production, which will increase the demand for workers and end the temporary unemployment that wage increases have brought about. This phenomenon is known as the Ricardo effect. Opponents of this line of analysis protest that it consists of a fundamental fallacy. It need not be the case that an increase in the use of machinery raises productivity. On the contrary, the optimum proportion of labor and capital is determined by the market. Attempts to overthrow this proportion by stepping up the use of machinery will result in malinvestment, not higher production.

The labor theory of value and the neo-Ricardian approach make wage increases much less problematic. By the terms of the labor theory of value, the price of labor—the cost of the laborer's subsistence—is a matter that is open to negotiation. The standard rate of subsistence is conventionally established, rather than fixed by nature; thus, scope for bargaining exists. The case is even clearer from the neo-Ricardian perspective, in which wages are not fixed at all by the constraints of the economic system and are entirely a matter of political and social determination.

This dispute about the effects of wage increases is an issue for microeconomics. If unemployment results from a rise in wages, then it is a question that affects the particular firms and industries in which the increases occur. Macroeconomics, the study of national economic systems as a whole, has also had its share of disagreements about wages.

The application of standard marginalist analysis to a depressed economy seems to generate a straightforward conclusion about wages. Even if massive unemployment results from an economic doctrine, there is a remedy: If capitalists can no longer secure as much income from selling their goods as they could previously, then the value product of labor has fallen. If so, laborers must reduce their wage demands if they wish to secure employment. By sufficient reductions in wages, it is possible to maintain full employment even in the midst of a depression.

This view reigned as accepted doctrine until the 1930's. John Maynard Keynes (1883-1946), in *The General Theory of Employment, Interest, and Money* (1936), advanced an entirely different position. He argued that reducing prices and wages would lead speculators to anticipate further reductions. As a result, they will respond immediately to wage cuts but will await further developments. Therefore, wage cuts will intensify a depression, not cure it. Instead, the level of spending should be increased and the monetary rate of wages should not be lowered. These views became orthodox during the 1940's and 1950's. Since the 1960's, they have been subjected to increasing challenge. The Austrian school, for example, holds that the marginalist approach is correct in macroeconomics as well as in microeconomics.

Context

During the late eighteenth and early nineteenth centuries, which saw the rise of economics as a scientific discipline, the labor theory of value held sway. Adam Smith (1723-1790), in *An Inquiry into the Nature and Causes of the Wealth of Nations* (1776), and David Ricardo (1772-1823), in *Principles of Political Economy and Taxation* (1818), both maintained that the price of a good was principally determined by its cost of production: Labor costs were the main element in these expenses. These economists, and their successors among the British classical school, did not work out a precise application of the labor theory to wages. Ricardo and his followers tended to see wages as not being amenable to much change. Should an increase in wages somehow be secured, the population would rise. As a result, wages would fall to their previous level, and they would tend to remain permanently at or near subsistence.

This grim view was made more systematic by Marx in *Das Kapital* (1867). His work soon aroused criticism and, partly in reaction to Marx's views, economists sought an altogether different theory of value.

The problems in Marx's labor theory were analyzed in great depth by the Austrian economist Eugen von Böhm-Bawerk (1857-1914). He challenged the Marxist account at its roots and claimed that an exchange of commodities was not an equality, as Marx had maintained. People exchange goods only if each values the good that he or she obtains more than the good that is given up. An exchange presupposes a double inequality, not an equality. Marx's pursuit of the underlying factor—labor—that explains the equality present in economic exchange is, in this view, the "solution" to a nonexistent problem. Böhm-Bawerk's criticisms were not confined to the rather abstract level of this contention. He discovered a detailed technical difficulty, the transformation problem, in Marx's system. Most economists thought that, after Böhm-Bawerk's assault, the labor theory had best be abandoned.

Meanwhile, a new theory was waiting in the wings. The marginalist revolution of the 1870's was accomplished by William Stanley Jevons (1835-1882), Léon Walras (1834-1910), and Carl Menger (1840-1921), an older colleague of Böhm-Bawerk. The marginalists dropped the labor theory altogether and explained wages by marginal productivity, which is ultimately traceable to consumer preference.

Marginalism has remained standard in economic theory since the 1870's. The Keynesian revolution of the 1930's did not repudiate marginalism's explanation of wages. Instead, Keynes claimed that the effects of expectations might interfere with the equilibrating role of changes in wages. He also saw workers as subject to a "monetary illusion": It was far better to reduce real wages while leaving monetary wages unchanged than to attempt a cut in the latter. Keynes accepted the standard explanation of wages and added to it that, in conditions of depression, special circumstances exist.

The major theoretical challenge to marginalism has come from neo-Ricardian economists. Defenders of the standard view often respond to neo-Ricardian attacks by assailing the weaknesses of the latter school's wage doctrine; because neo-Ricardians see wages as determined outside the economic system, they have no account to offer of the subject.

Bibliography

Blau, Francine D., Marianne A. Ferber, and Anne E. Winkler. *The Economics of Women, Men, and Work.* 3d ed. Upper Saddle River, N.J.: Prentice Hall, 1998. The authors explore in some detail the different experiences at work, in terms of wages and occupations, of men and women. They also explore the changing structure of the American family and how it has affected the employment situation.

Clark, John Bates. *The Distribution of Wealth.* New York: Macmillan, 1899. The most influential presentation of the view that marginal productivity theory shows that workers are not exploited in a capitalist economy. Argues that each factor of production receives its marginal value product and that workers cannot be exploited if they receive all that they produce.

Elster, Jon. *Making Sense of Marx.* Cambridge, England: Cambridge University Press, 1985. A detailed discussion of the labor theory of value. Most of the standard criticisms are given, as well as some new ones. Elster also raises difficulties for the marginalist case against exploitation, by asking why workers should receive only the value that is added by the last unit of labor.

Mises, Ludwig von. *Human Action.* Chicago: Henry Regnery, 1966. A massive treatise on economic principles by the leading twentieth century contributor to the Austrian school. Mises wholeheartedly accepts the marginalist analysis of wages. He claims to derive a value-free argument against wage increases not brought about by the market and criticizes the Ricardo effect.

Rothbard, Murray N. *Man, Economy, and State.* 2 vols. New York: D. Van Nostrand, 1962. A systematic presentation of economic principals. Rothbard offers a detailed defense of the marginalist approach against Keynesian objections. He claims that a depression need not be characterized by unemployment, as long as workers are willing to offer their services for reduced wages.

Steedman, Ian. *Marx After Sraffa.* London: Verson, 1977. A leading neo-Ricardian economist, Steedman gives a detailed critique of the labor theory's account of wages. He contends that the standard labor theory engages in circular reasoning and does not compare Piero Sraffa's system with marginalism.

Stigler, George J. *Production and Distribution Theories.* New York: Macmillan, 1946. A careful analysis of the main approaches to price and wage determination by a Nobel laureate. The neo-Ricardian school is not covered, but particularly valuable is Stigler's discussion of the controversy between John Bates Clark and Frank H. Knight. The latter questioned Clark's derivation of the justice of capitalism from the theory of marginal productivity.

Bill Delaney

Cross-References

Classical Economics, 74; Communism, 80; Economists, 164; Employment Theory, 180; Labor Economics, 353; Labor Theory of Value, 358; Marginal Principle, 390; Marginal Utility, 396; Marxist Economics, 412; Unemployment Causes, 600; Unions, 613.

WEALTH

Type of economics: General economics
Field of study: Economic theory

The notion of wealth provides a conceptual starting point for economics as a discipline. At the root of a long history of disagreement about the concept of wealth lie two conflicting opinions as to what the term implies.

Principal terms

LABOR: the human effort that is expended in the production (or exchange) of a good or service

MARKET VALUE: sometimes called exchange value; the price of a commodity in a free market

RICHES: a term that was used by David Ricardo to connote the pleasure or satisfaction that is provided by a good or service

SCARCITY: the preponderance of demand over supply

UTILITY: a term that is used by economists to connote the pleasure or satisfaction that a good or service provides to its possessor

VALUE: a term that was used by David Ricardo and others to connote the amount of labor that is required for the creation of a good or service

Overview

The concept of wealth is basic to the study of economics. Indeed, the question "What is wealth?" is probably the conceptual springboard for economics as a discipline. Despite its centrality, however, economists have never come to a consensus on the meaning of the term. The results of several centuries of controversy have been a continuing discussion that has captured the interest of economists because it calls into question the scope, and even the content, of both microeconomics and macroeconomics.

This protracted record of disagreement has birthed two different notions of what the word implies. What is wealth? When one speaks of a "wealthy nation," precisely what is meant? One of these conceptions of wealth, older than the discipline of economics itself, is still in general use. It can be summed up in the idea of material or tangible wealth. Many people suppose that wealth consists of "things," tangible assets. They have supposed that a well-functioning economic system produces "material wealth," such as automobiles, houses, footballs, tennis rackets, and myriad other products on which consumers spend their income. This objective conception of wealth is probably as old as recorded history.

Most economists, however, are not interested in ancient cuneiform records of slaves and gold artifacts, other than to be astonished at the variety of things that embodied wealth in Bronze or Iron Age communities. The analytic problem that is involved in this material conception of wealth is to establish a common denominator in all wealth that sums up the inherent value that is represented by a heterogeneous collection of objects from different cultures around the world. This is the problem that John Bates Clark (1847-1938) was referring to when he asked: "How great is the wealth of a nation?" In his commentary, he remarked that the "entire study of wealth is, indeed, meaningless unless there be a unit for measuring it."

In ordinary discussion, this so-called common denominator has always been money. For the economist, however, the challenging goal has always been to discover some measure that is more stable and less arbitrary than mere money. In the mercantilist period, William Petty (1623-1687) and Richard Cantillon (1697-1734) used what they called the "amounts" of land and labor that entered into the production of some good. Adam Smith (1723-1790) subsequently simplified these standards to labor alone. When he wrote in *An Inquiry into the Nature and Causes of the Wealth of Nations* (1776) concerning the value of a product, he indicated that its value to those who possess it, and those who want to exchange it for some new production, is precisely equal to the quantity of labor that entered into the production of the product.

From the very beginning, however, the concept of material wealth posed some extremely difficult problems, one of which had to do with the heterogeneous nature of labor itself. There are many different types of labor, which is a complex, rather than a simple, substance. It is not an interchangeable good and, therefore, serves poorly as a common metric for material wealth. In accounting for the decline of this objective view of wealth, it is best to focus on what is called the "myth of material wealth." While material things can contribute to wealth and are essential to the production of wealth in a community, however, there is no necessary correspondence between the increase of the wealth of a nation and the increments in the volume or weight of material objects in that nation. For example, Quechuan-speaking Indians in Peru may think that they are wealthy if they have enough land. Yet, land is patently valueless unless it produces income or other sustenance for its owner. At its root, the very concept of wealth is quite subjective. Pursuing this notion, the conclusion can be reached that one is wealthy because what one has fosters a belief that one is wealthy; it makes one believe that one is wealthy if it is endowed with what economists call "utility."

Smith referred to the idea that "every man is rich or poor according to how much his endowment is perceived by him as affording the necessaries, conveniences, and amusements of human life." It was the economist David Ricardo (1772-1823) who first pointed out some possible inconsistencies in Smith's views, in that the subjective utility that is provided by wealth (its "riches," as he called it) was not the same as the common denominator that he had specified, that is, the labor that was required for its creation. The quantity of labor determined its value.

In Ricardo's thinking, two countries might be equally rich, but the value of the riches of one country might be larger than the other if the former required more labor in their production. Ricardo's distinction between riches and value makes sharp the distinction between the subjective enjoyment of wealth and its objective embodiment in things. It helps to explain, for example, why a 3,500-year-old statue of the Phoenician goddess Astarte may be highly valued by a collector of Mesopotamian antiquities and yet be considered nearly valueless to a Bedouin tribesman who does not feel that the artifact enriches him.

From this perspective—the nonmaterial—the common denominator of the subjective conception of wealth—utility—has no objective existence. William Stanley Jevons (1835-1882) wrote concerning the fact that "we can never say absolutely that some objects have utility and others have not." What determines whether an object has utility is the appreciation that the possessors of the object perceive in the object. Lionel Robbins, in *The Nature and Significance of Economic Science* (1932), said the wealth is not necessarily wealth because of some inherent or substantial qualities—it is wealth because it is thought of as being scarce to the possessor.

This emphasis on the psychological elements in the equation of what constitutes wealth, as well as the role of scarcity in conferring desirability to goods, has assisted economists in clarifying many puzzling questions. For example, the ancient "diamonds and water paradox" may be paraphrased as the question: Why are diamonds, which are used mainly for ornamentation, so valuable in comparison with common tap water, which is so useful? The answer is that the pleasure of possessing the scarce commodity, diamonds, outweighs the pleasure that is inherent in drinking tap water. This subjective conception of wealth is not, however, without its own paradoxes. As the increase in utility or pleasure is normally directly proportional to scarcity, the adoption of this measure of wealth entails the conclusion that wealth, as a sum of enjoyments or pleasures, might increase as a consequence of the diminution of material abundance. Additionally, there is the awkward conclusion that replacing an objective standard of wealth with a subjective one in the aggregation of the wealth of individuals in a community or nation is ludicrous because it is tantamount to the aggregation of their feelings of pleasure or dissatisfaction. The frustration associated with these ambiguities led Robbins to state that the term "wealth" should be altogether avoided in economics.

In modern times, the measurement of national wealth has become a primary preoccupation for all advanced nations. Most countries define what they call their national product in statistical terms. If the income that is produced by a nation's storehouse of capital is defined as the wealth of that nation, then a nation's gross national product (GNP) can be used as a proxy variable for the wealth of a nation. The GNP in the United States can be defined as the total private, government, and net foreign spending in the nation, which is usually defined as the sum of consumption, investment, government spending, and net exports.

Applications

One aspect of wealth is often misunderstood: How is wealth created? It is the conventional wisdom of most ordinary citizens that agriculture and manufacturing are genuinely productive and do, indeed, create wealth. With trading and merchandising that involves middlemen, however, the issue is different. These activities involve only exchanges of one previously produced product for another and, therefore, are often thought to be less productive. They are not considered to be wealth-generating occupations, and in some societies, they have been called exploitive. Trading among merchants has had a long and unsavory reputation in the Western world. This attitude is probably the result of a combination of several elements. One of these is the long-standing prohibition against windfall profits and high interest rates by the medieval Christian Church in Western Europe. The other is more elusive and is probably the result of a deep-seated conviction that nothing can be gained by merely exchanging things. It follows that a middleman who gains from trading must be exploiting the community.

Trading, therefore, is sometimes thought of as social waste. The resulting problem is that many come to the wrong conclusion that what is being exchanged are things of equal value. Yet, the opposite is true: Exchange is never an exchange of equal values because if it were, it simply would not occur. Among informed participants who are exchanging goods in a market, both parties gain by trading what they have of lesser value for something that they subjectively consider to be more valuable. In other words, if Al swaps his tennis racket for Ed's baseball, then it is evident that Al values the baseball more than his tennis racket. Ed also exchanges because he values Al's tennis racket more than his baseball. The exchange is patently unequal, as viewed from either side of the transaction, and both participants are wealthier subsequent to the trade. In addition, the exchange itself is productive because it increases the wealth of both parties.

An argument might be raised, however, claiming that there was no real net increase in wealth. Al and Ed may believe that they are better off and may be happier, but the trade really "produced" nothing because there is still one baseball and one tennis racket. It is vital to point out that the manufacturers of the baseball and the tennis racket did not produce anything either: They fabricated or arranged an inventory of disorganized raw materials into more valuable forms. The input that goes into the production of Al's tennis racket and Ed's baseball is not different from the roles played by the tennis racket and the baseball in the exchange of the items between Ed and Al. The result of this productive process, which is called an exchange, was a product whose value was greater than the sum of the inputs that were donated by both parties. Nothing further is required to expand output and real wealth.

Context

From earliest times, most societies developed some conception of wealth that served their needs. Originally, Western society's concept of wealth revolved around the notion of tangible things of value, known as assets. Confronted by some of the inconsistencies in the definition of wealth as purely materialistic, the concept was broadened to include less tangible things of value, such as the services or amenities that are provided by capital assets. With the development, in the twentieth century, of sources of income that are associated with royalties, franchises, options, and other less tangible assets, this subjective concept of wealth that Ricardo called "riches" takes on real significance.

In the future, more and more intangibles will be subsumed under the definition of wealth. For example, is the clean air of a community an item to be included in the wealth of that community? Is the stress level or incidence of heart disease an item of wealth? Is the traffic congestion on expressways something that should be subtracted from the wealth of a community? These questions are generating an entirely new approach to the measurement of national and personal wealth.

Bibliography

Clark, John Bates. *The Distribution of Wealth: A Theory of Wages, Interest, and Profits.* 1899. Reprint. New York: Augustus M. Kelley, 1988. A classic text on economics written at the turn of the century. Deals with many fundamental concepts, including wealth.

Gazdar, Kaevan. *Germany's Balanced Development: The Real Wealth of a Nation.* Westport, Conn.: Quorum, 1998.

Gilder, George. *Wealth and Poverty.* New York: Basic Books, 1981. Contains very creative and interesting perspectives on the issues of wealth and poverty. Sometimes written a bit "tongue-in-cheek."

Heilbroner, Robert L. *The Essential Adam Smith.* New York: W. W. Norton, 1986. An excellent introduction to the basic works of Adam Smith. Very readable.

_____. *The Quest for Wealth.* New York: Simon & Schuster, 1956. A well-written and entertaining history of the acquisitive nature of Western culture. Delightful insights.

Heyne, Paul. *The Economic Way of Thinking.* 5th ed. New York: Macmillan, 1987. A brief text of microeconomics and macroeconomics. Quite sufficient without being compendious. The emphasis is on economic thinking rather than analysis or policy. Contains a good discussion on the "myth of material wealth."

Jevons, William Stanley. *The Theory of Political Economy.* 1871. Reprint. Charlottesville, Va.: Ibis, 1990. A classic text on economics by a renowned nineteenth century classical economist. Quite readable despite the outdated idioms. Presents excellent historical insights into the concept of wealth.

Robbins, Lionel. *An Essay on the Nature and Significance of Economic Science.* London: Macmillan, 1932. A learned treatise on the philosophical problems attending the study of economics as a discipline. Even though the text was written in the 1930's, its insights are still relevant.

Smith, Adam. *An Inquiry into the Nature and Causes of the Wealth of Nations.* Edited by E. R. Campbell, A. S. Skinner, and W. B. Todd. Oxford, England: Clarendon Press, 1976. The classic sourcebook on economic concepts. Contains many relevant insights on wealth.

Edward Sanford
Alfred J. Hagan

Cross-References

WELFARE ECONOMICS

Type of economics: Welfare economics
Field of study: Health, education and welfare theory

Welfare economics is the branch of economic theory that analyzes society's economic welfare. The primary focus of modern welfare economics is on economic efficiency. Economic welfare also involves equity, or fairness, but this concept is more difficult to access analytically than efficiency because equity standards require normative standards and value judgments that are untestable by fact and logic alone.

Principal terms

CARDINAL UTILITY: the assumption that individual utility is quantifiable and can be compared and added among different persons

MARGINAL RATE OF SUBSTITUTION: the rate at which a household can substitute one good for another without changing its economic welfare or utility

MARGINAL RATE OF TRANSFORMATION: the rate at which an individual producer or an economy must reduce the output of one good in order to produce more of another

NORMATIVE STATEMENTS: prescriptive statements that depend on value judgments concerning the way things ought to be and cannot be proven or disproven by fact and logic

ORDINAL UTILITY: subjective utility that cannot be compared or added among different persons

PARETO OPTIMUM: a state of the economy from which it is impossible to make anyone better off without making someone else worse off

POSITIVE STATEMENTS: statements that do not rest on value judgments and can be proven or disproven by fact and logic

PRODUCTION POSSIBILITIES CURVE: the locus of points defined by combinations of outputs that can be produced with full utilization of the economy's productive capacity

UTILITARIANISM: an important school of political philosophy that defined social economic welfare as the sum of individuals' welfare

Overview

Welfare economics is concerned with social economic welfare, or the economic well-being of a society or community. Social economic welfare has two dimensions—efficiency and equity. Efficiency includes the efficiency of the allocation of resources among firms and goods (productive efficiency) and the efficiency of the distribution of goods among individuals or households (distributive or consumptive efficiency).

It is not likely that one would view an economic situation as "best for the community" if it violated one's standards of equity or fairness. Equity standards, however, rest on value judgments of right and wrong. For example, one person's values may decry inequality of income and wealth as unfair, while another person may see the same situation as fair because people get what they deserve. One's value judgments may lead to normative or prescriptive arguments.

Unfortunately, economic theory has no means of evaluating personal, ethical, or moral values or value judgments. Similarly, it is possible to predict the economic consequences of actions that are based on values—for example, the effect of guaranteeing every person a minimum income—but economic analysis does not deal with value judgments or normative standards.

The difficulty of dealing with normative arguments analytically means that welfare economics is mainly concerned with the efficiency dimension of welfare. Pareto optimality is the widely accepted standard for economic efficiency. The economy reaches a Pareto optimum, or Pareto optimal state, if it is impossible to make changes that make some people better off without making others worse off. It requires no value judgment to say that making at least one person better off without hurting anybody else improves the community's economic welfare, but this is possible only if the initial situation is nonoptimal or inefficient. Unambiguous improvements in social economic welfare are possible only if it is possible to produce more of at least some goods without reducing the outputs of others—that is, if resources are allocated inefficiently among firms and goods—or it is possible to redistribute goods among individuals so that at least some are better off and others are no worse off—that is, if the initial distribution of goods is inefficient.

Goods are distributed efficiently among individuals or households when all households are willing to give up one good for another at the same rate, or when their marginal rates of substitution are equal. For example, imagine an economy that produces only two goods—food and clothing—and an initial distribution of goods among two households (A and B). Household A would be neither better nor worse off with four less units of clothing and an additional unit of food; that is, an additional unit of food is worth four units of clothing or an additional unit of clothing is worth one-fourth of a unit of food. Household B's preferences are such that it would be neither better nor worse off with two more units of clothing and one fewer unit of food; that is, one unit of food is worth two units of clothing or one unit of clothing is worth one-half of a unit of food to household B. If one unit of food is redistributed from B to A, and four units of clothing from A to B, B is better off and A is no worse. In other words, their joint welfare has improved because the initial distribution of goods was inefficient.

Yet, the distribution of goods is only part of the problem. It would be possible to make everyone better off, or at least some better off and others no worse, by producing more of at least one good and no less of the other. This is possible, however, only if the economy is underutilizing its productive capacity and operating inside its production possibilities curve (the combinations of outputs that can be produced if the economy's capacity is fully employed). In order to be on the production possibilities curve, each firm in the economy must utilize its capacity fully and the opportunity cost of producing each good must be the same for all firms.

Suppose that one firm (M) can produce one more unit of food by reducing its clothing output by six units; that is, the opportunity cost of the additional food is six units of clothing and the opportunity cost of the last unit of clothing that is produced by this firm is one-sixth of a unit of food. Another firm (N) must reduce its clothing output by only two units in order to produce an additional unit of food. Therefore, firm N's opportunity cost of producing an additional unit of food is two units of clothing and its opportunity cost of producing the last unit of clothing is one-half of a unit of food. If firm M reduced its food output by one unit, then it could increase its clothing output by six units. If N increased its food output by one unit, then its clothing output would fall by only two units. The net effect of these output changes is that their combined output of food remained the same and their combined clothing output increased by four units. Clearly, it would be possible to make at least one household better off by giving it the additional four units of clothing. Because no other households must give up any food or clothing, this is an improvement in welfare, but this results from the fact that the initial mix of outputs by the firms was inefficient.

Even if the economy is on its production possibilities curve and goods are allocated efficiently among households, this situation may not be Pareto optimal. For example, suppose that the economy's capacity is fully employed and the opportunity cost of an additional unit of food that is produced by any firm is two units of clothing. Furthermore, suppose that goods are distributed among households so that each household is willing to give up a maximum of four units of clothing for an additional unit of food. If any firm increases its output of food by one unit, then it must reduce its clothing output by two units. If any household is given an additional unit of food in return for two units of clothing, that household would be better off and the other households' welfare would be unaffected. In other words, Pareto optimality requires that the opportunity cost of the last unit of each good that is produced by each firm equal the value of the last unit of each good to each household. Once this condition is met, then it is impossible to make any household better off without hurting another household, and a Pareto optimal situation has been achieved.

Pareto optimality is only an efficiency criterion and not a complete basis for judging what is "best for society." Other things being equal, however, efficiency is better than inefficiency. If the economy is not at a Pareto optimum, then it is possible to improve economic welfare by moving to some Pareto optimal state; that is, there is at least one Pareto optimum that is clearly better than a nonoptimal state. Yet, there are many possible Pareto optima. If an economy moves from one Pareto optimum to another, then some people will be better off and others will be worse off. In this case, nothing can be said about the community's economic welfare unless a value judgment is made, and value judgments are not testable by fact and logic.

In reality, most economic changes do not generate unambiguous improvements in welfare because they make some members of the community better off and others worse off. Some economists argue that the welfare effects of these changes could be identified by asking whether those who are better off ("winners") could compensate those who are worse off ("losers") for their lost economic welfare.

The compensation principle asserts that, if it is possible for the winners from an economic change to compensate the losers, then the change is an improvement in the community's economic welfare—even if the losers are not actually compensated. Compensation tests do provide valuable information—for example, they can reveal if an economic change generated a very high value of benefits to winners and a very small value of losses to losers. Nevertheless, the compensation tests do not resolve the value judgments that ultimately must be made in order to assess welfare changes in these cases, and some benefits and costs are difficult or impossible to quantify in monetary terms. Moreover, even if benefits and costs were quantifiable monetarily, what is ultimately being gained and lost is utility, and modern utility theory holds that individual utilities are not additive.

Applications

One important area in the application of welfare economics is in the area of industrial organization and market structures. The structure and operation of markets have important implications for economic efficiency and welfare. A perfectly competitive economy reaches general equilibrium with all firms maximizing profit by producing at the point where the marginal cost of the last unit that is produced equals the price of the product. Each utility-maximizing household chooses the quantities of goods where the rate at which they are willing to give up one good for another equals the ratio of the prices of the goods. It can be shown that the perfectly competitive general equilibrium is Pareto optimal; that is, the last unit of each good that is consumed by consumers is just worth the cost (in other goods) of producing it. Moreover, perfectly competitive markets generate this result through the self-interest of buyers and sellers with no direction by the government. Some proponents of freely operating markets and a minimal role for government use this result to justify their faith that decentralized private markets generate the best results for society. Even in perfect competition, however, the Pareto optimal equilibrium is only efficient and not necessarily equitable.

If markets are not perfectly competitive, then freely operating markets will not generate a Pareto optimal equilibrium. If individual firms can affect the price at which they will sell—as is the case for monopolies and other imperfectly competitive markets—then they can maximize profit only by selling at a price that is above the marginal cost of the last unit that is produced. This means that there is no mechanism to ensure that the economy will produce outputs on its production possibilities curve, and the most likely consequence of imperfect competition is that the economy's outputs of goods will lie inside its produc- tion possibilities curve. Furthermore, if households choose their best combinations of goods, then the ratio of prices (the worth of one good to consumers in the terms of other goods) will not equal the ratio of the marginal costs of goods (the cost of the last unit of one good in the terms of other goods). Moreover, multiple prices (peak-load pricing and price discrimination) are possible in imperfectly competitive markets, which means that different households may pay different prices for goods. The main welfare implica- tion of multiple prices is that the final distribution of goods among households will be inefficient.

Cost-benefit analysis is another application of welfare economics. Cost-benefit studies attempt to quantify the monetary values of benefits and costs of economic changes. For example, a cost-benefit study of an airport expansion would try to quantify the value of the benefits to those who would gain from the expansion—frequent air travelers and local businesses that are dependent on the airport, for example—and the costs to those who would lose welfare from the airport expansion—such as households in the vicinity of the airport that would lose property values and incur greater costs of noise pollution, air pollution, and traffic congestion.

There are numerous applications of welfare economics in the areas of public finance and public policy. Pareto optimality says nothing about the normative desirability of income distribution or the distribution of goods. Public finance is concerned with providing goods and services through the public sector, subsidizing certain goods and services, and raising tax revenue, all of which alter the distribution of after-tax income and of goods and services among the members of the community. To the extent that tax and expenditure policies alter the final mix of outputs from the competitive equilibrium outputs, they drive a wedge between households' marginal rates of substitution and the economy's marginal rate of transformation.

For example, suppose that cigarettes are taxed and the tax revenue is used to subsidize food purchases by low-income households. Few people would question the equity or normative desirability of such a policy, but to the extent that the cigarette taxes reduce consumption and cause retail prices to exceed marginal costs, there will be a welfare loss from underproducing cigarettes. Furthermore, the food subsidy reduces the price of food below the marginal cost of producing it, and leads to overproduction and overconsumption of food in strict efficiency terms.

Welfare economics does not lead to the conclusion that society would be clearly better off if cigarettes were not taxed or basic food purchases by the poor were not subsidized. It does suggest, however, that a result that most would find equitable (except cigarette smokers and tobacco companies) conflicts with economic efficiency. In other words, the policy must ultimately rest on a value judgment that the gain in equity is worth the cost to efficiency.

Context

The formal theory of welfare economics is relatively new, and the major contributions to it have come in the twentieth century. Yet, defining society's economic welfare and identifying the economic arrangements that would make society as well off economically as possible have been central issues in economics since the birth of the discipline.

Adam Smith's famous doctrine of the "invisible hand" in *An Inquiry into the Nature and Causes of the Wealth of Nations* (1776) linked the pursuit of self-interest by buyers and sellers in competitive markets with a socially desirable outcome. This argument is partially supported by the Pareto optimality of the perfectly competitive equilibrium and continues in the argument of modern market-oriented economists who assign the largest possible role to decentralized, unregulated markets as the mechanism by which society makes its economic choices.

Utilitarianism, a school of English philosophical thought most popular in the first half of the nineteenth century, defined society's economic welfare as the sum of welfare of individuals. In cases in which economic changes made some better off and others worse off, the utilitarians argued that the improvements in welfare (additional pleasures) of those who were made better off could be added to the lost welfare (additional pain) of those who were made worse off, and differences would be the net effect of the change on society's economic welfare. If the additional pleasure from the change exceeds the additional pain, then society's economic welfare has improved. If the additional pain exceeds the additional pleasure, then society's economic welfare has worsened. Utilitarianism and its chief proponent, Jeremy Bentham (1748-1832), influenced classical economic thought mainly through James Mill (1773-1836) and his son, John Stuart Mill (1806-1873).

The notion of additive cardinal utility is implicit in the neoclassical theory of utility and value that was formulated by Alfred Marshall (1842-1924) in the late nineteenth and early twentieth centuries. It is also central to the concept of social economic welfare that was advanced by A. C. Pigou (1877-1959) in the early twentieth century. Pigou argued that economic welfare could be measured in monetary terms and that welfare changes for different individuals could be compared in order to determine the effect on society's economic welfare. The difficulty with this concept of welfare is that money can measure utility for different individuals only if money has the same utility for everyone, which is not the case.

Modern welfare economics, the so-called new welfare economics, stems from the theory of general equilibrium of Léon Walras (1834-1910) and the works of Vilfredo Pareto (1848-1923), particularly the *Manual of Political Economy* (1906). Pareto formulated the conditions for optimality or efficiency, and he showed that there are many possible optimal situations or states. He limited the focus of welfare economics to only those questions that could be answered without comparing the welfare of different persons, that is, to efficiency issues.

Although welfare economics (especially Pareto welfare economics) seems to be the domain of the strong proponents of unregulated private markets, important contributions have also been made by economists with quite different ideological and institutional orientations. The theory of market socialism, formulated in the works of Enrico Barone, Oscar Lange, Abba Lerner, and Maurice Dobb, established the possibility of achieving Pareto optimality in an economy in which capital and land are owned collectively and prices are set by a ministry of production (Barone) or a central planning board (Lange).

Bibliography

Bradley, Michael E. *Microeconomics.* 2d ed. Glenview, Ill.: Scott, Foresman, 1985. Chapter 12 of this introductory text is one of the few treatments of welfare economics at the elementary level. There is some technical economic analysis, but all required analysis is introduced earlier in the text.

Browning, Edgar K., and Jacqueline M. Browning. *Microeconomic Theory and Applications.* 3d ed. Glenview, Ill.: Scott, Foresman, 1989. A clear and technically undemanding intermediate microeconomic theory text. Chapters 5, 6, and 18 provide a good introduction to the elements of welfare economics.

Dobb, Maurice. *Welfare Economics and the Economics of Socialism.* Cambridge, England: Cambridge University Press, 1969. A very good introduction and critique of welfare economics by one of the most prominent Western socialists. Part 1 is a very sound but dense introduction to the elements of welfare economics. The technical level of the material varies, but a sound background in intermediate microeconomics is strongly suggested.

Feldman, Allan M. "Welfare Economics." In *The New Palgrave: A Dictionary of Economics,* edited by John Eatwell, Murray Milgate, and Peter Newman. Vol. 4. London: Macmillan, 1987. A very good brief survey of welfare economics and some areas of application. Parts are technically demanding, but the main arguments are understandable. Contains a useful brief bibliography.

Roth, Timothy P. *The Present State of Consumer Theory: The Implications for Social Welfare Theory.* 3d ed. Lanham, Md.: University Press of America, 1998.

Stiglitz, Joseph E. *Economics of the Public Sector.* New York: W. W. Norton, 1986. Chapter 3 is a good brief introduction to the basic propositions of welfare economics. The book also contains numerous applications of welfare economics to questions of government expenditures and taxes.

Michael E. Bradley

Cross-References

Classical Economics, 74; Economists, 164; Efficiency, 170; Environmental Economics, 187; Factor Analysis, 218; History of Economics, 295; Laissez-Faire, 366; Marginal Principle, 390; Politics and Economics, 476; Regulation and Deregulation, 526; Socialism, 544; Tax and Taxation, 569.

WORLD ECONOMIES

Type of economics: International economics
Fields of study: Country studies and international trade theory

The classification of world economies is a way of categorizing the economic system of a country. These "tags"—competitive capitalism, managed capitalism, centralized socialism, and decentralized socialism—are useful both to indicate where the power for economic decision making resides and to compare an actual system to its theoretical model.

Principal terms

CAPITALISM: a system characterized by a free market and private ownership and control of firms, with the goal of making profits; the system caters to consumers

CENTRALIZED SOCIALISM: a system characterized by state ownership of firms, with production and distribution decisions made by a planning board; the system is oriented toward the goal of rapid growth

COMMUNISM: an ideal system following capitalism espoused by Karl Marx; centralized socialism and "communism" in the Soviet Union are synonymous

DECENTRALIZED SOCIALISM: a mixed system of state and private ownership with more decisions made by the marketplace, but with emphasis on equality of income and overall planning

ECONOMIC SYSTEM: an organizational structure for making and implementing economic decisions

EFFICIENCY: output per unit of resources applied

ENTREPRENEUR: one who organizes, manages, and assumes the risk of running a business

KEY INDUSTRIES: industries vital to the country's survival; transportation, communication, banking, and steel manufacturing are key industries

RESOURCES: land or raw material, labor, or physical capital (plant, machines, and tools)

SECONDARY ECONOMY: businesses run by individuals and families after normal working hours, on a small scale; raising vegetables or livestock or tutoring students are such businesses

Overview

To classify world economies, economic systems need to be defined. An economic system is the organizational structure that directs how complex economic questions are answered and how these answers are communicated and coordinated toward society's goals. As Paul Gregory and Robert Stuart stated in *Comparative Economic Systems* (1989), "an economic system is a set of mechanisms and institutions for decision making and the implementation of decisions concerning production, income, and consumption within a geographical area." Thus, each economic system must answer basic economic questions: what goods and services to produce, how to produce those goods and services, and for whom those goods and services are made. None of these three questions is simple. What to produce involves decisions such as whether to produce certain shoes and in what colors, sizes, and styles. How to produce involves such questions as whether to employ more laborers or use robots.

For whom to produce is another complex question. Even if it is decided to distribute goods on an equal basis, questions remain such as whether the shoes be distributed equally in terms of per person or per family; whether everyone gets an orthopedic pair, regardless of what kind is needed; and whether a dictator distributes according to psychic wealth, even if one person gets much greater want-satisfaction (or utility) from another pair of shoes than does another person. The way the three questions of what, how, and for whom are answered will depend, first of all, on the desired goals and, second, on the structure built to meet those goals. Goals make a country partial to a certain kind of structure or system.

World economies can be classified with old, familiar "isms" (capitalism, communism, and the like), but modern comparative economists have resisted arbitrarily labeling a country's economy and have instead differentiated systems with various key criteria. That method is more exact, but it is more difficult for the public to interpet. This article uses both methods. To provide the reader with a handle for referring to an economy, four broad categories are used: competitive capitalism, managed capitalism, decentralized socialism, and centralized socialism. At the same time, the economy will be further defined through four key questions: where is the power center, what is the source of resources and entrepreneurship, what is the mode of communication and control, and who is the core group served.

Competitive capitalism refers to a system in which property is privately held, with individuals maximizing their position vis-à-vis profit or wages or purchasing power. The marketplace is the clearinghouse through which buyers express desires, and buyers and sellers find a mutually satisfactory price.

Managed capitalism is similar to competitive capitalism, but there are more large corporations in the picture, counterbalanced by a big government that regulates in key areas and uses monetary and fiscal policy to reduce business cycles.

Centralized socialism, or Stalinist communism, is at the opposite end of the spectrum. In this system, the state owns all resources (land and factories, for example) and decides what, how, and for whom through central planning. The planning board, not the marketplace, coordinates resources so that raw materials and labor will be in the right places to fulfill the plan. Efficiency and consumerism are given little consideration; rapid growth is a central goal.

In decentralized socialism, there is a mix of private and public ownership with many firms responding to the market system, leaving key industries like banking, transportation, communication, and steel under state direction. Promoting a more equitable society is the prime goal of most decentralized socialistic economies. Access to health care, education, culture, and a basic standard of living are advantages of this system.

Communism is not included as a system category because there is no country that has practiced communism as envisioned by its founder, Karl Marx (1818-1883). The Soviet Union, until the late twentieth century, was an example of Stalinist communism, not pure communism.

These broad categories give no hint, however, of the divergence within a category; both the United States and Japan would be listed under managed capitalism, but the economies are distinctively different. Thus, further criteria are needed such as the location of the power center and whether it will be centralized or decentralized; whether authority will be delegated; whether the public or a centralized committee will determine goals; and whether a mechanism is in place for enforcing the goals.

A second criterion includes the source of resources and entrepreneurship and who owns or controls resources; whether raw materials, labor, and productive capital are owned by individuals, society, or both; and whether ownership and control can be separated, as they often are in big corporations or in agricultural cooperatives.

A third criterion includes the mode of communication and control and what motivates entrepreneurs, management, and workers; in addition, once overall goals are defined, how will they be communicated to the rest of the economy, and how will information be kept correct and current. A final criterion is what core group will be served and when decisions are made both privately and some publicly, how these groups interact toward accomplishing the values of society. In addition, to the extent that emphasizing one set of goals gives rise to other kinds of problems, what modifications are made to address those problems? For example, if pushing for productivity leads to unemployment, what actions are taken to modify the hardship incurred?

Applications

In competitive capitalism, advantages are efficiency and motivation. Disadvantages are business cycles and income inequality. For an underdeveloped country that focuses its energies on growth, centralized socialism usually does better because the infrastructure must be built, surplus for growth extracted, and scarce talent concentrated at the top. Disadvantages are inefficiencies, poor communication and motivation, and a tendency toward bureaucracy and rigidity.

The Soviet Union has exemplified the difficulty that centralized socialism has in communicating current and correct information on which to make sound decisions. Bad information may especially be a problem when the motivation to deceive is strong, as when information would be used to change worker output.

Decentralized socialism attempts to overcome the difficulty of getting good information and motivating workers by introducing the marketplace and decentralization, with the state retaining control of only key industries. Decentralized socialism also emphasizes greater income equality.

In managed capitalism, business cycles are moderated through monetary and fiscal policy. To some degree, income is redistributed through tax policies or through governmental aid to the poor (see table).

In defining actual systems, the four criteria in the table help to highlight differences between economies. For example, in the United States and Japan, both economies are categorized as "managed capitalism." Both countries are individualistic, competitive, and responsive to the market system. In Japan, however, the Ministry of International Trade and Industry suggests that companies take actions to keep them more competitive so that, although the power is decentralized, the "top" also exerts an influence.

Another example includes the Soviet Union and Hungary, in which both were examples of centralized socialism until the late 1980's and early 1990's, and yet distinct differences existed between them. Hungary experimented with decentralization in 1968, and, although central control was reinstated in 1972, a secondary economy became strong. Those deviations from strict central control made the country more receptive to change in the late 1980's, when the country was in bad straits economically. Steps were taken to convert state-owned firms into the nonpublic sector (cooperatives, private firms, or joint ventures), and a totally new government was voted in. Thus, the power center became decentralized more naturally.

CRITERIA USED TO DEFINE THE FOUR MAJOR THEORETICAL ISMS

Criterion	Competitive Capitalism	Centralized Socialism	Managed Capitalism	Decentralized Socialism
Power	Marketplace	Central bureaucracy	Market and big business/ government	Top and market-place
Goals	Individual	Individual	Individual	Societal
Regulator	Marketplace competition	Marketplace competition	Competition and government	Competition and government
Source/ Resource	Individual/ private owned	State/state-owned	Individual/ private owned	Key industries; state/public and private
Communica-tion	Market transmits information	Plans from top down; infor-mation from bottom up	Market transmits information	Market and state directives
Control	Market and competition	State	Competition, laws	State and market
Motivation	Profit	Social goals	Profit	Profit and goals
Core group	Individuals	Leaders and goals of growth	Individuals	Society

On the other hand, the Soviet Union continuously had a rigid, centrally planned economy with little room for experimentation; thus, when the economy was unraveling in the late 1980's, it was very difficult to decentralize the power center. The population was split between those who wanted the reform to take place within the old, familiar structure and those who wanted very quickly to transform the economy into a market economy and perhaps secede from the Soviet Union.

Errors will be made in any system; the question arises whether one system will be prone to certain kinds of errors more often than another. Raaj Sah and Joseph E. Stiglitz examined this question in the *American Economic Review* (September, 1986) and concluded that more decentralized systems have a better chance of avoiding the error of rejecting a good project. On the other hand, centralized structures may pass up good schemes, but they will more often reject bad ideas.

Performance of a system is a significant determinant of whether a system endures or is modified. Reasonably acceptable achievement of full employment, price stability, and economic growth are imperative to the survival of most systems. Freedom, equality of income, education and health, safe environment, and satisfied consumers may be among the major or minor goals of a system.

Goals of the country will often make it partial to a certain kind of system. For example, if the country has attained a certain level of development and wants to be more competitive, the goal of efficiency may move the country toward capitalism, which embraces competition and responds to market signals.

The traditional "ism" concept has a strong influence on future policies. When the Soviets first faced the problem of shoddy goods and unmotivated workers, any solution which might label them as imitating "capitalists" was rejected. Similarly, because growth in centralized socialism was attained at the expense of the consumer, citizens preferred a market system which was perceived as more responsive to consumers. As J. M. Montias asserted in *The Structure of Economic Systems* (1976), "They (systems) live as symbols of clusters of symbols in the minds of participants in all modern systems . . . , and they may have a profound influence on the way actual systems change or on the reasons why they fail to change."

Context

There is some logic to the claim that the ideas of modern systems started with Marx's criticism of capitalism, which he believed would be replaced with communism. Marx and Friedrich Engels's *The Communist Manifesto* of 1848 gave impetus to many of the modern communist and socialist ideas of the modern day. In actuality, however, the word "socialism" was first associated with Great Britain and France sometime after 1825 and defined the doctrines of those who wanted social, rather than individual, control of life and work. These socialists wanted a different moral basis for society than individual gain.

Although Marx regarded some socialist experimenters and writers such as Robert Owen (1771-1858) and Claude-Henri de Rouvroy (1760-1825) as moralists and utopians, Marx, by contrast, set forth a historical sequence by which capitalism must fall, doomed by its own failures and alienation of the workers.

Marx's thesis brought the Hegelian cycle of thesis-antithesis-synthesis into full play. There were Stalinist communists who wrote to defend communism when it is forced on an underdeveloped country by a strong state playing a large role in the economy to promote growth (contrary to Marx's theory); while those in the Austrian school of economics defended capitalism as the only system that would allow efficient allocation of resources. In the middle of these extremes were those who tried to combine the best of both systems by combining central planning with the market system (for example, Oscar Lange and Jaroslav Vanek). Meanwhile, John Maynard Keynes concentrated on one of capitalism's main problems (according to Marx) and advocated governmental policy to reduce the severity of business cycles under capitalism.

Since none of the world's actual socialist systems conformed to the general picture of communism envisioned by Marx, some politicians looked at the apparent failure of "communist systems" in the early 1990's as a failure of Stalinist communism and sought revision of their economy toward a purer socialist system; others embraced a more capitalistic, market economy that retained some of the social benefits of socialism such as free medical care and reasonable housing for all. More than before, the 1990's presented the need to provide a number of different systems which might serve as models to countries in the process of revising the structures of their economies. Differing models were necessitated by differences in development, history, values, and goals for the future.

Perhaps future world economies will be closer together on the continuum between capitalism and socialism, as convergence theorists have long predicted. Market oriented societies have adopted some measures such as programs to control inflation and unemployment and give basic income programs to the disabled and elderly. At the same time, socialistic countries are discovering that being part of the marketplace community stimulates worker productivity, quality, and adoption of new technology in order to be competitive on world markets. Adaptation and evolution of systems appears to be the rule of survival.

Bibliography

Anderson, Ronald W., and Chantal Kegels. *Transition Banking: Financial Development of Central and Eastern Europe*. New York: Oxford University Press, 1998.

Caravan, Bernard. *Economics for Beginners*. New York: Pantheon Books, 1983. Although not strictly on economic systems, the book covers seven leading economists (including Karl Marx and John Maynard Keynes) and their views on labor theory of value, capital, and profit. The comic-book style allows for easy reading and comparison of theories and development.

Ebenstein, William, and Edwin Fogelman. *Today's Isms: Communism, Fascism, Capitalism, Socialism*. Englewood Cliffs, N.J.: Prentice-Hall, 1985. Gives a slightly different classification for systems and expands on the socialism of Owen and the Fabian socialists. It is, however, dated regarding specific countries and misses some of the better socialist theorists.

Elliott, John. *Comparative Economic Systems*. Belmont, Calif.: Wadsworth, 1985. This book covers in a comprehensive way important contributors to theory of economic systems, as well as the theoretical systems themselves. Geared to serious students of economics.

Gorbachev, Mikhail. *Perestroika*. New York: Harper & Row, 1987. In this book, Soviet president Gorbachev discusses the need for restructuring the Soviet system in the 1980's. The readable text provides insight into the thinking of the original architect of modern change in the Soviet Union.

Gregory, Paul, and Robert Stuart. *Comparative Economic Systems*. Boston: Houghton Mifflin, 1989. This textbook is one of the better ones in terms of covering both theory and operating systems (countries). Includes graphs and formulas that will be of interest to those with some economics background.

Leone, Bruno. *Socialism: Opposing Viewpoints*. 2d rev. ed. St. Paul, Minn.: Greenhaven Press, 1986. Under the broad term "socialism," Leone covers the thoughts of many authors on different forms of socialism and communism. He covers theoretical arguments as well as specific topics, such as "Socialism Is the Community of Christians." The book will not synthesize, but introduces different viewpoints.

Rius. *Marx for Beginners*. New York: Pantheon Books, 1974. Presents the theory of Karl

Marx in a fun, comic-book style. It gives thorough coverage of Marx's theory (history and origins, capital, labor, and the class struggle), presenting complex ideas in a digestible way.

Scott, Allen John. *Regions and the World Economy: The Coming Shape of Global Production, Competition, and Political Order.* New York: Oxford University Press, 1998.

Zimbalist, Andrew, Howard J. Sherman, and Stuart Brown. *Comparing Economic Systems: A Political-Economic Approach.* 2d ed. New York: Harcourt Brace Jovanovich, 1988. An examination of the economic systems of countries such as Japan, Sweden, the Soviet Union, China, Cuba, Hungary, and Yugoslavia up to 1987-1988, with a minimum of theory.

I. Lee Skov

Cross-References

Capitalism, 69; Communism, 80; Development Theory, 152; Growth Theory, 281; History of Economics, 295; International Trade, 343; Marxist Economics, 412; Models, 425; Socialism, 544; Undeveloped and Underdeveloped Countries, 593.

GLOSSARY

Ability-to-pay principle: The principle that a tax should be levied on the individual or entity that will be least hurt by the tax.

Absolute advantage: The situation that exists when a country can produce more of a certain good or service than another country with the same amount of resources.

Abstract labor: Labor in general, undifferentiated from any particular form of labor in production and equivalent when viewed from the perspective of capitalist social relations.

Accommodation: When the monetary authority increases the money supply in response to government deficits or private-sector wage and price increases so that interest rates do not increase and a recession does not occur.

Actual gross national product: The market value of goods and services that are actually produced in the economy during a specified period of time, normally a year.

Ad valorem tax: An excise or sales tax which is levied on a commodity as a fixed percentage of its market price.

Adjustable-rate mortgage: A long-term loan which has an interest rate that varies with changes in short-term interest rates.

Advertising: Any paid form of nonpersonal presentation and promotion of goods, services, or ideas by an identified sponsor.

Affirmative action: An antidiscrimination program designed to encourage the employment of women and minorities.

Aggregate demand: Total spending in a given period by households, businesses, foreigners, and government on currently produced final goods and services, as a function of the aggregate price level.

Aggregate supply: The total amount of goods and services that are produced and offered for sale at different price levels.

Aggregation: The process of combining individuals' demand functions into a single market demand function, or the process of combining the supply functions of many businesses into a single market or industry supply function.

Aid to Families with Dependent Children (AFDC): The major federal transfer program for the nonelderly in the United States, consisting of money payments to dependent children and their parents.

Allocation: A particular distribution of resources among the members of a population.

Allocative efficiency: The allocation of resources that accurately reflects and balances the preferences of buyers and the costs of production of desired commodities.

Amortization: A process which spreads the original cost of a long-term asset or loan over time.

Annuity: A series of equal payments from one party to another.

Antitrust laws: Laws that are designed to curtail private monopolistic practices in order to ensure competition among firms.

Arbitrage: The simultaneous buying and selling of an item at different prices in order to earn sure and certain profit.

Arrow's impossibility theorem: The theory that no voting system can combine the preferences of each individual citizen into a satisfactory preference ordering for the society.

Asset: Anything owned that has value, especially a resource that is possessed by an organization.

Asymmetric information: A situation in which some economic agents have useful private information that is not available to others.

Auction: A market institution with a set of explicit rules determining resource allocation and prices according to bids that are made by participants.

Autarky: A self-sufficient economy in which a country has no outside trade and must produce everything that it consumes.

Automatic stabilizers: Established programs, such as unemployment insurance, which automatically act to offset falling incomes in an economic downturn.

Automation: The control of machinery, processes, or systems by largely self-operating equipment that eliminates the need for constant human supervision or decision making.

Autonomous consumption: The portion of total consumption spending in a given year that is not related to aggregate disposable income.

Autonomous spending: The portion of total spending that does not depend on income, such as investment, government purchases, and exports.

Average cost: The sum of all costs divided by the amount of output, yielding the cost per unit of output.

Average propensity to consume: The ratio of total consumer expenditure to total disposable income.

Average tax rate: The total of taxes divided by the entire tax base, which may be income, property value, or consumption.

Balance of payments: A summary statement of all the economic transactions between a nation and the rest of the world during a specific time period, usually a year.

Balance sheet: An accounting statement which provides information on the level of assets, liabilities, and owner's equity in an organization.

Balanced budget: A budget which exhibits an equality between spending and revenue.

Bank holding company: A company holding a controlling interest in one or more banks.

Bank notes: Pieces of paper, issued by a private bank or a central bank, which may be either fiat money or commodity money.

Bank panic: A situation in which people lose confidence in banks and rush to withdraw their deposits.

Bargaining: Negotiations between interested parties about the terms of possible co-operation.

Bargaining structure: The scope of employees and employers who are covered or affected by a bargaining agreement.

Barrier to entry: Any obstacle that prevents a firm from starting a business in a particular industry.

Barter: The direct exchange of one good for another good without the use of money.

Benefit principle: The principle that a tax should be levied on the individual or entity that receives the benefits of the expenditures financed by that tax.

Bilateral agreement: A formal agreement between two independent units regarding a course of economic action to be taken by each.

Black market: The illegal trading of products in order to avoid government controls such as price ceilings and rationing.

Board of directors: A group, elected by shareholders, which sets corporate policy, governs the affairs of the company, and elects chief officers.

Bond: A publicly traded debt instrument which represents a loan that is made by the holder of the instrument to its issuer.

Boom periods: Economic fluctuations that exhibit high levels of production and low levels of unemployment.

Bourgeoisie: A dominant social group identified historically with increasing industrialization and urbanization, material values, and emergent capitalism.

Bracket creep: The phenomenon whereby taxpayers find themselves liable for a higher marginal tax rate because of inflation under an unindexed progressive income tax.

Budget: A statement of a government's or firm's proposed spending programs and expected revenue from taxes and other sources for its next year of operation.

Budget deficit: A budget which shows that spending will be greater than revenue collections.

Budget surplus: A budget which shows that spending will be less than revenue collections.

Bullionism: The belief that the political and economic power of a country is measured by its stock of gold and silver.

Business cycles: The recurring phases of upward and downward movements in the general level of economic activity.

Call option: The right to buy a security at a given price before the call expiration date, which is the last date on which an option may be exercised.

Capital: Any produced good that is designed to be repeatedly used in other production processes, or the money that must be saved in order acquire productive assets.

Capital account: The balance of payments account of intercountry money transfers that is connected with the purchase and sale of financial and ownership claims.

Capital budgeting: The process of planning for purchases of assets whose returns are expected to continue beyond one year.

Capital flight: The decision by firms to relocate productive assets from their home country to foreign locations, usually developing countries with low wages.

Capital gain: An increase in the market value of a share of common stock or other asset.

Capitalism: A system which is characterized by a free market and private ownership and control of firms with the goal of making profits.

Capitalist: One who owns the means of production or is an entrepreneur.

Cardinal utility: The assumption that individual utility is quantifiable and can be compared and added among different persons.

Cartel: A group of firms that collude in order to raise a product's price above the competitive price, to increase collective profits, and to thwart competition in an industry.

Central bank: A government-owned or -controlled bank which regulates and supports the banking system, implements monetary policies, and controls the money supply.

Ceteris paribus: A phrase meaning "other things being equal" which refers to conditions under which all variables but one are held constant and fixed.

Checkable deposits: Deposit liabilities that are issued by depository institutions and are payable on demand by writing a check.

Checking accounts: Accounts for which the deposited funds are available on demand; also called demand deposits or checkable deposits.

Classical economics: Developed between 1776 and 1875 in studies by Adam Smith, David Ricardo, Thomas Robert Malthus, and John Stuart Mill, the body of economic theory that argues for free market, or laissez-faire, economic principles.

Clearinghouse: A facility at a commodity exchange which matches all futures trades and sets initial margin requirements.

Coalition: A temporary alliance or union.

Codetermination: An arrangement whereby some of the members of the board of directors of a corporation are elected by employees, and others are elected by the holders of ownership shares.

Coincident indicator: A time series which has its turning points at about the same time as the turning points of the level of economic activity.

Collateral: An asset which is pledged by a borrower and which may be seized by the lender in the event of default in order to satisfy the unpaid balance of a loan.

Collective bargaining: A process by which labor and management negotiate contracts that deal with wages and conditions of employment.

Collusion: Any cooperation between sellers to set prices, sales levels, sales territories, or other business variables with the intention of raising prices or harming other competitors.

Colony: A region distinct and separate from, and politically subordinate to, the country that exercises actual sovereignty over the region.

Commercial bank: A financial institution which offers a wide variety of services, including deposit accounts and loans.

Commodity money: Bank notes or demand deposit accounts that may be redeemed by the owner for specie.

Common bond requirement: The requirement that the membership of any credit union have something in common, such as the same employer or the same occupation.

Common stock: A certificate of ownership in a publicly held corporation which provides voting rights and may provide dividends based on proportionate ownership.

Communism: A late stage of socialism in which goods have become so plentiful and human behavior so cooperative that social resources can be distributed according to need, not effort.

Comparable worth: An antidiscrimination program designed to ensure that individuals in occupations of equal value receive equal pay, regardless of the gender composition of the occupation.

Comparative advantage: The situation that exists when one country has a lower opportunity cost of providing a good or service than another country.

Compensation: The combination of wages and fringe benefits that a worker earns.

Competition: The situation that exists when firms in a given industry vie for a share of the market.

Competitive equilibrium: The simultaneous clearing of every market in an economy in which all participants are price takers.

Competitive price: The price that results when firms independently compete against one another in an attempt to maximize their profits.

Complement: A good or service which is used in conjunction with another good or service.

Compounding period: The time interval over which the bank calculates the interest on principal.

Concentration: The distribution of market shares across firms, measured to reflect the degree to which a small number of producers control sales or productive capacity.

Concrete labor: Productive activity of a definite kind that is exercised with a definite aim.

Conditionality: The requirements that are imposed on a borrowing country in return for easier repayment terms for its debt.

Conspicuous consumption: The purchase or use of goods or services in order to impress others with one's superior status, not because of need.

Constant returns: A circumstance in which the use of a factor of production results in the same quantity of returns as previous use of the factor.

Constrained optimization: The maximization or minimization of an objective function, subject to one or more constraints.

Constraints: Restrictions on capacities and the availability of resources.

Consumer sovereignty: A system in which a community's economic choices are made by consumers expressing their preferences in markets.

Consumer surplus: The difference between the amount that a consumer is willing to pay for a good or service and the amount that he or she actually pays.

Consumption: Expenditures on nondurable goods and services, plus the depreciation and interest costs that are associated with durable goods.

Consumption function: A theoretical relationship between aggregate household disposable income and aggregate household consumption spending in a given year.

Contractionary monetary policy: A central bank policy of restraining or reducing the money supply and raising the level of interest rates.

Convertibility: The legal right to exchange one asset for another asset at a fixed price, such as paper currency for a fixed amount of gold per unit.

Convertible bond: A bond whose holder has the right to exchange the bond for another security, usually a share of common stock, in a specified ratio.

Convertible currency: A currency which may be freely converted, without requiring a government license, into other currencies and thus is freely used in international trans-actions.

Cooperative: A form of business organization which is owned by its members and in which benefits are shared in the form of lower prices, better service, or the distribution of profits.

Corn Laws: Eighteenth century British legislation that limited imports of cheap foreign grain by imposing a sliding tariff.

Corporate bond: A debt security which represents an amount of finance capital that is borrowed by a corporation from the bondholder.

Corporation: A type of business firm, owned by stockholders, which is recognized by law as a legal entity separate from its owners.

Cost-benefit analysis: An attempt to balance costs against benefits, with the objective of bringing about optimal decisions for or against a particular activity.

Cost curve: A graphical depiction of the relationships between a firm's costs and its various levels of production.

Cost-of-living index: An idealized index of the relative money cost of a given level of consumption, satisfaction, or utility at different points in time.

Cost of production: The value of the resources that are engaged in order to produce output.

Countercyclical policy: Government policies that attempt to minimize the effects of business cycles by manipulating government expenditures, taxes, and the money supply.

Countertrade: An international trade transaction in which the seller agrees to accept partial or full payment in products or to provide investment or technology transfer as a condition of the sale.

Credit: The legal right to use money belonging to another person or firm.

Credit union: A cooperative financial institution which is organized by a group of people sharing a common bond.

Cross-subsidization: The use of profits in one product line or market to make up for losses in another product line or market.

Crowding-out effect: The argument that government deficit financing pushes up interest rates, which in turn diminishes or crowds out private spending.

Current account: The balance-of-payments account that covers international commodity transactions and services, such as tourist expenses and international interest payments.

Cyclical unemployment: Unemployment that occurs because of fluctuations in the overall economy.

Debt: A stock of goods, services, or money which is owed.

Debt instruments: Promises to pay, such as promissory notes or drafts.

Decision theory: An analytical technique which objectively describes the way that a decision maker processes data prior to making a decision.

Deductibility: The ability to deduct tax payments to one level of government from the tax base of another level of government.

Default risk: The threat that a borrower will not make a contracted payment to a lender.

Deficit: The situation that exists when spending exceeds revenue.

Deficit financing: A government policy of borrowing in order to support programs that could not otherwise be afforded.

Deflation: A decline in the average level of prices, which is associated with a serious recession or depression.

Deindustrialization: The loss of manufacturing or industrial jobs in a developed economy.

Demand: The quantities of a good or service that buyers are willing and able to purchase at various prices.

Demand curve: A graphed line which shows the different amounts of a good that would be demanded at various prices.

Demand for money: The amount of currency and deposits that people want and can afford to hold, usually expressed as a function of interest rates and income.

Demographics: The size, age, income, and other characteristics of a population.

Depletion: The process of amortization as applied to natural resources.

Deposit: A liability issued by a depository institution which can be redeemed by the depositor as contracted.

Depository institutions: Financial institutions, such as commercial banks, savings and loan associations, and credit unions, that accept deposits from the public.

Depreciation: A decrease in the value of capital because it wears out with use or with the passage of time.

Depression: A very severe downturn in general economic activity which lasts for several years.

Deregulation: A reduction in government intervention through the abolition or simplification of controls and regulation.

Devaluation: An increase in the price of foreign currency, measured in the terms of domestic currency.

Development: The process through which a society becomes increasingly able to meet its needs and ensure a higher standard of living and quality of life for its members.

Differentiated product: A type of good which exhibits significant differences in real or perceived characteristics or features.

Diminishing returns: A circumstance in which the use of a factor of production results in less output than previous use.

Direct taxes: Taxes that are intended to stay on the object of taxation and not be shifted.

Discount rate: The rate of interest used to determine the present value of sums of money that are expected to be received in the future; the interest rate that a central bank charges banks to which it lends reserves.

Discounting: The process of estimating the present value of a payment that is to be received in the future.

Discouraged workers: Workers who want jobs but have given up the hope of finding them.

Discretionary policy: A deliberate fiscal or monetary policy action taken with the intent of altering aggregate economic activity.

Discrimination: The setting of wages or job offers on the basis of factors other than worker productivity.

Diseconomies of scale: A condition in which small firms are more efficient than large firms.

Disequilibrium: The state of a market in which the quantity demanded of a product or service is not equal to the quantity supplied.

Disinvestment: A decline in productive capital.

Dislocated workers: Workers who lose their jobs because a plant closes.

Disposable income: After-tax income that is available for personal consumption or saving.

Diversification: The act of holding the stocks of many different firms; when a firm offers many related, though differentiated, products or acquires firms that do business within a different industry.

Dividends: Payments to stockholders from corporate profits.

Division of labor: The segregation of a production process into different specific tasks.

Duopoly: The exclusive control by two groups of the means of producing or selling a commodity or service.

Earnings: The money that is earned through employment, including wages, salaries, and bonuses.

Earnings differential: The ratio of average hourly earnings for two population groups.

Econometrics: A subdiscipline of economics which applies statistical methods to the study of economic data and problems.

Economies of scale: A condition in which large firms are more efficient than small firms, or economies in which the average production cost falls as more is produced.

Efficiency: An outcome which is achieved when marginal costs equal marginal benefits.

Elasticity: An indicator of the responsiveness or sensitivity of one variable to changes in some other variable when the two variables are functionally related.

Elasticity of demand: A measure of the responsiveness or sensitivity of a good's demanded quantity to a change in one of its determinants.

Elasticity of supply: A measure of the responsiveness or sensitivity of a good's supplied quantity to a change in one of its determinants, typically price.

Electronic funds transfer system: A technology for transferring money electronically, rather than by handwritten check.

Employment: Work for wages for at least one hour per week, or unpaid work for fifteen or more hours per week in one's own family business.

Enterprise zone: A depressed area in which a government attempts to create jobs by giving economic incentives to businesses that locate there.

Entrepreneur: One who organizes, manages, and assumes the risk of running a business.

Equilibrium: A stable market condition in which the quantity supplied and the quantity demanded of a given good or service are equal.

Equilibrium price: The price at which the quantity demanded by consumers equals the quantity supplied by producers.

Equity: Economic fairness, or the difference between the market value of a home and the outstanding principal that is left on the mortgage, or the interest in the assets of an enterprise that is left after all liabilities have been met.

Eurodollar: The practice of deposit creation in the currency of one country (the United States) in the commercial banking system of a second country or area (Europe).

European Economic Community (EEC): A European customs union consisting of twelve member nations: Germany, France, Italy, The Netherlands, Belgium, Luxembourg, Great Britain, Denmark, Ireland, Greece, Spain, and Portugal.

European Free Trade Area (EFTA): A free trade area whose members are Austria, Norway, Sweden, and Switzerland, with Finland as an associate member.

Excess burden: The burden that is imposed on an economy by a tax that is above the revenue that the tax raises.

Excess reserves: Bank reserves in excess of required reserves.

Exchange rate: The quantity of domestic currency that is exchanged for one unit of foreign currency.

Excise tax: A tax which is levied on each unit sold of a particular good or service.

Expansion: The phase of the business cycle when economic activity, production, and employment begin to increase.

Expansionary monetary policy: A central bank policy of expanding or increasing the money supply and lowering the level of the interest rate.

Expected return: The earnings or yield that an investor anticipates at the time that an investment is made, usually expressed as an annual percentage of the amount that is invested.

Expenditure: The purchase of goods and services over a given period, normally valued at current prices.

Expenses: The obligations that are generated because of the conduct of a business.

Explicit costs: Cash and barter costs.

Exploitation: A process whereby workers receive an income that is less than the value of the output that they generate.

Export: A good or service which is sold and delivered to a foreign customer.

Export promotion: Policies that are designed to increase the level of exports and stimulate domestic growth.

External benefit: A benefit to another person or persons for which payment cannot be required.

External cost: A cost to another person or persons for which compensation cannot be obtained.

External debt: A government-incurred debt which is held by persons or institutions outside the country.

External diseconomy: An unpriced side effect which harms another person or economic unit.

External economy: An unpriced side effect which benefits another person or economic unit.

Externalities: The actions of one economic agent that have external effects on other economic agents, or harms or benefits bestowed without compensation.

Face value: The amount of money that a bond will pay back as principal at maturity.

Factors of production: The elements that are used to produce a product or service, including land, labor, capital, and entrepreneurship.

Fair Labor Standards Act: An act which established a national minimum wage in the United States in 1938.

Family income: All the income that is brought into a household by its members.

Federal funds: The money that banks and other depository institutions lend to one another to help meet federal government reserve requirements.

Federal Reserve System: The U.S. system of central banking that is responsible for issuing currency, designing and implementing monetary policy, and regulating the financial system.

Fiat money: Money that is not based on or necessarily convertible into any commodity and is made legal tender by fiat of the government; also called paper money.

Final goods and services: Good and services that are purchased by their ultimate users.

Financial intermediary: A financial institution which transfers funds from ultimate lenders to ultimate borrowers.

Financial sector: The sector of the economy that is concerned with the transfer of funds from lenders to borrowers.

Fiscal policy: Government policy that is designed to influence the state of the economy by manipulating government spending or taxation.

Fixed costs: Those business costs that do not vary over the relevant range of production and that a firm must pay even if it produces no output.

Fixed exchange-rate system: An exchange-rate system whereby central banks agree to buy and sell their currencies at a fixed rate.

Flat rate: A fee which remains the same regardless of the usage of a product or service.

Flexible or floating exchange-rate system: An exchange-rate system whereby the demand and supply of foreign currency is allowed to determine the price of foreign currency.

Forecasting: Any technique that uses present knowledge in order to form an expectation.

Foreign exchange: Currency that is readily accepted by countries of the world, such as the U.S. dollar.

Foreign exchange rate: The amount of one currency unit that is required in order to purchase a unit of another type of currency.

Forward rate: The future price of a currency.

Foundation: An organization which distributes private wealth for public benefit and makes grants to nonprofit organizations.

Free-rider: An individual or firm that uses a resource without paying for it.

Free trade: The relatively uninhibited flow of imports and exports between countries without special restraints by governments.

Frictional unemployment: Brief periods of unemployment experienced by people moving between jobs or into the labor force.

Fringe benefits: Any form of compensation other than money wages, including insurance and vacations.

Full employment: The rate of unemployment in which only those workers who are either undergoing retraining or changing jobs are unemployed.

Fund-raising: The effort that is made to solicit contributions from individuals or organizations in order to benefit nonprofit groups.

Futures contract: An obligation to make or accept a delivery of a given quantity and quality of a commodity at a specific period in time.

Game theory: The study of strategic interactions among interdependent decision makers.

General Agreement on Tariffs and Trade (GATT): The international institution that serves as a forum for multilateral negotiation on the reduction of tariff and non-tariff barriers to trade.

General equilibrium: A system of prices and chosen quantities which results in all markets being in equilibrium at the same time.

General system of preferences (GSP): A set of tariffs on certain products from developing countries that are below the rates applicable to other sources of imports.

Giffen good: A hypothetical commodity which exhibits a positively sloped demand curve, so that higher quantities are demanded at higher prices.

Giffen's paradox: A situation in which the amounts that are demanded of a good vary in the same direction as changes in the price of the good; an exception to the general law of demand.

Glut: Overproduction that is caused by a lack of aggregate demand for goods and services, leading to unemployment.

Gold standard: A standard whereby the holder of a country's currency can freely convert that currency into gold at a fixed rate.

Government securities: Debt obligations that are issued by a government in the form of bills, notes, or bonds.

Grant: An approved amount of money given to finance a specific endeavor.

Gross national product (GNP): The total value of all goods and services produced by a country in a given year, measured as the sum of consumption expenditures, gross investment, government expenditures, and net exports.

Growth: The steady process by which the productive capacity of an economy is increased over time, bringing about rising levels of national income.

Hawley-Smoot Tariff Act: Legislation enacted in 1930 that placed the import duty of the United States at its highest level.

Health maintenance organization (HMO): An alternative to conventional health insurance under which health care is provided for a set fee.

Hedging: Eliminating risk from a future transaction by reaching an agreement to fix the value of an uncertain variable, often the price.

Hoarding: The stockpiling of products by consumers in the anticipation of short supplies, thereby causing the shortage to become more critical.

Horizontal merger: The acquisition by one firm of another firm that had been competing in the same product market.

Hostile takeover: The situation that exists when a firm's management opposes the purchase of its stock by another firm or individual.

Human capital: The sum of a worker's education, experience, training, and ability that allows him or her to be productive.

Illiquidity: A shortness of funds or assets that can be converted readily into funds.

Imperfect competition: The situation that exists in markets that contain elements of both competition and monopoly.

Implicit costs: The value of one's own resources, such as time.

Import: A good or service that is bought and acquired from a foreign producer.

Import substitution: The creation of a domestic industry to substitute for imports, usually by erecting entry barriers for imports such as tariffs and quotas.

In-kind transfers: Goods or services which are received from the government, rather than cash.

Incidence: An estimation of who pays a tax's burden, which may not be the intended object of taxation.

Income: Receipts from the sale of goods, services, and assets that take the form of wages, profits, rent, interest, or tax receipts.

Income effect: The change in the quantity of a good that consumers will purchase as its price changes, resulting from changes in their real incomes as a result of the price change.

Income elasticity: The responsiveness of consumer demand, measured by the percentage change in demand divided by the percentage change in income.

Increasing returns: A circumstance in which the use of a factor of production results in higher returns than from previous use of the factor.

Indexing: Increasing the values of economic variables such as wages in order to make up for price increases; constructing a number series that measures related variables, such as a price index.

Indicators: Economic trends, such as lagging, concurrent, and leading indicators, that are used by policymakers in forecasting the current and future state of an economy.

Induced consumption: The portion of total consumption spending in a given year that is related to disposable income, or disposable income times the marginal propensity to consume.

Industrial policy: A central government policy which is designed to aid in the revitalization of industry or increase investment in a particular industrial sector.

Industrialist: An individual who invests his or her capital in building an industry, usually involving a new product or manufacturing process.

Industry: A group of firms that produce products that are close substitutes for one another.

Infant industry: A new industry which cannot grow without protection from established foreign competitors.

Inferior good: A commodity which consumers are willing and able to buy more of when their incomes fall and less of when their incomes rise.

Inflation: A rise in the overall level of the prices of goods and services, which causes the purchasing power of money to fall.

Infrastructure: A country's systems of communication, transportation, finance, and other essentials which provide the basis for the operation of a market economy.

Innovation: The implementation of a new or improved product, process, or system.

Input: A product or service used alone or with other products in a production process.

Input-output analysis: A linear theory which models explicitly the interdependencies of the different sectors of an economy.

Insolvency: A situation in which a firm's liabilities exceed its assets, resulting in bankruptcy.

Insurance: The protection against pure risk through loss sharing.

Interest: The rate of return on capital, or a payment made for the right to use money belonging to another person or firm.

Interest rate: The annual rate at which a loan or debt security accrues interest.

Interest-rate parity: The theory that, in a free exchange market, the forward exchange rate will compensate for differences between the internal interest rates of various countries.

Interest-rate risk: The uncertainly of bank earnings that is caused by changes in interest rates.

Intermediate goods: Goods that produce final goods and services, such as human capital, physical capital, and partly finished goods and parts.

Internal rate of return: The discount rate that equates the present value of future cash inflows to an investment's costs.

International liquidity: The existence of a sufficient total stock of reserve assets to finance international trade by guaranteeing convertibility among currencies.

International Monetary Fund (IMF): The organization that encourages international monetary cooperation, facilitates the balanced growth of international trade, assists members in correcting balance-of-payments deficits, and promotes foreign exchange stability.

Invention: The usually purposeful discovery of knowledge, the application of which may be useful.

Investment: The acquisition of physical assets by a firm, including machinery, equipment, and plant.

Investment banker: A middleman between the investing public and companies or government units that need funds for expansion and development.

Investment tax credit: The amount by which a company may reduce its taxes because it has invested in new, more competitive equipment.

Invisible hand: A theory, set forth by Adam Smith in 1776, which claims that market competition transmutes selfish actions by individuals into the common good.

Iron law of wages: The proposition that the natural wage is the cost of the subsistence standard of living.

Job-specific training: Training that is applicable to a particular job and that cannot be transferred to another job.

Joint-stock corporation: An institution legally separate from its owners, who own it jointly and whose claims to the business depend on their share of the corporation's stock.

Keynesian economics: A school of thought which argues that market economies are not self-regulating and that government intervention becomes necessary to stabilize the economy.

Labor: The human effort that is expended in the production of a good or service.

Labor-management: An arrangement whereby the employees of a corporation or socialist enterprise elect the directors or make the directorial decisions by voting without participation by the holders of ownership shares.

Labor productivity: The level of output per unit of labor input.

Labor supply: The quantity of labor that individuals are willing to provide at different wage rates.

Labor theory of value: The theory that the values of commodities are determined by the amount of labor required to produce them.

Lagging indicator: A time series which has its turning points after the level of economic activity turns.

Lagrange multipliers: The variables that are associated with the constraints in the use of the Lagrangian technique of constrained optimization.

Laissez-faire: The doctrine that economic decisions are best left to individuals and that government intervention should be minimal.

Law of diminishing marginal utility: The law asserting that, as a consumer receives increments of a good, the increases in satisfaction or utility that result from those increments will eventually decline.

Law of diminishing returns: The law asserting that, as equal increments of some variable resource are added to a fixed amount of another resource, the additional output that results from each increment will eventually decline.

Leading indicator: A time series which has its turning points before the level of economic activity turns.

Legal tender: Currency that must be accepted as payment for all debts, as established by law.

Lender of last resort: The function performed by a central bank when it increases the quantity of its money in response to a generalized increase in the demand for liquidity.

Less developed countries (LDCs): Countries with levels of per-capita income that are far below those of industrial countries.

Liability: Anything that is owed, especially claims by other persons, companies, or the government against the assets of a firm.

Life-cycle hypothesis: The view that people determine their consumption levels by taking into account their expected lifetime wealth.

Limited liability: The legal principle that shareholders of a corporation and limited partners in a partnership cannot be held responsible, in a personal financial sense, for the actions of the corporation or partnership.

Limited partnership: A partnership in which at least one of the partners possesses a limited liability, usually as a trade-off for reduced opportunities to share in partnership profits or management.

Liquidate: To sell inventories of goods or assets for money.

Liquidity: The relative ability to convert an asset into cash on short notice and without much, if any, loss of value.

Liquidity preference: The preference for a portfolio composed primarily of liquid assets.

Loanable funds: Money made available for lending, principally for investment purposes.

Long run: A period which is sufficiently long that a firm can vary the quantity of all the inputs that are used in its production process.

Loss: An excess of expenses over incomes in a business.

M-1: A narrow definition of the money supply which includes checkable deposits, the currency that is in circulation, and traveler's checks.

M-2: A broader definition of the money supply which includes all the items in M-1 plus certain other financial assets, such as passbook savings accounts and money-market deposit accounts.

Macroeconomics: The branch of economics that concentrates on studying the overall level of economic activity, such as output, employment, and the general level of prices in the economy.

Malthusian population theory: A theory of Thomas Robert Malthus which states that population grows exponentially unless limited by "poverty, vice or moral restraint."

Marginal benefit: The additional benefit that accrues from an extra unit of consumption.

Marginal cost: The additional cost that is incurred from producing an extra unit of output.

Marginal product: The increase in total output that results from the addition of one unit of a variable factor of production.

Marginal propensity to consume: The change in consumption spending that results from a change in disposable income.

Marginal propensity to save: The change in savings that results from a change in disposable income.

Marginal revenue: The additional revenue that a firm obtains if it sells one more unit of output.

Marginal utility: The extra satisfaction that is derived from consuming an additional unit of a product.

Market: The dynamic process of interaction between those who supply a good or service and those who demand that good or service.

Market clearing: The assumption that prices and wages are sufficiently flexible to ensure that supply and demand are equal in all markets.

Market economy: An economic system which is characterized by the private ownership of resources, a limited economic role for government, and competitive markets.

Market failure: The failure of an unregulated market system to achieve an efficient allocation of society's resources.

Market power: The ability of one or more firms to have a noticeable impact on the price in a given market.

Market price: The price for a product or service that is determined by demand and supply, without government intervention such as price supports or target prices.

Market share: The proportion of total sales in a market that is held by a firm or group of firms.

Market socialism: An economic system which combines central planning with decentralized economic decision making.

Market structure: The characteristics of a market that affect a firm's selling conditions, such as the number of sellers, the extent of product differentiation, and the ease of entry.

Markup pricing: The addition by firms of a fixed percentage to their costs of production; also called cost-plus pricing.

Marshall Plan: The massive program of economic assistance that was provided to Western Europe by the United States at the end of World War II.

Mass production: The use of product-specific machines or assembly lines to produce standardized products.

Medicaid: The U.S. government program that pays medical and nursing home bills for the poor.

Medicare: The U.S. government program that pays hospital and physicians' bills for the elderly.

Medium of exchange: Something that is accepted as payment for purchasing goods and services; one of the roles performed by money.

Mercantilism: An economic theory of the seventeenth and eighteenth centuries which emphasized a balance-of-trade surplus and economic regulations that favored producers and restricted competition.

Merger: The combination of firms into singly owned entities, usually through the purchase of either the productive assets or ownership shares of one firm by another.

Microeconomics: The branch of economics that is concerned with the level of the individual firm or household.

Minimum wage: A floor imposed by legislation under which the wage rate cannot fall.

Mint: The place at which metallic coins are produced, which may be either a public or a private facility.

Monetarism: A policy which assumes that levels of economic activity can be strongly influenced, if not controlled, by adjusting the money supply.

Monetary authority: An agency which is responsible for controlling the money supply.

Monetary policy: Government policy that is designed to influence the state of the economy by controlling the money supply, credit, and interest-rate conditions.

Money: A medium of exchange which is used to pay for things and a form in which people can hold their accumulated savings or wealth.

Money markets: The markets for financial instruments that have maturities of under one year and are highly liquid.

Money multiplier: The change in economic activity that results from a change in the money supply.

Money supply: The amount of currency and deposits in existence at a given time.

Monopoly: An industry which is dominated by one seller that supplies an entire industry and that has no significant competitors.

Monopoly power: The ability of a firm or group of firms to influence the market price of a product by a significant amount for a significant time period.

Monopsony: An industry which is dominated by a single buyer, especially an employer in a labor market.

Monte Carlo simulation: A computer simulation of a given environment or behavior using random numbers generated by the computer.

Mortgage: A loan from a financial institution to a home buyer.

Most-favored-nation principle: The principle in a trade agreement that a country will impose no greater barriers on imports from one particular country than it imposes on imports from any other country.

Multilateral agreement: A formal agreement between several independent units regarding a course of economic action to be taken by each.

Multinational corporation: A business organization which has plant or production operations in one or more foreign countries and makes management decisions at a global level.

Multiplier: The number of dollars by which output expands as a result of a one dollar increase in autonomous spending, such as from a change in fiscal policy.

Mutual fund: An investment company which invests the funds of its shareholders in a diversified group of securities of other companies.

National banks: In the United States, commercial banks that obtain a charter from the Comptroller of the Currency, a U.S. Treasury department.

National debt: The sum of all past federal deficits and surpluses.

Natural monopoly: A situation in which very large fixed costs and low marginal costs make it unlikely that there will be more than one producer in an unregulated market.

Neoclassical economics: A school of economics which models the economy as determined by the actions of individual market participants.

Net exports: The value of a country's exports minus the value of its imports.

Net national product: The gross national product minus depreciation.

New-classical economics: A school of thought, developed in the 1970's and 1980's in reaction to Keynesian policies, that is grounded in the classical assumption that prices and wages adjust rapidly enough that price-wage equilibrium exists at all times.

New Deal: The policies of public-sector spending introduced by President Franklin D. Roosevelt during the Great Depression.

Nominal gross national product: The gross national product measured in current prices.

Nondiscretionary policy: Policies already in place to stabilize income and employment over the business cycle, such as progressive or proportional taxes and unemployment insurance.

Nonprofit organization: An association whose mission and goals are to serve a variety of socially desirable functions, rather than profit making.

Nonrenewable sources of energy: Sources of energy that are finite, such as fossil fuels.

Nontariff barrier: A trade barrier other than a tariff, such as a quota, a restrictive import licensing system, or a restrictive standards and quality import inspection procedure.

Normal good: A commodity which consumers are willing and able to buy more of when their incomes rise and less of when their incomes fall.

Normative science: A discipline which deals with what ought to be, including ethical judgments.

Obsolescence: The decrease in the usefulness of a piece of equipment or a process because of the development of better tools and methods of production.

Okun's law: A mathematical relationship between the rate of economic growth and a change in the rate of unemployment.

Oligopoly: An industry which is dominated by a small number of interdependent firms whose policies are determined by the expected actions of one another.

On-the-job training: Training that is completed while at work, either through a formal training program, teaching by coworkers, or learning by doing.

Open-market operations: The purchase and sale of securities, usually government securities, by a central bank.

Opportunity cost: The cost of sacrificing one opportunity in order to choose another opportunity, measured as the value of the forgone alternative.

Option: The privilege, bought for a price, of being able to choose the forward price or the spot (current) price.

Ordinal utility: The assumption that utility is subjective and cannot be compared or added among different persons.

Output: The consequence of the process of production, which is the creation of valuable physical objects and intangible services.

Pareto optimality: A situation in which no one can be made better off without making someone else worse off; in other words, efficiency in the use of resources.

Partial equilibrium analysis: A method which concentrates on the effects of changes in an individual, isolated market while assuming that all other factors in the economy are unaffected.

Partnership: A form of business organization in which two or more persons jointly form a business in order to take mutual advantage of the skills or resources of each partner.

Patent: A legal right conferred by government which enables a firm to exclude, for a set number of years, all others from duplicating a new and useful product or process.

Peak: The phase of the business cycle in which employment, prices, and output are at their highest levels.

Per-capita income: The total gross national product of a country divided by its total population, which is generally used as an economic indicator of development and standard of living.

Perfect competition: The market condition that exists when individual firms have no influence on price, there is perfect information, and entry and exit are free.

Permanent income: The average expected future income of a household, taking into account expected changes in income and transitory elements of income.

Permanent income hypothesis: The view that long-run income prospects are an important determinant of current consumption levels.

Phillips curve: The trade-off between lower unemployment and accelerating inflation that was discovered by A. W. Phillips.

Physical capital: Tangible investment goods, such as plant, equipment, machinery, and buildings.

Physiocrats: An eighteenth century school of French economists, led by François Quesnay, which emphasized the natural order and the primacy of agriculture in economic policy.

Planned economy: An economy which is controlled and directed by a central governmental authority.

Poor laws: British laws that helped the poor by providing guaranteed minimum income.

Portfolio: The sum of stocks and bonds that are purchased in order to obtain a return on investment, or the total assets and liabilities of a firm.

Positive science: The study of matters of fact, as opposed to the normative study of what ought to be.

Positive-sum game: A situation in which both sides benefit from an activity.

Potential gross national product: The market value of goods and services that an economy should be able to produce if all of its economic resources are fully and efficiently utilized.

Poverty line: The level of income below which an individual or family is deemed to be poor.

Preferred stock: A certificate which provides ownership, but not voting rights, in a corporation and pays fixed or variable dividends.

Premium: The price that is paid for an option.

Present value: The sum of money in the present that will be sufficient, at the given interest rate, to generate a specified flow of money in the future.

Price capping: A method of regulation whereby a firm's prices are set independently of its production costs.

Price ceiling: A maximum price which is arbitrarily set below the market price by a government.

Price controls: Maximum or minimum legal prices for goods and services that are determined by the government.

Price elasticity: A measure of the responsiveness of consumer demand to changes in price.

Price fixing: An agreement between sellers not to reduce a product's price below a specified minimum price level.

Price floor: A minimum price which is arbitrarily set above the market price by a government.

Price index: The number that shows how a weighted average of prices of a certain basket of goods has changed over time.

Price support: The minimum price for a product that is allowed by a government, which buys any resulting surpluses.

Prime rate: The benchmark interest rate for short-term business loans that is set by central banks and changed somewhat infrequently.

Principal: The beginning balance of a loan or the total unpaid balance at any point in the repayment process.

Privatization: The transfer of resources from collective to private ownership and control.

Product differentiation: The real or perceived differences between commodities within an industry.

Production function: The mathematical function that depicts the maximum amount of output that can be obtained from each combination of inputs at a specified point in time.

Productivity: The amount of output that can be obtained per unit of a given input, such as output produced per hour of labor.

Profit: An excess of incomes over expenses in a business.

Profit maximization: The behavior of a firm so that it may achieve a total revenue that exceeds its total costs by the largest possible amount.

Profit sharing: An arrangement whereby the employees of a company receive part of their pay in the form of a share in profits.

Progressive taxation: Taxation in which the tax rate increases as income increases.

Proletariat: The segment of society whose economic existence depends solely on the sale of its labor for wages.

Property rights: A set of rights which establishes ownership.

Property taxes: Direct taxes that are levied on land or buildings.

Proprietorship: A firm owned by a single individual, who has the sole claim on any earnings of the firm and who performs entrepreneurial functions for the firm.

Protection: The use of customs duties or nontariff barriers to keep the prices of foreign goods too high for them to compete with domestic production.

Public goods: Goods that can be consumed at the same time by more than one consumer and at no additional cost; it is usually difficult to exclude nonpayers from enjoyment of a public good.

Public sector: The portion of the economy that is under the direct control of the government.

Purchasing power parity: The theory that exchange rates can be set according to a rule which compares intercountry price indexes.

Pure competition: A market in which individual sellers cannot affect the market price.

Put option: A security which gives its owner the right to sell a specific amount of a specific asset at a specific price within a specific time.

Quantity theory of money: The argument that the price levels of commodities vary directly with the supply of money and the rate at which money changes hands and inversely with the levels of output.

Quota: A limit on the quantity of goods allowed into or out of a country, especially a limit on the quantity of imports.

Rate of return: An investment's average annual profit divided by the amount of capital that was invested.

Rational expectations: The formation of expectations about future market events based on all the available information that is relevant to the market.

Rationing: An artificial allocation of resources to consumers, especially in times of shortage or war.

Raw materials: Goods that have not yet been used in a production process but will be.

Real gross national product: The value of the gross national product in the constant prices of a base year, therefore adjusting for inflation.

Real income: The purchasing power of an individual's money income, expressed as the amount of goods and services that can be purchased, or nominal income divided by an appropriate price index.

Real wage: The actual or money wage rate, adjusted for the cost of living.

Recession: The phase of the business cycle when employment, prices, and production of goods and services are declining, or any sustained decline in economic activity.

Regression analysis: The method of fitting linear and nonlinear algebraic models to observed data for the purposes of testing hypotheses and forecasting.

Regressive taxation: Taxation in which the tax rate falls as income increases.

Renewable sources of energy: Sources of energy that are freely available in nature in nonexhaustible amounts, such as wind, wave, and solar power.

Rent: The return to a fixed factor of production that remains after the other factors receive their payments, especially a return to the owner of property by a tenant, or a payment to a factor of production above what is necessary to bring it to market.

Research and development: The undertaking of activities that are designed to yield new productive methods, products, or services.

Reserve requirement: The amount of reserves that the central bank requires commercial banks to keep in order to back up their deposits.

Reserves: The vault cash holdings of banks and their deposits at the central bank.

Resources: The productive services of land, labor, and capital used in producing other goods and services.

Retained earnings: The portion of a company's profit that is saved directly by the company in order to acquire new plant and equipment.

Returns to scale: The relationship between a firm's size and its efficiency.

Ricardian equivalence: The hypothesis that debt financing is equivalent to tax financing in its economic impact.

Risk: The possibility that expected earnings may not be achieved.

Risk-free asset: An asset characterized by a return which is known with complete certainty.

Roll over: To borrow money to repay an existing loan which has come due for payment.

Sales tax: A broad-based tax on the sales of consumer goods.

Saving: After-tax income that is not spent on the consumption of goods or services.

Savings account: An account which does not have a specific time limit before a depositor can withdraw funds.

Savings and loan association: A type of thrift institution which has traditionally emphasized savings accounts and home mortgage loans.

Say's law: the proposition that general overproduction or underproduction is impossible because supply creates its own demand.

Scarcity: Often used as a synonym for shortage; strictly speaking, scarcity exists when quantity demanded exceeds quantity supplied at a zero price of a good.

Seasonal adjustment: An adjustment to a monthly or quarterly time series of data which removes seasonal fluctuations from those data.

Seigniorage: The difference between the face value of money and the cost of its creation, the value of which accrues to the government.

Shareholder: An owner of one or more shares of stock in a corporation, who is in actual or potential possession of the company's stock certificates.

Sherman Antitrust Act: The first federal antitrust law in the United States to prohibit monopolization of an industry by a single firm and collusive agreements between firms.

Short run: A period which is so short that the quantity of at least one input into the production process cannot be varied.

Shortage: The situation that exists when the quantity demanded exceeds the quantity supplied.

Social costs: The sum of the costs that a private producer bears and those that it inflicts on others without compensation.

Social insurance: Benefits that are paid as a matter of right on the basis of objective eligibility criteria, such as age and lack of employment.

Social Security: The U.S. government program that pays cash pensions to retirees or disabled workers, their spouses, or their survivors.

Social welfare function: A mathematical statement which indicates how the well-being of society, taken as a whole, may be maximized.

Socialism: A type of economic system characterized by the collective ownership of a major part of a nation's resources and by the centralized managerial control of these resources.

Sole proprietorship: A form of business organization in which the firm and its owner are identical and inseparable.

Solvency: A situation in which a firm's assets exceed its liabilities.

Specialization: A concentrated effort in one area of production.

Specie: Money in the form of precious metals, such as gold and silver.

Speculation: The act of buying and selling in a market in the hope of profiting because of an expected change in the future market price.

Spot rate: The current exchange rate between two currencies.

Stabilization policy: An economic policy which is designed to eliminate or reduce inflationary and recessionary tendencies in the economy.

Stagflation: The simultaneous occurrence of high unemployment and rising inflation.

Standardized product: A type of good with little or no variation in characteristics or features; also referred to as a homogeneous product.

State banks: Commercial banks that obtain a charter from state banking commissions.

Steady-state growth: A situation in which all economic variables grow at the same constant rate.

Stochastic model: A model which uses random disturbances in order to describe the impact of changes in minor factors on a given economic system.

Stock: A financial asset representing the ownership of a corporation and a proportional claim on the earnings of the corporation.

Stockouts: The phenomenon that occurs when a purchasing order arrives and the firm cannot fill the order from either current production or inventory.

Store of value: Something that can store wealth over time, which is the second major function of money in addition to it being a medium of exchange.

Straight-line depreciation: An accounting method which explains the lost value of an asset that is used in production by assuming that an equal amount of value is used up each year.

Strike: A collective refusal by employees to work under the conditions that are required by their employers.

Structural unemployment: Unemployment that is caused by a mismatch between the skills or location of job seekers and the requirements or location of available jobs.

Subchapter-S corporation: An organization with a limited number of stockholders which elects to be taxed other than as a full corporation.

Subminimum wage: A lower wage floor for certain workers, such as young or inexperienced workers.

Subsidy: Any form of direct or indirect financial assistance provided by the government to a person, household, or firm for a specific commodity.

Subsistence wage: The level of wages that is just adequate to provide the minimum requirements to support a worker.

Substitute good: A product which is acceptable in place of another; an increase in the price of one results in an increase in the demand for the other, and vice versa.

Substitution effect: The change in the quantity of a good that consumers will purchase as a result of a change in the relative price of that good.

Sunk costs: Costs which, once incurred, cannot be recovered.

Superior good: A commodity which consumers are willing and able to buy more of, as a fraction of income, when their incomes rise and less of when their incomes fall.

Supply: The quantities of a good or service that owners are willing to offer for sale at various prices.

Supply curve: A graphed line which shows the relationship between the price of a good and the quantity of the good that is supplied to the market.

Supply-side economics: An economic policy approach which suggests that, in order to stabilize the economy, measures be taken to boost aggregate supply and output.

Surplus: The situation that exists when revenue exceeds spending.

Surplus value: According to the labor theory of value, the uncompensated time during which workers labor for capitalists, which accounts for the existence of profit.

Target price: A guaranteed price for a product which is set by the government.

Tariff: Government-mandated charges levied on imports and exports to increase revenue, restrain foreign competition, and indirectly subsidize sectors of the home economy.

Tax base: That which is taxed, such as income, wealth, and consumption.

Tax bracket: A range of income over which a specific marginal tax rate applies.

Tax credit: The amount that may be subtracted from tax liability.

Tax deduction: The amount that may be subtracted from the tax base prior to computing tax liability.

Tax evasion: The reduction of tax liability by illegal or fraudulent means.

Technology: The application of science to the solution of practical problems affecting human well-being, or the state of knowledge regarding how inputs can be combined in production.

Term to maturity: The time that elapses before the issuer of a financial asset must pay its maturity value to the holder of the asset.

Terms of trade: The prices of a country's export products relative to the prices of its import products.

Thrift institutions: Nonbank depository intermediaries, such as savings and loan associations, savings bank, and credit unions.

Time deposits: High-interest accounts that have a specific time period before which a depositor may not withdraw funds without facing an interest penalty.

Time series: A measure of the pattern of an economic activity over time.

Time series analysis: The statistical study of the lead-lag behavior between time series.

Total costs: The sum of fixed costs and variable costs.

Trade deficit: A situation in which the value of a country's imports exceeds the value of its exports, which results when a country spends more than it earns internationally.

Trade surplus: A situation in which the value of a country's exports is greater than the value of its imports, which results when a country earns more than it spends internationally.

Trademark: A unique word, logo, or insignia which identifies a company's goods or services as separate and distinct from other companies' goods and services.

Transaction costs: The costs of information and exchange that are necessary to complete an economic exchange.

Transfer payment: A government payment, such as unemployment compensation, welfare benefits, or social security benefits, for which the recipient does not furnish goods or services.

Transitory income: A change in income which is not expected to be permanent; according to the permanent income hypothesis, it should not affect consumption greatly.

Treasury bill: A short-term debt instrument which is issued by a national treasury, often priced at a discount from its face value.

Treasury bond: An interest-paying Treasury debt instrument which is issued for maturities from ten to thirty years.

Treasury note: An interest-paying Treasury debt instrument which is issued for maturities from one to ten years.

Trough: The phase of the business cycle in which employment, prices, and output are at their lowest levels.

Trust: A group of firms that turn over managerial discretion to a single, centralized management.

Unemployment: The situation that exists when a person is seeking work but is unable to find it.

Unemployment rate: The percentage of the labor force that is unemployed, which is a commonly used measure of labor market conditions.

Union: An association of wage earners which is organized for the purpose of maintaining or improving the conditions of their employment.

Use value: A commodity's ability to satisfy human wants, desires, and needs.

Utilitarianism: The idea that economies should be ranked based only on the cardinal or ordinal utilities of individuals in that society.

Utility: An abstract concept which expresses the satisfaction, usefulness, quality, or pleasure that is derived by an individual from consuming goods and services, as determined by that individual.

Value-added tax: Tax revenue based on the creation of value in the manufacturing process, measured as the difference between the final value of a product and the value of the resources that were used in its production.

Variable costs: Those business costs that vary over the relevant range of production and that can be avoided if no output is produced.

Velocity of money: The rapidity with which money changes hands, measured as the average number of times that each unit of currency is spent during a year.

Vertical merger: A merger of firms whose products are complements, usually when one supplies its products or equipment to the other.

Voluntary export restraint: An agreement worked out between two trading nations whereby the exporting country will limit its volume of exports, which is equivalent to a quota.

Wage ceiling: A legally imposed maximum wage, which is usually in effect only during wartime.

Wage floor: A legally imposed minimum wage, which exists in several U.S. states for certain industries and workers as well as in the Fair Labor Standards Act.

Wage-price spiral: The notion that an increase in product prices leads to increased wage demands, which raises costs and causes further price increases.

Wealth: A stock of funds which has been accumulated from past saving and represents the ability to spend beyond income.

Welfare economics: A field which investigates the principles by which alternative economic arrangements can be ranked in the terms of the welfare or common good of a community as a whole.

Write off: To depreciate.

Yield to maturity: The annual rate of return of a debt instrument which is held until its maturity date.

Zero-sum game: A situation in which a gain by one party can only be made through the other party's corresponding loss.

ECONOMICS
BASICS

LIST OF TITLES BY CATEGORY

INDEX

A page range in **boldface** type indicates a full article devoted to that topic.

A

Ability-to-pay criterion, 571
Ability-to-pay principle, defined, 645
Absolute advantage, defined, 86, 212, 645
Absolute poverty, defined, 593
Abstract labor, defined, 358, 645
Accommodation; defined, 146, 645;
  theory, 113
ACE hardware, 104
Acid rain, 189-190
Actual gross national product, defined, 645
Ad valorem tax, 520-521, 569, 571;
  defined, 645
Adjustable-rate mortgage, defined, 645
Adverse selection, defined, 124
Advertising, **1-5**; and communications
  theory, 2; defined, 1, 645; and market
  research, 2; and oligopolies, 462
Advertising Age, 4
AFDC. *See* Aid to Families with
  Dependent Children
Affirmative action, defined, 645
Afghanistan, 596
AFL-CIO. *See* American Federation of
  Labor and Congress of Industrial
  Organizations
Africa; debt problems, 591;
  decolonization of, 156; economic
  growth, 155; famine in, 243;
  government debt in, 49; population
  growth, 486; socialism in, 548
Agency bond, defined, 40
Agency cost, defined, 228
Agency for Economic Development, U.S.,
  100
Aggregate, defined, 180, 514
Aggregate demand, defined, 419, 645
Aggregate supply, defined, 419, 645
Aggregation, defined, 140, 563, 645
Agricultural Adjustment Act (1933), 265
Agriculture; and cooperatives, 103-104;
  and law of diminishing returns, 374;

and perfect competition, 406-407;
  products, 216; and quotas, 522; and
  resources, 534-536; and seasonal
  unemployment, 601
Agriculture, U.S. Department of (USDA),
  241
AID. *See* United States Agency for
  International Development
Aid to Families with Dependent Children
  (AFDC), 488, 491, 645
Airline Deregulation Act (1978), 408
Airlines, regulation of, 392, 408-409, 446,
  464, 530
Algeria, 597
Allocation, defined, 645
Allocative efficiency, defined, 645
American Airlines, 497
American Federation of Labor and
  Congress of Industrial Organizations
  (AFL-CIO), 616
American Telephone and Telegraph
  (AT&T); breakup of, 408
American Tobacco Company, 61
Amortization, 449, defined, 448, 645;
  negative, 453
Amortized loans, compared to bonds, 41
Anarchism; defined, 544, 546; and
  socialism, 546
Annual report, 106
Annuity, defined, 645
Anthropomorphic measurements, 239
Antitechnology, 584
Antitrust laws, defined, 645
Antitrust policy, **6-11**, 369; and Chicago
  School, 445-446; and corporations, 61;
  defined, 6, 442; and market structure,
  408-410; and trade unions, 369
Arab-Israeli War (1973), 340
Arbitrage, 208-209, 231, 259, 558-559;
  and commodity trading, 402; defined,
  206, 401, 645; and technology, 582
Archer-Daniels-Midland corporation
  (ADM), 109

D

under Mussolini, 82; taxes, 578; trade quotas, 522; unions, 614

ITT. *See* International Telephone and Telegraph

IVACG. *See* International Vitamin A Consultative Group

Ivory Coast, 596

J

Jamaica, 597; and barter with the United States, 38

Japan, 516; capitalism in, 640; corporations in, 60; economic growth, 66; and International Monetary Fund, 337-338; investment in, 65; and mercantilism, 297; Ministry of International Trade and Industry (MITI), 291-292; national income, 63-64; tariffs, 252; taxes, 231, 577-578; technology in, 583; trade, 589; trade quotas, 522; trade with United States, 254, 588; unions, 614-618; yen, 206

Jenkin, Fleeming, 143, 567

Jevons, William Stanley, 77, 173, 296, 298, 394, 429, 567, 624, 627

Job search policies, defined, 606

Job-specific training, defined, 657

Job Training Partnership Act (1982), 609

Johnson, Lyndon B., and War on Poverty, 491

Joint-stock companies, 109

Joint-stock corporation, defined, 657

Jordan, 597

"Junk bonds," 44, 231

Justice Department, U.S., and antitrust laws, 7, 9-10

K

Kalecki, Michal, 516-519

Kampuchea, 596

Kellogg, 1

Kennedy, John F., 610

Kenya, 596

Key industries, defined, 638

Keynes, John Maynard, 116, 138, 283, 381; on aggregate demand, 505; and budget deficits, 48; on capitalism, 642; on depressions, 518; on employment theory, 184, 603-604; on fiscal policy, 237; on Great Depression, 184; in history of economics, 298; influence on George E. Moore, 296; interest theory, 381; and International Monetary Fund, 337; and macroeconomics, 384; and microeconomics, 429; on money, 147; on poverty, 492; on recessions, 457; on saving, 542; on wages, 623-624

Keynesian economics, 149-150, 167, 185, 298; and business cycles, 52, 55; and consumption theory, 385-387; and deficit spending, 138, 267; defined, 657; and development theory, 156; and economic growth, 490; and employment theory, 184; and growth theory, 281, 283; and inflation, 116, 149-150, 265, 299; and investment, 66; and macroeconomics, 25, 52, 385; and monetary policy, 279; and "neoclassicial synthesis," 293; and saving, 64, 283; and social change, 291; and taxes, 579; and unemployment, 299, 609

Keynesian models, 55

King, Gregory, 143

Klein, Lawrence R., 429

Klein-Goldberger model, 249

Koran, 327

Kulaks, 415

Kuznets, Simon, 154, 284, 286, 290, 293, 304; and gross national product, 273

L

Labor; and capitalism, 359, 362; in communist theory, 81-82; defined, 626, 657; derived demand for, 353; horizontal division of, 160; marginal product of, 353-354; and productivity, 353-356; supply of, 354-356, 364; and wealth, 627

Labor Department, U.S., 277

Labor economics, **353-357**; applications, 355-357; study of, 356